St. Louis Brews

THE AMERICAN
BREWING
Co.
A.B.C.
TRADE MARK
REGISTERED
St. Louis
A.B.C. BEER.

St. Louis Brews
200 Years of Brewing in St. Louis, 1809–2009
by Henry Herbst, Don Roussin, and Kevin Kious

REEDY PRESS
St. Louis, Missouri

Wooden Barrels and Iron Men

I dare say there are many of our old timers who remember very well when the men started at four O'clock in the morning and worked until half past six, when they stopped for breakfast. At seven O'clock they went back to work and worked until twelve and then worked in the afternoon from one to six.

—James C. Cochran, *The Pabst Brewing Company*, 1948

In 1881, the brewery workmen of Cincinnati drew up a number of demands to be presented to the brewers. These were:
1. A reduction of the work day from thirteen to ten and a half-hours.
2. A reduction of Sunday work from eight to four hours.
3. A minimum wage of $60 a month.
4. Freedom for the worker to seek board and lodging wherever he liked.

—Herman Schluter, *The Brewing Industry and the Brewery Workers' Movement in America*, 1910

The work required for the production of one brew of beer was exceedingly protracted and difficult. The hauling, dipping, pumping, breaking, stirring and boiling were tiresome work for the laborers, indeed requiring 15 to 17 working hours every day, and making the brewer's occupation one of hard toil and almost unbearable labor.

—H. S. Rich and Company, *One Hundred Years of Brewing*, 1903

The new agreement with the employees, signed May 26 by the Anheuser-Busch and Lemp brewing companies, of St. Louis, runs for two years. Among the concessions made to the men are the following: The men are given a full holiday once a week, instead of a half holiday, as heretofore. Fifty minutes are allowed each morning for breakfast. Apprentices have to take their turn at being laid off during the slack season. Heretofore no apprentices were laid off when work became slack in the winter, but the men had to stand the loss. This agreement is the one which the syndicate breweries refuse to sign. A movement was started by the engineers, machinists, oilers and ice plant workers of the Anheuser-Busch brewery to try to get eight hours, but it fell through, because the Lemp men could not agree. The brewery men work ten hours.

—*The Western Brewer*, June 15, 1896

Authors' note: When co-author Henry Herbst began toying with the idea of doing a book on St. Louis brewing history, he thought that Wooden Barrels and Iron Men would make a good title, serving as something of a tribute to the vital "little guys" in the brewing industry. The above quotes illustrate the often-difficult conditions faced by early brewery workers, the "Iron Men" who helped develop the industry.

Simply put, there would have been no beer barons, the stars of this book, without the hard work and expertise of their employees. May this book also serve to preserve their efforts.

Dedication

For Elaine, my wife of 43 years, the love of my life and my best friend.

For my daughters Amy [Anthony] Graziano, Susan [Jeff] Wandishin and Kathleen [Denny] Arnett.

For my parents, Marion and George Herbst, my father was a member of the Brewers and Maltsters Local #6 and an employee of Anheuser-Busch Inc. from 1938 until his retirement in 1976 and for my great-grandfather Joseph Herbst who was employed locally during the nineteenth century as a cooper.

For my grandchildren; Jamie Wandishin, Meghan Arnett, Celeste Graziano, Zachery Wandishin, Tyler Arnett, and Nina "Queen Bee" Graziano. So they always remember that the legacy of their grandfather and his ancestors was embedded within the history of the St. Louis brewing industry.

—Henry Herbst

To the people who made the history—beer barons, brewers, workmen.

To the people who recorded and saved the history—journalists, authors, librarians.

To my parents, Parker Len and Roberta Kious, who always encouraged my love of words and paid for my books and education.

To the many teachers who encouraged me to write, including Pauline Watkins, Heidi Hardy, Shirley Naughton, Sue Van Kerre Broeck and Dr. James Davis.

To Gary "The Hacker" Zimmerman for introducing me to the breweriana collecting hobby.

To my wife Patty, for not just tolerating the hobby but embracing it.

And to June the cat, who was always in my lap.

—Kevin Kious

To my father, Donald, Sr., and mother, Bonnie Roussin, and uncles Dean Roussin and Douglas Roussin, who all taught me the importance of history, beginning with the exploration of our family tree.

To John A. White, ("J.A.W."), my English college professor in The Block, who stressed the joys of writing in his classes, which has inspired me to pick up the pen on a regular basis, in the years since.

To my sons Joseph and William, who have tolerated a basement full of beer cans their entire lives.

To my wife Mary Ellen, always supportive of my breweriana collecting and also joyfully sharing our many trips exploring long shuttered brewery buildings. In the best present I ever received, a copy of *100 Years of Brewing,* Mary Ellen wrote: "To use, with love, for the search of knowledge." Reading that gift set me on the path that led to my involvement, here, in the *St. Louis Brews* book project.

—Donald Roussin

Reedy Press
PO Box 5131
St. Louis, MO 63139, USA

Library of Congress Control Number: 2009935682

ISBN: 978-1-933370-91-0

Please visit our website at www.reedypress.com.

design by Nick Hoeing

Printed in Canada
09 10 11 12 13   5 4 3 2 1

Contents

ix Acknowledgments

xi Foreword ~ Tom Schlafly

xiii Introduction ~ William Vollmar, PhD

3 Chapter 1 The Chronological History of Brewing in St. Louis

30 Chapter 2 The Major Brewers in St. Louis:

32 Anheuser-Busch Inc.	90 Falstaff Brewing Corp.	144 Lemp Brewing Co.
52 Anthony & Kuhn Brewing Co.	102 Forest Park Brewing Co.	160 Liberty Brewing Co.
56 Bremen Brewing Co.	104 Gast Brewing Co.	162 Mutual Brewing Co.
58 Carondelet Brewing Co.	108 Green Tree Brewery	166 Louis Obert Brewing Co.
62 Cherokee Brewing Co.	114 Griesedieck Bros. Brewery Co.	176 Phoenix Brewery
64 Chouteau Avenue Brewery	122 H. Grone Brewery	179 St. Louis Brewing Association
66 City/Union Brewing Co.	124 Home Brewing Co.	182 Schilling & Schneider/Koch Brewery
70 Columbia Brewing Co	127 Hyde Park Breweries Assn.	186 Schorr-Kolkschneider Brewing Co.
75 Consumers Brewing Co.	135 Independent Breweries Co.	190 The Joseph Uhrig Brewing Co.
79 Empire Brewing Co.	137 Klausmann Brewery Co.	194 Wainwright Brewing Co.
81 Excelsior/American Brewing Co.	141 Lafayette Brewery	201 Winkelmeyer/Union Brewery

204 Chapter 3 Brewers Deserving Honorable Mention

233 Chapter 4 Weiss Beer Breweries

240 Chapter 5 Craft and Contract Brewers

247 Chapter 6 Affiliated Industries and Organizations

255 Chapter 7 The Choicest Product of the Brewers' Art

271 Bibliography

277 Index

Acknowledgments

The authors would like to extend our sincere thanks to the many people who provided support for this effort. The scope of the subject matter exceeded the ability of any one person to produce such a book. Many people offered a variety of assistance, which includes, but was not limited to, providing the following: access to their personal collections for the purpose of photographing and scanning items, family photos, research assistance, corporate information, logos, images, and technical advice. A special thank you to Tom Schlafly for graciously agreeing to write the foreword and to William Vollmar, PhD, for his efforts in providing the introduction. We would also like to thank Matt Heidenry and Josh Stevens of Reedy Press for their guidance through the minefield of book publishing. All effort has been made by the authors to provide complete and factual information. Any errors or omissions occurred without malice and are solely our responsibility.

—Don Roussin, Kevin Kious, and Henry Herbst

Susan Appel
Troika Brodsky
Mary Butler
Bob Chapman
Larry Chase
Tim Conklin
Barb Cook
Robbi Courtaway
Steve DeBellis
Curt Faulkenberry
William "Zelli" Fischetti
Joel Gandt
Marc Gottfried
Ray Griesedieck
Robert Griesedieck
Stephen Hale
Paul Haudrich
Tony Joynt
Bob Kay
Ray Klimovitz
Dan Kopman
John Kottemann
Kent Knowles
Rich LaSusa
Tracy Lauer
Richard Lay
Lauren Leeman
Dushan Manjencich
Sam Marcum
Michael Mattingly

H. James Maxwell
Carl Miller
Dave Miller
Bill Mitchell
Jim Mitchell
Bruce Mobley
Bryan Monaco
Brian Neville
Connie Nisinger
Don Powell
Jim Reichmuth
Herman Ronnenberg
Jeffery Sahaida
Tom Schlafly
Herb Schwarz
John Smallshaw
Lonnie Smith
Ron Snowden
Dan Stauder
John Sterling
Lee Stertz
Jerry Stevison
Mike Sweeney
Bob Thebeau
Charles Vick
Bill Vollmar, PhD
Davide Weaver
Rosemary Witte
Rick Zimmer

FOREWORD

*B*eer has been around for thousands of years. The brewing process is in one sense amazingly simple. The first beers were probably produced by accident when wild yeast found its way into jars full of water and grain, prompting the natural sugars to start fermenting. The process can also be incredibly complicated and can challenge some of the best scientific minds in the world today.

In the history of brewing, St. Louis is a relative newcomer, at least when compared with Sumeria and ancient Egypt. But the modern-day beer gods have smiled on St. Louis in many ways. We have been blessed with an abundance of fresh water, which is essential in brewing beer. We sit atop a network of limestone caves, which provided a cool place to store lagers before the advent of refrigeration. And we have experienced wave upon wave of German immigrants who brought both an appreciation for beer and a talent for brewing it very well.

Just as many St. Louisans take the bounty of the Mississippi and Missouri rivers for granted—while billions of people around the world are faced with a severe shortage of clean, fresh water—many have also not fully appreciated our city's rich tradition of brewing. A lot of folks know next to nothing about the two hundred-year history of brewing in their home town. Too bad. This is a fascinating story that should interest everyone, including those who don't consider themselves connoisseurs of beer.

A lot of Americans are taking an increased interest in knowing where their food comes from. *St. Louis Brews* satisfies the same sense of curiosity with respect to beer. It doesn't focus on the raw ingredients, but rather on the individuals, families, and events that built and shaped the world of beer as it is today in St. Louis.

It's fitting that our city was both a cradle of jazz and America's beer capital. Jazz, in contrast to orchestral music, is an improvisational medium. Musicians and their audiences expect the unexpected. The story of brewing in St. Louis has been similarly unscripted. Most changes have been unpredictable. Some breweries and retailers have adapted successfully to changing circumstances. Some have not. Consumer preferences have been alternatingly fickle and fiercely loyal.

St. Louis Brews, 200 Years of Brewing in St. Louis, 1809–2009 is a book to savor and enjoy, like a glass of good, local beer.

Tom Schlafly
President
The Saint Louis Brewery Inc.

INTRODUCTION

Over its long history St. Louis has exhibited a variety of personas including frontier outpost, fur trading center, raucous river town, gateway to the West, transportation hub, and, not least, brewing mecca. From 1809 when John Coons set up a primitive brewery on what is today the site of the Gateway Arch to Carlos Brito's audacious takeover of Anheuser-Busch, St. Louis has been known as a city where beer was king.

In technocentric modern America where what is found on the internet or heard on *Larry King Live* is often held to be the fount of all knowledge, many might think that beer and St. Louis means Anheuser-Busch and the Budweiser Clydesdales. That would be as far from the truth as possible. While the influence of Anheuser-Busch is critical to the history of brewing in St. Louis there is so much more to the story than that. Over one hundred breweries have existed in and around the Mound City during the past two centuries. Many were small, obscure operations that lasted but a few years while others grew to be national and international behemoths. All contributed to the American brewing industry and to the rich, vibrant history of beer in St. Louis.

Like most American cities, the origins of brewing in St. Louis were humble; a few small, two or three person operations producing only a few dozen or so barrels each year to be sold in local taverns and saloons. It was not until the influx of German immigrants in the 1840s that brewing became a significant business. Among those newcomers was Adam Lemp who introduced lager beer to St. Louis and, some contend, to the United States. Eventually his Western Brewery would become one of the largest in the country. By 1860 there were forty breweries in St. Louis producing 200,000 barrels annually. Among the smaller of these was the Bavarian Brewery owned by a local soap merchant named Eberhard Anheuser. In 1869 Anheuser's son-in-law, Adolphus Busch, became his partner forming the name that would become synonymous with beer—Anheuser-Busch.

The twenty-five years following the Civil War saw a tremendous expansion of brewing in St. Louis with the city becoming the third largest producer of beer in the country. As the Industrial Revolution took hold in America in the late 1800s, the brewing industry experienced rapid growth through such technological innovations as pasteurization, artificial refrigeration, refrigerated rail cars, and a coordinated system of railroad distribution. These innovations permitted breweries that were local or at best regional in scope to transform themselves into national marketers. St. Louis breweries, led by Anheuser-Busch, were at the forefront of this transformation.

The years between 1890 and 1910 were the Golden Era of brewing in the United States and in St. Louis. Anheuser-Busch became the world's largest brewer. Lemp and the American Brewing Company were national brewers. The St. Louis Brewing Association, a combine of eighteen metro breweries, was in full operation and many small local breweries thrived in a city whose population had reached 687,000. But even as St. Louis brewers enjoyed their greatest prosperity, disaster was about to strike them. Within a decade America's favorite beverage was declared illegal and all brewing activity in St. Louis ceased. National Prohibition existed for thirteen years. Most local brewers simply went out of business; while larger concerns kept operating by producing soft drinks, baker's yeast, ice, near beer, table syrup, and similar products.

On April 7, 1933, beer was re-legalized. Where twenty breweries had operated in St. Louis in 1919, only eight reopened in 1933. Anheuser-Busch, Falstaff, and ABC were among the national brewers to return. The city's greatest loss to Prohibition was its oldest lager brewer—the William J. Lemp Brewing Company, which closed its doors and never reopened, eventually selling its property for eight cents on the dollar.

Beer was back but post-Prohibition brewing was nothing like it had been in its Golden Era. Large national brewers were beginning to dominate in a country that was ever shrinking due to radio, television, air travel, and the automobile. The small local and regional brewer, geared to deal with only his immediate market, was doomed. In 1935 America had 700 breweries; by 1950 there were less than 400; by 1970 only 125; and in 1980 a scant forty breweries produced 181 million barrels of beer. Modern business and marketing practices, combined with changing demographics, meant that only brewers who could produce and market on a massive scale could hope to prosper in a new national marketplace.

St. Louis mirrored the nation. A city that had known over one hundred breweries in its history reached a post-Prohibition high of eleven and by the mid-1950s had only two functioning plants—Anheuser-Busch and Falstaff. Both were strong national brewers, ranking third and fourth in 1948. Where Anheuser-Busch anchored its national structure on newly constructed, strategically located regional plants, Falstaff sought to fashion its power-base by buying and refitting regional breweries that were going out of business. While both companies continued to grow, ranking first and third nationally in 1958, Falstaff's base proved to be unsound. Its older facilities required major financial support and ultimately the company began to decline in both sales and profits. In 1975, Falstaff sold out to the General Brewing Company of Corte Madera, California. On November 4, 1977, General Brewing closed the old Falstaff plant on Gravois Avenue leaving Anheuser-Busch as the only brewery operating in St. Louis.

In 1957, under the leadership of Gussie Busch, Anheuser-Busch recaptured its status as America's leading brewer, a position it would retain for over half a century despite serious challenges from Falstaff, Schlitz, and Miller. Its network of breweries spanned the country while its sales continued to climb. By the time of Junior's retirement in 1975, Anheuser-Busch was brewing over 35 million barrels annually and nearly every fourth beer consumed in America was an A-B product.

Under August Busch III the brewery continued to expand its sales and markets, even going international in the 1980s. By 1991 Anheuser-Busch controlled over 44 percent of the American beer market. That year was also noteworthy as it saw a new phase of St. Louis brewing history begin when Tom Schlafly opened his Saint Louis Brewery on the west end of the city's downtown. It was a return to the beer business much as it had been in the mid-1800s—a small brewery producing limited quantities for local sale and consumption including consumption at the site of production. Over the next fifteen years other small breweries and brewpubs began operation in the St. Louis area. These new/old breweries certainly were no challenge to the powerhouse on Pestalozzi Street, but they did offer St. Louis beer drinkers an alternative and found for themselves a solid niche market.

There was, however, something else that did present a challenge, in fact a fatal challenge, to Anheuser-Busch—the mega international brewing conglomerate. Much as technology altered the American marketplace in the late nineteenth century, globalization changed the business world in the twenty-first century. To all it appeared Anheuser-Busch was secure as America's number one brewer. However, in 2008, in less time than it takes to lager two brews of Budweiser, the house that Adolphus Busch built lost its independence, finding itself a subsidiary of the global brewer InBev. From first rumor to final acquisition, abdication took a scant fifty-two days. One hundred and fifty-six years of brewing history ended in less than two months and

a family that had virtually created modern American brewing ceased to be part of that industry.

St. Louis no longer has a king, but it still has its heritage of beer and what that product of companionship has contributed to both the city and the nation. Henry Herbst, Kevin Kious, and Don Roussin are not professional historians, but their love of and fascination with the history of St. Louis breweries has caused them to devote a good portion of their lives to researching and studying the city's breweries. They have combined their efforts and produced a comprehensive history of St. Louis brewing that documents two hundred years of achievement. Here are the great and the grand along with the small and the forgotten. Together they weave a rich tapestry of high accomplishments, flamboyant, larger-than-life characters, quaint anecdotes, unsolved mysteries, tragedies, successes, and failures. So pour yourself a Bud or, if you prefer, a Schlafly and enjoy the history of beer in St. Louis.

William Vollmar, PhD
Historian Emeritus
Anheuser-Busch

St. Louis Brews

Chapter 1

The Chronological History of Brewing in St. Louis

*A*drian Block and Hans Christiansen established the first known brewery in the New World around 1612 on the southern tip of what is now Manhattan, New York. Due to its geographical location, the brewing industry in St. Louis began much later than that. In the 1700s the location of the village of St. Louis, on the west bank of the Mississippi River, was the far West, and did not even belong to the United States. Pierre Laclede's men came to the future site of St. Louis in 1764 and built log huts for themselves and a warehouse for Laclede's furs, which he purchased from the Native Americans. The village, as laid out, was three blocks wide and one mile long. By 1770 it held five hundred residents.

In the early days, primarily French settlers inhabited St. Louis, then part of the Territory of Louisiana. Its remoteness was highlighted by an Indian attack on the village in 1780. But by 1800, the village was home to one thousand residents.

As an indication of early 1800s life in St. Louis we can cite Stephen Ambrose, who wrote in his book *Undaunted Courage*, "A critical fact in the world of 1801 was that nothing moved faster than the speed of a horse. No human being, no manufactured item, no bushel of wheat, no side of beef, no letter, no information, no idea, order, or instruction of any kind moved faster. Nothing ever had moved any faster, and, as far as Jefferson's contemporaries were able to tell, nothing ever would."

The Louisiana Purchase, signed in 1803, transferred ownership of the territory from France to the United States. Locally, the citizens celebrated what is known as Three Flags Day on March 9–10, 1804, when Spain turned the territory over to France, whose flag flew overnight before it ceded the territory to the United States the following day.

Under the direction of President Thomas Jefferson, Meriwether Lewis, William Clark, and their "Corps of Discovery" left St. Louis on May 14, 1804, in an attempt to find a passage across the uncharted West. Returning to St. Louis on September 23, 1806, they would later report their discoveries to the president.

In 1809, St. Louis was incorporated as a town, with boundaries of Franklin, Poplar, and Seventh streets. That year also marks the first evidence of commercial brewing in the town. The arrival of the first steamboat in St. Louis would not occur until eight years later, when the *Zebulon M. Pike* made its way up the Mississippi River.

The recorded history of the St. Louis brewing industry can be divided into eight distinct phases:

Phase 1 1809–1840 **A Cottage Industry**: Begins historically on October 19, 1809. The industry during this time is a cottage industry, composed of small, primitive breweries. Their product is small or common beer, "strong" beer, ale, and porter. "Strong" beer is what we would refer to today as 5 percent beer; in the 1800s it was the first brew made with the mash while "small or common" beer was of lower alcoholic content and was a weaker beer, generally the second or third brew made with the mash. It would be like using a tea bag two or three times.

Phase 2 1840–1865 **The Germanization of St. Louis**: Starts around 1840 when an influx of Germans arrive in St. Louis. The brewing of lager beer begins, while the industry remains a highly manual operation. The brewers support the Union in the Civil War.

Phase 3 1865–1889 **The Glory Days**: Begins in 1865 with the end of the Civil War. The industry expands, modernizes, becomes unionized, and national and international shipping begins. The small and medium-size breweries close or consolidate.

Phase 4 1889–1920 **The Beginning of the End**: Following the first consolidation of 1889, the city sees new breweries open before another consolidation in 1907. The brewers take part in the 1904 World's Fair. The Prohibition movement gains strength during World War I and eventually prevails.

Phase 5 1920–1933 **The Dark Days of Prohibition**: During this time, the few breweries that survive do so by producing a variety of products such as ice, malt, near beer, soda, and yeast.

Phase 6 1933–1957 **Happy Days Are Here Again**: Beer is back! Anheuser-Busch and Falstaff roll out the first legal beer since 1920. The smaller local breweries—ABC, Griesedieck Brothers, Hyde Park, Obert, Columbia, Schorr-Kolkschneider, and Gast—make their return.

Phase 7 1957–1991 **Toward a National Expansion**: Anheuser-Busch becomes the industry leader after expanding nationally by building new and modern breweries. Falstaff expands nationally by purchasing existing older breweries, makes a play for the top spot, becomes noncompetitive, and finally closes its St. Louis headquarters and brewery.

Phase 8 1991–Present **The Craft Brewers Arrive**: On December 26, 1991, the Saint Louis Brewery, Inc., opens its Tap Room, becoming not only the first brewpub to open in St. Louis, but also the first new brewing facility to operate in the city in more than fifty years. In 2008 InBev buys out Anheuser-Busch, the city's remaining large brewery.

Phase 1
1809–1840
"A Cottage Industry"

The brewing of some type of fermented malt beverage was surely begun in St. Louis at a very early date; unfortunately, this information was never recorded. The village's first newspaper began publishing in 1808, and it is from this publication that we learn of the first documented brewer to operate in the city of St. Louis.

On October 19, 1809, an ad appeared in the *Missouri Gazette*, which read:

Barley and Hops.
Purchased at John Coon's brewery and at the Printing Office.

The ad ran again on November 30, 1809, in the *Louisiana Gazette*, the new name of the *Missouri Gazette*.

John Coons was the second American-born citizen to reside in St. Louis. It is documented that he settled there as early as 1786 and resided within the city until 1811. He is listed in early St. Louis history books as a carpenter and joiner. He and his wife would later move to what is now St. Louis County. While Coons's brewery operated for at least two years, its actual closing date remains unknown.

The second documented brewery associated with St. Louis was actually located north of the city in what was then the village of Belle Fontaine. Constructed of logs, it was owned and operated by Jacques Marcellin de St. Vrain and Victor Habb (also spelled Hab or Hobb). A longtime resident, St. Vrain was well known among the citizens of St. Louis. He had aligned himself with the moneyed class and purchased a significant amount of land as an investment following the Louisiana Purchase. Habb was a brewer by trade, and upon the demise of St. Vrain's brewery would find employment in other local breweries. On April 26, 1810, the *Louisiana Gazette* ran an article congratulating the citizens of St. Louis on the acquisition of this "new establishment for making porter and strong beer."

On May 3, 1810, this ad appeared in the *Louisiana Gazette*:

TABLE BEER & PORTER
Manufactured by St. Vrain & Habb, at Belle Fontaine, near St. Louis. Those who wish to be supplied will please direct

their orders to the brewery, or to Edward Hempstead Esq., St. Louis who will always have a quantity in his cellar ready for sale. Customers who may want a large supply will please to give a timely notice.

On June 21, the following expanded ad appeared for the first time:

STRONG & TABLE BEER
Manufactured by St. Vrain & Habb, at Belle Fontaine, near St. Louis. The price of strong beer, will be ten dollars in cash or twelve in produce. Five dollars in cash for table beer or 6 in produce delivered at the brewery at the following prices

wheat-----------52 ½ cents
barley----------50 cents
rye-------------62 ½ cents
corn------------25 cents
green hops-----10 cents

cattle and pork at market price will also be taken and three months credit shall be given to purchasers provided he give an endorsed note to the satisfaction of the brewers.

Unfortunately, St. Vrain and Habb's brewery was a short-lived affair, for it burned down in 1812.

No known brewery operated in St. Louis between 1812 and 1815. But in 1815, Joseph Philipson began what was called the St. Louis Brewery. This brewery was located on Main Street, at the north end of town, in a two-story frame building. Philipson employed Victor Habb as his brewer and sold his product for six dollars per half-barrel and eleven dollars per barrel. His ale was offered for 12 cents per quart. Philipson also shipped his ale to Ste. Genevieve and sold it through his brother's store there. The primitive nature of these early breweries is described in J. Thomas Scharf's *History of Saint Louis City and County*. He states that at the Philipson brewery, "the beer was cooled in a dug-out canoe, which lay on the north side of the building."

In 1816, St. Louis had three thousand residents, and the city spread from St. Charles Street south to Spruce Street and west to Seventh Street. In the spring of 1819, Victor Habb advertised in the newspaper that "he would be operating a cart through the streets of St. Louis daily to supply the residents with beer and vinegar by retail."

During 1820, Philipson sold his interest in the St. Louis Brewery to Matthew Murphy and James Nagle. Shortly thereafter, Murphy and Nagle sold out, and once again Philipson became sole owner. Being the only brewer in town, he had no competition from local concerns, but he did have to contend with imported beer. This beer was brought to St. Louis on a regular basis by steamboats plying the Mississippi River and its tributaries. Brewers from Pittsburgh, Cincinnati, Poughkeepsie, and elsewhere were eager to supply the local market.

St. Louis was incorporated as a city in 1822, with five thousand residents. That same year Philipson, his brewery having been partially damaged by fire, was forced to sell to John Mullanphy, a prominent local businessman. Mullanphy leased the brewery to Simon Philipson, brother of Joseph, who operated it for three years. The Philipsons retired from the brewing business in 1824. Thomas Biddle, Mullanphy's son-in-law, ran the brewery for a short time thereafter. Mullanphy next operated the brewery with Matthew Murphy as his brewer until 1829, when it too was destroyed by fire.

In the latter part of 1826, James C. Lynch opened a new St. Louis brewery, from which he supplied the city with beer, ale, and porter. The retail price in 1827 was 75 cents per dozen bottles. This was a very successful concern, with Lynch expanding his brewery yearly. In 1831 he advertised that he had eight hundred barrels on hand and had also begun his own bottling. Unfortunately, in 1835 Lynch had to sell his brewing facilities to satisfy creditors.

The city's population had grown to almost six thousand by 1830. The following year, Ellis Wainwright, who had migrated from Yorkshire, England, began the Fulton Brewery. His products were the traditional types of English ale.

James and William Finney began operating the City Brewery in 1834. The Finney brothers, who had been in St. Louis since 1818, had initially operated a general store where they had been involved with the importing of beer from eastern breweries. The Finneys would remain in operation at their original location until around 1848.

The rise of German immigration to St. Louis began in the mid-1830s, around the same time a new brewery began operation. Known as the St. Louis Brewery, it was operated by Isaac McHose and Ezra English. The location at 316 South Second Street produced traditional ales and porters, and the brewery became the most popular in the city.

The last brewery to begin operation during Phase 1 was the Missouri Brewery. Started in 1837 in the northern part of the city, it was owned and operated by Small and Rohr and produced ale, beer, and porter. It ceased to exist in 1841.

Around 1840, the first era of pioneer brewers

was ending. Highlighted by the manufacture of top fermented ales and porters and people entering and exiting the industry at will, it was all done on a small scale. In 1839, only four local breweries were in operation: James and William Finney's City Brewery, McHose and English's St. Louis Brewery, Wainwright's Fulton Brewery, and Small and Rohr's Missouri Brewery. The total production of the St. Louis breweries in 1840 was three thousand barrels. They had an assessed value of nine thousand dollars.

Left: Brewery worker's cellar candle, 1860s.

Bellow: Brewery worker's oil cellar lamp, 1860s.

Phase 2
1840–1865
"The Germanization of St. Louis"

The beginning date of this era actually is unclear. Various St. Louis historians have given the date as 1838, 1840, 1841, and 1842. The fact remains that this phase started whenever Johann Adam Lemp (known as Adam), a native of Eschwege, Germany, began brewing bottom-fermented lager beer in his grocery store at Sixth and Morgan streets. He thereby earned the title of "The Father of Lager Beer in St. Louis."

Lager, which in German means "to store or age," requires the use of bottom-fermenting yeast and a lengthy storage time (to gain clarity and brilliance), and was particularly suited to manufacturing in St. Louis. It was brewed during the winter months and stored in underground caves or cellars until the summer drinking season. There being no means of mechanical refrigeration at the time, the beer was chilled in the naturally cooler temperatures of these caves, as well as by ice that was cut from the frozen Mississippi River during the winter months, hauled to the caves, and packed in straw. The presence of the river and natural caves thus gave aspiring St. Louis brewers a leg up on the competition.

By 1840, the city's population had jumped to more than sixteen thousand residents. The city limits extended from Montgomery Street on the north to Lynch Street on the south, and westward to Eighteenth Street. As the city continued to grow, many more breweries were established over the next two decades. While some operations were fly by night, others served as the foundations for local and even national industry leaders.

Adam Lemp began brewing in a twelve-barrel brew kettle. His beer met with such wide acceptance by the local populace that he soon had to build several new buildings to permit increased output. Quickly exhausting the facilities on Second Street, Lemp began to search for a better site for building a new and larger brewery.

Lemp's contemporaries included Michael Kuntz, who began brewing around 1842 in the area of Eighth and Carr. This brewery was later moved to Cass Street where it was operated by William Nolker, Franz (Frank) Griesedieck, and Theodore Brinckwirth. Also known as the Lafayette Brewery, it would be absorbed into the St. Louis Brewing Association (SLBA) in 1889.

In 1843, Julius Winkelmeyer and Frederick Stifel began operating a brewery at 352 S. Second Street. In 1847, they opened a new facility at 1714 Market Street. Later known as the Union Brewery, its caves extended north under Market Street. This site is now the location of the "New" Post Office. The Union Brewery would also be included in the 1889 consolidation.

In 1845, Adam Lemp selected a site south of the city limits for his new Lemp's Western Brewery, near what is now South Broadway and Cherokee Street. The property had a natural cavern system beneath it. This cave was first expanded to store the output from the Second Street brewery. Newspapers of the time stated that the cave had been expanded to a height of fifty feet, a width of twenty feet, and a length of one hundred yards.

During this time period, McHose and English began one of St. Louis's first beer gardens near what is now Benton Park. They used the natural caves there to store their beer. In an effort to attract customers, they also provided entertainment, including bands, ten-pins, and walkathons.

In 1846, Joseph Uhrig bought a plot of land

on the southwest corner of Eighteenth and Market streets. Extending 100 feet west and 142 feet south, the property was purchased for $525. One year later Uhrig would open the Camp Spring Brewery, overlooking Chouteau's Pond. The brewery's storage caves were a short distance away at what is now the corner of Jefferson and Washington avenues. Located west of the city limits, the caves became a popular gathering place for St. Louisans, offering entertainment in the form of band concerts, operas, picnics, and tours. The brewery was absorbed into the St. Louis Brewing Association in 1889 and was closed in 1891 to make way for the construction of Union Station. The St. Louis Coliseum was erected on the site above the caves in the early 1900s.

About 1848, Charles Stifel took over ownership of James and William Finney's City Brewery. Stifel would erect a new brewery on Fourteenth Street in 1859. Charles Stifel was very active in the local and national brewing industry. In 1867, he served as chairman and presiding officer of the seventh convention of the United States Brewers Association in Chicago. In 1889, he sold the City Brewery to the SLBA syndicate.

Samuel Wainwright, who had joined his brother Ellis in the St. Louis brewing business, took control of the Fulton Brewery upon the death of his brother in 1849. In 1857, he purchased half of the former George Busch brewery located on Gratiot Street between Ninth and Tenth streets. In the late 1850s, he and partner Charles Fritz abandoned the production of ale and began brewing lager beer. Samuel died in 1874, with his son Ellis taking over operation of the brewery. In 1889, the brewery was sold to the SLBA, with Ellis becoming president of the association. Ellis Wainwright also served as president of the United States Brewers Association in 1891 and 1892.

In 1850, St. Louis was home to seventeen operating breweries with a total capacity of sixty thousand barrels per year. The city's population had swelled to over seventy-seven thousand inhabitants, with German immigrants accounting for more than twenty-two thousand of them. The influx of Germans had a lasting effect on the city. Brewery historian James Lindhurst nicely summarized this influence, stating that "the large German population in St. Louis was to make itself felt in the life and customs of the growing city in many ways, but perhaps in no way more than in the brewing industry."

Around this time the Arsenal Brewery was started by Guido and Adelbert Steinkauler. It was later purchased by Louis Obert. Located on the cor-ner of Twelfth and Lynch streets, it operated as an independent brewery until and after Prohibition.

In the early 1850s, William Stumpf began brewing at a site that over the years would carry a variety of names: Stumpf's, Thamer Brewing Company, Anton Griesedieck, Miller Brothers Brewery, Consumers Brewing Company, Griesedieck Brothers Brewing Company, and the Falstaff Brewing Corporation. This brewery holds the distinction of being involved with both local consolidations. In 1889, operating as the Miller Brothers Brewery, it would be included in the St. Louis Brewing Association merger. It was operated by the SLBA only until 1890. Six years later another company purchased the property with the idea of constructing a new brewery there. Reopened as the Consumers Brewing Company, the entirely new facility was operated until 1907, when it joined nine other breweries in a second local consolidation, known as the Independent Breweries Company (IBC).

In 1852, George Schneider built a small brewery on a hillside in south St. Louis, located on the east side of what is now South Broadway, between Lynch and Dorcas streets. In 1856, Schneider moved his brewery to a site on the west side of Eighth Street between Crittenden and Pestalozzi. With the new location came a new name—the Bavarian Brewery. Schneider was overextended financially when in mid-1857 a severe economic depression fell upon the country. Unable to secure sufficient capital to continue operations, and with a production of only five hundred barrels per year, Schneider was forced to sell the brewery. On December 11, 1857, Phillip Hammer, a local cooper, purchased it. Within a week, Phillip entered into a partnership with his brother Carl. The firm's name was changed to C. and P. Hammer Company. Soon a third brother, Adam Hammer, joined the partnership. Then Adam Hammer formed a new partnership with Dominic Urban. The new firm, Hammer and Urban, set out on an immediate expansion program for the Bavarian Brewery, including a new brick brewhouse.

By 1860, production had reached 3,200 barrels a year, ranking twenty-ninth out of the forty breweries operating in the city. Again misfortune struck the owners of the Bavarian Brewery, for they soon realized that production capacity far exceeded the demand for their product; they were forced to declare bankruptcy. During subsequent proceedings, two of the brewery's creditors took over its operation. E. Anheuser and Company, the new operator, represented an equal partnership between Eberhard Anheuser, a successful candle and soap manufacturer, and William D'Oench, a wholesale druggist. D'Oench became a silent partner while Anheuser assumed immediate control of the Bavarian Brewery.

Disaster struck local beer drinkers in 1854, "the year the beer ran out." Local newspapers estimated that 18 million glasses of beer had been drunk in the city between March 1 and September 17. This represented the entire capacity of the local brewing industries' sixty thousand barrels. The papers reported that no more beer would be available until the end of October. The following reasons were given as to why St. Louis was without beer:

- The summer had been one of the hottest in memory.
- There had been a dramatic increase in the number of Germans immigrating to St. Louis.
- The previous year's barley crop had been a poor one.

In response to the 1854 shortage, more breweries began to spring up. Construction of the Gambrinus Brewery on Victor Street was begun in 1855 by Anton Jaeger (also spelled Yeager). The construction was met with some local opposition until a compromise was reached: the brewhouse would be built in the Gothic style, so that if the brewery were not successful, it could be turned into a church. Jaeger's Gambrinus Brewery did succeed, and it would later become the Anthony and Kuhn Brewing Company.

Also in 1855, the Green Tree Brewery was started by Joseph Schnaider and Max Feuerbacher. The partners later moved from downtown to the Soulard neighborhood. One of the city's more successful breweries, Green Tree was absorbed by the SLBA in 1889.

In 1857, Carl Klausmann began brewing at a location on South Broadway in Carondelet, a community located just south of the city. That same year, Joseph Uhrig made St. Louis's first bock beer at his Camp Spring Brewery. The original Excelsior Brewery also started operation in 1857. Located on South Broadway just north of Pestalozzi Street, the Excelsior name would have the distinction of later being used by two other local breweries.

The *Daily Missouri Republican* reported in 1857 on the St. Louis brewing industry and the effects of German immigration: "a sudden and almost unexpected wave of immigration swept over us, and we found the town inundated with breweries, beer houses, sausage shops, Apollo gardens, Sunday concerts, Swiss cheese and Holland herring. We found it almost necessary to learn the German language before we could ride in an omnibus or buy a pair of breeches and absolutely necessary to drink beer at a Sunday concert." The paper went on to list the city's thirty largest breweries, which included Mound, Oregon, Philadelphia, Arsenal, Rocky Branch, Pittsburgh, Iron Mountain, Eagle, and the Wash Street Brewery, among others.

In the late 1850s, Christian Staehlin, Jr. took

The oldest known piece of advertising from E. Anheuser & Co. showing the brewery buildings, underground caves, and the bottling department, circa 1860–1875. Used with permission of Anheuser-Busch InBev. All rights reserved.

over management of the Phoenix Brewery from his father. This brewery was located at Eighteenth Street and Lafayette Avenue and was later swallowed up by the SLBA. In 1859, Louis Koch established a brewery at Tenth and Sidney streets. Later known as the Schilling & Schneider Brewing Company, it would likewise be absorbed into the SLBA syndicate in 1889.

On May 30, 1860, the *Daily Missouri Republican* reported that the forty breweries operating that year in St. Louis were valued at over $1 million. They were producing more than two hundred thousand barrels of beer annually. In order of output, they were:

The Operating Breweries of St. Louis—1860

	Brewery	*Owner*	*Output*
1	Union Brewery	Winkelmeyer & Schiffer	16,000 barrels
2	Phoenix Brewery	Ch. Staehlin	15,500 barrels
3	Busch's Brewery	Fritz, Wainwright & Co.	15,000 barrels
4	Camp Spring Brewery	Joseph Uhrig & Co.	14,000 barrels
5	Arsenal Brewery	G. Steinkauler	9,000 barrels
6	Steam Brewery	F. Boyd & Co.	8,500 barrels
7	Western Brewery	A. Lemp	8,300 barrels
8	Pittsburgh Brewery	Coste & Leusler	8,000 barrels
9	Green Tree Brewery	Joseph Schnaider & Co.	7,500 barrels
10	Stern Brewery	Ch. Longuemare	7,100 barrels
11	Wash Street Brewery	Hamm & Hoppe	6,500 barrels
12	City Brewery	Chr. G. Stifel	6,100 barrels
13	Schnerr's Brewery	Constantine Schnerr	6,000 barrels
14	Iron Mountain Brewery	Adolph Gebhard	5,300 barrels
15	Jefferson Brewery	Bruning & Wettekamp	5,000 barrels
16	Oregon Brewery	Stock Brothers	5,000 barrels
17	St. Louis Brewery	E. English	5,000 barrels
18	Broadway Brewery	G. G. Zoller & Co.	4,800 barrels
19	Bellefontaine Brewery	Pearson, Smith & Co.	4,500 barrels
20	Lafayette Brewery	Theodore Brinckwirth	4,500 barrels
21	New Bremen Brewery	Spangler & Smith	4,500 barrels
22	National Brewery	Fred Wagner	4,500 barrels
23	Rocky Branch Brewery	Charles Zoller	4,500 barrels
24	German Brewery	Eckerle & Weiss	4,300 barrels
25	Stumpf's Brewery	William Stumpf & Co.	4,200 barrels
26	Southern Brewery	Keitz, Schricker & Co.	4,100 barrels
27	Pacific Brewery	Kuntz & Hoffmeister	4,000 barrels
28	Philadelphia Brewery	A. Deutelmoser	4,000 barrels
29	Bavarian Brewery	Gottschalk & Co.	3,200 barrels
30	Excelsior Brewery	Chr. Kohler & Co.	2,500 barrels
31	Gambrinus Brewery	Anton Jaeger	2,500 barrels
32	Franklin Brewery	Tinker Brothers & Co.	2,200 barrels
33	Washington Brewery	Ch. Schneider & Co.	1,950 barrels
34	Jackson Brewery	Jacob Steuber	1,500 barrels
35	Fortuna Brewery	Bergesch, Feric & Co.	1,300 barrels
36	Laclede Brewery	Ch. Stolzh	1,300 barrels
37	Hickory Brewery	Conrad Elliot	1,000 barrels
38	Missouri Brewery	G. Bautenstrauch	800 barrels
39	Schlop Brewery	L. Koch	500 barrels
40	Schumann's Brewery	Ch. Schumann	<u>500 barrels</u>
			212,400 barrels

At this time the larger breweries were using steam power, while most smaller breweries were still being run by hand and horse power. The city's population had risen to 160,000. Because of an increase in production and lower barley prices, the public and the local press campaigned for—and got—a reduction in the price of beer to two glasses for a nickel.

Arriving in St. Louis in 1857, Adolphus Busch found employment on the levee in one of the commission houses. Within a couple of years, he had begun specializing in hops and malt. As a supplier to Eberhard Anheuser, he came to know and admire Anheuser's daughter Lilly. On March 7, 1861, in a double wedding ceremony, Adolphus married Lilly, and his brother Ulrich married Lilly's older sister Anna. Shortly after the wedding, with the Civil War beginning, Adolphus Busch enlisted in the Union army as a private. Other St. Louis brewers to enlist in the Union army included Charles Stifel, who served as a colonel; Anton Jaeger, also a colonel and who was killed at the battle of Lexington, Missouri; William Lemp (son of Adam Lemp) and Otto Lademann (son-in-law of Joseph Uhrig), who both served as captains.

In 1862, William Moran began operating a brewery in north St. Louis that in 1876 was purchased by Robert Jacob, and in 1878 sold again to Marquard Forster. He changed the name to the Hyde Park Brewing Company and operated it under that name until 1889, when it was merged into the St. Louis Brewing Association. Henry Grone and partners likewise began brewing in the early 1860s. Their Clark Avenue Brewery, also known as H. Grone and Company, was also absorbed into the SLBA conglomerate.

Adam Lemp passed away in 1862, at which time his son William took over the operation of the family brewery.

The United States brewing industry, in an effort to help support the Union in its war efforts against the Confederacy, would in 1863 agree to a tax of one dollar per barrel. This was the first national tax on alcohol. The brewers also volunteered to police their own industry to ensure that proper payments were made to the federal government.

In 1864, William Lemp oversaw the construction of a new brewery on the site of the caves his father had developed. That same year William D'Oench, Eberhard Anheuser's silent partner, sold his 50 percent interest in the Bavarian Brewery to Anheuser's son-in-law, Adolphus Busch.

The end of the Civil War in 1865 brought a close to this phase of St. Louis's beer history, which featured a great influx of Germans into the St. Louis area, and along with them the introduction and popularization of lager beer. The industry was still made up of many small breweries serving the local market. For those who were ready, the next decades would bring economic growth, expansion of trade, and a gradual movement toward national and international markets.

Phase 3
1865–1889
"The Glory Days"

The third phase began in 1865 with Joseph Schnaider, formerly associated with the Green Tree Brewery, building a new brewery at Chouteau and Mississippi avenues. It would operate under the name Joseph Schnaider's Chouteau Avenue Brewery until 1889, when it was merged into the St. Louis Brewing Association. Charles Becker started the Liberty Brewery in 1865. A few years later it was purchased by John Heidbreder. Located at 2534 Dodier, it too would be merged into the SLBA.

In 1868, the United States Revenue Department issued a statement regarding the "free beer" supplied to brewery workers. It took the position that "the beer would not be taxed, providing it was not used as an inducement for them to work for less wages or as a part of their wages." This custom continued unchanged at Anheuser-Busch until 1986, when the practice was ended by mutual consent of the company and the unions.

The new but short-lived second site of the German Brewery, founded by Theodore Eckerle and constructed in 1869, was located at Miami and Salena streets. It would operate only until 1871. In need of additional capacity, E. Anheuser and Company purchased the idle brewery

and operated it as a branch of its Bavarian Brewery until 1879. A new brewery called the Home Brewing Company was constructed on the site in 1892. It operated under that name until it was merged into the Independent Breweries Company (IBC) in 1907. The IBC closed the brewery in 1909. Today, the site is a parking lot for the Brewers and Maltsters Local #6 Union Hall.

In 1870, St. Louis annexed the village of Carondelet, and its population stood at 310,000. The same year, Henry Anthony and Francis Kuhn purchased the brewery formerly owned by Civil War casualty Anton Jaeger. Renamed the Anthony & Kuhn Brewing Company, in 1889 it was merged into the SLBA.

There were fifty operating breweries in the city in 1870, with an assessed valuation of $5 million. These breweries employed more than seven hundred workers. William Lemp's Western Brewery had become the city's largest.

The 1870s saw the brewers begin the use of brand names, logos, and trademarks. E. Anheuser & Company registered the "A and Eagle" logo in 1872. Not long after, Adolphus Busch, with much foresight, took immediate advantage of the discovery of pasteurization. This discovery, originally intended to

help the French wine industry, was even more of a boon to the brewing world. Pasteurization provided for the stability of beer, allowing it to be bottled and stored for longer periods of time than was ever before possible. The bottles, sealed with corks by hand, allowed brewers to ship their products to distant markets, forever providing competition to the local brewer. When pasteurization was combined with the use of icehouses and railcars, the brewers who wished to export could greatly expand their production, sales, and profitability. Adolphus Busch was one of the first brewers in the United States to pasteurize, bottle, and ship his beer to other parts of the country and around the world. William Lemp would not be far behind in taking

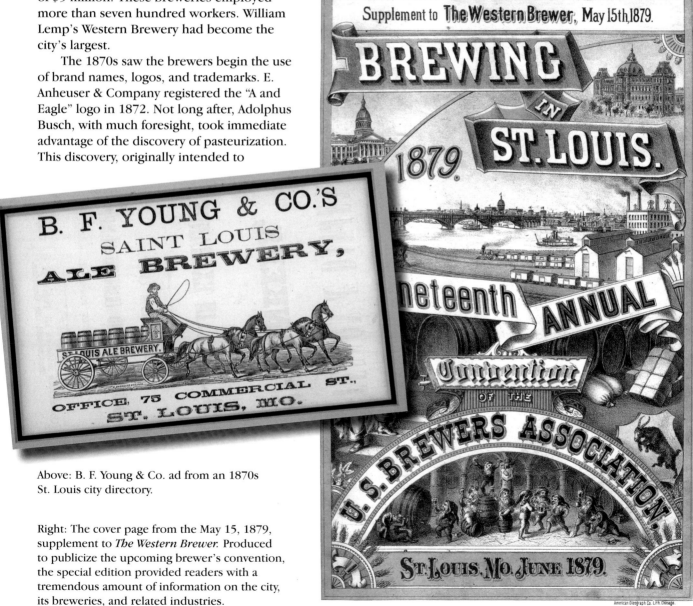

Above: B. F. Young & Co. ad from an 1870s St. Louis city directory.

Right: The cover page from the May 15, 1879, supplement to *The Western Brewer.* Produced to publicize the upcoming brewer's convention, the special edition provided readers with a tremendous amount of information on the city, its breweries, and related industries.

advantage of this discovery and likewise expanding his markets worldwide.

The E. Anheuser & Company changed its name to E. Anheuser Co.'s Brewing Association in 1875. The following year, at the Centennial Exhibition in Philadelphia, the refrigerated railway car debuted. One year later, Anheuser was reported to be using forty of them for beer shipments. In the centennial year, St. Louis expanded its city limits westward to Skinker Boulevard and adopted a resolution separating its urban self from the agrarian population in St. Louis County. Meanwhile, Adolphus Busch and his friend Carl Conrad developed and received U.S. Patent 6376 for a new brand of beer they called Budweiser. Anheuser was reported in the same year to be selling its St. Louis Lager brand in the western town of Denver, Colorado.

By 1877, the local and national brewing industry was beginning to evolve, with small, poorly managed breweries having fallen by the wayside while the better-managed ones expanded. *The Western Brewer* reported that the local brewing industry had produced 421,026 barrels for the year.

The Largest Operating Breweries in St. Louis—1877

William Lemp's Western Brewery	61,299 barrels
E. Anheuser Co.'s Brewing Association	44,961 barrels
Wainwright Brewery	33,000 barrels
Joseph Schnaider's Brewery	25,820 barrels
Charles Stifel's Brewery	25,797 barrels
Winkelmeyer's Brewery	25,473 barrels
H. Grone Brewery	23,970 barrels
Green Tree Brewery	22,200 barrels
Brinckwirth, Griesedieck & Nolker	20,935 barrels
Anthony & Kuhn Brewery	20,189 barrels
Excelsior Brewing Co.	16,707 barrels
St. Louis Brewery	12,000 barrels

On June 4, 1879 (a year in which local brewers produced 528,424 barrels), the United States Brewers Association held its nineteenth annual convention in St. Louis. More than 150 members attended, coming from eighteen states and the District of Columbia. Attendees included Christian Moerlein of Cincinnati; Fred Miller and the Uihlein brothers of Milwaukee; Fred Lauer from Reading, Pennsylvania; and Gustavus Bergner and Charles Bergdoll of Phildadelphia. The official reception and meetings took place at the Germania Club Hall located at Gratiot and Eighth streets. The first evening's entertainment was held at Schnaider's Garden, with local citizens joining the brewers

for a night of festivities, the grand finale being a fireworks salute to the brewers. While in St. Louis, visitors toured the larger local breweries and the city, traveling by carriage to Lafayette Park, Tower Grove Park, Shaw's Garden, Forest Park, and on to a grand reception at the Fairgrounds Park. The final evening, the brewers took an evening steamboat ride to Carondelet and back to the St. Louis riverfront, receiving salutes from workers as they passed the breweries of Anheuser and Lemp.

The importance of export shipping for the local breweries of Lemp and Anheuser can be sensed by *The Western Brewer*'s convention issue detailing the fact that Lemp was shipping bottled beer to all of the South American ports, and Lemp's beer could be purchased in Calcutta, Yokohama, Hawaii, Shanghai, Sidney, Melbourne, London, Paris, and Berlin. Anheuser's product, meanwhile, could be found in the East and West Indies, Central America, Japan, China, Australia, Africa, and the Sandwich Islands. Anheuser's bottling capacity was listed as 100,000 bottles per day.

In addition to the local brewers, *Western Brewer* saw fit to highlight the local brewers' supply trade. Those mentioned included: Charles Ehlermann & Company, C. F. Hermann & Company, and Robert Jacob & Company, all supply houses; Mississippi Glass Company, bottle manufacturer; Fairbanks & Company, brewers' scales; Kupferle Brothers, brass foundry; Conrad Seibel, copper works; L. P. Fries & Son, brass works and beer pumps; Caldwell & Watson, grain conveyors; C. Hoppe & Son, maltsters; John Kimpel, brewers' wagons; St. Louis Refrigerator and Wooden Gutter Company, ale and beer coolers; and the renowned E. Jungenfeld, brewery architect.

It was also in 1879 that the E. Anheuser Company's Brewing Association changed its name once again. The new name was the Anheuser-Busch Brewing Association, reflecting the co-ownership position that Adolphus Busch had assumed. Eberhard Anheuser passed away the next year, and full control of the brewery passed to Busch.

By 1880, the city's population had risen to more than 350,000, and the local brewers produced a combined total of 627,275 barrels, ranking St. Louis as the third-largest brewing city in the United States. Only New York City, with a whopping 2,384,884 barrels, and Philadelphia, with a total production of 765,884 barrels, ranked ahead of St. Louis. The same year Carl Conrad took the Joseph Uhrig Brewing Company to court over the latter's unauthorized use of the Budweiser brand name. Uhrig was ordered by the court to cease using the name Budweiser. This would prove to be the first of many court cases that Anheuser-Busch would pursue over the use of the name. To date, the company has been successful in defending its rights to Budweiser in all but one case within the United States, but has met with mixed results overseas.

In the early 1880s, mechanical refrigeration was one of the latest inventions. Anheuser-Busch and Lemp were the first brewers in St. Louis to take advantage of this technological innovation. Artificial refrigeration allowed brewers to stop using their underground caves, enabled year-round production, provided more stable and more easily controlled storage temperatures, and allowed the use of above-ground insulated storage cellars.

The decade of the 1880s was certainly an interesting one in the St. Louis brewing industry. During this ten-year span, no new breweries of any significant size were introduced. The existing breweries were in a race to expand and modernize their facilities. Mechanical methods of bottling, pasteurization, artificial refrigeration, and export shipping

not only increased the cost of doing business for the existing breweries, but also raised the entry cost for anyone with a desire to get into the brewing business. Numerous ownership changes took place among the existing breweries, and five weiss beer breweries were started, but these were small brewing operations and short-lived enterprises.

While owners were attempting to expand, the brewery workers were trying to organize local trade unions. Although paid well in comparison to workers in most other industries, workers dealt with long hours and hard working conditions. The demands of one brewery workers union in 1881 were:

- A reduction of the workday from thirteen to ten hours.
- A reduction in Sunday work from eight to four hours.
- A minimum wage of sixty dollars per month.
- The right of each employee to seek board and lodging wherever he liked.

The first brewers union was formed in New York

The St. Louis Brewing Association

Anthony & Kuhn Brewing Company	Menard between Sidney and Victor streets
Bremen Brewery Company	3913 North Broadway
Brinckwirth-Nolker Brewing Company	1820 Cass Avenue
Cherokee Brewing Company	Cherokee Street and Iowa Avenue
Excelsior Brewing Company	Eighteenth and Market streets
Green Tree Brewery Company	Sidney Street between Eighth and Ninth streets
A. Griesedieck Brewing Company	Eighteenth Street and Lafayette Avenue
H. Grone and Company	2211 Clark Avenue
Hyde Park Brewing Company	Sixteenth and Salisbury streets
Klausmann Brewery Company	8639 South Broadway
Liberty Brewing Company	2534 Dodier Street
Miller Brothers Brewery Company	Gravois and Shenandoah avenues
Schilling & Schneider Brewing Company	822 Sidney Street
Joseph Schnaider's Chouteau Ave. Brewery	2000 Chouteau Avenue
C. G. Stifel Brewing Company	Fourteenth and Howard streets
Wainwright Brewing Company	Tenth and Gratiot streets
Julius Winkelmeyer Brewing Association	Seventeenth and Market streets
Heim's Brewery Company	Tenth Street and Illinois Avenue (East St. Louis)

City in 1885, while in St. Louis the Brewers and Malt-sters Local #6 was organized on March 28, 1886.

Along with the crosscurrents of unionization, modernization, increased production, and expansion of trade areas, came the inevitable—price wars. Concerted efforts were made to sustain the existing price structure by the larger brewers around the country, but in an effort to compete, the small and medium-size brewers had but one recourse: consolidation.

Consolidation of most local breweries came about in June of 1889. At that time, eighteen St. Louis–area companies were merged to form the St. Louis Brewing Association. The combined output of these plants the previous year had been 800,000 barrels.

The only significant brewers to remain independent were the Anheuser-Busch Brewing Association, William J. Lemp's Western Brewery, and the Arsenal Brewery of Louis Obert.

In November of 1889 a second shock wave hit the St. Louis brewing industry, when it was announced that an English syndicate had purchased the St. Louis Brewing Association for $10.5 million, with local brewer Ellis Wainwright named to head the American wing of the association. Why a British syndicate? For a number of years there had been an economic depression in Great Britain, and English financiers became interested in foreign investments. In keeping with similar trusts set up in the oil and railroad industries, English investors would within a period of two years set up separate brewing syndicates in twenty-one U.S. cities. The SLBA in St. Louis represented their largest and most expensive investment in the American brewing industry. Attempts were also made by foreign investors to consolidate the Anheuser-Busch Brewing Association and William J. Lemp's Western Brewery with the Pabst, Schlitz, and Miller breweries, all of Milwaukee. This effort at national consolidation was unsuccessful. Meanwhile, the local syndicate took immediate steps to become competitive with the larger shipping breweries. The older and less efficient breweries were closed, production was moved into the newer and more cost-efficient plants, management was consolidated, and bulk purchasing was established in an attempt to cut the cost of raw ingredients.

The SLBA consolidation brings an end to the third phase of the St. Louis brewing industry. It had been an era marked by modernization, national expansion, unionization, and finally the consolidation of the local brewing industry.

Phase 4
1889–1920
"The Beginning of the End"

The 1890s began with St. Louis housing three major independent breweries and the syndicate of eighteen other local breweries. Anheuser-Busch and Lemp had been national shippers of beer for a number of years and had both built extensive networks of depots and bottling plants across the country. (Some of the SLBA's breweries exported considerable amounts of beer as well.) From St. Louis their beer could be shipped to these facilities in bulk, then repackaged and bottled for local distribution. Lemp had sixty-four depots in Texas and more than two hundred nationwide. Adolphus Busch, in addition to setting up depots around the country, also began to purchase an interest in out-of-town breweries. At one time or another, he held a position in the Alamo and Lone Star breweries of San Antonio, the Texas Brewing Company of Fort Worth, the American Brewery of Houston, and the Shreveport Brewery and Ice Company of Shreveport, Louisiana.

In 1890, the population of St. Louis had risen past four hundred thousand, and the local breweries' total production continued to make St. Louis the nation's third-largest brewing city. The top six brewing cities as listed by *The Western Brewer* that year were:

New York City	4,257,978 barrels
Chicago	1,673,685
St. Louis	1,613,215
Milwaukee	1,527,032
Brooklyn	1,508,144
Philadelphia	1,458,846

Following the SLBA consolidation, most of the prior brewery owners had continued as members of the local board of directors and managers of their respective breweries. Dissatisfaction with this arrangement became obvious in 1890 when all of the brewing interests of a branch of the Koehler family were merged to form the American Brewing Company. A new brewing facility was built on the site of the former Excelsior Brewing Company to be operated by Henry, Hugo, and Oscar Koehler. They represented just the first brewing family to leave the SLBA to begin a new and independent brewing operation; more would follow. The American Brewing Company would be part of the second consolidation of St. Louis breweries when in 1907

it became a part of the IBC.

By 1892, Lemp was producing more than three hundred thousand barrels per year, while Anheuser-Busch was selling more than seven hundred thousand barrels per year. Both brewers operated their own local railroad companies in order to facilitate the movement of freight.

On February 2, 1892, William Painter, a Baltimore machine shop owner, received a patent on a newly designed bottle closure that was to revolutionize the brewing industry and lead to the creation of the Crown Cork and Seal Company. Called by Painter a "crown cork," it would lead to the standardization of the packaging industry and to the brewing industry's adoption of high-speed filling machines. A superior closure, it soon replaced ceramic and rubber stoppers. With the exception of the internal seal no longer being made of cork and the optional ability to twist the cap off, the design remains unchanged today.

Another new brewery was constructed in 1892 at Twentieth and Madison streets. Known as the Columbia Brewing Company, it was a model for the entire industry. Officers of the new brewing facility were Casper Koehler, president; Rudolph Limberg, secretary; and Zach W. Tinker, treasurer. The Columbia Brewing Company would also be merged into the IBC in 1907.

In 1893, the Pabst Brewing Company of Milwaukee became the first brewer in the world to produce more than 1 million barrels of beer in a year (Anheuser-Busch would not reach this milestone until 1901). St. Louis was also the site of what *The Western Brewer* deemed a "Beer War" in 1893. In "a contest between the independent American interests and the English syndicate that for three years attempted to gain control of the beer market by purchase," the price of beer to retailers had been reduced considerably. Saloon patrons were insisting that the retail price go down accordingly. An SLBA-tied saloon owner was quoted as saying:

Unless the syndicate comes to our relief, I do not see how this beer war can continue any length of time without doing retailers incalculable injury. We do not experience much difficulty with people who call for a glass of beer, but it is the bucket trade that is beginning to hurt us, and that is, in St. Louis, the heavier trade of the two after you get beyond the heart of the city. We have been selling one quart and a quarter for five cents, and now our customers expect us to sell two quarts and a half for five cents.

The introduction of what were to be two of St. Louis's most popular and enduring brands of beer occurred in the 1890s. In 1896, Anheuser-Busch introduced Michelob, a draft beer supposedly developed for connoisseurs. Its distribution would be tightly controlled, and it was permitted to be served only at finer establishments. In 1899, Lemp introduced the Falstaff brand, which would soon become its flagship label, and after Prohibition would give its name to the Falstaff Brewing Corporation.

A different type of brewery merger took place in 1897, when Hilda Lemp, daughter of William Lemp Sr., married Colonel Gustav Pabst, son of the founder of the Pabst Brewing Company of Milwaukee. When Hilda's sister Elsa married an Englishman, the stage was set for the English to once again unsuccessfully attempt to consolidate the Pabst and Lemp breweries.

The Union Brewing Company started a plant in St. Louis in 1898. Otto Stifel, son of Charles Stifel, resigned from the presidency of the SLBA to take over the Union facility in 1906, establishing Otto F. Stifel's Union Brewing Company. Located at Gravois Avenue and the southwest corner of Michigan Avenue, the plant, which began making oleomargarine when Prohibition neared, was used by Falstaff afterward.

Paulus Gast, a longtime St. Louis wine manufacturer, opened a brewery in 1900 at 8541 North Broadway with an annual capacity of seventy-five thousand barrels. Known as the Gast Brewing Company, it would also be part of the Independent Breweries Company merger.

During the spring of 1901, the Empire Brewing Company began operating at Sarah Street and Duncan Avenue. With a capacity of one hundred thousand barrels per year, it would operate as an independent brewery until 1907, when it too was merged into the IBC.

Crusading prohibitionist Carrie Nation visited St. Louis on July 5, 1901. She was on her way to Crawfordsville, Indiana, to answer charges of attempting to wreck a saloon there. As she approached Oheim Brothers' saloon on Walnut Street, she began lecturing against drink to some men standing nearby. Nation removed the famous nickel-plated hatchet from her purse but was dissuaded from using it, instead choosing to address the crowd that had gathered. The bartender summoned police, who took Nation to their station in a patrol wagon. She was released after being admonished not to stir up any more trouble.

The first in a series of tragedies destined to befall the Lemp family also occurred in 1901, when Frederick Lemp, the favorite son of William Lemp Sr., died of a heart attack at the age of twenty-eight. An 1893 electrical engineering graduate of Washington University who also completed studies at the United States Brewers' Academy (he trained at the family and European breweries as well), Frederick had been groomed to take over the lead role in the Lemp Brewing Company. His older brother William would then inherit that duty.

In 1902, Jacob Schorr and Henry Kolkschneider, two men who had long been associated with the local brewing scene, opened the Schorr-Kolkschneider Brewing Company. Located on Natural Bridge Road and Parnell Street, it would operate as an independent brewery until it was (at least supposedly) closed in 1919 for Prohibition.

In 1903, the William J. Lemp Brewing Company formally registered the Falstaff name and shield logo. The next year, William J. Lemp Sr., still despondent over the untimely death of his son, and also the passing of his close friend and fellow brewer Frederick Pabst, took his destiny into his own hands. On the morning of February 13, 1904, he committed suicide in his upstairs bedroom at the Lemp Mansion. The late Lemp's estate would be valued at over $10 million.

Later in 1904, St. Louis welcomed citizens from all over the world to its Louisiana Purchase Exposition. Between opening day (April 30) and the closing ceremony on December 1, more than

Above: Budweiser Barley Malt Syrup was a Prohibition-era product from Anheuser-Busch.

Left: A postcard view showing the grounds of the German Tyrolean Alps venue at the 1904 St. Louis World's Fair.

19 million visitors came to town to see what became popularly known as the 1904 World's Fair. The local brewers did their part to make the fair a resounding success. Adolphus Busch served on the board of directors, in charge of European matters. He used his international reputation and influence to convince many of the European nations to exhibit at the fair. William J. Lemp Jr.

ner Brewing Company into the IBC, would again set out on his own. In 1910, Wagner and his son opened the Forest Park Brewing Company on the south side of Forest Park Boulevard, just west of Grand Avenue. It would in later years become the cornerstone of the Falstaff Brewing Corporation.

At this time, Carrie Nation, the Woman's Christian Temperance Union, and the Anti-Saloon

---

The Independent Breweries Company

American Brewing Company	2814 S. Broadway	St. Louis, MO
Central Brewing Company	Eighteenth Street and E. Broadway	East St. Louis, IL
Columbia Brewing Company	Twentieth and Madison streets	St. Louis, MO
Consumers Brewing Company	1900 Shenandoah Avenue	St. Louis, MO
Empire Brewing Company	Sarah Street and Duncan Avenue	St. Louis, MO
Gast Brewing Company	851 Hornsby Avenue	St. Louis, MO
Home Brewing Company	Miami and Salena streets	St. Louis, MO
National Brewery Company	Eighteenth and Gratiot streets	St. Louis, MO
Wagner Brewing Company	2101 Adams Street	Granite City, IL

---

also served on the board of directors and on the Agriculture Committee. In conjunction with the fair, the city also played host to the annual United States Brewers Association and the Master Brewers Association of America conventions that year.

The local brewers also joined forces to construct and host the World's Fair's German Tyrolean Alps. Located next to the main entrance, it recalled the Bavarian Alps and operated as the largest dining and entertainment venue at the fair.

On June 26, 1907, the *St. Louis Globe-Democrat* advised local citizens that a second consolidation of the local brewing industry, which had been rumored for over a year, was at last completed. Most of the smaller breweries begun since the 1890s had found themselves unable to grow large enough to compete in what was by this time not only a very competitive local market, but also a national and international marketplace. Taking a cue from the earlier English syndicate, nine local brewers merged to form the Independent Breweries Company.

The output of these combined plants was estimated to be 650,000 barrels per year, with a total capacity of 800,000 barrels. The total value of the assets for the nine breweries was listed at $6.8 million; they employed around 1,500 men. Henry Griesedieck Jr. of the National Brewery Company was elected to serve as IBC president, and one person from each brewery was to serve on the board of directors.

Edward Wagner, who had merged his Wag-

League were campaigning even harder for national Prohibition and were winning many converts to their cause. The "golden era" of the U.S. brewing industry was about to come to an end.

The last completely new brewery to be constructed in St. Louis prior to Prohibition was the Mutual Brewing Company, located at Boyle and Duncan avenues. Mutual beer was first available to the local populace on August 22, 1913. The company would survive only until 1917, when its assets were sold at a public auction.

One way for the brewers to fight the dry movement was to preach economics. In 1916, Hugo Koehler, president of the Independent Breweries Company, told *American Brewer* that over the past ten years St. Louis breweries had average expenditures over $1.1 million per year for new buildings and machinery. He also stressed that the twenty-one St. Louis breweries had 9,617 employees earning more than $5 million a year. Plus, they paid $3.3 million in federal taxes and $785,230 in city and state taxes annually.

In addition to the pressures of the prohibitionists, the brewers, who were primarily of German ancestry, would face the wave of anti-German feelings that swept the country as a direct result of the war in Europe. At one time celebrated citizens of their community, they now found some of the local population turning against them.

In spite of all of the negative happenings in the brewing industry, in 1917 "Papa Joe" Griesedieck purchased the failing Forest Park Brewing

Company and renamed it the Griesedieck Beverage Company. At the time it had only one brew kettle, with a capacity of 125 barrels. Annual production stood at ten thousand barrels.

The United States entered World War I in 1917, and immediately government limits were placed on the amount of grain that could be allocated to brewers. Amid severely restricted output, anti-German feelings, and the daily strengthening of the Prohibition movement, the nation's brewers prepared for the inevitable. The Anheuser-Busch Brewing Association changed its corporate name in 1919 to Anheuser-Busch, Incorporated. Many of the local breweries began to or continued to produce various types of non-alcoholic beverages. Soon, malt tonics, near beer, malt syrup, and the like were the only types of malt products they could legally manufacture.

On January 16, 1919, the necessary thirty-sixth state in the Union ratified the Eighteenth Amendment to the U.S. Constitution. It prohibited the manufacture and sale of all forms of alcoholic products: ale, beer, wine, and whiskey. Prohibition went into effect one year after ratification, on January 16, 1920, and was soon backed by the enforcement provisions of the Volstead Act. Only those breweries willing to violate the law—and some were—could try to sneak real beer out the door.

Prohibition brought an abrupt end to the fourth phase of St. Louis brewing history. The "golden era" of brewing in St. Louis and in the United States had come to a screeching halt.

Phase 5
1920–1933
"The Dark Days of Prohibition"

The next historical phase begins with Prohibition in full swing. All of the breweries were required by law to cease producing beer with an alcoholic content greater than 0.5 percent. Thousands of employees were laid off, and the majority of the breweries closed. Attempts were made by some to shift production to other products. The St. Louis Brewing Association closed all but one of its breweries and tried to survive on near beer and soft drinks. The Independent Breweries Company met with some success in the area of soda manufacturing. Their soda brand IBC root beer had decent sales in the local market. This brand name was revived a number of years ago and is still with us today.

At Lemp, company ownership was split among various family members, all of them independently wealthy and having no desire to struggle through Prohibition. William J. Lemp Jr. unceremoniously shut down the Lemp Brewing Company. Employees arrived at work one day only to find the plant locked. Lemp made no attempt to enter any other form of manufacturing. In 1920, Elsa Lemp followed in her father's footsteps by committing suicide.

Anheuser-Busch, Inc., and the Griesedieck Beverage Company did not sit idly by. They both made an active effort to survive the great national experiment. Anheuser-Busch produced and aggressively marketed near beer, malt tonic, soda, ice, malt, wagons, refrigerated cabinets, and diesel engines. The mood was such that A-B would do almost anything to keep its employees working and to generate income. Some of the brewery buildings were even rented to other manufacturers in an attempt to remain solvent. The Griesedieck Beverage Company followed suit. It manufactured near beer, soda, and malt tonic, and even went so far as to use the brewery facilities to cure hams.

In 1920, William J. Lemp Jr. and "Papa Joe" Griesedieck met in Lemp's office to discuss Griesedieck's possible purchase of the Falstaff name and logo. An agreement was reached, and Falstaff was sold to Griesedieck for twenty-five thousand dollars. Lemp was paid five thousand dollars in cash with a promise that the balance would be paid

within nine months. Shortly thereafter, the name of the Griesedieck Beverage Company was changed to Falstaff Corporation.

In 1922, the Lemp Brewing Company complex was sold at auction to the International Shoe Company for about 10 percent of the facility's estimated value. On December 29, William J. Lemp Jr. committed suicide in the same room of the Lemp Mansion where his father had killed himself in 1904.

In March of 1927, after much planning, Anheuser-Busch, Inc., converted its idle stockhouse #3 into a plant for the production of baker's yeast. Sales were discouragingly slow during the first couple of months, but by the end of the year, the company was operating more than twenty distributor branches in ten states. Production in December of 1927 exceeded two hundred

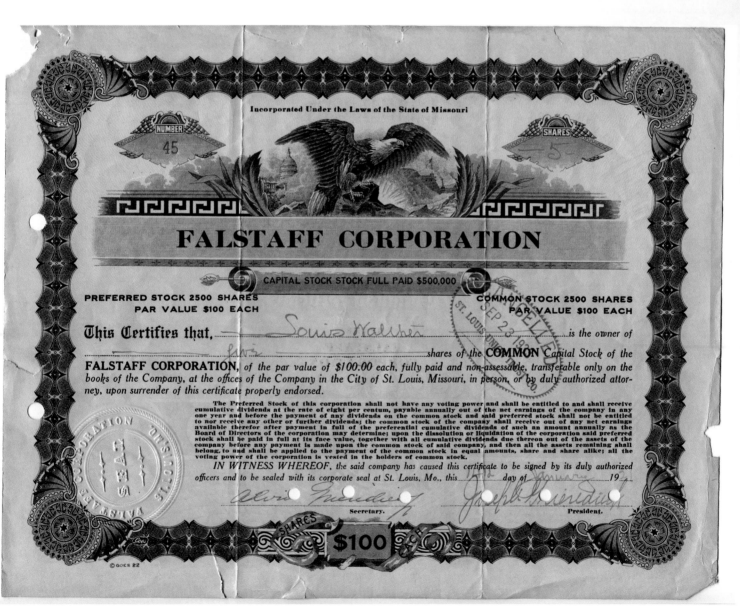

An original Falstaff Corporation stock certificate belonging to brewmaster Louis Walther and signed by Alvin and Joseph Griesedieck.

thousand pounds. Within four years sales had grown to such heights that the capacity of the St. Louis facility had been reached, and yeast sales accounted for more than one-third of A-B's total sales revenue. It was at this time that the company built a new yeast plant production facility in Old Bridge, New Jersey.

During the election of 1932, one of the Democratic Party's campaign promises was to repeal Prohibition. With Franklin D. Roosevelt winning the White House, the Democrats made good on their platform. They had public sympathy behind them, as most citizens had come to realize that the "noble experiment" had become not only an embarrassment, but also a total failure. In preparation for the Repeal of national Prohibition, on January 16, 1933, the Falstaff Corporation changed its name to the Falstaff Brewing Corporation. The Twenty-first Amendment to the Constitution, designed to undo the Volstead Act, was introduced on February 14, 1933, and ratified by the House of Representatives. The required three-fourths of the states voting in favor of Repeal would not happen until December 5, 1933. But for the nation's brewers, Repeal would come early. The Cullen-Harrison bill was passed on March 22 and allowed for production of 3.2 percent beer, deemed "non-intoxicating." The brewers had been given a head start and were allowed to begin brewing in preparation for "New Beer's Eve," set for midnight, April 7. At last, the "Dark Days of Prohibition" had drawn to a close, heralding an end to the most dismal phase of St. Louis brewing history.

Phase 6
1933–1957
"Happy Days Are Here Again"

April 7, 1933—"Beer Is Back!" and the next phase of St. Louis brewing began. Anheuser-Busch, Inc., and the Falstaff Brewing Corporation were ready and immediately began serving the local market, supplying St. Louisans with their first legal beer in more than thirteen years. The Schorr-Kolkschneider Brewing Company was back in operation shortly thereafter.

Falstaff, operating from its original small facility on Forest Park Boulevard, quickly found itself unable to keep up with demand. In April, Falstaff began negotiations with Carl Stifel to lease the former Otto F. Stifel's Union Brewing Company. An agreement was reached and the plant was reopened on July 1, 1933. The Hyde Park Breweries Association would provide its Hyde Park brand to local residents beginning on December 12, 1933.

On March 31, 1934, the Columbia Brewing Company reopened, returning the Alpen Brau brand on draft to the local citizenry, followed soon by the ABC Brewing Corporation in May and the Obert Brewing Company in June of the same year. By September of 1934, the Gast Brewery, Inc., Griesedieck Brothers Brewing Company, and the Carondelet Brewing Company were all in operation. The local brewing industry, which in 1919 had produced more than 3 million barrels, was back up and running. Its importance to the area economy is illustrated by the fact that in just eighteen months local brewers had invested

1936 original Budweiser can design.

more than $5 million in the construction and modernization of their facilities.

Having guided Anheuser-Busch through the troubled times of Prohibition, and with brighter days ahead for the brewing industry, a physically ailing August A. Busch Sr. committed suicide in 1934. The brewery came under the control of Adolphus Busch III, who in 1927 had handled the successful entry of Anheuser-Busch into the yeast market.

On January 24, 1935, another major innovation came to the brewing industry. On that day in Richmond, Virginia, the G. Krueger Brewing Company of Newark, New Jersey, introduced to the world Krueger's Ale and Beer packaged in cans. Krueger was reluctant to test this new package in its local marketing area, and Richmond was considered far enough away that if the idea failed, it would not adversely impact Krueger's sales. The success of canned beer is history, and within months many other brewers had followed Krueger's lead. The following year the ABC Brewing Corporation

became the first St. Louis brewery to begin marketing beer in cans. Anheuser-Busch and Falstaff would follow this trend shortly thereafter. Beginning a move toward national expansion, in February 1935 the Falstaff Brewing Corporation purchased the failing Krug Brewing Company of Omaha, Nebraska. Falstaff would acquire its fourth brewery (including the leased Stifel plant) in 1937, purchasing the National Brewing Company of New Orleans. In 1936, the Obert Brewing Company in St. Louis went out of business. For a variety of reasons, other local breweries began to fail. The ABC Brewing Corporation closed its doors in 1938, reopen and then close again, while the Schorr-Kolkschneider Brewing Company was shuttered in 1939, followed by the Carondelet Brewing Company in 1941.

World War II saw restrictions again placed on the U.S. brewers' use of grain, with a resulting reduction in beer production. In 1942, the federal government also placed restrictions on the use of metal for bottle caps and beer cans; no canned

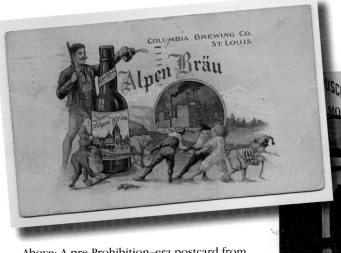

Above: A pre-Prohibition–era postcard from the Columbia Brewing Company showing the brewery, gnomes, and the Alpen Brau label design.

Right: April 7, 1933, "Beer is Back" and Adolphus Busch III, August A. Busch Sr., and August A. "Gussie" Busch Jr. are shown with the first case of bottled beer and a "Certificate of Priority," which was inserted into each case produced on the first day following Repeal.

beer was sold domestically between 1942 and 1946. The brewers also adjusted production to package more beer in quart containers in order to reduce the quantity of metal crowns used. The government did allow the brewers to package beer in cans for overseas shipment to military personnel. Along with everything else during the war, the beer cans shipped overseas were olive drab in color.

In 1943, William Lemp III died of a heart attack. He had loaned his name to a brewery in East St. Louis that resurrected the Lemp brand; it went out of business a couple of years later. In 1944, the Falstaff Corporation completed the purchase of the former Otto Stifel brewing facility, which it had been leasing since 1933. Adolphus Busch

III, who had guided Anheuser-Busch, Inc., since 1934, passed away in 1946. Succeeding him was his younger brother, August A. "Gussie" Busch Jr.

When the war was over and all government restrictions were lifted, the race began to see who would become the new leader in the U.S. brewing industry. Anheuser-Busch would begin its national expansion by constructing new breweries, while Falstaff would resume its growth by continuing to purchase older facilities. In 1948, Anheuser-Busch was the nation's fourth-largest brewer, producing more than 4 million barrels of beer. Falstaff ended the year in fifth place with a total production of over 2.9 million barrels, including the production from the Columbia Brewing Company facility,

Top 5 U.S. Brewers—1948

Joseph Schlitz Brewing Co.	Milwaukee, WI	4.6 million barrels
P. Ballantine & Sons	Newark, NJ	4.1 million barrels
Pabst Brewing Co.	Milwaukee, WI	4.1 million barrels
Anheuser-Busch, Inc.	St. Louis, MO	4.0 million barrels
Falstaff Brewing Corp.	St. Louis, MO	2.3 million barrels

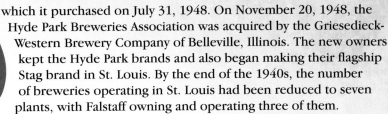

which it purchased on July 31, 1948. On November 20, 1948, the Hyde Park Breweries Association was acquired by the Griesedieck-Western Brewery Company of Belleville, Illinois. The new owners kept the Hyde Park brands and also began making their flagship Stag brand in St. Louis. By the end of the 1940s, the number of breweries operating in St. Louis had been reduced to seven plants, with Falstaff owning and operating three of them.

The 1950s would witness the changing of the guard insofar as who could lay claim to being the nation's largest brewer. In 1950, St. Louis remained a huge player in the American beer business, with four of the nation's top twenty brewers operating plants in the city: A-B (#2), Falstaff (#7), Griesedieck-Western (#11), and Griesedieck Brothers (#20). The city became the second-leading beer producer in the country, behind only Milwaukee.

In 1951, Anheuser-Busch began operating its first brewery outside of St. Louis, opening its new brewing facility in Newark, New Jersey. In 1952, Falstaff closed the former Otto Stifel facility on Gravois and Michigan, which was no longer needed following Falstaff's acquisition of the more modern and larger Columbia plant.

In an effort to expand westward, in 1952 Falstaff purchased the San Jose, California, facility of Wieland's Brewing Company. This was followed by the 1953 acquisition of the Berghoff Brewing Cor-

Top 5 U.S. Brewers—1956		
Joseph Schlitz Brewing Co.	Milwaukee, WI	5.9 million barrels
Anheuser-Busch, Inc.	St. Louis, MO	5.8 million barrels
P. Ballantine & Sons	Newark, NJ	3.9 million barrels
Falstaff Brewing Corp.	St. Louis, MO	3.8 million barrels
Pabst Brewing Co.	Milwaukee, WI	3.4 million barrels

poration facility in Fort Wayne, Indiana.

In 1954, Anheuser-Busch also expanded westward, opening a new brewing facility in Los Angeles. Late in the year the Carling Brewing Company, another company with national aspirations, acquired the two Griesedieck-Western facilities in St. Louis and Belleville.

Anheuser-Busch introduced a "popular priced" brand in 1955. Originally called Busch Lager, the name was later changed to Busch Bavarian and still later simplified to just Busch. Meanwhile, Falstaff was expanding into Texas with a pair of 1956 purchases—the Gulf Brewing Company of Galveston and the Mitchell Brewing Company of El Paso.

The year 1957 saw many significant changes involving St. Louis brewers. While Anheuser-Busch would become the "King of Beers," the year also saw the Carling Brewing Company close the former Hyde Park plant in November. In December, Falstaff, which opened a new office complex at 5050 Oakland Avenue, entered into a friendly takeover of the Griesedieck Brothers Brewing Company, and with the added sales volume they became the nation's third-largest brewer.

Since Prohibition's end, the nation's brewing industry sales leader had switched several times among Anheuser-Busch, Pabst, and Schlitz. In the early 1950s, A-B firmly set its sights on being the industry leader, and with Gussie Busch leading the way, they succeeded in overtaking Schlitz in 1957. A-B has continued as the U.S. industry leader ever since.

Anheuser-Busch's ascension to the top brings a close to this sixth phase of St. Louis brewing history. The nationwide industry shakeout of the smaller brewing companies was now nearly complete. Many had been under-capitalized, some had poor management, and some had tried to use pre-Prohibition equipment and wound up making poor quality beer. The expansion of the post–World War II economy and the migration of families to the suburbs also helped hasten the demise of many of the small brewers.

Phase 7
1957–1991
"Toward a National Expansion"

The next historical era saw the requirements for those who desired to stay in the brewing business change. A national market would be required in order to reach an economy of scale, and television advertising would begin playing a major role in bringing the brewers' marketing messages to the entire country.

Anheuser-Busch, wanting to develop market share in the southeastern portion of the United States, purchased the American Brewing Company's plant in Miami on February 6, 1958. A 400,000-barrel-capacity brewery, it would be used to manufacture the Busch Bavarian brand as well as Regal Beer, which had been American's flagship brand. While the purchase was being challenged on anti-trust grounds by the Federal Trade Commission, Anheuser-Busch began construction of a completely new brewery in Tampa. The Tampa facility delivered its first beer in 1959, and in October of 1961, A-B sold the Miami brewery to the National Brewing Company of Baltimore.

A 1950s die-cut cardboard in the shape of the Falstaff shield, featuring a couple aboard a boat.

In 1958, Falstaff closed down operations at its original brewery on Forest Park Boulevard. At this time Falstaff was operating both the former Columbia and the former Griesedieck Brothers facilities in St. Louis. Although Anheuser-Busch was the largest brewery on a national basis, Falstaff was still the top seller in the local market. For the year 1962, Falstaff maintained a 37 percent share of the beer market in the state of Missouri, while Anheuser-Busch held 27 percent.

In 1964, as part of the St. Louis Bicentennial celebration, Falstaff opened its International Museum of Brewing, located in the lower level of a new visitor and hospitality center across the street from the main brewery. Not far away, on December 15, Gussie Busch drove the bung into his brewery's 10 millionth barrel. A-B had become the first brewer to ever produce 10 million barrels of beer in a single year.

In 1965, Falstaff purchased the Narragansett Brewing Company of Cranston, Rhode Island. At the time, Narragansett was the largest brewer on the East Coast, and Falstaff felt that the purchase would provide the market penetration and production facilities required to enter the competitive northeastern beer market. Unfortunately, the Federal Trade Commission felt otherwise, and they filed an antitrust lawsuit that would drag on until 1972. In the end, the purchase was allowed to stand, but the battle had cost the Falstaff Brewing Corporation dearly. In turn, industry analysts thought that Falstaff had paid twice the amount it should have for Narragansett.

In 1966, Anheuser-Busch opened a new brewery in Houston, and the company finally overtook Falstaff in the Missouri market, obtaining a 31 percent market share relative to Falstaff's 28 percent share. The year would also be the high-water mark for Falstaff as far as the number of barrels of beer produced. Nationwide, the company produced

more than 7 million barrels, to rank as the nation's fourth-largest brewer. But the stage was set for Falstaff's demise, and its status as one of the leading breweries in the country was about to collapse.

In 1967, Falstaff discontinued brewing operations at the former Columbia plant. At this time, all local operations were consolidated into the main plant, the former Griesedieck Brothers facility.

Anheuser-Busch continued its national expansion program in 1968, opening a new brewery in Columbus, Ohio. In 1969, A-B brought yet another new brewing facility online in Jacksonville, Florida. That same year saw the beginning of a major change in the U.S. brewing industry, when the W. R. Grace Company sold its 53 percent interest in the Miller Brewing Company to the Philip Morris Company.

Philip Morris purchased the remaining 47 percent of Miller in June of 1970. All told, the company had paid $227 million to acquire the brewer. Meanwhile, Anheuser-Busch opened a new brewery in Merrimack, New Hampshire, and in November produced its 20 millionth barrel for the year, becoming the first brewer to reach that milestone. The year also saw the last of the Lemp brothers, Edwin, die on November 30 of natural causes.

The Falstaff Brewing Corporation witnessed its Missouri market share fall to 17 percent in 1972, while Anheuser-Busch led the market with 37 percent of the state's beer sales. A-B opened a new brewery in Williamsburg, Virginia, while Falstaff purchased the trademarks, brands, and trade names of the P. Ballantine & Sons brewery of Newark, New Jersey. This was another attempt by Falstaff to strengthen its market position on the East Coast and to try to bring its brewing facilities back to full operating capacity.

The Ballantine purchase cost Falstaff $4 million, plus an agreed-upon payment of 50 cents for each barrel produced over the next six years.

Top 5 U.S. Brewers—1957		
Anheuser-Busch, Inc.	St. Louis, MO	6.1 million barrels
Joseph Schlitz Brewing Co.	Milwaukee, WI	6.0 million barrels
Falstaff Brewing Corp.	St. Louis, MO	4.3 million barrels
P. Ballantine & Sons	Newark, NJ	3.9 million barrels
Theo. Hamm Brewing Co.	St. Paul, MN	3.3 million barrels

Top 5 U.S. Brewers—1966		
Anheuser-Busch, Inc.	St. Louis, MO	13.5 million barrels
Joseph Schlitz Brewing Co.	Milwaukee, WI	9.4 million barrels
Pabst Brewing Co.	Milwaukee, WI	9.0 million barrels
Falstaff Brewing Corp.	St. Louis, MO	7.0 million barrels
Carling Brewing Co.	Baltimore, MD	5.1 million barrels

Around this time, Meister Brau, Inc., of Chicago had declared bankruptcy. Meister Brau had but three assets to sell: its Chicago brewery, its San Francisco brewery, and its brand names. In July, Falstaff purchased the San Francisco brewery for $2.5 million, and Miller Brewing purchased, for an undisclosed amount, the Buckeye and Meister Brau brand names plus a little-known brand of low-calorie beer called Lite. The following year, 1973, marked the first year that the Miller Brewing Company broke into the nation's top five brewers.

Top 5 U.S. Brewers—1973		
Anheuser-Busch, Inc.	St. Louis, MO	29.8 million barrels
Joseph Schlitz Brewing Co.	Milwaukee, WI	21.3 million barrels
Pabst Brewing Co.	Milwaukee, WI	13.1 million barrels
Adolph Coors Co.	Golden, CO	13.1 million barrels
Miller Brewing Co.	Milwaukee, WI	10.9 million barrels

Anheuser-Busch continued its domination of the U.S. brewing industry in 1974, producing more than 30 million barrels of beer. That same year, August A. Busch III was elected president of the company, succeeding his father. During the elder Busch's run as corporate president, A-B had added eight new breweries, and annual beer sales had risen from 3 million barrels to more than 34 million.

Falstaff had closed its San Jose brewery after acquiring the Meister Brau plant in San Francisco, but was unable to reach the West Coast sales volume needed to keep the 1.5-million-barrel-capacity brewery operating profitably. So in October 1974, the San Francisco plant was sold to San Francisco–based General Brewing Company, headed by Paul Kalmanovitz. Terms of the sale called for General to produce the Falstaff brand under contract.

In 1975, a modern-day beer war began. The Miller Brewing Company, assisted by its parent corporation Philip Morris, began heavily promoting its recently acquired Lite beer brand. With the stated intention of replacing Anheuser-Busch as the industry leader, Miller began construction of new breweries. Miller's strategy was one of market segmentation, where a company tries to divide the existing market into smaller segments so that, from a sales standpoint, it has products to offer to a wider variety of consumers. Philip Morris had been successful in this type of marketing within the cigarette industry, and now applied the same techniques to the brewing industry. In addition, Philip Morris would apply profits from its other divisions toward the marketing of the Lite beer brand. Overall, Miller began spending $1.58 per barrel on advertising, while Anheuser-Busch was spending $0.98 per barrel and Falstaff was spending just $0.48 per barrel. Meanwhile, the owners of Falstaff, faced with declining sales and profits, agreed to sell controlling interest in the company to Paul Kalmanovitz in March for $10 million cash, plus an additional $10 million to pay current debts.

In 1976, Anheuser-Busch opened a new brewery in Fairfield, California. But backed by Philip Morris money, Miller was starting to make a dent in Anheuser-Busch's supremacy.

By 1977, Falstaff's share of the Missouri beer market had fallen to 7 percent, while Anheuser-Busch's share was 35 percent. Anheuser-Busch would also enter the "lite/light" beer segment of the market that year with the introduction of its Natural Light brand, positioned to compete head-to-head with Miller Lite. Falstaff sold its remaining stock to Paul Kalmanovitz, and on November 4 the St. Louis brewery was closed forever. Gabe and Walker, Falstaff's advertising cowboys, had ridden off for the last time.

The Miller Brewing Company moved into second place in U.S. brewing industry sales in 1977. The next year Anheuser-Busch became the first brewer to exceed the 40-million-barrel mark, producing 41.6 million barrels. Miller produced 31.2 million barrels, drawing to within 10 million barrels of the leader. However, this would be the closest that Miller would ever get to Anheuser-Busch. By 1980, A-B would pass the 50-million-barrel mark and widen the gap over Miller to 13 million barrels. The race was over.

Miller had constructed a new brewery in Trenton, Ohio, hoping it would be needed to meet increased demand for its products. But by the time it was finished in 1981, Miller's sales had turned flat, and the completed brewery sat idle until finally opening ten years later. Anheuser-Busch, meanwhile, opened its eleventh brewery, this one in Baldwinsville, New York, in 1983. That same year A-B sold more than 60 million barrels of beer.

A new low-alcohol brand called LA was introduced by A-B in 1984, and that year the company produced a record 64 million barrels. This represented 34.6 percent of the beer manufactured in the United States. Its breweries accounted for 82.9 percent of the Anheuser-Busch Companies' sales and 96.5 percent of operating income. *Fortune* magazine ranked Anheuser-Busch as the nation's fifty-third-largest industrial company. Truly, the little Bavarian Brewery had come a long way.

Anheuser-Busch passed the 70-million-barrel production mark in 1986. On March 28, 1988, the first shipment of beer was made from its newly completed brewery in Fort Collins, Colorado. In 1989, A-B became the first brewer to exceed the 80-million-barrel mark in sales, producing 80.7 million barrels. For the year 1990, sales reached 86.5 million barrels, commanding a 43-million-barrel lead over second-place Miller. A-B's national market share represented 43.7 percent of industry sales. The Anheuser-Busch Companies achieved $11.6 billion in gross sales, with a net income of $842 million. For 1990, *Fortune* magazine ranked the business as the forty-fourth-largest industrial company in the United States by sales. The goal of controlling half of the nation's beer industry was beginning to look possible.

U.S. brewing industry sales stayed flat in 1991, and Anheuser-Busch maintained its hold on the number-one sales position with total production of 86 million barrels. This phase of the history of brewing in St. Louis closes with Anheuser-Busch holding firm to its leadership position for the thirty-fifth straight year.

Top 5 U.S. Brewers—1984		
Anheuser-Busch, Inc.	St. Louis, MO	64.0 million barrels
Miller Brewing Co.	Milwaukee, WI	37.5 million barrels
Stroh Brewing Co.	Detroit, MI	23.9 million barrels
G. Heileman Brewing Co.	LaCrosse, WI	16.7 million barrels
Adolph Coors Co.	Golden, CO	13.1 million barrels

Phase 8
1991–Present
"The Craft Brewers Arrive"

The next phase of St. Louis brewing history began on December 26, 1991, when the Saint Louis Brewery, Inc., opened its Tap Room brewpub for business.

This new segment of the U.S. brewing industry had begun in California in the early 1980s. Brewpubs performed both the brewing and selling of beer and ale on their premises. Many of them also served food. Liquor laws in the state of Missouri had to be changed to allow this type of business. The Saint Louis Brewery was the first to take advantage of the new statutory changes that were put into effect in the summer of 1991. The company was incorporated on August 22, 1989, by Tom Schlafly, Dan Kopman, Charles Kopman, and Joe Tennant, who had set out in search of a location even before the law was changed. The partners settled on purchasing the former John S. Swift Building at 2100 Locust Street, which had been used as a backdrop in the 1981 movie *Escape from New York*. Listed on the National Register of Historic Places, and having survived a neighborhood fire in 1976, the building was in need of major renovations. Schlafly and associates began by renovating the south end of the building only.

The thirteenth Anheuser-Busch brewery came online in 1993 with the opening of a brewery in Cartersville, Georgia, that could produce 7 million barrels per year. A-B continued to lead the industry with record sales of 87.3 million barrels. This represented a 44.3 percent share of the U.S. beer market. Total sales for the Anheuser-Busch Companies had reached $13 billion, with net income (before special charges) of $980 million.

The city of St. Louis was behind the curve when it came to the opening of brewpubs, but it would see its second such establishment in 1995 with the September 1 opening of the Morgan Street Brewery on Laclede's Landing. Lance Lierheimer served as the first head brewer for owners Steve and Vicki Owings and partners Dennis and Randy Harper.

A-B's Tampa brewery, in operation since 1960,

was closed in December of 1995. The decision was based on the fact that the Cartersville brewery, online since 1993, was ramping up toward maximum capacity, along with the fact that the Tampa plant was situated in the middle of Busch Gardens. Busch Entertainment had an interest in expanding the park, and the brewery was expendable.

In June of 1996, the Saint Louis Brewery announced that, beginning with the pale ale and oatmeal stout styles, it would have its Schlafly brands bottled under contract by the August Schell Brewing Company of New Ulm, Minnesota. Distribution was in place for selling these brands in St. Louis, St. Charles, and Columbia, Missouri.

Davide Weaver, owner of the Bacchus Brewing Company, started his brewpub at a location in Union Station formerly occupied by Dierdorf & Hart's Steak House. Bacchus opened in April 1999 and operated only until early 2000. It was quickly reopened in May of 2000 as the Route 66 Brewery and Restaurant, formerly located in suburban Crestwood. This brewpub stayed open until January 2005. Owners of both establishments cited the high rental cost per square foot and a lack of nearby parking as reasons for their demise.

In 2001, Anheuser-Busch became the first brewery in history to reach the milestone of 100 million barrels of production in a single year. Cracking into the top five of U.S. brewers that year was the Boston Beer Company. It was the brainchild of Jim Koch, a descendant of nineteenth-century St. Louis brewer Louis Koch. The formula for Jim Koch's Samuel Adams Boston Lager was derived from an old recipe used at the family's Soulard brewery.

The Saint Louis Brewing Company, in need of greater production capacity and with a desire to bring its bottled beer production home, opened the Schlafly Bottleworks on April 7, 2003. Located

in a former Safeway grocery store in the St. Louis suburb of Maplewood, the facility doubles as a brewpub and a bottling plant.

The brewpub business finally began taking off in St. Louis in the twenty-first century. Holding the modern record as the shortest-lived brewpub is the City Grille and Brewhaus, located in the former Playboy Club building at 3914 Lindell Boulevard. Opened in December of 2005, it was sold the next month and quickly closed in March of 2006. Steve and Molly Neukom, owners of the Augusta Brewing Company in Augusta, Missouri, opened the Square One Brewery at 1727 Park Avenue in the Lafayette Park neighborhood on February 20, 2006. In 2008, a distilling operation was added to this brewpub.

February 1, 2007, was the effective date for Anheuser-Busch to begin serving as the U.S. distributor for InBev. The brands included Beck's, Bass, and Stella Artois. With financial support from the Anheuser-Busch "Here's to Beer" campaign, the first St. Louis Brewers Heritage Festival was held in Forest Park in May 2007. The event featured beers from seven local breweries. To honor this event and the rich brewing heritage of St. Louis, the Missouri History Museum hosted an exhibit called *From Kettle to Keg*, featuring many St. Louis pre-Prohibition brewery items. The exhibit was open from April 2007 through January 2009. The second St. Louis Brewers Heritage Festival, in May 2008, once again supported by A-B's "Here's to Beer" campaign, featured more than sixty beers from eight local breweries, along with samplings from the St. Louis Brews, the local home brewers' organization.

Opening day for Dushan Manjencich's Buffalo Brewing Company was St. Patrick's Day, March 17, 2008. Located at 3100 Olive Street near the Saint Louis University campus, the brewpub, while con-

Top 5 U.S. Brewers—1993		
Anheuser-Busch, Inc.	St. Louis, MO	87.3 million barrels
Miller Brewing Co.	Milwaukee, WI	44.0 million barrels
Adolph Coors Co.	Golden, CO	19.8 million barrels
Stroh Brewing Co.	Detroit, MI	12.5 million barrels
G. Heileman Brewing Co.	LaCrosse, WI	8.9 million barrels

Top 5 U.S. Brewers—2001		
Anheuser-Busch, Inc.	St. Louis, MO	100.0 million barrels
Miller Brewing Co.	Milwaukee, WI	40.1 million barrels
Adolph Coors Co.	Golden, CO	22.7 million barrels
Pabst Brewing Co.	Milwaukee, WI	9.2 million barrels
Boston Beer Co.	Boston, MA	1.1 million barrels

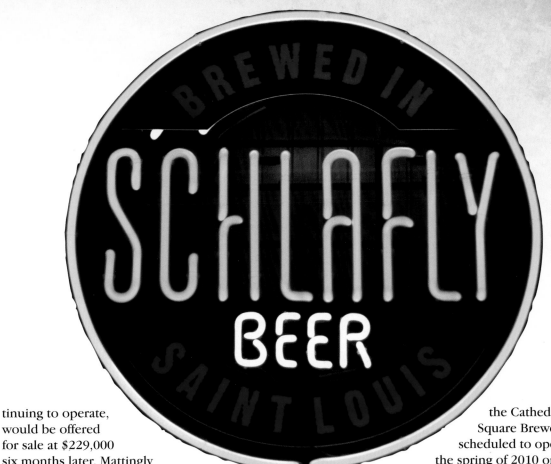

tinuing to operate, would be offered for sale at $229,000 six months later. Mattingly Brewing Company at 3000 South Jefferson had its grand opening in June 2008. With the belated arrival of the brewing equipment, the brewpub began serving its own beers that November, with Drew Huerter serving as brewer. The Amalgamated Brewing Company, doing business as The Stable, would open its doors on June 21, 2008, in the former stable building of the Lemp Brewing Company. The brewing equipment would not arrive until January of 2009, with the house brews placed on tap on May 29, 2009.

Following months of a rumored merger between InBev and Anheuser-Busch, the plans were unveiled in late May of 2008, with InBev announcing a planned takeover of A-B. Following weeks of back and forth negotiations, an agreement was reached on July 13, 2008, whereby InBev would acquire the outstanding shares of Anheuser-Busch stock for $70 per share. This placed a value on the company of $52 billion.

The summer and fall of 2008 saw the Schlafly Bottleworks add additional brewing and fermenting equipment, raising capacity to forty-one thousand barrels per year. Distribution of the Schlafly brand by then extended to ten states.

The latest entry into the local brewing scene, the Cathedral Square Brewery, is scheduled to open in the spring of 2010 on Lindell Boulevard in the location formerly occupied by the City Grille and Brew Haus.

As we commemorate the history of 200 years of brewing in St. Louis with the publication of *St. Louis Brews*, we look forward to the future. These are truly exciting times for beer and brewing in St. Louis. The city today is home to the North American headquarters of the world's largest brewer, as well as the location of one of the largest breweries in the world. The local microbreweries are running their bottling lines at full capacity, while the area brewpubs continue to grow in number. St. Louis now has two major beer festivals along with a host of smaller events. On the internet, beer aficionados are served by numerous websites and by two blogs that cover the local brewing scene and host lively discussions: www.stlhops.com and www.stltoday. com/lagerheads. Local homebrewers seem to be multiplying in number, and interact closely with their commercial counterparts.

Best of all, the availability of a wide variety of locally made beers is at an all time (at least post-Prohibition) high. Lovers of the city's beer and brewing history can hopefully look forward to recording and documenting the next two hundred years of brewing in St. Louis.

Chapter 2

The Major Brewers in St. Louis

This chapter is devoted to the breweries that in the authors' opinions represent the major St. Louis brewing firms. These brewers were also around long enough and late enough that most received ample mention in both local histories and industry publications such as *American Brewer* and *The Western Brewer*. Some were involved with the 1889 consolidation and others the consolidation of 1907. Some returned after Prohibition; sadly, most did not. These breweries also did plenty of advertising, which has kept their names alive in the collections of breweriana buffs as well as historians.

Well over thirty breweries qualify as notable in the two hundred years of brewing in St. Louis. This number alone marks the city as a great brewing center. They are presented here with a few of their individual histories covering more than one enterprise. The smaller breweries and today's craft brewers will be covered in subsequent chapters.

A lithograph from the E. Anheuser Co.'s Brewing Association, circa 1875–79. This litho features a factory scene with the brewery moved east in an effort to show the Mississippi River, a bottle of their flagship brand St. Louis Lager, the bottling department, and bottle wielding cherubs. Courtesy Missouri History Museum, St. Louis.

Anheuser-Busch Incorporated

#1 Busch Place

George Schneider	1852–1857
Philip Hammer	1857–1857
Philip & Carl Hammer	1857–1857
Philip, Carl, & Dr. Adam Hammer	1857–1858
Dr. Adam Hammer	1858–1858
Dr. Adam Hammer & Dominic Urban	1858–1859
Gottschalk & Co.	1859–1860
E. Anheuser & Co.	1860–1875
E. Anheuser Co.'s Brewing Association	1875–1879
Anheuser-Busch Brewing Association	1879–1919
Anheuser-Busch, Inc.	1919–2008
Anheuser-Busch InBev	2008–

Top: Eberhard Anheuser, 1805–1880, founder and president 1860–1880. Used with permission of Anheuser-Busch InBev. All rights reserved.

Bottom: The brewhouse clock tower, showing the original design including the observation deck. The building was placed on the Register of National Historic Landmarks in 1967. Used with permission of Anheuser-Busch InBev. All rights reserved.

FROM HUMBLE BEGINNINGS IN SOULARD

"It was indeed a very primitive affair—a hole in the ground, supported by neither brick nor stone wall, being the cellar, with a board shanty over it, for the brew house." This description, given in 1903 by H. S. Rich and Co. in the groundbreaking work *100 Years of Brewing*, describes the original 1852 brewery of George Schneider. From such humble beginnings the "hole in the ground" grew to become the brewing division of the Anheuser-Busch Companies, which in 2007 had sales in excess of $18 billion. That year A-B's brewing division had worldwide beer sales of 128 million barrels and ranked 149th on the *Fortune* 500 listing of the top American corporations. When Belgium-based InBev's cash takeover offer of $70 per share was accepted in July of 2008, the SEC filings placed a value on the Anheuser-Busch Companies Inc. of $52,274,585,107.24. The merger set the stage for the new company to take an even fuller part in the global marketplace. From humble beginnings, in 156 years the company had risen to the top.

The George Schneider who opened the Bavarian Brewery on the east side of Carondelet Avenue (now South Broadway) between Dorcas and Lynch streets in 1852 is believed by most local brewery historians to have been the same George Schneider who had previously operated the Washington Brewery, beer garden, and saloon located at Third and Elm streets. With the men stationed at the nearby United States Arsenal as a steady source for customers, Schneider met with enough success to construct a new brewhouse in 1856 near what is today Eighth and Crittenden streets. For unknown reasons, Schneider ran into financial problems the following year, leading to a three-year series of brewery ownership changes. Interim owners included Philip Hammer; then Philip Hammer and Carl Hammer; next Phillip Hammer, Carl Hammer, and Adam Hammer; then just Adam Hammer; followed by a partnership of Adam Hammer (a local physician) and Dominic Urban (president of the St. Louis Board of Assessors). In 1859 and 1860, the brewery was briefly operated by the firm of Gottschalk and Company, headed by Charles W. Gottschalk, whose day jobs included St. Louis city registrar and president of the Washington Mutual Fire Insurance Company. On May 30, 1860, the *Daily Missouri Republican* listed the forty operating breweries in St. Louis, showing the Bavarian Brewery ranking twenty-ninth in size with an annual production of thirty-two hundred barrels.

The ownership changes ended that year when Eberhard Anheuser and his friend William D'Oench, a pharmacist, took over the Bavarian Brewery and renamed it the E. Anheuser and Company Bavarian Brewery. Anheuser, born in Kreuznach, Prussia, on September 27, 1805, came to St. Louis in 1842, where he became a successful soap manufacturer. As a silent partner, William D'Oench represented the "and Co." part of the ownership.

TWO NEW SONS-IN-LAW

During a double wedding ceremony on March 7, 1861, Adolphus Busch married Anheuser's daughter Lilly, and Adolphus's brother Ulrich Busch married Lilly's sister Anna. Adolphus, born July 10, 1839, in Kastel, near Mainz in the Grand Duchy of Hesse, immigrated to the United States in 1857. Arriving in St. Louis, he began work on the riverfront as a clerk in the wholesale supply business. Eventually, he formed a partnership with Ernst Wattenberg and opened the wholesale commission house of Wattenberg, Busch, and Company. Ulrich and Anna moved to Chicago, where he engaged in the brewery supply business. Adolphus enlisted in the Union army for three months shortly after his wedding. Returning from the war, he re-entered the supply business and in 1864 began part-time work as a salesman for the Bavarian Brewery.

In 1869, Adolphus Busch sold his share in Wattenberg, Busch, and Co. and used the funds to purchase William D'Oench's half-interest in the Bavarian Brewery. The brewing company was restructured, with Anheuser maintaining the position of president and Busch becoming secretary. With his new ownership position, Busch began taking a more active part in the management and growth of the brewery.

Top left: Adolphus Busch, 1839–1913, president 1880–1913. Used with permission of Anheuser-Busch InBev. All rights reserved.

Bottom left: Pre-Prohibition–era photo of the Anheuser-Busch Brewing Association bottling department. Note the women outnumber the men and boys.

Below: Carl Conrad ad. Used with permission of Anheuser-Busch InBev. All rights reserved.

THE 1870S AND 1880S

Anheuser may have backed into the beer business, but Busch was knowledgeable in the industry as well as the process. During the 1870s and 1880s, Busch seized upon many of the latest scientific and industrial innovations. These included pasteurization, which allowed a brewery to package, store, and ship products with a much longer shelf life, and mechanical refrigeration, which allowed the brewers to build their stockhouses above ground, no longer requiring the use of underground caves. These innovations allowed the brewery to begin bottling its product in 1872 under Busch's guidance, and an article in *The Western Brewer* ten years later called him the "father" of lager beer bottling.

In 1875, the Bavarian Brewery's corporate name was changed to E. Anheuser Co.'s Brewing Association. The next year, at the Centennial Exposition in Philadelphia, refrigerated railcars were exhibited, and within one year the brewery owned a fleet of forty such cars. This paved the way for the southern and westward expansion of the brewery's sales territory. This was accomplished by the construction of numerous icehouses along the railroad rights of way where ice in the cars could be replenished, guaranteeing the safe arrival of beer to distant destinations.

Carl W. Conrad, 1843–1922, the original owner of the Budweiser brand name. Used with permission of Anheuser-Busch InBev. All rights reserved.

THIS THING CALLED BUDWEISER

The year of America's centennial, 1876, saw the introduction of Budweiser lager beer, brewed by E. Anheuser Co.'s Brewing Association but bottled and distributed by Carl Conrad, a local wine and liquor merchant doing business as C. Conrad & Company. Carl Conrad registered the trademark "Budweiser" in the U.S. Patent Office on July 16, 1878. In January 1883, Conrad declared bankruptcy and licensed the Budweiser name, bottling, and marketing rights to what had become known as the Anheuser-Busch Brewing Association. It was his largest creditor and held a ninety-four thousand–dollar lien. In January 1891, A-B legally acquired all rights to the Budweiser name and trademark from Conrad and his wife; the Busches and Conrads would remain lifelong friends.

For more than 130 years, A-B has defended the ownership of the name Budweiser in courts around the world (including an early victory over the Joseph Uhrig Brewing Company of St. Louis). Not always successful in this defense, the company's argument stems from the claim that the name Budweiser is a brand name and a registered trademark. However, the Czech Republic brewer Budejovicky Budvar N.P. (which began brewing in 1895) makes a counter-argument that its Budweiser is a style of beer based on the geographic origin of the product. A-B has on a number of occasions failed in its attempt to purchase the Czech brewery outright, so the battle continues to this day.

During the late 1800s, many American brewers such as Miller, Schlitz, and others sold a beer they called Budweiser based on the claim that Budweiser is a style of beer. However, all were blocked in their attempt to use the name. Only the tiny DuBois Brewing Company of Dubois, Pennsylvania, won a lawsuit that entitled it to use the name, which lasted into the 1970s when DuBois was purchased by the Pittsburgh Brewing Company. Pittsburgh continued usage of the label only to have the lawsuit reopened; following the court's decision, its use of the Budweiser name was terminated.

THE SHIPPING BREWERIES

From 1870 to 1900 the population of the United States nearly doubled. The city of St. Louis was seeing dramatic growth as well, making it a good time to be in the local beer business. Further, with technological changes beginning in the 1870s, growth for those breweries located on the less populated western fringe of the United States, such as St. Louis, could occur by

E. ANHEUSER CO'S BREWING ASSOCIATION
BOCK

ST. LOUIS, MO.

Above: A lithograph from the E. Anheuser Co.'s Brewing Association, circa 1875–1879. This litho depicts five goats propelling King Gambrinus and the introduction of the springtime seasonal bock beer. During the late nineteenth century, all St. Louis breweries produced bock beer and traditionally introduced their version on May 1. Courtesy Missouri History Museum, St. Louis.

Right: Reverse-on-glass hanging sign from the 1890s.

City	Barrels	Population
New York, NY	2,987,811	1,911,698
Philadelphia, PA	765,844	847,170
Chicago, IL	458,894	503,185
St. Louis, MO	627,275	350,518
Cincinnati, OH	584,431	255,139
Milwaukee, WI	577,992	115,587

1880 beer production in barrels versus population (ranked by population)

expanding markets to the south and west (and for that matter, everywhere else).

The above table shows how the major eastern brewing centers of New York and Philadelphia, along with Chicago, were large population centers. Hence, the brewers there had a vast local market in which to sell. Meanwhile, the brewing centers of St. Louis, Cincinnati, and Milwaukee had a much smaller population base and, therefore, looked beyond their local markets to increase sales.

Not surprisingly then, the large shipping breweries grew to include Anheuser-Busch and the William Lemp Brewing Company of St. Louis (many other St. Louis breweries shipped to a lesser extent); the Valentine Blatz, Joseph Schlitz, and Pabst brewing companies of Milwaukee; and the Christian Moerlein Brewing Company of Cincinnati.

With additional capacity needed, in 1871 E. Anheuser & Co. purchased the former German Brewery located just a couple of miles south of the main plant and operated it as a branch brewery until 1879. The brewery's efforts to expand its market paid off quite handsomely. Production rose from 31,545 barrels in 1875 to over 200,000 in 1881. By 1887, A-B was the number-one brewery in the world, selling an incredible 456,511 barrels. Such monumental sales required constant expansion and modernization at the brewery. A-B kept a series of local architectural firms such as E. Jungenfeld and Company; Widmann, Walsh & Boisselier; and Janssen & Janssen quite busy. An 1886 article in *The Western Brewer* discussed some of the company's new buildings, including a new stockhouse designed by the recently deceased architect Edmund Jungenfeld. It called A-B's growth "the wonder of the country . . . never apparently completed, the buildings of this vast concern continue to spread out in every direction, until they form, like some of the great establishments at Burton-on-Trent in England, a village by themselves, within the heart of a city."

Two of the numerous methods of delivering Anheuser-Busch products that have been used over the years. The horse-drawn buckboard below shows the delivery of beer in the West circa 1880s.

With their demand for railcars increasing, in 1878 Adolphus Busch and three other St. Louis businessmen established the St. Louis Refrigerator Car Company for the purpose of buying, building, leasing, and operating refrigerator cars. In 1880, the use of these railcars helped Anheuser-Busch's beer to become the exclusive U.S. beer sold on draft at the new Metropolitan Concert Hall in New York City. Sent in a car that could hold eight hundred barrels, the brew was kept uniformly cold from the St. Louis brewery to the "lips of the consumer." By 1883, the fleet size was up to two hundred cars, and the company was building its own refrigerator cars. By 1888 it was operating a fleet of 850. Manufacturers Railway Company was formed in 1887 to handle the local switching of railcars between the brewery and the main rail lines. To reach the national market and complete the expansion to the south and west, a network of distribution was established that included local agents, branches, storage depots, icehouses, and bottling works. The transportation methods basically followed the Mississippi River south to New Orleans and the established railways to the west and southwest.

For A-B, selling beer in remote markets proved to be entirely different from selling it in St. Louis, where its established name and reputation were known. Selling beer to people who did not know of the company required advertising. In addition to print ads, point-of-sale material had to be created and distributed by sales agents. With this branding in mind, the "A and Eagle" logo had been created in 1872. Brand names were also established during this time period, one of the most famous being St. Louis Lager, with the reputation that St. Louis had as a great brewing city bringing immediate recognition to the name. Of course any brewery in St. Louis could produce something called "St. Louis Lager," so the Budweiser brand name would later replace St. Louis Lager as A-B's flagship brand.

To reflect the new ownership position and growing influence of Adolphus Busch, the brewery was renamed the Anheuser-Busch Brewing Association in 1879. The following year, Eberhard Anheuser, the company's principal founder, passed away. A-B's rapid growth continued, and by the mid-1880s sales had overtaken those of the Lemp Brewing Company, its chief local rival.

THE GOLD MEDAL AND THE BLUE RIBBON

Throughout the nineteenth century the worldwide competition for medals at expositions and fairs was hotly contested. At the World's Columbian Exposition held in 1893 in Chicago, regarded by the brewers as the most important competition of the century, the rivalry came to a head. At the time, Pabst was the largest brewer in the United States, with A-B holding second place. At one point in the competition, A-B had been awarded six medals with Pabst having received five. The grand prize was still to be awarded, and the judges' scrutiny was intense. A dispute flared over the makeup of the judges' panel and the method of awarding points; the brewers, interested only in product quality, disputed the fact that points were to be awarded for "commercial importance." Ultimately, A-B's Budweiser was awarded the highest award over Pabst's Blue Ribbon beer. This decision was later reversed based on a chemical analysis supposedly showing that Budweiser contained impurities: the award was then given to Pabst. Outraged, Adolphus Busch appealed the decision, and the exposition commission then announced that no award would be given. With Busch threatening legal action, the commission again reversed itself and gave the award to Budweiser. Once more, Pabst complained and again was declared the winner. Busch pursued one judge across Europe in an effort to get him to change his mind. In late 1894, the commission announced its refusal to reconsider the decision, and Busch was quoted as saying, "Prizes are not given to the goods meriting same but are secured by money and strategy." This statement speaks volumes as to why the Anheuser-Busch Brewing Association did not have any entries in the beer judging at the World's Fair held in St. Louis in 1904.

In addition to the judging controversy, the 1893 World's Fair was significant to A-B for the lavish display it mounted, consisting primarily of a fifteen thousand dollars facsimile of the entire plant. Designed by E. Jungenfeld & Company on a scale of 1 inch to 4 feet, it included details such as all the brewing equipment, pipes, and railway cars. The model brewery was hooked up to electricity and actually ran, but the one-barrel brew kettle could not produce beer because of federal regulations. Surrounding the entire mini-brewery was an ornate pavilion decorated with bottles of six different A-B brands: Budweiser, White Label, Pale Lager, Columbian Muenchener, Anheuser, and Liquid Bread (the latter an extract of malt sold exclusively by David Nicholson of St. Louis).

CUSTER'S LAST FIGHT

In addition to his many other talents, Adolphus Busch was a master when it came to advertising and marketing. A-B would produce and distribute calendars, pocketknives, openers, corkscrews, and postcards all featuring the name or image of the brewery. But without question the most lasting and famous advertising piece was the artwork known as *Custer's Last Fight*. The original painting was done in St. Louis in the 1880s by Cassilly Adams, and it passed through several owners, ending up on the wall of a saloon on Olive Street. Adolphus Busch had admired the work and eventually acquired it. He commissioned F. Otto Becker, an artist employed by the Milwaukee Lithographic Engraving Company, to create a new drawing based on Adams's work to be lithographed for mass distribution. In 1896, the same year that A-B introduced its super-premium brand Michelob, thousands of copies of Becker's version of *Custer's Last Fight* were distributed. Over time, more than a million copies were produced, making it one of the most popular pieces of artwork in American history.

THE ST. LOUIS 1904 WORLD'S FAIR AND THE RUSH TO PROHIBITION

The new century would get off to a great start for the Anheuser-Busch Brewing Association, as in 1901 it overtook national competitor Pabst and first reached 1 million barrels in annual production. With preparations being made for St. Louis to host the 1904 Louisiana Purchase

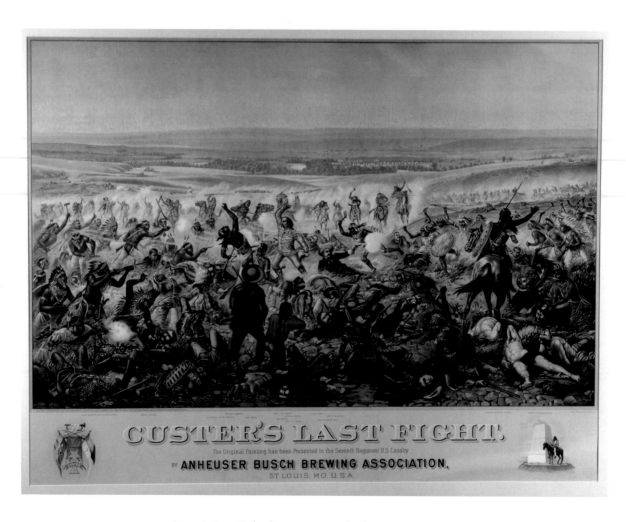

Custer's Last Fight, from an original oil painting by Cassilly Adams, litho by F. Otto Becker. With the exception of the Clydesdales, the most recognized piece of Anheuser-Busch advertising. Used with permission of Anheuser-Busch InBev. All rights reserved.

Exposition, Adolphus Busch accepted the position of World's Fair director. In addition, many of the local brewers, led financially by Busch, came together to create the German Tyrolean Alps, the fair's largest entertainment venue. Located on the east end of the "Pike" and next to the main entrance, the Alps covered in excess of six acres and proved to be one of the most popular attractions of the fair. But behind the scenes, there were numerous disputes between the Alps owners and the management of the fair. These included trash pickup, blocking of the service entrance by railroad cars, the width of the walkways, and the cost of electricity and water. The disputes festered throughout the summer, with letters going back and forth between the two sides, all of which led to Busch's resignation in November of 1904. In addition to taking part in the Alps venture, A-B also had an exhibit in the fair's Palace of Transportation.

While it is interesting to note that no St. Louis brewers submitted their beers for judging at the fair (and no reason has been unearthed as to why), brewers from seventeen different countries did enter the competition. Although only nine breweries from the United States were represented, the Indianapolis Brewing Company's Dusseldorfer brand was awarded the grand prize. To celebrate, its employees were given a day off, and soon the brewery was displaying a facsimile of the medal on its etched glasses.

Following the closing of the fair, many of the state and national buildings were put up for sale or were simply demolished. Busch saw to it that the brewery purchased the Belgium national building. It was moved onto A-B's property and reconstructed for use by the Adolphus Busch Glass Manufacturing Company.

In 1905, A-B announced plans for a $1.2 million expansion program, most of it in the form of a new seven-story stockhouse. The company, which had suffered several recent losses from fire, opted to insure the plant for $6 million, ten times the previous amount. By 1907 production had risen to nearly 1.6 million barrels, more than one-third of it bottled Budweiser. It took 173 million bottles to contain the 560,000-plus barrels filled.

Adolphus Busch and his wife, Lilly, celebrated their golden wedding anniversary in 1911 at their home in Pasadena, California. In honor of the occasion, the brewery was closed to give its five thousand employees a day off. Among those

sending presents to the couple were President William Howard Taft, former president Theodore Roosevelt, and Emperor Wilhelm II.

With the gathering storm clouds of Prohibition becoming more and more ominous, Anheuser-Busch, other national brewers, and various brewing organizations worked to separate the brewing industry from the hard liquor industry. They eventually failed. Brewers also began producing low- and non-alcoholic beverages. A-B trademarked the Bevo brand, a non-intoxicating malt-based beverage, on August 31, 1908.

Suffering from ill health, Adolphus Busch died on October 10, 1913, while on a trip through Europe. His body was returned to St. Louis where funeral services were held on October 25. It took twenty-five trucks to haul all of the funeral flowers to the cemetery. A crowd estimated at twenty-five thousand gathered around the brewery to pay tribute to Busch, who was laid to rest in Bellefontaine Cemetery. Obituaries noted Busch's lifelong charitable donations and an estate valued at over $50 million. With his death, the control of A-B passed on to August A. Busch Sr., who continued the fight against the Drys. Residing at his country estate known as Grant's Farm and traveling back and forth to the brewery each day, he would continue to direct the brewery's attempts to distance itself from the poor reputation of some saloons by constructing and operating three local restaurants of upscale design. These included the Stork Inn, located at 4527 Virginia Avenue and opened in 1910; the Gretchen Inn, now known as the Feasting Fox, located at 4200 South Grand, which opened in 1913; and the Bevo Mill, located at 4749 Gravois and opened in 1918.

In 1916, A-B shipped out 150 carloads of beer in a single day, a record for a U.S. brewery. Late that year construction was started on a new bottling plant. The project took longer than expected and ended up costing $10 million. Named the Bevo Bottling Plant, it finally opened in 1918 as the largest bottling facility in the world. The next year saw A-B sell a reported 3.9 million bottles of Bevo, although sales would quickly dwindle through the 1920s. As the brewing industry wound down in preparation for the coming of Prohibition, a new corporate name, Anheuser-Busch Incorporated, was adopted on November 22, 1919.

PROHIBITION

A-B ceased brewing operations on December 1, 1918, in response to President Woodrow Wilson's wartime proclamation prohibiting the use of any food product for making malt beverages. The brewery had enough beer in storage to sell until running out in the middle of 1919. By then, the Eighteenth Amendment calling for Prohibition had already been passed and was set to go into effect on January 16, 1920.

What does a brewery do when it cannot legally make beer? Throughout the nation, some brewers saw the glass as half empty and simply abandoned their plants and went off to other endeavors. Other brewers, seeing the near-beer glass as half full, did

everything within their power to keep facilities open and employees working. August A. Busch Sr. can be counted among the latter group. Between 1919 and 1933, he worked within the laws to repeal Prohibition. He lobbied local, state, and national officials on behalf of Anheuser-Busch and the brewing industry. Busch felt that Prohibition would eventually be repealed, he just didn't know when. To keep his people employed and to generate a revenue stream, Busch ventured into a variety of products, including baker's yeast, corn products, ice, ice cream, near beer, ice cream cabinets, malt

Above: August A. Busch Sr., 1865–1934, president 1913–1934. Used with permission of Anheuser-Busch InBev. All rights reserved.

Left: The distinctive Bevo Mill, located at 4749 Gravois and constructed under the supervision of August A. Busch Sr., opened in 1918.

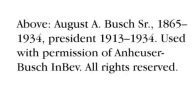

syrup, refrigerated trucks, non-alcoholic malt-based beverages, motor truck bodies, ginger ale, grape soda, and root beer, along with coffee- and chocolate-flavored drinks.

Prohibition was finally seen as an utter failure (from a financial, ethical, and/or moral point of view) by a majority of citizens, and even by many politicians. The Democrats included the repeal of Prohibition in their 1932 presidential election platform, and following Franklin D. Roosevelt's victory were quick under his leadership to enact a modification to the Volstead Act. This allowed for the production and sale of beer with an alcoholic content of 3.2 percent or less by weight beginning on April 7, 1933. On "New Beer's Eve," as the day became known, A-B and Falstaff were the only two St. Louis brewers ready to sell beer. Remaining open during the dark years had enabled A-B to quickly resume the production of real beer. To commemorate the repeal of Prohibition, on the afternoon of April 7, 1933, outside the main office on Pestalozzi Street, August A. Busch Jr. presented to his father a gift of six Clydesdales pulling a beer wagon loaded with kegs of Budweiser. The Clydesdales would go on to represent Anheuser-Busch and become one of the most famous and loved corporate icons. They have appeared seemingly everywhere, from the Calgary Stampede to the Rose Bowl Parade.

After receiving the required votes of three-quarters of the states, the passage of the Twenty-first Amendment on December 5, 1933, completely repealed the Eighteenth Amendment. It stands as the only amendment to the Constitution that has ever been repealed. August A. Busch Sr. had been handed the reins of the brewery upon the death of his father in 1913 and had overseen its continued growth. He had steered it through Prohibition and lived to see that era end. His business had been vindicated, but he was suffering from health problems and committed suicide on February 13, 1934. A-B's presidency was handed over to Adolphus Busch III. It was his responsibility to guide the brewery through the remainder of the Depression and World War II.

Just as before Prohibition, the brewery began a lengthy period of continuous expansion and modernization. From 1933 to 1936, nearly $8 million was spent on such efforts. In 1936, the company reported around $3 million in

Above: Adolphus Busch III, 1891–1946, president 1934–1946. Used with permission of Anheuser-Busch InBev. All rights reserved.

Below: The Clydesdales and beer wagon shown alongside the stables in St. Louis, April 1933. Originally, the hitch was made up of six horses. Used with permission of Anheuser-Busch InBev. All rights reserved.

profits. Two years later a similar amount was spent on yet more improvements. Annual sales ballooned to over 2 million barrels.

Following the introduction of the beer can in Richmond, Virginia, on January 24, 1935, A-B began canning the Budweiser brand in this innovative package in August of 1936. The cans featured instructions on how to open them, and to ensure that customers would succeed in opening the cans, openers were supplied with every case of beer.

Brewery expansions in the early 1940s included another new stockhouse. In 1941, company vice president and general manager August Busch Jr. noted that "our architect and our master brewer have been running an unending race."

Having helped steer the brewery through years of tremendous growth following Repeal, Adolphus Busch III passed away after a battle with cancer on August 29, 1946. With his passing, control was handed over to August A. "Gussie" Busch Jr. Under his leadership, the brewery began a long period of national expansion. The company also spent $9.5 million on improvements to the St. Louis brewery in 1947.

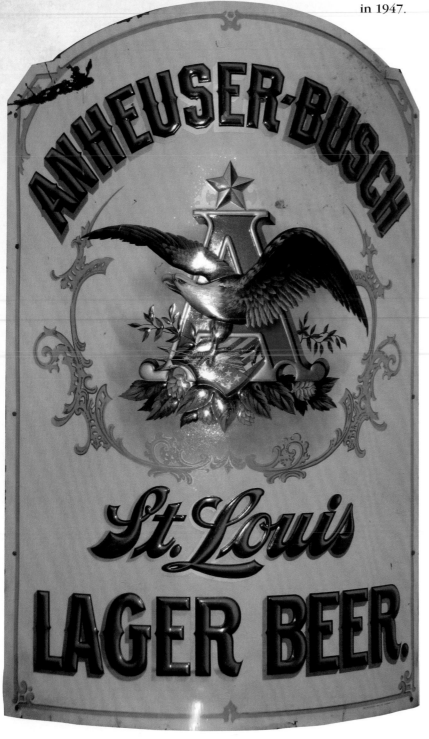

THE FIRST OF MANY

𝓘n 1946, A-B bought a fifty-acre tract in Newark, New Jersey, with an eye toward building a new brewery. These plans were soon abandoned, though, as the company decided it needed a larger plot of land. The groundbreaking ceremony for A-B's first new brewery was held in Newark on March 30, 1950. The New Jersey brewery would come online with a capacity of 1.25 million barrels and release its first beer on June 4, 1951.

On March 10, 1953, A-B announced that it had purchased the St. Louis Cardinals baseball club from Fred Saigh for $3.75 million. Saigh had been convicted of tax evasion and needed to sell the team but wanted to keep the franchise in St. Louis. In order to do so, he declined bids from Houston and Milwaukee groups that were higher than A-B's offer. This was followed by A-B's purchase of Sportsman's Park from St. Louis Browns owner Bill Veeck.

The Griesedieck Brothers Brewery held the contract to serve as the Cardinals radio broadcast sponsor through the 1953 season; A-B honored the last year of the contract.

Anheuser-Busch embossed and lithographed tin corner sign showing the A & Eagle and featuring St. Louis Lager beer.

Gussie wanted to change the name of Sportsman's Park to Budweiser Stadium. Baseball commissioner Ford Frick denied this request as being too commercial, so the name Busch Stadium was adopted. In the spirit of goodwill and local cooperation, Griesedieck Brothers, which also held the television broadcasting rights, relinquished those rights to A-B. Typical of the era, during the 1952 season, only two Cardinals games had been televised in St. Louis, so they were not giving much up. The real value was in the radio broadcast.

In June of 1954, A-B's second satellite brewery, with a capacity of 1 million barrels, went online in Los Angeles. The year also saw the implementation of an ill-advised price increase which turned out to be one of the worst mistakes ever made by Gussie Busch. The wholesale price was raised 15 cents a case, which translated into a retail increase of $1.20 per case, and sales declined over 800,000 barrels as no other brewers followed their lead. In his normal fashion, Gussie addressed the shareholders and took sole responsibility for the error.

To pump up sales, Gussie Busch and Dick Meyer later embarked on the ultimate road trip, a nine-month-long meet and greet to visit all 650 nationwide wholesalers. Locally, he also hosted get-togethers for eleven thousand St. Louis–area A-B salesmen, wholesalers, and tavern owners at Grant's Farm, with one thousand people attending each night for eleven consecutive nights.

August A. Busch Jr., 1899–1989, president 1946–1971.

BUSCH LAGER— BUSCH BAVARIAN—BUSCH

With only two brands (the many other pre-Prohibition brands having been discontinued), the ultra-exclusive, draft-only Michelob and premium priced Budweiser, A-B was in need of a "popular" priced beer to compete with others in that huge segment of the market. Industry-wide sales in 1955 totaled 85 million barrels, of which 68 million barrels were in the so-called popular-priced field. In an effort to gain entry into this market, following much fanfare, A-B introduced Busch Lager on March 15, 1955. Complete with a new package design, point-of-sale materials, plus print, radio, and TV advertising, the rollout was well planned and the test market was begun. *Brewers Journal* reported in August 1955 on a surprise move in which a new brand called Busch Bavarian would be introduced in test markets on August 24. The short-lived Busch Lager brand would be withdrawn in November. Busch Bavarian had its own package design, name,

and advertising agency, all with the purpose of distinguishing it from the Budweiser and Busch Lager brands. After successfully defending itself in a number of lawsuits over the Bavarian part of the name, the brand name was changed in 1979 to simply Busch Beer.

WE'RE NUMBER 1

One of the most innovative marketing campaigns ever conceived helped launch A-B to the number-one position among U.S. brewers. Conceived by the D'Arcy advertising agency, it was introduced in 1956. Known simply as "Pick-a-Pair," the promotion played a dominant role in the summertime advertising of A-B for many years. Consumers were urged to "Pick-a-Pair-of-Six-Packs, buy Bud." And buy Bud they did.

With a single exception, the three U.S. brewing industry leaders every year since the 1933 repeal of Prohibition had been Pabst, Schlitz, and A-B. Each had been in first place at some time, but Schlitz, which had led in both 1955 and 1956, gave up the lead to A-B for good in 1957. With production that year of 6.1 million barrels, the St. Louis company took over the number-one slot and never looked back. Indeed, it would grow to dominate the industry, the position it maintains to this day.

The next year was a big one for the company, with sales of over $257 million and an impressive increase in production to nearly 7 million barrels. Helping spur 1958 sales of Budweiser was an advertising budget in excess of $12 million. This was just a sign of things to come, as A-B continued flexing its marketing muscles in subsequent decades. Some of the company's ad campaigns became the stuff of at least temporary legends. These included "Where There's Life . . . There's Bud"; "That Bud . . . That's Beer"; and "When You Say Budweiser, You've Said It All." Memorable advertising icons in later years included Louie the lizard, Spuds McKenzie, the Budweiser frogs, and of course the Clydesdales. Under A-B's marketing efforts the "Bud Bowl" became an annual winter ritual, TV spots included "Whassup" and "Dude," and radio listeners heard about the "Real Men of Genius."

Top: Introduced in 1955 as a "popular priced" beer, the Busch Lager brand lasted less than a year.

Bottom: Beer brewers on the stairs of the Starting Cellar, circa 1950. The gentleman kneeling at lower right in the white lab uniform is George Herbst, father of co-author Henry Herbst.

In an effort to increase its position in the Florida beer market, in 1958 A-B purchased a Miami brewery owned by the American Brewing Company. The U.S. Justice Department filed suit against A-B, charging the purchase to be in violation of federal antitrust laws. Meanwhile, A-B was constructing a new brewery in Tampa with a capacity of 500,000 barrels. It went online in May of 1959. On October 2, 1961, under court order to dispose of the Miami plant, A-B sold it to the National Brewing Company at a loss estimated at $900,000.

A-B became the first brewery in history to reach the 10-million-barrel mark in annual production, an event that was celebrated on December 15, 1964. The company was on a roll, with new breweries planned and under construction. A brewery with an annual capacity of 1 million barrels was opened in Houston, Texas, in May of 1966, followed by openings in Columbus, Ohio (1.7 million barrels), in June of 1968; Jacksonville, Florida (1.9 million barrels), in May of 1969; and Merrimack, New Hampshire (1.7 million barrels), in June of 1970.

Meanwhile, back in St. Louis, the A-B brewhouse (1892), stables (1885), and schoolhouse (1868) received landmark status and were placed on the registry of National Historic Landmarks in 1967.

August A. Busch III, 1937– , president 1974–2002. Used with permission of Anheuser-Busch InBev. All rights reserved.

"BRING LOTS OF MONEY"

The stability of the U.S. brewing industry was to change in the 1970s. Philip Morris purchased a 53 percent share of the Miller Brewing Company from the W. R. Grace Company for $130 million in 1969. Miller was languishing in seventh place among U.S. brewers with an annual production of 5.4 million barrels. The following June, Philip Morris completed its purchase by acquiring the remaining 47 percent for $97 million.

A-B brought its new Williamsburg, Virginia, brewery, with a capacity of 2 million barrels, online in June of 1972. Later that month Miller announced that it had acquired several brands and assets from Meister Brau, Inc., of Chicago. These included the Meister Brau, Buckeye, and Lite beer brands. In addition, Miller purchased inventories and certain other assets, most notably the distributor Better Brands of Illinois. A brewing industry report by the *Research Corporation of America* stated that the purchase price was six times more than the average annual sales of the brands and the distributor for the years 1971 through 1973.

No one within the U.S. brewing industry could begin to comprehend the massive changes to the competitive balance that the industry was about

to undergo. A real beer war was about to unfold. Miller's sales were up 28.8 percent in 1973, while profits at A-B were down for the first time since 1963. In the spring of 1974, Gussie was serving as A-B board chairman and chief executive officer, while his longtime personal friend Dick Meyer was serving as president, having been elevated to that position in 1971. August A. Busch III was serving as executive vice president/general manager of all brewery operations, and in a cost-saving effort he made the decision to fire a large number of upper-level managers. Gussie and the board supported the proposal, but Meyer objected and resigned over the magnitude of the cost-reduction measures. Following Meyer's resignation, the board of directors appointed August III as president. August began by naming six new vice presidents, among them two future A-B presidents, Dennis "Denny" Long and Patrick Stokes. Sales for A-B in 1974 rose 14 percent, but once again, profits declined. On May 8, 1975, a press release announced the fact that the A-B board had designated August III to serve as both president and chief executive officer,

Postcard aerial view of the one hundred–acre Anheuser-Busch complex, circa 1980.

replacing his seventy-six-year-old father in the latter position.

For Miller, sales in 1974 rose an astonishing 31 percent to 9 million barrels, moving the company to fifth place in the industry; its profits or losses were not disclosed by parent Philip Morris. Even though there had been several brands of light beer on the market for a number of years, all had met with rather limited success. It would take the 1975 introduction of Miller Lite, fueled by massive amounts of advertising money, to convince American consumers that what they really wanted in a beer was one that had "great taste" yet was "less filling." Russell Cleary, chairman of the G. Heileman Brewing Company, referred to Philip Morris as the "cigarette Santa Claus" in relationship to its funding of Miller Brewing Company advertising.

If the battle against Pabst and Schlitz was not enough, the added threat of the Philip Morris/Miller combination was bringing the beer wars to an entirely new level, and it took an incredible amount of energy and money for A-B to remain number one in the brewing industry. August III would bring that energy, and A-B brought the money. He was quoted in *Business Week* on November 8, 1976, as stating, "If Miller wants a fight, tell Miller to come right along, but bring lots of money." The magazine reported that Miller, now being run by former Philip Morris people and fueled by the profits made by the cigarette division,

was changing the face of the brewing industry with heavy advertising, market segmentation, and new product proliferation. With the small regional breweries unable to compete at this level, most were due to fail, and the big would become bigger. A month later, A-B brought a new brewery located in Fairfield, California, online with a capacity of 3.6 million barrels.

The ongoing competitive battle became known at A-B as the "Kill Miller" era, and was led by August III with Denny Long (then vice president and general manager) and Mike Roarty (vice president of marketing). They were ready to fight for every advertising space that was available, but they did not see the changing beer market relative to the creation of the light-beer segment. August III believed it to be a fad and originally declined to create a product offering in the category. Left alone, Miller not only created the segment but also controlled the market. Late to respond, A-B in 1977 finally entered the light-beer market with what was then known as Anheuser-Busch Natural Light, later shortened to simply Natural Light. This was followed closely by the introduction of Michelob Light in February of 1978.

"DRINK SCHLITZ OR I'LL KILL YOU"

Having seen its market position fall to third place, Schlitz was in need of major help. The company made several critical mistakes. To reduce raw material costs, it switched to liquid corn syrup as a substitute for barley malt, then introduced a production change—accelerated-batch fermentation—that shortened the brewing process. This was followed up by dropping the successful "When You're Out of Schlitz, You're Out of Beer" campaign in favor of ads featuring a bunch of tough-looking guys, known in the advertising trade as the "Drink Schlitz or I'll Kill You" campaign. The ads were pulled after ten weeks, but Schlitz had lost its momentum and was doomed to suffer a slow and painful corporate death. Over the next two years, Schlitz would see sales declines of over 4 million barrels, while A-B sales increased over 16 million barrels and Miller rose to assume the number-two position with increased sales of over 19 million barrels. Finding itself with excess capacity after having overbuilt, Schlitz closed a sale on October 31, 1979, with A-B agreeing to buy its brewery in Baldwinsville, New York, for $100 million. While A-B embarked on a four-year modernization program to bring that brewery up to its standards, Schlitz left the brewing industry in 1982, when it was purchased by the Stroh Brewing Company of Detroit. The redesigned Baldwinsville brewery opened in February of 1983 with a staggering capacity of 7 million barrels.

The marketing expenditures required to keep up with the spending of the Miller Brewing Company were highlighted in 1978, when Denny Long, speaking at a financial analysts conference, stated that for 1977, A-B had spent more than $79 million on advertising and was prepared to increase that by 33 percent to over $106 million in 1978. By comparison, they had spent $49 million in 1976 and $41 million in 1975. The 33 percent increase in the advertising budget was based on the fact that Miller had released its 1978 plans to its wholesalers, which called for spending over $100 million on advertising.

ORGANIZATIONAL CHANGES

As the beer wars continued unabated, Miller, in anticipation of ever-increasing sales, announced plans in 1979 for the construction of a new 10-million-barrel brewery (estimated to cost over $400 million) to be located in Trenton, Ohio, with a targeted completion date of 1983. At A-B, a new organizational structure was created in October of 1979. A holding company

known as Anheuser-Busch Companies, Inc., was set up, with the brewery to be known as Anheuser-Busch, Inc., operating as a subsidiary of the parent company. Dennis Long was named president and chief operating officer of Anheuser-Busch, Inc., with August III serving as president and chief operating officer of Anheuser-Busch Companies. In 1980, Anheuser-Busch, Inc., became the first company to ever produce 50 million barrels of beer in a year.

Rumors of the sale of A-B had circulated for many years. Listed among potential buyers were the Bronfman family of Canada, which owned Seagram's; Brascan Ltd. of Toronto; General Mills, Inc.; Unilever N.V.; and Australia's Elders IXL, Ltd., maker of Foster's lager. In 1985, the board adopted a "poison-pill" strategy as a defensive mechanism to hold off any unwanted suitors.

A-B's new entry into the light-beer market came on April 29, 1981, when Budweiser Light (soon renamed Bud Light) was introduced to test markets. The national rollout took place in April 1982. A-B was now fully committed to challenging the dominant position of Miller Lite by having entries in all three price categories of the light beer segment.

"THE BEER WARS ARE OVER"

In its issue of February 21–27, 1983, the *St. Louis Business Journal* declared at the top of its front page, "The beer wars are over, to Anheuser-Busch go the spoils." Reporting on the 1982 performance of A-B and Miller, they stated that A-B, whose marketing budget had grown to around $220 million, had continued to grow, while Miller had seen its market share decline. A-B controlled more than 32 percent of the U.S. beer market, while Miller's share had slipped to 21 percent. Once again, the industry's overcapacity had reared its ugly head, and the new Trenton, Ohio, brewery constructed by Miller and scheduled to open in 1983 was mothballed.

In September of 1986, A-B paused to acknowledge the fact that it had reached a cumulative production total of 1 billion barrels since its humble beginnings in 1852. The following year, a scandal broke with the disclosure that several middle-level managers had been on the receiving end of gifts from an advertising agency that did business with A-B. The internal investigation culminated in what could best be described as the classic "taking one for the team," when Denny Long assumed full responsibility and resigned his position as president of the brewery. He had never been implicated in the affair, and people who knew him strongly believed that he resigned simply because the misdeeds had happened on his watch. Long, who had been with the brewery for more than thirty years and had risen from office boy to brewery president, had led the fight in the trenches against Miller. August III now assumed the role of president of A-B, Inc., in addition to his other duties.

CHANGES ARE COMING

The construction of new breweries continued, and in March of 1988 A-B brought its latest brewery in Fort Collins, Colorado, online with a capacity of 5.4 million barrels.

Upon the September 29, 1989, death of August A. "Gussie" Busch Jr. at the age of ninety, some people in St. Louis felt like they had lost their best friend. Although few had actually met him, many felt as if they knew him. His life had been an open book, lived to the fullest in front of everyone. He worked hard, and he played hard. His philosophy was that you were either trying to help him sell more Budweiser or you were in his way. Life was black and white. He was the closest thing to royalty that had ever come out of south St. Louis. The brewery, Budweiser beer, the Cardinals, Busch Stadium, horses, gin rummy, four wives, eleven children, WWII veteran, Grant's Farm, the Clydesdales—his name and his image were everywhere. There was never a local charity or event in need of sponsorship that he and A-B were not a part of. Who could ever forget the sight of him riding into Busch Stadium on opening day or before a playoff game, sitting atop an A-B beer wagon being pulled by his beloved Clydesdales? At the time of his death, he controlled over 35 million shares or 12.5 percent of the common stock of Anheuser-Busch Companies, Incorporated.

After eight years in mothballs, Miller finally opened its 10-million-barrel brewery in Trenton, Ohio, with limited production during the summer of 1991. The last new brewery to be brought online by A-B was its Cartersville, Georgia, plant, which opened in 1993 with a capacity of 6 million barrels. The brewing business and other industries were at this time becoming increasingly global in nature. The cover of A-B's 1993 annual report noted "An Expanding Global Presence."

In October 1995, A-B announced corporate changes that would allow the company to concentrate on its core beer business. These changes included the closing of the Tampa brewery and the sale of both the baked-goods division and the baseball St. Louis Cardinals. The closure of the Tampa brewery occurred in December of 1995, in part because of the desired expansion of the Busch Gardens facility, which would have been difficult with the brewery sitting right in the middle of the property. In addition, with the Cartersville brewery up and running, there was enough capacity within the system to handle the sales volume. The baked-goods division was spun off to shareholders, and despite an estimated value of $300 million, the baseball team, Busch Stadium, and its parking garages were sold for $150 million to a group of investors headed by Bill DeWitt Jr., Drew Baur, and Fred Hanser. Part of the sales agreement provided that the Busch Stadium name be retained.

Having needed more than 134 years to produce its first billion barrels, A-B would produce an additional billion barrels between 1986 and 1998. The company was edging ever closer to controlling 50 percent of the U.S. beer market. Forty years earlier it had controlled less than 8 percent.

Toward the end of the millennium, the country was seeing the growth of smaller brewers as the brewpub and microbrewery industry began taking off. To keep up with the small but growing presence of these craft brewers, A-B once again began producing a variety of beer styles, just as it had done in the nineteenth century. To this end, under the name American Originals, they reintroduced their Faust, Black & Tan, Muenchener, and American Hop Ale brands.

August Busch III was approaching sixty-five years of age in 2002, and with it, a self-imposed deadline to relinquish the position of president of the holding company (Anheuser-Busch Companies) and the brewery (Anheuser Busch, Inc.). He became the chairman of the board of A-B Companies effective July 1. Pat Stokes, who had joined A-B in 1969, became the new president. Thirty-eight-year-old August A. Busch IV was appointed president of Anheuser-Busch, Inc., and from that position, he ran the brewing operations.

BREWING INDUSTRY GLOBAL CONSOLIDATION

A-B's twenty-first-century strategy was to lead the U.S. market, sign international export/licensing agreements, and buy minority interests in foreign breweries. Over the years, agreements had been reached in Canada, Mexico, England, India, Vietnam, South Korea, Chile, China, Russia, Japan, Spain, and other countries. But under modern corporate standards it was no longer good enough to be number one in the United States; success was all about what could be done in regards to global ownership. In what today could best be described as a harbinger of things to come, in April of 2002 Pat Stokes, then senior executive vice president, was quoted in the *St. Louis Post-Dispatch* as telling the *Wall Street Journal*, "If an international acquisition will not enhance A-B's earnings growth . . . then we will not do it."

In 2002, Philip Morris sold its Miller Brewing division to the South African Breweries (SAB) for $3.6 billion, forming a new corporation known as SABMiller. This merger moved the new company to the number-two position in the world, behind A-B but ahead of Belgium-based Interbrew. Another brewing conglomerate, to be known as InBev, was formed in 2004 with the merger of Brazilian brewer AmBev and Interbrew. With headquarters in Leuven, Belgium, the new company controlled 14 percent of world beer sales, making it the global industry sales leader.

Anheuser-Busch's efforts at dominating the U.S. beer market reached their apex in 2003, when sales of over 102 million barrels represented 49.8 percent of the market. A-B came close to the goal of controlling half of the domestic market again in 2004, but the next few years saw its share slip below 49 percent.

In August of 2004, Anheuser-Busch and the St. Louis Cardinals baseball club signed a twenty-year agreement, the terms of which were not revealed, concerning the new baseball stadium scheduled to open in 2006. The agreement extended the name Busch Stadium through 2025.

In May of 2006, A-B purchased the Rolling Rock brand and trademarks from InBev for $82 million. Rolling Rock had been brewed in Latrobe, Pennsylvania, since 1939 and had a solid nation-wide base of loyal, young beer drinkers. Following the purchase, A-B transferred production of Rolling Rock to its Newark brewery. Also in 2006, Molson Incorporated of Canada merged with the Adolph Coors Company of Golden, Colorado, to form the Molson Coors Brewing Company.

With the November 30, 2006, announcement of the retirement of both Pat Stokes and August Busch III and the promotion of August IV to president and chief executive officer, came further word that an agreement had been signed with InBev. This would allow for A-B to be the exclusive U.S. importer of nineteen InBev brands, including Bass, Beck's, and Stella Artois. The agreement was set to become effective on February 1, 2007. Over the next year and a half this friendly agreement would set in motion numerous speculative rumors of the possibility of a merger between InBev and A-B.

On April 7, 2008, A-B celebrated the seventy-

August A. Busch IV, 1964– , president 2006–2008. Used with permission of Anheuser-Busch InBev.

fifth anniversary of the return of legal beer (and the Clydesdales) by shutting down the entire brewery for the afternoon and hosting a private party on Pestalozzi Street, in front of the main entrance to the Bevo Plant. Leading the Clydesdale team down Pestalozzi Street were the highly energetic and entertaining Mystic Sheiks of Morocco, brought in from Busch Gardens in Tampa for the event. With no public acknowledgment, owing to other more pressing developments, A-B surpassed the 3-billion-barrel mark of cumulative production in 2008.

On July 1, 2008, SABMiller PLC and Molson Coors Brewing Company merged their North American operations under the new corporate name of MillerCoors LLC. The stage was set for even bigger news.

INBEV AND THE PESTALOZZI ACQUISITION CORPORATION

A-B's stock closed at $52.58 per share on the afternoon of May 22, 2008. The next morning, news broke on *The Financial Times of London* Alphaville website that InBev was making preparations for a takeover bid of A-B. Less than three weeks later, on June 11, InBev submitted a cash offer to the A-B board of directors of $65 per share; the offer had a total value of $47.5 billion. With InBev having set up a wholly owned subsidiary known as the Pestalozzi Acquisition Corporation, for the exclusive purpose of effecting the merger transaction, it was "game on."

As would be expected, on June 26, 2008, A-B rejected InBev's offer and announced its own cost-reduction plan, along with a statement that the offer was too low. This announcement was met with little interest, but the posturing continued back and forth between the two parties. When on July 9 InBev raised its all-cash offer to $70 per share, representing a total value of $52 billion, it was "game over." August IV flew to New York to discuss the terms of the takeover with InBev chief Carlos Brito. Upon his return, the A-B board of directors, along with legal and financial advisers, held a meeting on July 13, 2008. At the conclusion of the meeting it was announced that they had agreed to the buyout by InBev. On that same day, the InBev board of directors approved the merger. Following the execution of the merger agreement the companies issued a joint press release announcing the transaction.

In the end, the A-B board of directors determined that their fiduciary duties to their shareholders required them to accept the offer as being in the best interest of the shareholders. No better offers were available. Globally, SABMiller and Molson Coors were in the midst of their own merger, Grupo Modelo of Mexico was resisting talks of a takeover, and Heineken of the Netherlands and Carlsberg of Denmark were working through a $15.3 billion takeover of Scottish & Newcastle of the United Kingdom. Additionally, the low value of the dollar relative to the euro helped seal the deal.

The InBev shareholders voted in favor of the merger on September 29, followed by a November 12 meeting of A-B stockholders in Secaucus, New Jersey. There they approved the merger with InBev in a meeting that lasted a total of twenty-five minutes. There were an estimated 150 shareholders in attendance at the meeting conducted by August Busch IV (who together with his father controlled only 1.7 percent of the company stock) and Pat Stokes. Of the 497 million votes, 96 percent were cast in favor of the merger. This action left only the approval of the United States, China, and U.K. governments. Events were now happening at a rapid pace, as on November 14 the U.S. Justice Department gave approval to the merger, while requiring InBev to sell its Labatt USA distribution subsidiary to an independent third party. On the same day (November 18, 2008) that China gave its approval, the merger was completed and A-B stock was removed from the New York Stock Exchange. The new stock began trading under the symbol ABI on the Euronext Brussels exchange on November 21. And thus was born Anheuser-Busch InBev. Carlos Brito, the Belgium-based CEO, appointed Luiz Fernando Edmond to lead the North American region as zone president and Dave Peacock to assume the position of president of Anheuser-Busch.

THE TIMES THEY ARE A-CHANGING

An announcement penned by Edmond and Peacock was made on December 8, 2008, stating that 1,400 employees system wide were to be laid off, with approximately 1,000 of that number coming from the St. Louis operation. This was in addition to the 1,000-plus employees who took voluntary retirement. They also stated that 250 open jobs would remain unfilled and that 415 contractor positions would be eliminated. These layoffs, although anticipated for months, still came as a shock to the employees involved and to the local community. The departments most affected by the move were engineering

E. Anheuser & Co. Bavarian Brewery, bottling department employees, 1875, featuring a bucket full of corks and St. Louis Lager brand containers.

and information technology.

Worldwide adjustments to the operating breweries of A-B InBev began to take place almost immediately, with the announcement that a brewery located outside of St. Petersburg, Russia, one of the ten operating breweries in Russia, would be closed. This was followed by the January 2009 announcement that the fabled Stag Brewery in London, England, would be closed. Also, the company sold a 19.9 percent share of the Tsingtao Breweries of China to the Asahi Breweries of Japan for $667 million. It still maintains a 7 percent interest in Tsingtao.

Around the same time, the Busch Entertainment division announced that it would no longer offer two free beers to adult visitors at the company's theme parks and would renovate the hospitality rooms and remove displays featuring the history of the brewery at those locations. Following discussions that had started prior to the merger, it was announced on January 8, 2009, that A-B InBev would donate the historic Bevo Mill restaurant to the St. Louis Development Corporation. By mid-March, the leased restaurant had ceased operations. The city immediately began seeking a new management company to operate the restaurant.

A-B InBev announced that New York City had been selected as the location of its office to help manage its global brewing interests. This move would transfer some of the day-to-day global operations there from its headquarters in Leuven, Belgium. St. Louis would remain the headquarters of North American operations and the home of Budweiser.

In a letter dated January 14, 2009, A-B InBev advised its suppliers that they no longer would be paid on the standard 30-day terms, but in the future, payment would be made on 120-day terms. Their statement went on to say that this policy was in keeping with other multinational companies and would help them to better manage their business.

In accordance with the agreement with the U.S. Justice Department relative to the merger, Anheuser-Busch InBev reached an agreement in February 2009 to sell Labatt USA, the U.S. importing

*When the Pilsener Princes
and Light Lager Lords
set sail on a sea of suds
there were Millers and Pabstses
and Schlitzes and Blatzes
and oceans and oceans of Buds.*

*In the board rooms of Schnitzel,
the Duchy of Pretzel,
reigned the marvelous Barons of Beer:
Miller and Ruppert and Busch
Then Miller retired to the vats in the sky,
and Ruppert expired with a Ruthian sigh,
leaving but one of the Beer Barons Three,
August Anheuser Busch.*
St. Louisan, January 1976, Stephen Darst

division of the former InBev, to KPS Capital Partners, a private equity group. The completion of this agreement on March 13, 2009, coincided with the announcement that their Foshan brewery located in southeastern China was up and running.

IN RETROSPECT

On the international business world, it is obvious that the attempt to take over Anheuser-Busch had been in the planning stages for a long time. Details, which became available later, showed that InBev had two plans. Plan A, code named Project Aluminum, was the plan to take over Anheuser-Busch. Plan B, code named Project Barium, was the backup plan, calling for a takeover of SABMiller. InBev had gotten to the point of identifying two possible companies that could potentially challenge these plans. One was Diageo-Guinness, code named Duck, and the other was Heineken, code named Helium.

Only time will tell if the business strategy of InBev, based on debt and acquisition, was the right way, or if A-B's strategy of signing licensing agreements and purchasing partial ownerships may have been the correct strategy. In regards to the Busches—Adolphus, August Sr., Adolphus III, August Jr., August III, and August IV—their lifelong commitment and dedication to the single task of wanting to sell more Budweiser is without question. Their world was black and white; you were either part of the solution or part of the problem. The 156-year survival of Anheuser-Busch as an independent company had been an industrial example of Darwin's theory of evolution. The company was always willing to change and adapt to economic, social, and industrial developments. Over the many years, it survived fires, labor problems, local competition, two world wars, Prohibition, the Great Depression, Lemp, Pabst, Schlitz, and Miller, but in the end, the corporate giant failed to adapt to the brewing industry's global consolidation strategies. Being number one in the United States was just not good enough.

Anthony & Kuhn Brewing Company

10th Street between Sidney & Victor

Anton Jaeger	1855–1861
Jaeger's (Gambrinus) Brewery	1861–c. 1864
Grone & Co.	c. 1864
Charles A. Huber	c. 1864–1866
Huber & Apel	1866–1868
Charles A. Huber	1868–1870
Anthony & Kuhn	1870–1883
Anthony & Kuhn Brewing Company	1883–1889
Anthony & Kuhn branch, SLBA	1889–1899

Top: View of the Anthony & Kuhn brewery, from a city directory ad.

Bottom: Anthony & Kuhn embossed glass, goblet style.

Though not as well known as some of their contemporaries, brewing partners Henry Anthony and Francis Kuhn were still major players in the nineteenth-century St. Louis beer business. While the brewery where they flourished was located in Soulard, their original location was at the crosstown Philadelphia Brewery.

Henry Anthony's first job related to the local beer business was as a maltster in partnership with William Linze. The latter had briefly been a co-owner of the Philadelphia Brewery at Twenty-sixth and Morgan streets. While at the Philadephia Brewery, Anthony became a partner with William Oberschelp shortly after the Civil War. Francis Kuhn replaced Oberschelp as Anthony's junior partner in 1867.

Kuhn was born in the city of Phalsbourg, province of Lorraine, France, in 1837. Upon leaving school at age fifteen, he began serving a three-year apprenticeship, without pay, at a banking house in his hometown, after which he relocated to Paris.

In 1859, Kuhn and his parents migrated to St. Louis. The Kuhns must have been a fairly well-to-do family, as they bought Francis's way out of the draft for the French army, spending twenty-four hundred francs to hire a substitute in order to satisfy their long-cherished wish of coming to America.

For the next eight years, Kuhn demonstrated his business acumen, first by successfully serving as business manager of a soap/candle/lard oil manufacturer; then by working for a woodenware maker; and next by operating a restaurant. Why he decided to enter the beer business is unclear, but it proved to be a wise career change.

Anthony and Kuhn kept the old Philadelphia Brewery tag for a couple of years but then started doing business under the Anthony & Kuhn brewery name.

NEW LOCATION

In August of 1870, Anthony and Kuhn, sensing a better opportunity, closed their old Philadelphia plant, and for $65,000 purchased what was still called (after its original owner) Jaeger's Brewery. It was located on Tenth Street between Sidney and Victor, and brewing at the location went back to 1855, when Anton Jaeger moved from the Laurel Brewery to establish a new plant.

Jaeger named his new enterprise the Gambrinus Brewery, after the possibly mythical Flemish king often credited with the invention of lager beer. It was a fairly substantial facility, as the 1857 *Handels-Zeitung* brewery list shows annual production of 6,500 barrels, ranking eleventh out of twenty-nine local breweries. In addition to the two-story brewhouse, the site included a four-room brick dwelling and a large saloon. Jaeger's Garden was also an attraction, as many German societies held summer festivals there. After a dance hall was built, winter balls were hosted as well.

Top: A view of Anthony & Kuhn Brewing Co. pictured as if looking from the southeast corner to the northwest, note the statue of King Gambrinus on his pillar in the foreground. Image is from the May 15, 1879, edition of *The Western Brewer*.

Bottom: Circa 1890 litho, featuring a beautiful woman wearing a pendant necklace in the shape of the Anthony & Kuhn shield. Copies of the company's Peerless Special and Pale Lager bottle labels are in the background.

The Gambrinus Brewery was something of a family affair, with Ambrose and Nicholas Jaeger joining Anton. Production in 1860, however, dropped considerably from 1857 levels, indicating a possible fire or other disruption in the business.

Anton Jaeger's brewery was destined to outlive him, as he joined the Union army and was killed in 1861 at the Battle of Lexington, Missouri. Ironically, at the same skirmish where Jaeger became a war casualty, St. Louis brewer Charles Stifel became a war hero.

Following Jaeger's death, his brewery had a series of owners. Henry Grone and partners apparently operated there in 1864 prior to building a new plant on Clark Avenue. Grone was succeeded by Charles Huber and his partner, Herman Apel. Huber had become sole owner by the time of the sale to Anthony and Kuhn.

At first, the new owners continued calling their new plant the Gambrinus Brewery. One corner of the brewery grounds featured a prominent statue of Gambrinus, depicted in the traditional manner wearing his crown and royal robes holding aloft a foaming glass of beer. The brewery was also notable for its unusual Gothic-style brewhouse. The design was a result of Anton Jaeger's agreement with the local Catholic clergy that, should the brewery fail, the building would be converted to a church. As fate would have it, the bishops never got their free brewhouse.

According to St. Louis brewery historian Steve DeBellis, Henry Anthony claimed to be a descendant of Gambrinus, with a secret family formula for brewing his fine lager beer. Relative or not, the Gambrinus name was dropped in 1873 in favor of simply Anthony & Kuhn (A&K).

YEARS OF GROWTH

The partners spent over $150,000 on improvements to the brewery in the 1870s, beginning with the enlargement of the brick-lined underground cellars. During the same period, the brewhouse was improved and extended and a malt house added. Thus began a period of steady growth for the brewery.

By the early 1870s, more than fifteen thousand barrels a year were being produced. Thirty employees were on the payroll, and Anthony & Kuhn was shipping its product to points south and west. Annual output had doubled to thirty thousand barrels by 1879.

Instrumental to the brewery's success was the adjacent mammoth beer garden, with enough tables to seat three thousand. Said to command a magnificent view, and also home to a bowling alley, the garden was described by an early source as "one of the most attractive places of resort for ladies and gentlemen in the city. There are few gardens that can compare with it in beauty of location, shade and other appointments."

With streetcar stations nearby at Gravois and Carondelet, the ease of access boosted attendance at the garden. The garden included a forty-by-forty-

Above: Portrait and signature of Francis Kuhn, from *St. Louis: History of the Fourth City (1763–1909)*, by Walter B. Stevens.

Below: Unusual cardboard bottle case.

foot grand pavilion, and during summers Postelwaite's military band played both matinee and evening performances. Anthony & Kuhn also operated a saloon and depot at 110–12 North Fifth Street (later renamed Broadway) and had another beer garden on Morgan Street, just west of Jefferson, at the old Philadelphia Brewery location. The considerable number of embossed Anthony & Kuhn XXX pilsner-style glasses still in existence—probably the most common of the style from any pre-Prohibition St. Louis brewery—attests to the large crowds that frequented the brewery's facilities.

A&K continued its aggressive exporting efforts when a bottling house was completed in August 1882 for packaging its XXX lager beer. According to brewery publicity, "shipping in car load lots" was a specialty. While most of the beer, described by one source as "excellent and delicious," was sold within three hundred miles of St. Louis, some was shipped as far west as Idaho and Wyoming and as far south as Galveston, Texas.

In 1883, the business was formally incorporated as the Anthony & Kuhn Brewing Company. However, the new company quickly found itself in dire financial straits. In October 1883, *The Western Brewer* reported that A&K's "financial embarrassment" had been settled, with the stock transferred to the trustees to whom the brewery owed money. While Anthony and Kuhn remained at their brewery's helm, the trustees would chart the course. The company was soon back on its financial feet, and by 1889 production reached fifty thousand barrels. A city directory ad from that year said that A&K were "sole bottlers of XXX Lager, Culmbacher and Malt Nectar."

BOUGHT BY THE BRITS

*L*ater that year, Anthony & Kuhn was one of many breweries sold to the St. Louis Brewing Association (SLBA), a British investment syndicate. Francis Kuhn left the brewing industry soon after to devote his attention to banking, distilling, and a streetcar line. Henry Anthony, however, continued as brewery manager until 1897.

The following year, Anthony became one of the organizers of the new Union Brewing Company in St. Louis. He didn't get to enjoy his new brewery for long, though, passing away late in 1899 at age sixty-seven, leaving a widow and seven children.

Francis Kuhn lived longer but saw some misfortune in his later life. His wife, the former Maria Thannberger, died in March of 1881, leaving him with a son and three daughters. A few years later, he was remarried to Mathilde Thannberger, a sister of his first wife, but the marriage was short-lived as his new wife died just three months later.

In November of 1897, as president of the Ravenswood Distillery Company, Kuhn had to deal with the aftermath of the plant's burning, which destroyed more than three hundred thousand gallons of bonded whiskey. Still, Francis Kuhn persevered over these tragedies until passing away in 1911.

The SLBA had ended production at its Anthony & Kuhn branch in 1899. The brewhouse was converted to use as the bottling shop of the nearby Green Tree Brewery branch, with the malt house taken over by the Frank Feuerbacher Malting Company. *The Western Brewer* gave the old plant one final mention in 1922, disclosing that it had been sold to a laundry. The short-lived Royal Breweries, Incorporated, which brewed weiss beer right after Repeal, may have used one of A&K's old buildings, but the historical record is unclear on the point.

According to Soulard-area folklore, the brewery's cellars were still accessible until the late 1930s. At that time, they were sealed for good, supposedly in reaction to two boys entering them on a lark and then disappearing. In any case, presumably the underground vaults are still intact forty feet below the ground, but the rest of the brewery has gone the way of so many others that once graced the neighborhood. The exception of course is Anheuser-Busch, which still provides the area with the cheery beery smells it has long enjoyed. For many years, the old Anthony & Kuhn site has been home to one of the city's Boy's Clubs, with a baseball diamond located behind it where the beer garden had been.

Business partners in life, Henry Anthony and Francis Kuhn remain close in death, fittingly buried only a few yards apart in Bellefontaine Cemetery in north St. Louis.

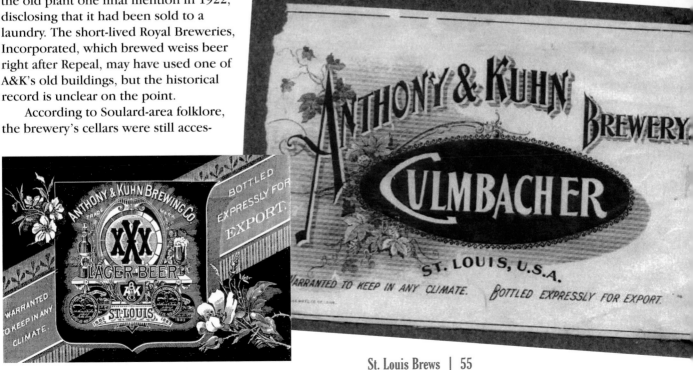

Bremen Brewery Company

3905 North Broadway

Louis Spori	1853–1856
Spori & Spengler	1856–c. 1860
Spengler & Schmid	c. 1860
Tobias Spengler, Bremen Brewery	c. 1860–1872
Tobias Spengler & Son	1872–1879
T. Spengler & Co.	1879–1886
Bremen Brewery Company	1886–1889
Bremen branch, SLBA	1889–1903

TOBIAS SPENGLER

Top: Artist's conception of the Bremen Brewery, taken from *The Western Brewer.*

Bottom: Photo of Tobias Spengler Sr., from the *St. Louis Globe-Democrat.*

While the Bremen Brewery made beer in St. Louis for about sixty years, it has an origin as obscure as most of the shorter-lived plants. The classic tome *100 Years of Brewing* states that the small lager-beer brewery was founded "about 1842" by Tobias Spengler. The problem is, Tobias Spengler did not arrive in the United States until 1850!

Spengler was born in Baden, Germany, in 1816 and apprenticed to a soap manufacturer. He moved to Belleville, Illinois, in 1852, where he started a soap plant. But just like Eberhard Anheuser across the river, Spengler soon traded in his soap suds for suds of a different sort. A later biographical sketch says that Spengler sold his soap business in 1856 to move to St. Louis, where he purchased a brewery previously operated by a brother-in-law. This must have been Louis Spori (also spelled Sperri), whom brewery historian James Lindhurst states began the New Bremen Brewery in 1853. Other sources indicate that Spori started the brewery in 1842, after spending the previous sixteen years at a brewery in nearby Manchester, Missouri. The 1857 *Handels-Zeitung* list still gave Spori as the name of New Bremen's proprietor, but shortly thereafter Francis Schmid replaced Spori as Spengler's associate.

Schmid was soon gone as well, leaving Spengler to run the Bremen Brewery by himself. The "Bremen" name (the brewery was variously called "Bremen" and "New Bremen") refers not only to the street near the brewery, but also to the name given to the entire north St. Louis neighborhood surrounding the plant. In fact, the town of Bremen did not incorporate with St. Louis City until the mid-1850s, which could conceal the earlier opening date for the Bremen Brewery.

Typical of many early brewers, Tobias Spengler also ran a saloon and lived on the brewery grounds. His son, Tobias Jr., joined the business in 1872 as it continued a slow but steady growth. By 1879, annual production was nearing ten thousand barrels, and the firm name was changed to T. Spengler and Company, reflecting the growing influence of William Schreiber.

Schreiber was a practical brewer, a term used to indicate someone well versed in the actual process of brewing rather than just a capitalist bringing money to the table. He was born in Germany in 1843 and had learned the brewer's trade in Munich. Schreiber worked at a brewery in Belleville, Illinois, after immigrating to the United States. Following service in the Civil War in 1864–65, he was hired at the Bremen Brewery by Tobias Spengler. Schreiber conveniently married Spengler's daughter, Kate, in 1876.

By 1884, annual production had increased to about seventeen thousand barrels, and Bremen had established itself as one of many midsize breweries able to prosper in the ever-growing city of St. Louis. Two years later, the business was incorporated as the Bremen Brewery Company with seventy-five thousand dollars of capital stock split between the Spenglers, Schreiber, and Edward Breitner.

Above: Bremen factory scenes from E. Jungenfeld's 1895 architectural portfolio.

Right: New Year's Day die cut card with three children on a sled, "Compliments of Bremen Brewery, January 1, 1895, St. Louis, Mo." Note carved lion on sled.

Tobias Spengler Sr. died in 1887, just two years before Bremen became one of many breweries merged into the St. Louis Brewing Association (SLBA) conglomerate. William Schreiber continued as brewery manager and as an SLBA director until his death in 1895. Paul F. Young replaced him as Bremen branch manager.

The SLBA must have liked the Bremen site. In 1890, a $250,000 improvement project was started, including many new buildings. The St. Louis brewery architectural firm of E. Jungenfeld & Company did the design work. But the SLBA began suffering from over-capacity, and the Bremen Brewery branch was closed in 1903, although parts of the plant continued to be used for storage.

In 1907, the SLBA transferred the Bremen property to its realty division for redevelopment. In the twenty-first century, the site has served a trucking company, while the brewery buildings have disappeared without a trace.

Carondelet
Brewing Company

2025 Gravois Avenue

1933–1941

FRED N. HOELZER
President
Carondelet Brewing Co.

Top: Newspaper ad informing readers that Carondelet's krausened brew was "A natural beer, not carbonated."

Bottom: Fred Hoelzer photo taken from the *St. Louis Star,* June 6, 1934, special feature section on local breweries.

Of the numerous St. Louis breweries that came and went after Prohibition, one of the shortest lived was the Carondelet Brewing Company. Located just down the street from the Falstaff-leased Stifel Union Brewery, Carondelet was the brainchild of a trio of men—Fred Hoelzer, William Compton, and Nick Ems.

National Prohibition officially ended in April 1933 with the legalization of 3.2 percent beer. A couple months later, the Carondelet Brewing Company (CBC) was incorporated with a mere twenty thousand dollars in capital. Hoelzer, who was connected with the St. Louis theater business, and Ems, a longtime general-store operator from Kimmswick, each held four hundred shares of corporate stock and became company president and secretary-treasurer, respectively. Compton had worked for the Klausmann Brewery in south St. Louis prior to Prohibition, and during the dry years he had operated a bowling alley. He was named corporate vice president as well as brewmaster and held the remaining two hundred shares of original stock. Three of his five assistant brewers had likewise worked at Klausmann.

The brewery name came from the historic south St. Louis neighborhood. Carondelet had been a separate town back when the Klausmann Brewery began there in the mid-nineteenth century. While CBC was not actually in Carondelet, the operators opted to stick with the name in honor of the locale in which they had made their brewing reputations.

Rather than taking over the old Klausmann property, the brewery was set up in a building designed as a meat-packing house. CBC entered into a five-year lease on the site from the Laclede Packing Company, which had built but apparently never operated the facility on Gravois near McNair and Shenandoah. Enough brewing equipment was installed to provide for an annual capacity of fifty thousand barrels per year.

Brewing commenced at Carondelet in the fall of 1933. From the outset, the brewery emphasized that CBC beer would be fully krausened. The term refers to beer that is naturally aged to undergo a secondary fermentation, providing natural carbonation. While krausening had been common before Prohibition, afterward many brewers elected to inject carbon dioxide directly into the brew to produce additional fizz. A November 1933 newspaper article mentioned that the seventy-seven vats at CBC were all filled with aging beer. The story stated that this brew would be placed on the market once the krausening process had been allowed to give the new CBC beer a mellower flavor.

At first only draft beer was produced, but bottled beer sales began on July 31, 1934. CBC beer would be packaged in both clear bottles and brown "steinies." In the meantime, additional stock had been sold, bringing aboard as minority investors Joseph Kovarik, George Schmaltz, and John Grimm.

In 1935, Nick Ems and Fred Hoelzer exited the company. Hoelzer sold his stock to brewmaster/ vice president Bill Compton, who then took over as corporate president. Ems sold out to R. G. Strutmann, who replaced him as secretary/treasurer and on the board of directors. Existing correspondence sent to CBC from its lawyers shows a company that either suffered from inattention to detail or else tended to play fast and loose with government rules. Letters and minutes also detail additional ownership changes. George Ernst came aboard as corporate vice president in 1935, only to be replaced by Arthur Dill in 1936.

While so much corporate shuffling typically indicates internal problems, this didn't seem to be the case at CBC. Late in 1935, President Compton announced the purchase of the old Phoenix Brewery at Eighteenth and Lafayette streets. Phoenix had sat idle for about twenty years prior to the sale, although in 1934 an entity called Marth Brewing Corporation had attempted (and failed) to reopen the plant. Compton stated that Carondelet would begin rehabbing the Phoenix plant starting in January 1936. The company planned to spend two hundred thousand dollars on improvements and new equipment at the site. CBC hoped to be brewing there by mid-1936, with designs of eighty employees and a one hundred thousand–barrel annual capacity. But for whatever reasons, most likely a lack of cash, the move to Phoenix never occurred, and CBC continued operating at its original location.

Little is known about what went on at the brewery over the next couple years, but in 1938 Carondelet began production of Green Tree brand beer, a venerable St. Louis label originated in the nineteenth century by the Green Tree Brewery. Green Tree never reopened after Prohibition, but the brand's lapsed trademark had been revived in 1933 by Christian Buehner and other local investors calling themselves Green Tree Breweries, Inc. While their plans for building a brewery never took off, they did contract with the Peerless Brewing Company of Washington, Missouri, to produce Green Tree beer. Peerless had purchased the rights to brew and market the Green Tree brand west of St. Louis on April 1, 1937. Green Tree Breweries, Inc., later contracted with CBC to produce its beer for St. Louis and points east. In late 1938, CBC submitted plans to the government for converting a former garage into an addition to its bottling shop, perhaps in hope that sales of Green Tree beer would take off. With both Peerless and Green Tree on the verge of insolvency, Carondelet officers Bill Compton and Arthur Dill decided to purchase Green Tree Breweries, Inc. This enabled them to maintain the trademark, which otherwise would have reverted to Peerless.

At some point, Nick Ems came back into the CBC fold, taking over his old role as vice president. Records from 1939 reveal a company in turmoil. In June, it was announced that the Phoenix property had been sold to Harold Sanders for twelve thousand dollars. Notes from a meeting of CBC stockholders and board members a few days later show that the company consisted of just four

These four bottles illustrate label variations for two of Carondelet's flagship brands, CBC and St. Louis Select Lager.

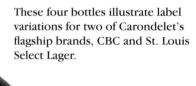

people: President Arthur Dill, Secretary/Treasurer Nick Ems, and a pair of vice presidents—Elsie Ragan and Mary O'Neil. How and why these ladies had come aboard is anybody's guess, as is the disappearance of Bill Compton. At this meeting, the company elected to take out a chattel mortgage of just over twenty thousand dollars. At a November 1939 board meeting, Ems and Dill were forced to cover this mortgage with their personal funds. It was the only way CBC could continue functioning, as creditors and suppliers were refusing to extend additional credit.

Matters were soon further complicated. At a meeting held the day after Christmas, Arthur Dill announced that CBC could not complete the

purchase of the Phoenix property as it was unable to pay both an outstanding deed and its share of the real estate taxes. CBC turned to Marie Wesley (another mystery woman), who loaned it twelve thousand dollars to repay Harold Sanders, thus taking over the old Phoenix deed. The dismal news at this meeting continued, with Dill noting that sales of Green Tree beer were slumping. The CBC board opted to lower prices in an effort to stimulate the shrinking sales numbers.

Carondelet continued to struggle through 1940. The brewery was producing Hampton Springs Krausened Bohemian beer for the local Roebock Liquors store, but profits were insufficient to keep the brewery from having to take out another loan, for forty-five hundred dollars, in May. In October, CBC was named as a defendant in a federal lawsuit filed by Schott Breweries, Inc., of Highland, Illinois. Schott sought to stop CBC from using the name Bohemian Beer and alleged that the St. Louis brewery was using a label designed to be "deceptively similar" to that of the Highland Bohemian brand.

Injury was added to insult when CBC president Dill suffered severe burns in a horrible accident on December 16. The forty-two-year-old had struck a match upon entering his garage, igniting fumes from gasoline that had apparently leaked from his

car. Dill was seriously burned on his arms, legs, and chest; the garage and his auto were destroyed beyond repair.

Carondelet soon met an inglorious ending, when on April 30, 1941, it voluntarily surrendered its brewing license. This decision came amid charges by the State of Missouri that the brewery was avoiding taxes by failing to cancel beer stamps and reusing previously canceled ones. In announcing CBC's closing, Dill mentioned that the brewery had not been operating since February, when vandals had entered the plant and destroyed machinery.

CBC never reopened. It continued on in name only until the end of 1946, all the while being hounded by creditors and lawsuits. Eventually, its few remaining assets were sold off and its krausened beer became just a distant memory. Company cofounder Nick Ems went on to own the former Central/Lemp Brewery in East St. Louis for a couple of years in the mid-1940s. He sold out to St. Louis's other CBC, the Columbia Brewing Company. As for Carondelet's physical plant, an insurance map from around 1950 shows that part of it was finally being used as a meat processing plant, with another part serving as a body shop. The former brewery site remains to this day and is currently being used by a vending machine company.

Above: Seldom-seen Carondelet "pony" keg, 1/8-barrel size. Sealing bung hammered into the keg at the brewery is still in place.

Middle: Matchbook cover for CBC beer, "On Tap and in Bottles." Carondelet payroll check, signed by Corporate Vice President Arthur Dill.

Right: The last of its kind? This is the only example known to the authors of this CBC Beer back-bar light-up sign.

Cherokee
Brewery Company

2726 Cherokee

Cherokee Brewery, Meier Brothers	1866–1867
Cherokee Brewery, Herold & Loebs	1867–1877
Cherokee Brewery Company	1877–1889
Cherokee Brewery, branch, SLBA	1889–1899

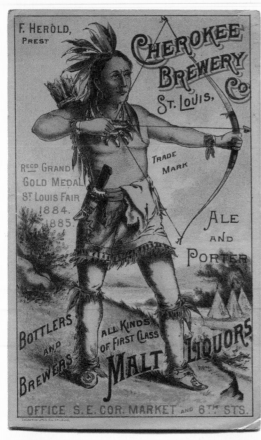

Top: Cherokee Brewery trade card, noting St. Louis Fair Gold Medal wins of 1884 and 1885.

Bottom: Cherokee Brewery, from E. Jungenfeld & Co.'s 1895 *Portfolio*.

While the Cherokee Brewery Company would gain some local prominence under the ownership of the Herold and Loebs families, it was founded in 1866 by the Meier brothers. Ferdinand Herold and George Loebs purchased the brewery the next year.

Ferdinand Herold was born on New Year's Eve, 1829, in Merxheim, Germany. His father was a physician and surgeon. Young Herold attended the preparatory department at Heidelberg University, then went to work for a mercantile establishment in Hamburg, a job at which he stayed for six years. He came to the United States in 1852, spending two years in New York City while working as a clerk for a large wholesale and retail grocery. When Herold came to St. Louis in 1854, he worked at a dry goods store. Two years later he moved to Mascoutah, Illinois, to become co-owner of a mercantile and grocery store, which he ran for ten years. He served as Mascoutah's postmaster during the Buchanan administration, dabbled in real estate, and then established a soda factory. As Mascoutah had several breweries during this era, perhaps he also enjoyed a brew or two as he plotted his next career move.

Herold took a trip to Europe in 1866, and upon his return to St. Louis bought into the Cherokee Brewery. His partner, George Loebs, presumably brought the brewing savvy to the firm of Herold & Loebs, since he served as plant manager. After the business was incorporated around 1877, Loebs became company secretary, with Herold serving as president and treasurer. Assisting the company was Leo Rassieur, a corporate director in charge of the brewery's depot, office, and saloon, all at 413–15 Chestnut (the depot/office later moved to 526 Market Street). Like many St. Louis breweries, Cherokee also featured an on-site beer garden.

After producing 13,508 barrels during the 1873–74 brewing season, ranking Cherokee thirteenth out of twenty-nine St. Louis breweries, annual production leveled off to just over eleven thousand barrels during the late 1870s. It is unclear whether this is indicative of a sales slump, or if the company was simply content with that production level. In any case, the brewery would soon see considerable increases in production.

Cherokee was unique among St. Louis breweries during this period, as a producer of ale- and porter-style brews in addition to lager beer. Lager had truly become king in St. Louis, and most of the small ale producers had gone out of business by 1880. Cherokee likewise employed a unique marketing strategy. While the company's ale, porter, and half-and-half were available only in draft form, its lager was put out strictly in bottles.

The brewery was not content to do business just in St. Louis. In 1882, a depot and refrigerator were erected in Litchfield, Illinois. The structure had space for four hundred kegs of beer and was designed by St. Louis architect O. J. Wilhelmi, a relative of the Winkelmeyer brewing clan.

Cherokee's sales strategies must have been clicking,

for by 1884 production had increased to over eighteen thousand barrels. The brewery would also provide jobs for many members of the Herold and Loebs families. Ferdinand Herold brought his two oldest sons, Theodore and Robert, into the business, while Jacob Loebs succeeded George Loebs as superintendent, with Henry Loebs serving as brewery foreman.

In 1883, Ferd Herold bought George Loebs's share of the business, and Theodore Herold replaced Loebs as corporate secretary. The next two years brought a pair of honors to the brewery, which it quickly chose to brag about on its corporate letterhead: in 1884 and 1885 a Cherokee brew was awarded the Grand Gold Medal at the Great St. Louis Fair.

An 1885 guide to St. Louis industries discussed the brewery in some detail. The main building was said to be two stories tall and measure 200′ × 175′. Among other tidbits: Cherokee's forty to fifty employees produced Herold's Malt Extract for the Richardson Drug Company, the brewery housed two ice machines, and there were three "commodious" cellars located forty-five feet underground. The guidebook also revealed that, just a few months prior to publication, Cherokee had decided to start bottling its ale, porter, and half-and-half, which were previously available only on tap. With the brewery capable of filling three hundred to four hundred dozen bottles a day, such an operation was described as the only one of its kind in the nation west of Chicago.

Like so many of their fellow brewery owners, the Herolds opted to sell out to the St. Louis Brewing Association (SLBA) syndicate in 1889. The SLBA would end up closing a number of its breweries over the next couple of decades, and the Cherokee branch ceased brewing in the fall of 1899 (although its appearance in city directories until 1902 likely indicates the SLBA was at least up to something at the location). Evidence also seems to point to continued production of ale and porter styles at Cherokee following the SLBA purchase. John Michael Friedrich, who served as Cherokee brewmaster from 1892 until its demise, moved over to the old Liberty Brewing Company location to help start the Burton Ale and Porter Brewing Company

immediately after Cherokee closed.

Theodore and Robert Herold stayed in the St. Louis brewing industry as part-owners of both the Home and Consumers breweries. Their father, Ferdinand, took a brief respite from the business world following the SLBA sale. But he soon entered into a venture with Peter Hauptmann, building a passenger and freight steamboat named (of all things) *Cherokee*, the first steel-hulled craft to ply the Mississippi. He next built a steamer with a one-thousand-ton carrying capacity named *Ferd. Herold*, and with partner Hauptmann incorporated the Cherokee Packing Company. Now attached with the new nickname "Commodore," Herold would go on to have numerous other business interests. He died at the age of eighty-two in 1912.

As for the Cherokee brewery itself, a 1909 Sanborn insurance map indicates that the brewhouse had already been torn down, but most of the other buildings remained. Tenants occupying some of them included a sausage factory, a livery stable, and a carriage paint shop. Other buildings were vacant, including the large former stockhouse. Adjacent to the stockhouse was the two-story former office building, shown as being used for "motion pictures." The latter two buildings still stand on the site.

When the husband and wife cave exploring team of Hubert and Charlotte Rother visited the remnants of the Cherokee Brewery Company in 1964, they were directed to a trap door in the basement that they hoped would lead to the brewery's storage cellars. These vaults were thought to have been part of a natural cave complex. The manager of the store, however, was unable to find a key to the locked door. The Rothers were later told that when the brewhouse was demolished, the rubble was used to fill in the cellars. They apparently never did gain access to what was beneath the trap door.

Above: Label for Herold's Porter, dating to the late 1880s, rated "XXX."

Chouteau Avenue Brewery

2000 Chouteau Avenue

Chouteau Avenue Brewery, Joseph Schnaider	1865–c. 1867
Chouteau Avenue Brewery, Schnaider & Henry Breidenbach	c. 1867
Chouteau Avenue Brewery, Joseph Schnaider	c. 1867–1879
Joseph Schnaider Brewing Company	1879–1889
Schnaider branch, SLBA	1889–1892
Chouteau Avenue Branch, SLBA	1892–1893

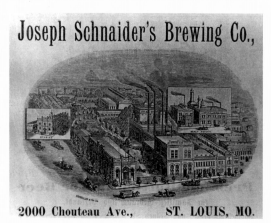

Top: Steel cut lithograph portrait of Joseph Schnaider, from *The Makers of St. Louis: The Mirror,* 1906.

Bottom: 1880s brewery scene newspaper ad, publisher unknown, with images of nearby stables and malt house included as inserts.

Joseph Schnaider began his St. Louis brewing career at the Philadelphia Brewery in 1854. He soon went out on his own as a partner in the Green Tree Brewery. Schnaider and Max Feuerbacher built a new Green Tree Brewery in 1863, but Schnaider didn't stick around long, selling out in 1865.

Schnaider's next business move was to build his own brewery on the south side of Chouteau Avenue near Mississippi Avenue. A large beer garden was established adjacent to the brewery, which became instrumental to its success. By 1874, Joseph Schnaider's Chouteau Avenue Brewery was the fifth largest in the city, ranking just ahead of his old Green Tree plant by producing slightly less than twenty-five thousand barrels.

The German-style beer garden was already on its way to becoming nationally famous. A lover of music, Schnaider established a light opera company that performed at the garden, partly to compete with the St. Louis Browns baseball team, whose success had been eroding his profits by attracting away customers. In addition to delicious food and drink, the garden featured both popular bands and symphonies, some of which later combined to form the St. Louis Symphony Orchestra.

Schnaider became a well-known public figure and benefactor, a real estate magnate who developed many houses near his brewery, and president of the Market Street Bank. In 1873, he built an Italianate mansion at the intersection of Hickory and Dillon streets in St. Louis, where he and his wife, Elizabeth, raised their seven children who survived infancy and mourned the seven who did not. According to Mary Bartley's *St. Louis Lost*, the interior of the Schnaider home was described in a newspaper article (on the occasion of Joseph being presented with a gold-headed cane by the Market Street Bank's board of directors) as follows:

> . . . every apartment was gorgeously and magnificently furnished—mirrors, portraits, and fancy paintings adorned the walls; and, in a word, we doubt there is a more complete and convenient family residence in the city. The wine cellar which, perhaps, is unsurpassed, was next visited, where the new board of directors found samples of the very best of foreign wines, and they agreed unanimously to hold their monthly meetings in this place thereafter.

Unfortunately, Schnaider's days in the spotlight were numbered, as he began suffering from ill health in the late 1870s. To consolidate his affairs, in 1879 the Joseph Schnaider Brewing Company was organized. Schnaider then stepped down from active management of the brewery while continuing as corporate president. His oldest son, Joseph M. Schnaider Jr., who had studied brewing in

Germany as well as at home, was named secretary-treasurer and assumed most of his father's duties, with Fred Wahl, who had worked for Schnaider for thirteen years, named manager. A number of improvements were also started at the brewery around this time, too.

The 1879 annual convention of the U.S. Brewers Association was held in St. Louis, with brewers from all over the country in attendance. After delegates were given a tour of the many Soulard-area breweries (where an incredible number of plants were located within a few blocks of one another), they were among a huge crowd attending an evening concert at Schnaider's Garden. Following the music was a fancy fireworks display, the highlight of which was a thirty-foot-tall image of Gambrinus, the unofficial patron saint of beer. While the reporter for *The Western Brewer* was a bit miffed that the normally free garden charged 25 cents admission for the occasion, he did allow that the concert had done Joseph Schnaider "lasting honor."

In the summer of 1881, Joseph Schnaider Sr. returned to Germany. He died there a few months later at the young age of forty-nine. His body was returned to St. Louis for the funeral, with the list of pallbearers reading like a Who's Who in St. Louis brewing—William J. Lemp, Casper Koehler, Henry Anthony, Henry Kunz, Charles Stifel, Tony Straub, Henry Grone, Lawrence Lempel, George Schilling, and John Heidbreder.

The Western Brewer had some interesting comments following Schnaider's death:

> He was a man of excessive nervous temperament, proud of his success as he had a right to be, possessed withal of a warm and kindly nature, which, however, men who did not understand him rarely succeeded in finding. But he had many friends closely attracted to him, and his demise leaves a vacant chair at the hospitable board of St. Louis brewers.

To honor the late brewery founder, a piece of artwork was installed at Schnaider's Garden. *The Western Brewer* reported that on May 9, 1883, "an excellently executed bust of the late Joseph

Schnaider . . . was unveiled . . . with appropriate ceremonies." This unusual piece of breweriana has yet to surface in any area collections.

Joseph Schnaider Jr. continued at the helm of the Chouteau Avenue Brewery until it became part of the St. Louis Brewing Association (SLBA) merger in 1889. The SLBA used the plant as a brewery only briefly, ending production in 1893. It continued on, however, as the Chouteau Avenue Crystal Ice and Cold Storage plant, producing ice using water from an underground stream in the natural lagering cave. In the years before Prohibition the former brewery also served as home to the Prudential Bar Fixture Company, which produced items for the many brewery-owned taverns of the day. Into the 1940s the old Chouteau Avenue Brewery continued in the ice business and was also the site of the local office of the SLBA, which had evolved into a real estate company. Most of the buildings were torn down in 1960.

Until recently, much of the property was covered by a parking lot where semi-trucks were being offered for sale or lease. The site was owned by two of the partners who were also redeveloping the Lemp brewery complex. The tract is now home to a number of attractive single-family row houses, constructed to match the nineteenth-century style of the neighborhood. Across the street is a restaurant named Vin de Set, with a rooftop bar and bistro. It was opened in the former Centennial Malt House building, an annex of Schnaider's brewery. Constructed in 1876, and restored by Paul and Wendy Hamilton, the building is located at 2017 Chouteau Avenue. Visitors to this address will also find, among other businesses, the Moulin (French for mill, an appropriate name for a one-time malt house) Events and Meetings banquet hall, and the Grand Petite Market, a specialty gift, culinary, and wine shop.

While the Chouteau Avenue Brewery is long gone, there is one Schnaider family brewery still in business. In 1891, Joseph Schnaider Jr. left St. Louis to found (with partner Isaac Garza) the Cerveceria Cuauhtemoc in Monterrey, Mexico. It was the first Mexican brewery to be built as a lager beer facility, and by 1897 it had become the biggest brewery in Mexico. It is still a major player in the Mexican brewing industry.

City Brewery/Union Brewing Company

1. City Brewery
38–40 Cherry Street

Finney Brothers	1834–c. 1840
Finney Bros. & Dory	c. 1840–c. 1848
Stifel, Berscht & Co.	c. 1848–c. 1852
Charles G. Stifel	1852–1879
(new brewery opened 1859 at	
Fourteenth and Chambers streets)	
C. G. Stifel Brewing Company	1879–1889
Stifel branch, SLBA	1889–1905
City branch, SLBA	1905–1920

2. Union Brewery
3126 Gravois Street

Union Brewing Company	1898–1906
Otto F. Stifel's Union Brewing Company	1906–1919
Falstaff Brewing Corporation, Plant #2	1933–1952

Above: Portrait of Otto Stifel.

Facing page: Colonel Charles G. Stifel's portrait, originally published in Scharf's *History of Saint Louis City and County*.

hough they are now largely forgotten, members of the Stifel (pronounced STEE-full) family played a role in the St. Louis brewing industry for over a century. The colorful clan descended from Frederick Stifel, who operated a small brewery in Neuffen, Kingdom of Wurttemberg, Germany, in the early 1800s. It was there that Charles G. Stifel was born in 1819. He came to the United States in 1837, eventually landing work on a farm in Newark, New Jersey. He then was able to find a brewery job in Wheeling, West Virginia, where he started out making twelve dollars a month. Several of his brothers and two of his sisters likewise ended up in Wheeling.

EARLY STRUGGLES

harles Stifel stayed at the brewery in Wheeling for a few years then moved on to New Orleans. He became quite ill for several weeks after arriving in the Crescent City and found himself nearly broke. But he soon found success in the egg business, operating in both New Orleans and Nashville. He was able to afford a holiday in Germany, but he had to beat a hasty retreat from officials trying to draft him into the German army.

In the meantime, Charles's brother Frederick, along with partner Julius Winkelmeyer, had done well at a brewery they had launched in St. Louis in 1843. The latter also became a part of the Stifel family by marrying his partner's sister Christina. Frederick Stifel and his wife were both victims of the local cholera epidemic in 1849. That same year, Charles and brothers Jacob and Christopher all decided to move to St. Louis. While Christopher went to work at the brewery of brother-in-law Winkelmeyer, Charles opted to join a rival enterprise.

He invested eighteen hundred dollars in the Finney Brothers ale brewery on Cherry Street, which had opened in 1834. James and William Finney operated a local grocery and "boat" store in addition to the brewery. In the 1840s they had a partner named John Dory (also spelled Drury).

At first Charles Stifel and a partner named Berscht rented the Finney facility; brother Jacob Stifel also was involved in the enterprise. In addition to cream ale, the new owners began producing the lager-style brew that was sweeping the St. Louis market. Charles bought out his partners in 1852 to become sole owner of what was by then called the City Brewery. Business must have been booming, as Stifel began operating a branch brewery on the east side of Carondelet between Lesperance and Picotte streets. Nothing is known about this operation except for its appearance in city directories in 1853 and 1854.

By 1859, demand for his beer had grown to the point that Stifel, acting as his own architect, built a new brewery and malt house on Fourteenth Street in an area that was then surrounded by woods and where Stifel had previously built aging cellars. Despite this rustic location, Stifel continued using the City Brewery moniker, and the city would later grow around his brewery. For a couple of years brewing took place at both the new and the old facilities, and even after all production had been moved to the new site, the original plant remained home to the brewery's office.

CHARLES AT WAR

As the Civil War began to heat up, pro-Union forces started organizing in Missouri. Many members of the local German turnverein (gymnastic societies) were called to service. One of them was Charles Stifel, and in anticipation of local conflict he bought fifty muskets and conducted military exercises inside his brewery's malt house. While the largely pro-Union city of St. Louis would later prove to be a safe haven during the war, a riot between rival sympathizers occurred early in the conflict. The day after this melee, Stifel marched his regiment to the recently liberated federal arsenal, where they were christened the Fifth Regiment of the U.S. Reserve Corps, with Charles being made a colonel (which would become his nickname for the rest of his life).

Colonel Stifel and company then marched into the tense city, where the regiment was fired upon by rebel foes. While two of Stifel's men were killed and seven wounded, the other side had thirty-eight casualties. During the skirmish, many St. Louis residents opted to flee to the county or into Illinois.

A week later Stifel and his troops headed out to Boonville, Missouri, where their ranks swelled to three hundred men and two steamboats. These Union forces routed the Confederate troops at Lexington, Missouri, and Stifel continued his army career in western Missouri. But when word reached him that his business affairs back in St. Louis were going downhill, he decided to resign his commission and return to the brewery. Colonel Stifel was able to get the business back on its feet, and thus began a long era of prosperity for the City Brewery. The 1866 convention of the United States Brewers Association was held in St. Louis, and the hot topic was the recently enacted federal tax stamp system that the brewers saw as unworkable. Stifel was active at the convention and was held in

such high esteem by his peers that he was selected as chairman and presiding officer at the next year's convention in Chicago. He served the same group as a vice president in 1885.

GLORY YEARS

The 1870s and 1880s were a glorious and growing time for the brewing industry in the thriving city of St. Louis. Annual production at the City Brewery had grown to nearly twenty thousand barrels by 1874, ranking it tenth out of the twenty-nine local brewing firms. In 1879, with output up to thirty thousand barrels, the business was incorporated as the C. G. Stifel Brewing Company, and many improvements were undertaken. A new ice and refrigerating house was built, three new cellars were dug, with a new office building and giant grain elevator added soon thereafter. Stifel served as president of his namesake company, with assistance from corporate treasurer Richard Bosewetter and brewery superintendent Jacob Schorr. Their efforts were clearly paying off, as the Stifel/City brewery produced more than forty thousand barrels in 1884, moving the company up to the number-four slot in St. Louis brewing. In addition, Charles Stifel had shown off his engineering expertise by inventing a new type of mash machine as well as a unique keg-bunging apparatus.

THE PRODIGAL SON

Charles Stifel's son, Otto, was born in St. Louis in 1862. Prior to becoming a partner in his father's brewery, he graduated from Washington University in St. Louis, then went abroad to study at the School of Technology in Stuttgart, Germany. He also studied brewing at schools in Chicago, Milwaukee, and New York. As his father grew older, Otto's role in the brewery became more and more prominent.

In 1889, the City Brewery was among many absorbed by a British investment group known as the St. Louis Brewing Association (SLBA). Charles Stifel remained at the brewery until his retirement in 1892. Son Otto continued on, serving as vice president (and later president) of the stateside directorate of the SLBA. Like most beer barons, the Stifels had other business interests in addition to the brewery. Otto was active in politics and ran the East St. Louis Ice and Cold Storage Company, while Charles owned a huge amount of property and was longtime president of the Northwestern Savings Bank in St. Louis.

Colonel Stifel passed away in 1900 at the age of eighty-two. In addition to his many accomplishments, his obituary in *The Western Brewer* noted that he had donated a monument of poet Friedrich Schiller to the city. At his death, Stifel was survived by his wife, Louise, whom he had married back in West Virginia in 1847, and his three children. By this time his old City Brewery had become one of the SLBA's primary facilities, churning out some ninety thousand barrels per year. It stayed open until becoming a victim of Prohibition in July of 1920.

A NEW STIFEL BREWERY

In addition to his brewing duties at the City Brewery and with the SLBA, Otto Stifel had quite a reputation as a sportsman. St. Louis had thriving racetracks for many decades, and Otto became a lifelong lover of the ponies. His interest in horse racing reached a pinnacle in 1904, when in conjunction with the World's Fair the local jockey club put up a huge fifty thousand dollar purse for a race dubbed the World's Fair Handicap. The outstanding horse Hermis, shipped in from New York, was the heavy favorite, but Otto's mare Colonial Girl swept by him in the stretch to take the top prize (a horse owned by Memphis brewer John Schorr, formerly of St. Louis, finished third). Sadly for Stifel, by the next year puritanical forces shut down the local track so he had to race his stable elsewhere. With this outlet for his energies stifled, it was perhaps inevitable that Otto turned his attention elsewhere, in this case another brewery.

The Union Brewing Company, at Gravois Avenue and Michigan Street in St. Louis, was founded in 1898 by partners Christian Beck, F. W. Schumacher, and Henry Anthony (the latter of Anthony & Kuhn Brewing Company fame). Beck was a player in the Columbia Distilling Company, and the new brewery was designed to provide independent saloonkeepers with their own source of beer.

In 1906, following his resignation as president of the SLBA, Otto Stifel and partner Julius Bongner purchased this brewery. Stifel affixed his well-known name to the plant, doing business as the rather wordy Otto F. Stifel's Union Brewing Company. A new stockhouse and bottling shop were constructed in 1908, and Stifel became noted for good treatment of his employees.

Stifel's interest in horse racing continued. In 1912, he purchased a large farm on Dougherty Ferry Road near Valley Park and spent considerable money improving the property. A twenty thousand dollar barn was built, as was a six-room bungalow for the farm manager, with one of the rooms kept for Stifel to use during overnight stays. He kept some of his racehorses at the farm and continued racing a stable in Kentucky and elsewhere. He was prominent in other areas of the sporting world as well. In 1913, he bought an interest in the St. Louis Terriers baseball club of the upstart Federal League. In 1915, while construction continued on a new two-story bottling house at the brewery, Stifel was part of a group that purchased the St. Louis Browns baseball team.

OTTO'S DEMISE

The last years of World War I were not kind ones to the brewing industry. Business was hobbled by wartime restrictions on grain and coal. Soon things got even worse with the enactment of the Eighteenth Amendment outlawing beer. Once again prohibitionists were raining on Otto Stifel's parade, this time with fatal results.

Brewing was halted early in 1919, and prior to the onset of Prohibition part of the Union Brewery was converted into an oleomargarine factory. This was not as illogical a path for the brewery as it might seem, for in addition to keeping horses on his farm, Stifel also raised Ayrshire cattle, which provided much of the milk used at the plant. This alternate business was apparently rather successful.

All was not well with Otto Stifel, however, especially financially. Friends noted that he had been suffering considerable gambling losses over the last few years. He was in debt to the tune of $150,000 and having difficulty raising funds. On August 18, 1920, Stifel was supposed to meet with brother-in-law Edwin Conrades to discuss the affairs of the former brewery and to close the sale of some of his stock from the company operating his late father's estate. The night before the scheduled meeting, Stifel stayed at his farm. The next morning he took an early train to St. Louis but returned before the meeting. Around noon, his farm manager walked into the house and found Stifel's body on one of the twin beds in his room—the victim of a self-inflicted gunshot wound to the mouth, the revolver still in his hand.

Otto Stifel had left numerous suicide notes to family members and associates. Several of the notes were stuffed in a brewery logo envelope left on a nightstand. An open slip of paper sitting on the same table read simply, "To my wife and son: I think this is best." A rambling open note blamed some of his friends and relatives for taking advantage of his poor financial and mental conditions. Whether or not the fifty-seven-year-old brewer was simply deluded is unclear. As a parting shot, Stifel requested that his longtime attorney, Theodore Rassieur, attempt to nullify some of his recent business transactions to enable his creditors to "get an honest share of my residue."

BACK IN BUSINESS

Charles "Carl" Stifel was just twenty-three years old when his father committed suicide. While it is uncertain what went on at the brewery during the remaining thirteen years of Prohibition, following Repeal he was ready to get back into the brewing business.

The Falstaff Brewing Corporation had come flying out of the gate in 1933 and was having great success with its namesake brand. Unable to keep up with demand and desperate for additional brewing capacity, Falstaff entered into an agreement with Carl Stifel to lease the facility of the former Otto F. Stifel's Union Brewing Company.

Once again the Stifel family began feuding over finances, and a May 1936 lawsuit filed against Carl Stifel by his aunt Mrs. Louise Conrades afforded details about the lease between Falstaff and Stifel.

Of the 3,250 shares of Stifel brewing stock, Carl owned 1,703, his aunt 1,103, and several small shareholders the rest. Mrs. Conrades's lawyers contended before Circuit Judge John W. Joynt that Carl owed the company $55,532. They alleged that Carl had an under-the-table deal with Falstaff to receive $2 per barrel produced rather than the contractually agreed upon $1.25 per barrel for the first year and $1 thereafter. Whatever its merits, this lawsuit did not succeed, and Carl Stifel survived the challenge to his reign as company president.

In February of 1944, Falstaff reached an agreement with Carl Stifel to purchase the brewery for $600,000 cash. Production continued at the brewery only until 1952. By then Falstaff had purchased the Columbia Brewing Company in north St. Louis, and the former Union Brewery was no longer needed. Portions of the brewery were used as an advertising warehouse and offices until 1957. The brewhouse was later torn down to make way for a gas station. Other parts of the old brewery remain, however, including the office building; among its current occupants are a lot of cats. A shelter-type facility called the Clowder House Foundation has been established on the site, which offers felines for adoption and also serves as a home for cats whose late owners have arranged for them to live out their nine lives in comfort.

The Stifel name lives on in the St. Louis area in the form of the well-known investment company of Stifel Nicolaus. This firm takes its name from Herman Stifel, son of Otto's brewing uncle Christopher, who entered the stock and bond business in 1897 (the Nicolaus portion of the name comes from Henry Nicolaus, who spent many decades in the St. Louis brewing industry and was forced to turn to his other investments during the dry days of the 1920s). Currently a subsidiary of Stifel Financial Group, today's Stifel Nicolaus no longer mentions its brewing roots on its corporate resume.

Above: Stifel's Union delivery truck, manufactured circa 1911 by Reliance Motor Truck of Owosso, Michigan, with driver and two deliverymen.

Right: Brewery workers photo, taken in front of the Stifel's Union brewery about 1910. Otto F. Stifel can be seen in the first row, second from left (man with beard).

Columbia Brewing Company

2000 Madison Street (Twentieth and Madison)

Columbia Brewing Company	1892–1907
Columbia branch, IBC	1907–1921
Columbia Brewing Company	1934–1948
Falstaff Brewing Corporation, Plant #5	1948–1967

Top: Factory scene from *The Western Brewer*, 1892.

Bottom: Photo taken in June 2008 of the arched brickwork above the former main entrance of the Columbia Brewery.

A rather late addition to the pre-Prohibition roster of St. Louis breweries, the Columbia Brewing Company opened in 1892. It was the brainchild of a pair of brewing veterans, Casper Koehler and Zach Tinker. They chose the Columbia name in conjunction with the four-hundredth anniversary of the journey to North America by Christopher Columbus.

Columbia was built using plans drafted by E. Jungenfeld & Company, the famous St. Louis architectural firm specializing in brewery construction. The plant was built to last, with solid brick walls forty inches thick at the base, and equipped with state-of-the-art brewing and refrigerating equipment. The owners of the new brewery must have been confident in their ability to sell beer, as Columbia opened with the third-largest production capacity of some two dozen local breweries.

Casper Koehler had first entered the St. Louis brewing scene around 1860 at the Excelsior Brewery, where he remained for a number of years. He returned to Europe for a while, next headed to Davenport, Iowa, to brew with his brother Henry, and then came back to Excelsior, which was sold to the St. Louis Brewing Association (SLBA) conglomerate in 1889. Like several other St. Louis brewers who had sold their plants to the British syndicate, Casper Koehler quickly jumped back into the beer business, organizing Columbia in 1891. His son-in-law Rudolph Limberg was likewise a major stockholder, with his son Julius Koehler serving as brewery superintendent. Their partner Zachariah Wainwright Tinker, born in St. Louis in 1853, was the son of pioneering St. Louis maltster George Tinker. In addition to operating malt houses, George Tinker had also owned the Franklin Brewery. Zach tried his hand at a few non-brewing jobs prior to joining his father at the Tinker and Smith Malting Company. That company's Spring Water Malt House, established in 1866, became associated with the new brewery when Columbia was formed.

Early brands produced by the Columbia Brewing Company included Columbia Pale, Standard, Extra Pale, and Muenchener. They were joined by the bottled brands Carlsburger, Wuerzberger, Export, and Banner. The latter label was introduced in 1902 with advertising that used both a rooster and a flag as symbols.

One of the most elaborate attractions at the 1904 St. Louis World's Fair was the German Tyrolean Alps concession area. Located at the entrance to the amusement section, the 250,000-square-foot enclosure was sponsored by the St. Louis brewing industry. Basically a reduced version of a German alpine village (complete with a castle, homes, and churches with fake mountains in the background), but filled with actual native artisans, the structure was said to have cost $500,000. The Alps also included a huge restaurant with a seating capacity of three thousand. The local breweries took full advantage of the opportunity to sell their beers to thirsty fairgoers. In honor of the fair, the Columbia Brewing Company introduced a new brand of beer,

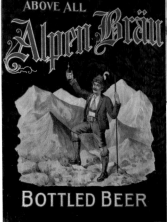

appropriately named Alpen Brau. It would become one of the region's best-known brands, and the brewery would continue to use the symbol of the Tyrolean Alps for the duration of its existence.

Columbia was one of numerous St. Louis breweries merged into the Independent Breweries Company (IBC) in 1907. It became one of the chain's major production facilities, and Alpen Brau beer quickly emerged as the chain's leading brand. Within a few years of the IBC merger, Alpen Brau (described in ads as "amber, topped with rich creamy foam, sparkling, delicious, with just the proper tang to tickle the tongue") was being produced at several of the company's breweries.

In anticipation of the Eighteenth Amendment, in 1919 the IBC began producing IBC root beer, a soda that survives to this day. The Columbia Brewing Company, however, closed its doors at the end of 1921.

Many of St. Louis's well-heeled brewers turned to their other investments to make a living during the dark days. Part of the IBC was spun off into the Independent Realty Company, which occupied itself by managing the extensive real-estate holdings of the ex-brewers, including the numerous

brewery-owned (former) taverns. The realty company still owned most of the IBC's former breweries in 1933, when it once more became legal to make beer. They were a bit slow out of the blocks, but finally in June it was announced that Mark C. Steinberg had brought together a number of local businessmen to purchase the Columbia plant. The partners brought $300,000 cash to the table and expected to spend $150,000 rehabbing the plant.

REBIRTH

Casper Koehler had died in 1910, but his nephew Hugo Koehler, who had been involved in the family's American Brewing Company and had for many years been president of the IBC, was among the new investors. The re-established Columbia Brewing Company began making beer again in 1934. Assisting Koehler at the helm were President J. Spencer McCourtney, who had joined the Independent Realty Company in the 1920s; Vice President Frank Forster, who had worked at his family's Hyde Park brewery in St. Louis prior to Prohibition; and Mark Steinberg, corporate treasurer and likewise a major stockholder, who was also a bigwig in the Independent Realty Company. Karl K. Vollmer, who had married into the Koehler family, was named assistant treasurer and distribution chief. Vollmer, a native of Davenport, Iowa, brought some rather unusual credentials to the brewing business, having graduated from Cornell University and possessing an MBA from Harvard.

Things started out somewhat slowly for the new Columbia Brewing Company, which eked out small profits its first couple years but actually lost money in 1937. Despite these problems with the balance sheet, Columbia launched an expansion program in 1937 and began advertising extensively on the radio and in print. The slogan "Nothing Finer out of a Bottle" was featured in these ads. Whether increased sales were due to these marketing efforts or to the delicious taste of Alpen Brau, the next year saw the brewery make a profit of over sixty thousand dollars. Further brewery expansions were started in December of that year.

Columbia had a banner year in 1939, with an astounding 282 percent increase in Alpen Brau sales and over $325,000 in profits. Much of the money was put back into the company. By the time a four-year expansion program was completed in 1941, over $800,000 had been spent on buildings and equipment. Around this same time, Columbia introduced perhaps its best-remembered slogan, "It's The Tops!" This motto had something of a double meaning, since Alpen Brau labels had traditionally shown the "tops" of mountains, and now the "tops" (or crowns) of Alpen Brau bottles could be used in advertisements featuring the new theme.

Clever marketing by Columbia no doubt was a factor in the sales increases of Alpen Brau beer. One example occurred in the spring of 1935, when heavy rains caused flooding on the Missouri River. This in turn rendered impassable roads leading to territories covered by the Alpen Brau distributor in Flint Hill, Missouri. Sensing a great publicity opportunity, the brewery arranged for cases and kegs of its beer to be flown into the affected area, so that inhabitants might not be "deprived of their favorite brew." The company ended up spending much more money publicizing the delivery in newspaper ads than was spent on the flight itself. The stunt, perhaps not coincidentally, happened to tie in nicely with the ongoing Alpen Brau ad slogan "Above All."

Two years later Columbia launched an aggressive push to open new accounts to sell its bottled beer. The campaign included an exclusive agreement with the Eagle Stamp Company. Two Alpen Brau bottle caps could be swapped for one Eagle Stamp, which could then be exchanged for a wide variety of prizes, including clothing, furniture, and even gasoline. It doesn't appear that anybody at Eagle kept the crowns when the promotion was over, though, as collectors can attest to the fact that Alpen Brau caps are hard to find.

Top: Alpen Brau cloth uniform patch from the 1930s.

Above and left: Two seldom-seen tin signs issued in the 1890s.

Right: Alpen Brau bottle label, commemorating the 1904 World's Fair.

Below: Label, circa 1905, with Columbia's shield logo printed in the center.

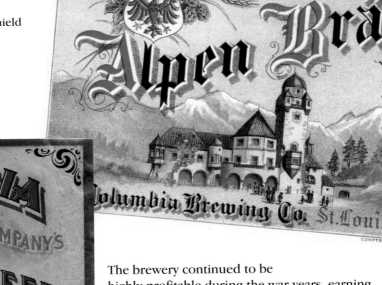

The Columbia Brewing Company was also a strong advocate of radio advertising, sponsoring 120 programs a week by 1940. During one March of Dimes pledge drive, the brewery sought to garner local goodwill by having its radio commercials say, "Deprive yourself of one bottle of Alpen Brau and send your dime to President Roosevelt, [and] you will enjoy the next bottle that much more." In October 1940, one of Columbia's on-air programs made national news, though not necessarily in a way the company would have liked. Hollywood movie star George Jessel, while being interviewed in St. Louis on an Alpen Brau–sponsored live radio program, announced, "I am very happy to be on this Hyde Park [a competing local brewery] program." According to a contemporary account in *American Brewer*, Columbia executive Karl Vollmer, who was standing outside the broadcast booth, "almost fainted at Jessel's faux pas." The head of the advertising agency handling the show tried to save the day by telling switchboard operators responding to callers asking about the flub to say, "Jessel's bull was just one of his little jokes."

Columbia did its part for the war effort in 1942 with the giant lighted Alpen Brau sign on the brewery smokestack programmed to alternate with a "Buy War Bonds" message complete with a fifteen-foot-tall red, white, and blue *V* for victory.

The brewery continued to be highly profitable during the war years, earning $177,115 in profits in 1945. But despite continued sales increases, only $98,000 was netted in 1946.

At the beginning of 1947 it was announced that Columbia was planning to merge with the Ems Brewing Company of East St. Louis, Illinois. Like Columbia, Ems had been a part of the old Independent Breweries Company back in the pre-Prohibition era, when it was called the Central Brewing Company. Columbia President McCourtney revealed that master brewer J. Adolph Mertens, former Ems president, had been elected first vice president of Columbia and would also take over as general manager of the St. Louis branch. A few months later Mertens was elevated to company president, with McCourtney taking the title of board chairman. Karl Vollmer was advanced to first vice president, with F. P. Rollins Jr. and L. A. Fruend also named vice presidents.

There are various possible reasons for Columbia's interest in the Ems plant (named after Nick Ems, who had rescued it from the defunct Lemp Brewing Company in the mid-1940s). First, Columbia may have wanted increased capacity for producing Alpen Brau. Second, J. Spencer McCourtney was interested in launching a namesake brand called Courtney's Ale and may have believed that the East St. Louis facility was better adapted to ale production than the St. Louis brewery. Finally, it appears that Columbia wanted Adolph Mertens running its operations, so the merger looked to be a good way of accomplishing that.

At the close of 1947, Columbia's ledger showed a loss of $4,923. A write-off on the inventories of the Ems plant was said to have cost $68,000. Despite this, the company still had big plans for its future and for the St. Louis brewery, as construction began on a new $1.5 million bottling plant. The new building was constructed in the striking International style, said to be the first of the design built west of the Mississippi River. The final step in this construction project was to be a third packaging line, which would for the first time in company history be used to fill cans.

Amid these changes, 1948 marked the end of the line for both the Columbia and Alpen Brau names, when the mighty Falstaff Brewing Corporation swept in and effected a merger with Columbia. The St. Louis brewery became Falstaff Plant #5. The Alpen Brau label was quickly killed. The East St. Louis brewery, which had brewed both Courtney's Ale and Alpen Brau, had already been closed by Columbia before the Falstaff deal was finalized.

The former Columbia Brewing Company plant was eventually expanded to produce more than five hundred thousand barrels a year. It continued under the Falstaff flag until 1967. Owing to the outstanding bottling plant, it served Falstaff as an exclusively package facility, filling both twelve- and sixteen-ounce cans and various sized bottles. After Falstaff dumped the Alpen Brau label, it

was eventually acquired by the Potosi Brewing Company in Wisconsin, which made the brand from 1960 to 1971.

The St. Louis brewery was acquired by the city's land reauthorization authority in the 1970s, although it sat vacant until the 1980s. Then, with federal assistance, it was converted into an eighty-four-unit apartment complex. Brewery Apartments continues serving that purpose to this day. Now, on a warm summer afternoon, in the open courtyard where Columbia Brewing Company employees once enjoyed lunch and a refreshing Alpen Brau beer, children can be found enjoying the refreshing coolness of a large swimming pool, certainly not a bad fate for the former brewery.

Right: Miss Columbia unveiling a bottle of Banner beer, introduced by the brewery in the early 1900s.

No brewing location in St. Louis has a more colorful or convoluted history than that of the Consumers Brewing Company, which itself only operated from 1896 to 1909. Breweries on the site took part in both of the major St. Louis brewing mergers, and more than a century of beer-making occurred there.

The story of the brewery on Shenandoah Avenue began elsewhere, in the Soulard neighborhood, on the southwest corner of Ann Avenue and Decatur (later Ninth) Street. A brewery was opened there by German immigrant William (Wilhelm) Stumpf. While *100 Years of Brewing* gives an 1850 start date for Stumpf's Brewery, the *Handels-Zeitung* 1857 newspaper list recorded an 1853 opening date. The latter source also credits the brewery with annual production of ten thousand barrels, ranking it fourth in production out of twenty-nine local firms. This list also includes a pair of Stumpf partners named Hazen and Krug. Local maltster Charles Hoppe was also said (by *100 Years of Brewing*) to have been a brewery partner in the early years. Two different 1860 industrial censuses indicate a smaller production total for that year. It is unclear if this reflects shrinking sales for the brewery, some kind of production problem such as a fire, or simply some inaccuracies with the numbers given.

William Stumpf soon took on a new brewery partner—a young William Lemp, who was also involved in the downtown St. Louis brewery of his father Adam Lemp. Son William was Stumpf's partner for a number of years, even after his father passed away in 1862, leaving him in charge of Lemp's Western Brewery.

Typical of the brewing business, Stumpf's brewery was also a family affair, with Frederick and Otto Stumpf both employed there. In addition to the brewery, the company operated a storage cave and beer garden at the southwest corner of Buena Vista (now Lemp) and Arrow streets. Called simply Stumpf's Cave, it was a major attraction in its day, and William Stumpf's home was located nearby. Yet another outlet for Stumpf's beer was Union Park, a beer garden and saloon near the brewery. Herman Bachmann was a partner with William Stumpf in this enterprise. In his 1902 book *Mercantile, Industrial and Professional St. Louis*, historian Ernst Kargau said the partners made Union Park "a splendid place of recreation," featuring concerts, shade trees, and lovely flower beds.

NEW BREWERY LOCATION

In 1870, William Stumpf built a new brewery on the southwest corner of Buena Vista Street and Shenandoah Avenue. The old site continued to be used as a malt house, which by the late 1870s was being run by Anton Wagenhaeuser. A 1908 newspaper article discussed the then still-standing original brewery and malt house, parts of which were being used by the American Molding and Frame Manufacturing Company. William Stumpf's son

Consumers Brewing Company
(and predecessors)

Southwest corner of Ninth Street and Ann Avenue

Wilhelm (William) Stumpf	c. 1853–1857
William Stumpf & Company	1857–c. 1860
(Stumpf, Hazen, & Krug)	c. 1857
(Stumpf, Hoppe, & Krug)	?
Stumpf & Lemp	c. 1860–1866
Stumpf's Brewery, William Stumpf	
(aka Stumpf & Co.)	1866–1870

2301 Buena Vista Street—new brewery at new location

Stumpf's Brewery, William Stumpf	
(aka Stumpf & Co.)	1870–1875
Stumpf & Thamer	1875–1877
Thamer Brewing Company	1877–1878
A. Griesedieck & Co.	1878–1880
A. Grieseideck Brewing Company	1880-1883
Miller & Wagenhaeuser	1883–1885
Miller Brothers Brewery Company	1885–1889
Miller Brothers branch, SLBA	1889–1890
Consumers Brewing Company	1896–1907

(1900 Shenandoah Avenue)

Consumers branch, IBC	1907–1909
Griesedieck Brothers Brewing Company	1911–1924
Griesedieck Brothers Brewery Company	1933–1957
Falstaff Brewing Corporation, Plant #10	1957–1977

Consumers Pale Lager beer label, from the 1890s.

William still owned the property, lived next door, and operated a saloon on the corner. The famous 1896 tornado had torn part of the old brewery's roof off, but it had been repaired to match the old structure. This article also mentioned that the elder Stumpf had operated a brewery in Fayetteville, Illinois, prior to moving to St. Louis, and that the record books from the St. Louis brewery were still in his son's possession. The younger Stumpf also had hanging in his house a certificate proclaiming his father, who passed away in 1894, a lifetime member of the United States Brewers Association. The current whereabouts of these mementos is unknown.

The old brewery wasn't around much longer. A March 1909 article in *American Brewer* noted that it was being sold by the city of St. Louis. Two bids had been made on the property the month before, but with the highest being only $275, they were not accepted. Interestingly, this article states that the Stumpf Brewery was where William J. Lemp "made his first beer" and that the brewery site was going to be used as part of a public park. The site remains the location of Pontiac/Soulard Park to this day.

Production at William Stumpf's new brewery for the 1873–74 brewing season was 11,155 barrels, ranking it fourteenth out of twenty-nine St. Louis breweries. In 1875, Stumpf sold a half-interest in the brewery to Julius Thamer for forty-five thousand dollars. Thamer was a longtime St. Louis maltster, who as early as 1860 was operating two local malting plants and was still running a malt house at 311 Destrahan Street.

On Valentine's Day, 1877, the company name was changed to Thamer Brewing Company, indicating that William Stumpf was no longer involved in the business. A mere 1,260 barrels were produced by Thamer the year after the takeover, with sales the next year amounting to around 8,000 barrels. The Thamer Brewing Company proved to be a short-lived enterprise, for in December of 1878 the brewery was sold for $20,000 to three new partners—Anton Griesedieck, August W. Koehler, and Robert Miller—who would operate under the mantle of A. Griesedieck & Company. Slightly more than 3,500 barrels of beer were produced by the new partners in 1879.

Anton Griesedieck was yet another St. Louis maltster, having operated (with his brother Henry) a malt house at 1210 Park Avenue. Anton would later run this business with his sons. Another brother, Bernard, had also worked in the malting business, and by 1881 he was corporate secretary at the brewery, which had incorporated as A. Griesedieck Brewing Company the previous year. It was capitalized at fifty thousand dollars. The Griesediecks' malting company was incorporated at the same time for a like amount. The Griesediecks decided to depart and set up business at the larger Phoenix Brewery facility in 1883, selling their shares in the brewery to Herman Miller and Anton Wagenhaeuser, two men who were already partners in a malting plant at 716 S. Third Street. Wagenhaeuser only stuck around for a couple of years before selling out to partner Miller. That left the brewery ownership solely in the hands of Herman and Robert Miller, who opted to again change the name of the business, which naturally became the Miller Brothers Brewery Company.

Top: Consumers metal tray with a portrait of Admiral Dewey. Not surprisingly, this tray dates to the time of the Spanish-American War.

Right: Miller Brothers Brewery account book.

Facing page: Consumers Brewery scene, the nineteenth-century building still stands.

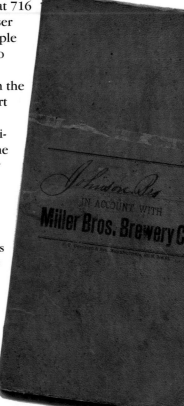

By 1884, the Miller brothers had increased the brewery's output to more than sixteen thousand barrels. Their plant was one of many merged into the St. Louis Brewing Association (SLBA) in 1889. The SLBA must have had little interest in continuing production at the brewery, as it was closed and sold in May of 1890 to Gustav Cramer Dry Plate Manufacturing.

BEER RETURNS

It may have seemed unlikely, but brewing would return to the site within six years. In 1895, a new brewing company was formed. The Consumers Brewing Company was capitalized at $150,000 and organized by five partners—corporate President Theodore Herold; Vice President Frank Nagle, a restaurateur; Secretary-Treasurer Ernest Wagner, a brewer from Rock Island, Illinois; Louisa Sproul, the widow of Frank Sproul, formerly of Anheuser-Busch; and plant superintendent Robert Herold.

Consumers purchased the property from Gustav Cramer, tore down the old buildings, and in 1896 completed construction of a new brewery. It was one of numerous so-called vacuum breweries established worldwide around this time. The term refers to the beer's fermentation process, which took place in special tanks under vacuum pressure. This supposedly kept the brew exceptionally pure and retained natural carbonation so gas didn't have to be added later. The new plant was built with a sixty-five-thousand-barrel capacity.

Theodore and Robert Herold were sons of well-known St. Louisan Ferdinand Herold, who for many years had operated the Cherokee Brewery. That brewery was part of the SLBA merger in 1889. The sons had learned the business at their father's brewery. Theodore had also worked for the Budweiser Beer and Wine Company. After leaving Cherokee in 1890, Theodore Herold went on to help organize and become president of the Home Brewing Company, where he and brother Robert stayed until 1895. When the Herold brothers left Home, rumors were already swirling that they were going to start a new brewery. In reference to these rumors, an 1895 article in *The Western Brewer* quoted Robert Herold as saying that "he and his brother had been brought up in the brewery business, and that they would probably continue in it."

Theodore Herold was born in 1863 in Mascoutah, Illinois, where his father was in the mercantile and soda factory business. In 1886, he married Louisa Griesedieck, a daughter of Frank Griesedieck. Herold became further involved with that family in 1897, when Henry C. Griesedieck became a partner at Consumers. For a number of years Henry had been the manager of the Heim Brewery in East St. Louis, but he departed to replace Ernest Wagner on the Consumers management team.

The three primary brands produced by Consumers were Bohemian, Pale, and Standard lagers. Two beer depots were established by the company, one at Seventh and Clark streets and the other at Grand and Natural Bridge.

Theodore Herold began suffering from ill health after the turn of the century, with brother Robert assuming the lead role in the brewery. Theodore passed away in 1907 at only forty-four years of age. The same year Consumers Brewing Company became a part of the second St. Louis brewing syndicate, a nine-brewery merger known as the Independent Breweries Company (IBC). The IBC apparently had little use for the Consumers plant, closing it within a couple years. However, it was strangely destined to continue playing a large role in St. Louis brewing history.

On December 18, 1911, the IBC sold the property to Henry Griesedieck Jr. for $115,000. Ten days later it was transferred to the Griesedieck Brothers Brewing Company. The Griesediecks reopened the plant and would operate there until the 1950s, when they merged with the Falstaff branch of the Griesedieck family. The brewery became Plant #10 of the Falstaff Brewing Corporation. Falstaff operated the brewery until 1977, more than one hundred years after William Stumpf had first started brewing at the site.

Abandoned by Falstaff, the buildings, which are largely intact to this day, became a treasure trove of breweriana. Numerous visitors gathered both collectibles and corporate records from inside. Some have fond memories of rummaging through massive file cabinets while standing atop a mountain of moldering Falstaff stock certificates. Others explored the brewery's storage cellars, a trip which requires some care, as zealous collectors even removed some of the iron steps reading "Consumers Brewing Company."

Right: Front view of Consumers trade card.

Bottom: Reverse of same trade card, showing brewery, stables, sternwirthe, and depots.

One of the last additions to the pre-Prohibition lineup of St. Louis breweries, the Empire Brewing Company was organized in 1901. Capitalized at $250,000, the company was run by Louis H. Haase as president, Jacob Moerschel as vice president, Frank Laubketter as secretary, Frank Wellman as treasurer, and Otto Moeller as plant superintendent. Henry Heil soon replaced Laubketter as secretary.

Empire's beer first hit the market on January 31, 1902. It must have met with a good reception, as corporate stock was increased to four hundred thousand dollars just a few months later and a new stockhouse quickly built. In 1904, the brewery doubled its ice-making capacity and erected a new office building and bottling shop north of the main plant.

Brewery President Louis Haase was a St. Louis native, born in 1861. Along with his father and brothers he helped run the long-lived A. C. L. Haase and Sons Fish Company. Louis had first worked in the packing room, then as a traveling salesman; he later became vice president of the fish company.

Jacob Moerschel had arrived in St. Louis from Germany in 1867 and immediately began work in the brewing business. He had operated the Spring Brewery in St. Charles, Missouri, prior to helping start Empire, and he later ran the Capitol Brewing Company in Jefferson City.

When Empire merged with eight other area breweries to form the Independent Breweries Company (IBC) in 1907, Haase was named vice president of the conglomerate. The Empire location was a desirable one for the IBC. The buildings and equipment were practically new, it was located right along the tracks of the Wabash Railroad, and there was room for expansion. IBC made frequent improvements to the plant. Under brewmaster A. P. Otto Moeller, the Empire plant brewed Empire lager, Alpen Brau, and American Bohemian brands.

Brewing at Empire ended less than twenty years after it began. With Prohibition on the horizon, the IBC closed the brewery in the spring of 1918.

Empire Brewing Company

Sarah Street and Wabash Railroad

| Empire Brewing Company | 1901–1907 |
| Empire branch, IBC | 1907–1918 |

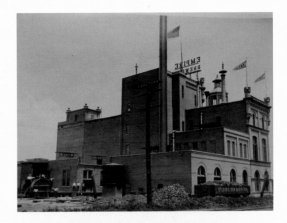

Top: Scene showing rear of Empire Brewing Company. Image is not reversed, illuminated "Empire Brewery" sign faced towards the front of the brewery.

Bottom: A storefront proudly displays Empire beer outdoor signs.

Left: Employees from Empire's Engineering Department. Used as the book's cover photo, each worker holds or is connected to tools of his trade, such as ice tongs, an anvil, and an oil can. Also note the man in the back row far left is holding a cat. The gizmo the worker to the immediate right of the Empire sign is holding is something of a mystery.

A group of investors came together in 1933 and bought the property for $150,000 with intentions of reopening. Directors of the new operation were H. L. Winterman, J. Reynolds Medart, W. J. Drosten, Henry Antler, and Nellson N. Tracy. Their plans never got off the ground, and eventually they defaulted on the mortgage. The brewery went back into the hands of the IBC, which continued to try to sell the ten-building complex. In April of 1936, a nearby grass fire spread to the brewery, damaging several buildings. The IBC decided to tear down most of the brewery shortly thereafter, reportedly to save on property taxes.

Fortunately the office building was spared. It has recently been used as the office for the U.S.

Metals and Service Company, a steel business that operates on part of the former brewery property. Located just off Route 40/I-64, and near the Metrolink tracks at Sarah Street and Duncan Avenue, the building has changed little in the last one hundred years. Visitors can still enjoy the beautifully sculpted lioness heads, which served as Empire's corporate symbol, incorporated into the architecture.

Five tradesmen smile admiringly at a bottle of Empire beer.

The large American Brewing Company in St. Louis was the crowning achievement of the Koehler (pronounced Kay-ler) family, whose ownership role in local brewing began in 1860 at the Excelsior Brewery. Located on the east side of Seventh Street near Lynch, Excelsior was founded in 1857 by Charles Hoelzle, who was not a brewer himself. It is unclear who manned the brew kettle for Mr. Hoelzle. In 1860, Casper Koehler and a partner identified as J. Huber purchased the plant. Koehler, who was just twenty-one years old at the time, had grown up in Frankfurt, Germany, and arrived in the United States in 1858. He had worked for a time at his brother Henry's brewery in Fort Madison, Iowa, about 120 miles up the Mississippi River from St. Louis.

While there are enough holes and discrepancies in the accounts of Casper Koehler's early years to drive a beer wagon through, he may also have spent some time farther upriver in Rock Island, Illinois. An 1860 St. Louis city directory indicates that was where his partner Huber lived. As Ignatz Huber owned a brewery in Rock Island, the "J. Huber" may actually have been a reference to him.

Excelsior was a small brewery even by mid-nineteenth-century standards. An 1860 industrial census states that the company had only six thousand dollars invested in it, employed three workers for a thirty-dollar monthly cost of labor, and used a four-horsepower steam engine to power the plant. Casper Koehler soon had a new partner in the brewery, as around 1863 his brother Henry joined him in St. Louis. The new partnership operated Excelsior under the business title of H. Koehler and Brother.

Henry Koehler would have a long, successful, and interesting career in the brewing business. Born in 1828, he had served the traditional three-year brewing apprenticeship beginning at age fifteen in the German town of Mainz. He next worked as a journeyman at breweries in Mainz and Frankfurt. Following the unsuccessful German Revolution of 1848, Henry must have seen greater promise in the United States. He migrated to New York City, briefly working as a cooper for five dollars a month. Displeased with his situation, Henry drifted west through such brewing towns as Cincinnati and Louisville before reaching St. Louis, where he worked for a time at Lemp's Western Brewery. Upon learning that the man running the brewery in Fort Madison had left for California in 1851, Henry arranged to lease that plant. He remained there for eleven years. At one point, prohibitionists had arrested all the saloon owners in Fort Madison, leaving the brewery as the only local sales outlet for his beer. The "drys" also threatened to storm the brewery but were deterred by Henry and an armed contingent of workmen and friends. Sensing that St. Louis might be a city more friendly to brewers, Henry found someone to sublet the Fort Madison plant and left to join brother Casper at Excelsior.

Under Henry's leadership the brewery began a period of growth. Casper Koehler sold his interest to Philip

Excelsior Brewery / American Brewing Company

Excelsior (East side of Seventh Street near Lynch)

Charles Hoelzle	1857–1860
Casper Koehler & J. Huber	1860–1863
H. Koehler & Brother	1863–1866
Henry Koehler & Philip Hehner	1866–1870
Henry Koehler & Jacob Hiemenz	1870–1874
Casper Koehler & Jacob Hiemenz	1874–1875
Excelsior Brewing Company	1875–1880

(moved to former Joseph Uhrig Brewing Company site 1880–1891, then to former Winkelmeyer site 1891–1917, branch of SLBA from 1889 to closing)

American Brewing Company

Henry Koehler Brewing Association	1880–1882
American Brewing Company	1890–1907
American branch, IBC	1907–1920s
ABC Brewing Corporation	1934–1937
Terre Haute Brewing Company	1937–1938
ABC Brewing Company	1939–1940

HENRY KOEHLER, ESQ.

Portrait of Henry Koehler, reproduced from a late 1870s issue of *The Western Brewer*.

Facing page: ABC pop-up card, shows one scene when opened, another when closed.

Top right: Peter Saussenthaler.

Bottom right: Oscar Koehler.

Below: Peter Saussenthaler's Excelsior Brewery business card.

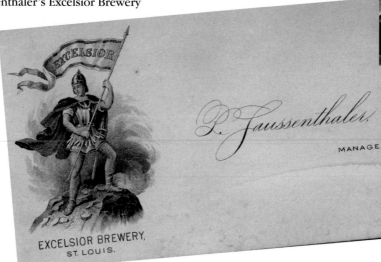

Hehner after the Civil War, returning to Europe to work at breweries in Prague and in Germany. Hehner in turn sold out to Jacob Hiemenz in 1870. Disaster struck the next year when the brewery was destroyed by fire, but the new partners quickly rebuilt. When the footloose Koehler opted to head upriver to Davenport, Iowa, in 1872 to operate the Arsenal Brewery, brother Casper returned to the United States to help him there. In 1874, Casper returned to St. Louis and the Excelsior Brewery, with he and Hiemenz renting the plant from Henry.

Production that year amounted to 9,314 barrels, ranking Excelsior nineteenth out of the twenty-nine breweries in St. Louis. The next year, the eighteen employees raised production to twelve thousand barrels. Soon thereafter the business was incorporated as the Excelsior Brewing Company. Veteran brewers John W. Schorr and plant superintendent Peter Saussenthaler joined Koehler and Hiemenz as stockholders and corporate officers.

Bottled beer was important to the Excelsior Brewery even as early as 1875, when an industrial guide mentioned that, though the brewery had five wagons for city delivery, its "outside trade is, if anything, far ahead of home consumption." As federal law required brewers to have their bottling shops separated from their brewhouses, the Excelsior Bottling Company was formed, with Jacob Hiemenz as president. Increased sales soon led Excelsior to lease the nearby plant of the closed Pittsburgh Brewery, which was then converted into a malt house.

The year 1880 brought a big change to the Excelsior Brewing Company, when it purchased the financially ailing Joseph Uhrig Brewing Company in St. Louis. Production of the flagship Red Feather brand was shifted to that plant, while brewing at the old plant continued under the auspices of the newly formed Henry Koehler Brewing Association. Joining corporate president Henry Koehler in that enterprise were Simon Ittel as vice president, F. Lipsius as superintendent, and Henry Koehler's son Oscar Koehler as secretary. This enterprise was short-lived, ceasing operations in 1882. It would only mark a temporary end to brewing at the location, however.

The Excelsior Brewing Company, meanwhile, continued operating out of the old Uhrig plant. Sales had slipped, however, as only around 13,000 barrels were produced in 1884, a far cry from the 23,284 barrels cranked out of the old plant in 1879. Casper Koehler and partners Schorr and Saussenthaler must not have been too worried, however, as early the next year they purchased the Tennessee Brewing Company in Memphis for $18,000. The trio of owners stayed on at the new Excelsior site until selling out to the St. Louis Brewing Association (SLBA) syndicate in 1889. The SLBA operated the brewery for only two years, whereupon it was torn down to make way for Union Station, the city's palatial new railroad depot. The venerable Excelsior name continued until early 1917, however, as the SLBA trotted the name down the street to its Winkelmeyer plant after the closing of the former Uhrig facility.

Not content to just passively watch the St. Louis brewing scene, the Koehler family soon began again, choosing as a location for a new brewery the familiar property that had housed the original Excelsior Brewery. Oscar Koehler and partners had been operating the Sect Wine Company out of the old brewery for a number of years. As a sign of things to come, by 1888 malting had restarted at the facility, with the production of Missouri wine gradually phased out.

The site had not seen brewing activity for eight years. All of that soon changed, as the three sons of Henry Koehler (and nephews of Casper Koehler) formally incorporated to operate a new brewery in January 1890. They chose the name American Brewing Company, with Henry Koehler Jr. elected corporate president, Oscar C. Koehler vice president, and Hugo A. Koehler secretary-treasurer. The enterprise was truly a "home industry" (to use a popular phrase of the day), as all of the stock was held exclusively by St. Louisans. An account published shortly before the brewery opened stated, "It will be the endeavor of the officers of the company to produce beers of the highest class only, and to obtain patronage by furnishing only such an article."

Most of the old Excelsior Brewery buildings were torn down in order to build the new brewery. Only the malt house continued as part of the American Brewing Company plant. The Koehlers spared little expense in the brewery's construction, purchasing the most modern equipment available for the new enterprise. Mostly local firms were hired. The buildings were designed by the well-known architectural firm of E. C. Janssen. The foundation onto which the plant was built was a handsome stone called broken ashler, which was laid out by Geisel and Company. The brick brewery walls were erected by Koenig and Sons. In the brewhouse, some of the largest copper kettles ever manufactured (up to the time) came from the Seibel-Suessdorf Manufacturing Company. The elevators, mash machines, and much of the other brewing equipment came from the Felber Machine Works, and new boilers were installed by the John O'Brien Boiler Works Company.

The American Brewing Company office building was put up on the site of the original Koehler family home. The machine house was designed with huge plate-glass windows embedded into the exterior walls, providing passersby a great view of the giant steam engines and ammonia compressors as they hissed and whirled around. This view of the American plant would end up becoming a top tourist draw.

Construction of the new brewery went quickly. On February 28, 1890, the Standard, Muenchener, and Bohemian brands were placed on the market. Soon Pale Export, Wuerzberger, and Bock brands would be added to the company's stable of labels. A formal dedication of the new American brewery took place on February 26, 1891. Many prominent citizens of St. Louis, including Mayor Edward Noonan, delivered speeches during the ceremony. Guests were lavishly entertained by the corporate officers, with the malt house floor used as a banquet room.

While American was primarily operated by the three sons of Henry Koehler, the previous generation of the family was far from done with the brewing industry. In 1891, Casper Koehler became president of the new Columbia Brewing Company in St. Louis. His son Julius H. Koehler joined him in that business, taking on the role of general superintendent. In addition, Casper and his partners had built a larger facility at the Tennessee Brewing Company in 1892, with a design similar to that of the new Columbia Brewery. His brother Henry had also stayed in the beer business. The esteem in which Henry Koehler was held by his fellow brewers in the Mississippi Valley is evidenced by his five-year reign as president of the St. Louis Brewers Association and an even longer spell as president of the Brewers Association of Iowa. Henry retired from the brewing business in 1894, after the Arsenal Brewery in Davenport was absorbed into the Davenport Malting Company. After that he spent much time traveling Europe and looking after his other investments.

Henry's son Oscar brought a sterling background to the American Brewing Company. Born in Fort Madison in 1857 (while his father was running the brewery there), he traveled to Europe and obtained a diploma from the brewing academy at Worms. He then studied at the University of

Leipzig, earning a doctorate in chemistry. Armed with this knowledge, Oscar returned stateside, joining his father at the Arsenal Brewery in Iowa and at the short-lived Henry Koehler Brewing Association, and then forming the Sect Wine Company. He returned to brewing with the formation of American, serving as plant superintendent as well as corporate president before returning to Davenport in 1894.

The three sons of Henry Koehler would see the new American Brewing Company grow quite prosperous. They specialized in bottling their beer, which was then shipped all over the United States and internationally. Assisting the Koehlers at American was plant superintendent Ed Wagner, known throughout the brewing industry as inventor of the "St. Louis model" pasteurizer and bottle soaking apparatus. Later, Wagner, his son Ed Jr., Henry Koehler Jr., and brewery architect Janssen would open the Wagner Brewery in Granite City, Illinois. The Wagners also started the Forest Park Brewing Company in St. Louis, from where the Falstaff dynasty would be launched after Forest Park's failure.

As American expanded its distribution across the country and around the world, it began to specialize advertising toward the new markets. Point-of-purchase displays sent to South America included phrases in Spanish. The fact that American was exporting beer worldwide was itself highlighted in advertising. One great magazine ad features a photo of a long train of the brewery's boxcars pulling away from the huge shipping department building. The ad reads:

The St. Louis A.B.C. Beers are Famous the World Over. (This) photograph showing a solid train of 35 cars "St. Louis A.B.C. Bohemian Bottled Beer," shipped to Manila, P.I. [Philippine Islands], November 22, 1898.

Closer to home the company targeted women in advertisements, focused on a more bawdy element in other ads, and even advertised to a group that would no doubt cause howls of public indignation if tried today—children. American placed advertising on the back cover of the children's

Excelsior Brewery scene from *The Western Brewer*, June 1879.

book *First Book of A.B.C.'s.* When the child reading this book finished the last page ("Z is for the Zeal to be shown in good things, Be it little maids, peasants or kings"), he or she could continue the education on kings by seeing one on the back cover proclaiming that American was the "King of All Bottled Beers." American would take the "king" theme further in some of its other advertising by utilizing a lion (the "king" of beasts) as an icon.

These advertising schemes were successful; in 1903 the capital stock of the company was increased from $300,000 to $1.25 million in order to enlarge the plant and build new bottling works, cooperage shops, and a larger ice factory.

A second major consolidation of St. Louis breweries took place in 1907, when nine operations combined to form the Independent Breweries Company (IBC). At the time American joined the ranks of the IBC, it was producing 120,000 barrels of beer per year, making the Koehlers powerful players in the new company. Hugo Koehler, who had served as American's vice president since 1890, was named IBC corporate treasurer and succeeded Henry Griesedieck Jr. as president in 1911. The conglomerate established its home office in the American brewery offices at 2825 South Broadway, and the plant served as one of its primary production facilities. When the IBC decided to close most of the bottling shops in its breweries in order to increase efficiency, one of the two kept open to serve the entire chain was at American.

Casper Koehler was getting up in years and was able to gracefully exit the brewing business following the 1907 IBC merger (the new company included his Columbia Brewing Company as well as his nephews' American). Later that year he suffered a stroke while visiting London, but he returned to St. Louis and eventually recovered. In 1910, as Casper was leaving St. Louis to spend the summer in Berlin, he remarked to friends before he left that, once gone, he did not expect to ever see St. Louis again. The words of the man who had spent parts of seven decades in the city's brewing business were prophetic, as three weeks later in Berlin he suffered a fatal stroke. An obituary in *American Brewer* spoke highly of Casper, stating, "He was an exceedingly cultured man and a great reader and a friend and patron of music and the arts. His old home, on Dillon Street,

Above: Pre-Pro ABC tri-fold trade card.

Right: Lithograph of an angel offering pearls from a clamshell, and marked with "Our Greeting 1901."

Below right: Another Excelsior lithograph of about the same vintage, this one featuring a cherub-faced girl sitting in a giant clamshell.

below Chouteau Avenue, was the rendezvous of many persons of culture and ability, and he delighted in entertaining."

Henry Koehler Jr. passed away just a couple of years after his uncle Casper. This left his brother (and IBC president) Hugo the only member of the brewing family still in St. Louis.

The formation of the IBC had come at a time when the brewing industry was under increasing pressure from the anti-saloon movement. The group took pains to announce that the taverns under its control would follow all saloon regulations. Such announcements did little to placate the prohibitionists. States, counties, and towns across the nation were voting themselves dry, a particular blow to shipping breweries like American. After the United States entered World War I, restrictions were placed on the brewing industry regarding the use of fuel and materials. Thus, it was an ailing and confused beer business that was made illegal by the enactment of national Prohibition.

For a considerable period into the 1920s the American plant produced cereal beverages and soft drinks. A 1927 newspaper report indicated that most of the IBC's plants had been boarded up, and "the only one which has been operating steadily has been the American . . . where beverages and malt are produced."

Hugo Koehler remained in St. Louis during the dark decade of the Volstead Act. His survival strategy was similar to that of other well-heeled brewers—to ride out the beerless years by managing his real estate and investment company, as well as a railroad. He also stayed in what remained of the Independent Breweries Company.

In the early 1930s, with the end of Prohibition on the horizon, the then-bankrupt IBC saw a golden opportunity not just to reopen facilities, but also to unload some of its old breweries to investors and thus recoup some of its debt. Later, with reports of the wild profits being generated by reopened breweries after beer became legal again, IBC was besieged by investment groups anxious to buy viable breweries that could be quickly rehabilitated. The former American Brewing Company plant certainly fell into that category.

In June 1933, a Chicago syndicate headed by A. D. Plamandon agreed to pay $275,000 to purchase the former American Brewing Company plant from the General Mortgage Bondholders' Protective Committee of the IBC. Plamandon had formerly been involved in two Windy City concerns, a malting house and the local Federal League baseball team. Whether his group was unable to find a brewery in the Chicago area, or if American just

seemed like a good investment, is not known.

A few weeks later, in early July, the ABC Brewing Corporation was chartered under the laws of Delaware (still a common practice due to that state's favorable business laws) with an authorized capitalization of three hundred thousand dollars. Why the ABC name was chosen instead of American is unclear. Plamandon was elected president of the new company, which was said to be expecting to begin operations within two or three months. However, three months came and went, and brewing had not yet resumed. Perhaps because beer was failing to get out the door, Plamandon was shoved down the corporate ladder, as on December 7 it was announced that Richard S. Hawes Jr. was the new ABC president. Hawes was the scion of a prominent St. Louis family. His father, Richard Sr., was vice president of the First National Bank, and his uncle was former U.S. Senator Harry B. Hawes. Also of note, his wife, Marion, was a direct descendant of Adam Lemp, founder of the Lemp family's former St. Louis brewing dynasty.

Rounding out the top ABC management team were Earl P. Morton as vice president and general sales manager, Dwight D. Thomas as secretary, and Henry B. Wellenkoetter as superintendent and brewing director. The board of directors was staffed by a number of prominent St. Louis–area businessmen, including James A. Dacey and A. S. Knapp. Former president Plamandon had stuck around after losing the top spot, accepting the position of corporate secretary. Brewmaster Wellenkoetter brought extensive experience to the ABC brewhouse. Before Prohibition he had been an employee of the SLBA, working primarily at the Wainwright Brewery. During the dry years he had established a brewery in Canada and was continuously active in that country's brewing industry until his return to St. Louis.

It is unclear what role the original buyers of the brewery, the "Chicago syndicate," were still playing in the company after Richard Hawes began sitting in the president's chair. In any case, it would not be the last time that Chicagoans were involved in running ABC.

By the end of 1933, President Hawes announced that one hundred men were engaged in installing the newest type of brewing equipment in the plant. The owners were spending $125,000 to modernize ABC, which once brewing resumed would have the capacity to produce 165,000 barrels of beer annually. Hawes told the press that ABC would be ready to start production of draft and bottled beer by the end of January 1934.

Hawes's projected start-up date proved to be

overly optimistic, as rehabbing took about three months longer than expected. Finally, on May 26, 1934, ABC beer was placed on the market. Public demand for the new brew was so great that sixty brand new trucks were kept busy making deliveries all over the St. Louis metropolitan area. These trucks had closed, insulated bodies with built-in cooling units, an advanced and innovative design for the time. While the brewery initially focused its marketing muscle on selling beer in the immediate St. Louis area, soon it announced plans to expand distribution throughout the Midwest.

In order to raise additional cash to pay for all the improvements being made, ABC made application to list its stock on the St. Louis Stock Exchange. By June 1934, the company was offering 250,000 shares of this stock for sale to the public. More cash had been provided by an earlier stock sale plus a bond issue of $183,000 that was set to mature in 1938.

At an autumn 1934 board meeting, Richard Hawes stepped down as corporate president. He was succeeded by R. D. Robinson, a former Indianapolis investment banker. Changes were also made to the board of directors at this time, signaling that all might not be well at the company. Unfortunately, while beer sales were relatively good, the company's public announcements were not matching its financial performance. The one-year delay in bringing ABC beer to market had given competitors a significant head start in establishing marketing beachheads that ABC found difficult to storm.

Stating that "cut-throat" competition had followed Repeal, resulting in "excessive sales costs and financial difficulties," on April 3, 1935, the ABC Brewing Corporation filed a debtor's bankruptcy reorganization petition with the federal court. Assets were listed at about $1.2 million, facing liabilities of $917,000. The biggest creditor was the Independent Realty Investment Company, the remnant of the old Independent Breweries Company, which held a first deed of trust for 20 percent of the debt. ABC's reorganization plan postulated that, since all of its debts could not be paid at once, the obligations needed to be stretched out over time in order to facilitate the company's financial recovery. As presented to the federal court, the proposal extended the maturity date on the first mortgage from 1938 to 1945. Other debts would be settled on the basis of 50 percent cash, 16 2/3 percent one-year notes, and 33 1/3 percent stock. The plan also proposed increasing ABC's $1 common stock from 300,000 to 450,000 shares, and issuing 12,000 new shares of preferred stock at $5 a share.

By September 1935, the required two-thirds of the creditors and a majority of the stockholders had approved the reorganization plan. On September 20, Federal Judge Charles B. Davis (who was getting to know a number of St. Louis–area brewery executives due to the filing of several bankruptcy petitions) approved the plan, and ABC was again off and running.

However, they were not running for long under the then-current management. On November 23, 1935, Oscar Baur, president of the Terre Haute Brewing Company, announced that he had turned his attentions west and was purchasing controlling interest in the ABC brewery. Baur was not looking to expand production of his Indiana brewery's flagship brand Champagne Velvet. Instead, he stated that beer manufactured at the ABC plant would continue to be sold under the long-established ABC Bohemian brand name. Baur also announced that the brewery would again be rebuilt with "new machinery and equipment." Oscar Baur became ABC president and brought with him Robert Baur as secretary-treasurer.

Hopes were high at ABC when it was announced that the brewery would become the first in St. Louis to package its beer in cans. The company chose to use flat-top cans rather than cone tops. It was a bold business move on the company's part, as a flat-top canning line was an expensive investment. It would have cost much less to convert an existing bottling line to fill cone tops, but the trade-off was that the "flats" were cheaper to ship. With ABC's tradition of exporting beer far and wide, lower transportation costs were no doubt a factor in this decision. Still, while beer in cans had been selling well across the industry since its debut on January 24, 1935, at that time it was hard to say whether it was a fad or a trend.

ABC would ultimately can a number of brands, starting around 1936, using American Can Company's "Keglined" cans. Surviving examples are quite rare. Among the labels are ABC Old English Ale, Old St. Louis Beer and Ale (the "Steamboat cans"), and Triangle Beer. Some controversy also exists as to whether some of the later brands were filled in St. Louis, or if some of them came out of the Manhattan Brewing Company in Chicago. ABC was among several breweries that produced the Black Dallas brand in cans. It is interesting to note that Manhattan also canned this label in a similar design, but with "Chicago" replacing "St. Louis" on the face of the can. This helps support the contention that there was a corporate link between the two companies, a link that, at least judging from the Black Dallas cans, the owners were not taking great pains to hide.

In May 1937, Oscar Baur presented his fellow stockholders a plan to dissolve the ABC Brewing Corporation and transfer its assets to the Terre Haute Brewing Company. Baur's sales pitch was that the company had struck out business-wise the prior year when it had lost seventy-three thousand dollars. He expected the merger would substantially reduce operating expenses, putting ABC back in the brewing ballgame. The majority of ABC stockholders agreed to Baur's plan. However, as in any game, there are frequently players who like to cry foul, and in this case it was minor league ABC stockholder James T. Murphy, who held just two hundred shares. Murphy filed a lawsuit in federal court seeking to block the merger, claiming that there was a "taint of unfairness" in the purchase of ABC stock by Terre Haute. Judge Davis again entered the playing field and dismissed Murphy's lawsuit, stating there was no legal reason to block the merger. More to the point, the judge said the sale of ABC had enabled the troubled brewery to be loaned a substantial amount of money, capital necessary for the required continuing (and seemingly endless) rehabilitation of the facility.

Terre Haute's reign over the ABC plant proved to be brief, as late in 1938 the new owners shut down the brewery portion of the ABC complex. The site was not abandoned, however, as for several months the Terre Haute Brewing Company distributed Champagne Velvet beer shipped in from Indiana out of its former St. Louis branch.

In March 1939, the brewery changed hands again, to another out-of-town group. A syndicate of Chicago investors, headed by Louis Kanne, purchased the ABC plant from Terre Haute via a mortgage for an undisclosed amount. Kanne, quickly elected president of the new company after the deal, announced that the new ABC Brewing Company would reopen with seventy-five employees within a week of obtaining a brewing license from the city of St. Louis. Kanne was confident about being able to so quickly resume operations because ABC was, in his mind, an up-to-date brewery in which half a million dollars had been spent on improvements before it was closed.

Louis Kanne may have been

new to the business scene in St. Louis, but he was not a newcomer to the brewing industry. Before coming to ABC, Kanne had resigned as treasurer and general manger of the Manhattan Brewing Company of Chicago, a position he had held for over five years. Prior to that, he had been engaged in the banking business. In a newspaper article at the time, Kanne described the new company as a "family affair," with his brother Benjamin Kanne corporate vice president and brother-in-law Meyer Lazarus as secretary-treasurer.

Louis Kanne and his associates first had to survive the scrutiny of local excise commissioner Lawrence McDaniel before the brewery could resume operations. At a hearing, Kanne denied that Manhattan had been a "Capone brewery" and that the new ABC had devious intentions of shipping beer into dry areas of nearby states. Two weeks later, McDaniel announced that he would issue ABC its operating permit since investigators had found "no reason why a permit should be denied."

The sales territory planned for the new company was composed of Missouri, Illinois, Kansas, Texas, Louisiana, and Arkansas. Kanne further stated that he expected an additional one hundred thousand dollars would be spent on improvements, including the purchase of approximately twenty-five delivery trucks and "additional motorized equipment . . . when business warrants it."

As the brand name ABC Bohemian had remained the property of the Terre Haute Brewing Company, it was announced that Kanne's new company would market its product as simply ABC Beer. Hopes were high that the new ABC would soon be operating the brewery at its annual production capacity of three hundred thousand barrels.

While the brewery seemed to be on the road to recovery, it actually was about to go off a cliff. The ABC Brewing Company terminated all business on January 31, 1940. In a statement of affairs signed by President Louis Kanne and filed in U.S. District Court that same day, assets were listed at $18,529 and liabilities at $29,600. In February 1940, the

Left: Old St. Louis Beer, one of the rarest St. Louis beer cans.

ABC Brewing Company was back in federal court when three creditors filed a petition of involuntary bankruptcy. They alleged the brewery owed them $13,878 and had committed acts of bankruptcy in making preferred payments to other creditors. Kanne's new company had defaulted on its mortgage, and ownership of the brewery reverted back to the Terre Haute Brewing Company, which in turn unloaded the property to investor Arthur H. Fuldner. The end had come.

While the ABC brewery was closed forever, its giant next-door neighbor was continuing to expand, both in terms of sales and the size of its complex. In September 1943, Anheuser-Busch purchased from Fuldner the ABC tract and buildings, which took up the area bounded by Broadway, Dorcas, Seventh, and Lynch. Finally, in May of 1952, Anheuser-Busch razed all the old ABC buildings, and much of the area was resurfaced as a parking lot. Few today realize that when parking on A-B InBev's lot off South Seventh and Broadway that they are truly visiting the home of the "King of All Bottled Beers."

DID THE ST. LOUIS MOB VANDALIZE THE ABC BREWERY?

On July 28, 1939, St. Louis Police Captain Arthur L. McGuire of the Lynch Street district reported that his department was investigating a "machine wrecking raid" by "vandals" that had occurred the previous week at the ABC Brewery. McGuire reported that the trespassers had damaged two bottling machines, poured grease into pasteurizing equipment, and broken a temperature control. Was the St. Louis mob sending the Al Capone mob a message?

Lou Kanne had called the new ABC Brewing Company a "family affair," a phrase perhaps more apt than he was willing to admit at the time. Both Lou Kanne and Lou Greenberg were well known as alleged "capos" of Al Capone. Greenberg was said to be Capone's financial wizard. By November 1939, however, when Capone was released from Alcatraz, the "Capone mob" was Capone's in name only, as his grip on the organization was slipping away along with his syphilis-infected mind.

Kanne had at one time been a major shareholder in the Manhattan Brewing Company in Chicago. He had obtained his Manhattan shares from the sister of "Hymie" Weiss after that famous bootlegger had been killed during Prohibition. Kanne eventually sold his shares in Manhattan to Greenberg in 1937. Lou Greenburg would later suffer the same fate as Weiss, gunned down while on a stroll just a few blocks from the Manhattan brewery.

Some historical sources insist that the trashing of the St. Louis bottling house was a blow from which ABC never recovered. But a reading of contemporary newspaper accounts indicates that this line of thought is overblown. Brewery operations were supposedly suspended for just twenty-four hours after the crime, and an officer of the company estimated damage at a mere two hundred dollars.

Was the vandalism attack mistakenly made against a legitimate business? For years afterwards, Lou Kanne never wavered from stating that at the time he was president of ABC, he was no longer associated with the Manhattan Brewing Company. He insisted that his interest in the St. Louis brewery was a personal one, not an extension of Capone, Incorporated.

However, in October 1977, as the Manhattan brewery was being prepared for demolition, Chicago brewery historian Rich LaSusa rescued thirty file drawers full of company records. Upon examination, the Manhattan documents were found to be chock full of papers concerning the proposed operation and advertising of the ABC brewery. Contrary to Lou Kanne's pleadings, these records show at least some evidence that the strings of the final ownership of ABC were being pulled by the officers of Manhattan. In hindsight, the suspicions held by local law enforcement officials that the July 1939 trashing of the ABC bottling house was really the work of the St. Louis mob were probably correct—in effect, a notice to the Chicago Capone mob to get out!

Falstaff Brewing Corporation

Plant #1 — 3662–84 Forest Park Boulevard
(formerly Forest Park Brewing Company)

Falstaff Corporation	1920–1933
Falstaff Brewing Corporation	1933–1958

Plant #2 — 3181 Michigan Avenue
(formerly Otto F. Stifel's Union Brewing Co.) 1933–1952

Plant #5 — 2000 Madison Street
(formerly Columbia Brewing Company)   1948–1967

Plant #10 — 1900 Shenandoah Avenue
Falstaff Brewing Corporation   1957–1977
(formerly Griesedieck Brothers Brewery Company)

Above: Oil painting of Falstaff Brewery founder Joseph "Papa Joe" Griesedieck, commissioned shortly after his death in 1938, artist unknown.

Facing page: Plastic wall hanging plate, featuring Sir John Falstaff.

Lemp's Falstaff

The Falstaff brand was surpassed only by Budweiser in terms of spreading the fame of the St. Louis brewing industry. The story of Falstaff also combines the saga of two famous local brewing names—the Lemps and the Griesediecks.

Falstaff was the brainchild of the William J. Lemp Brewing Company, which introduced the brand in June of 1899. Why the name of the Shakespearean character was chosen is a mystery. The great punster Shakespeare certainly selected the name at least in part as a reference to the sexual performance expected from the hard-drinking Falstaff. Historian Stephen Walker suggests that brewery President William J. Lemp viewed the Sir John Falstaff character as the embodiment of the "good life," a quality he wished to be associated with his beer. St. Louis actor Ben de Bar's acclaimed portrayal of the character was likewise said to have been an influence. Lemp may also have been familiar with Falstaff through the Verdi opera of the same name, first performed in the United States in 1895. In a 1901 advertisement appearing in a program at the World's Fair in Buffalo, the Falstaff brand was just one of eight Lemp bottled beers. The company didn't bother registering the trademark until 1902.

During the two decades before national Prohibition, breweries began concentrating on single brands. This certainly simplified marketing, and perhaps the brewers were growing so tired of fighting the dry movement that they lacked the energy to push multiple brands. Lemp promoted the Falstaff label heavily at the 1904 St. Louis World's Fair, and it quickly became the company's flagship bottled brand. Similarly, Budweiser became the flagship brand of Anheuser-Busch, Alpen Brau that of the Independent Breweries Company (IBC), and Hyde Park that of the St. Louis Brewing Association (SLBA). Lemp continued emphasizing Falstaff, "The Choicest Product of the Brewer's Art," until the brewery was closed in anticipation of Prohibition.

Enter Papa Joe

Meanwhile, Joseph Griesedieck had pursued a successful career in the St. Louis beer business. Born into a brewing family in Stromberg, Germany, in 1863, he was one of thirteen children of Anton Griesedieck. Soon thereafter, the family came to St. Louis, along with Anton's brother Henry. Another brother, Frank, had preceded them in 1859. While Frank worked at the Lafayette Brewery, Anton and Henry operated a malt house at Twelfth and Park streets.

Anton Griesedieck and partners later bought and operated the former Stumpf Brewery, and it was there in 1878 that Joseph Griesedieck began his career as a brewer at age fifteen. Following his local apprenticeship Joseph headed east, working in 1880 at the Bergner-Engel Brewery in Philadelphia, then attending a new brewing school opened by Anton Schwarz in New York City (later named the U.S. Brewers Academy). Griesedieck was a member of the first graduating class of eight in 1882.

In 1892, Papa Joe Griesedieck, as he would become known, opened the National Brewing Company in St. Louis along with brothers Henry and Bernard. When that brewery was merged into the IBC, Joe Griesedieck served as a general manager for the parent company and later worked at the Griesedieck Brothers Brewing Company, started by brother Henry and sons in 1911.

In 1917, Papa Joe and his three nephews (Tony, Raymond, and Henry) purchased the bankrupt Forest Park Brewing Company. In March they formed the Griesedieck Beverage Company, with Joe holding 750 shares, Henry 200, and Anton and Raymond 150 each. It was capitalized at $125,000 with $105,000 representing the property's purchase price, paid for with $5,000 cash and bank notes.

The Griesediecks did some renovating at the plant and reopened it. In addition to brewing beer there as Griesedieck Brothers Plant #2, the company introduced Hek non-alcoholic cereal beverage to the market on April 19, 1917. Hek was named after a malt beverage produced in ancient Egypt. The brand name provided for some entertaining advertising for the company, but not a lot of revenue.

Papa Joe's Son

*A*lvin Griesedieck was born in St. Louis in 1894. He was the only child of Joseph Griesedieck, not what someone would expect from a fellow nicknamed Papa Joe, but a historical fact nonetheless. Noted for his tenor singing voice and his eight children, Alvin graduated from Cornell University in 1916 with a degree in agriculture. He returned to the family farm in St. Louis County and began raising hogs. With Pro-

hibition just around the corner it seemed a wiser career choice than brewing. However, Alvin was destined for a brewing career.

In his 1951 book *The Falstaff Story*, Alvin Griesedieck recalled that Hek, unlike Anheuser-Busch's non-alcoholic Bevo, was dealcoholized rather than produced by the so-called check fermentation process. This supposedly imbued the product with better flavor and stability. Initial sales of Hek were good, though they soon slumped. But by expanding its sales territory, Griesedieck Beverage was still able to increase sales.

Just as demand began exceeding supply, production problems arose due to faulty bottling equipment. The Griesediecks scrambled for money and investors to help pay for repairs. But in October of 1920, with beer already illegal, the company went into receivership, unable to satisfy mechanics' liens. Griesedieck Beverage was soon declared bankrupt. Still, Papa Joe was confident that legal beer would someday return to the United States. Out of the wreckage of his bankrupt company, the Falstaff Brewing Corporation would be built.

Papa Joe was a friend of William Lemp Jr., who had taken over presidency of the Lemp Brewing Company following his father's 1904 suicide. In 1920, Joe decided to approach Lemp with the idea of buying the Falstaff trademark and label "as a nucleus around which to raise money for a new company," according to Alvin Griesedieck. Alvin recalled accompanying his father to Lemp's office across the street from the shuttered brewery, where they were greeted by longtime Lemp corporate secretary Henry Vahlkamp. Billy Lemp was not at first agreeable to selling the Falstaff name, but he soon came around. Alvin later wrote in *The Falstaff Story* of Lemp: "I believe in spite of his reputation for hardness and coldness in his business dealings, he consented to negotiate terms purely out of sympathy and a kindly feeling for my Dad."

Lemp's directors soon approved the sale, with terms of five thousand dollars cash and twenty thousand dollars due in nine months. With the sale of the bankrupt Griesedieck Beverage Company set to take place on December 17, 1920, Joseph and Alvin Griesedieck organized the Falstaff Corporation. With personal friends of Papa Joe providing most of the cash, the new company scraped together a successful bid of $140,000. The former Forest Park brewery was back in the Griesediecks' hands.

Dry Days

For over a decade the new Falstaff Corporation struggled to stay alive, "usually one jump ahead of the bill collector," as stated by Alvin Griesedieck in *The Falstaff Story*. Despite attaching the Falstaff brand to its near beer, sales of such brews by any name were generally a failure. Production never amounted to more than thirty thousand barrels a year. The company briefly produced medicinal beer (until the government yanked permission for such a thing) and also for a short time produced a malt tonic. Other products included dry lemon soda, ginger ale, and root beer. Falstaff even cured and smoked hams and bacon, and bottled non-alcoholic beer for the Griesedieck-Western Brewery Company of Belleville, Illinois, and the Tennessee Brewing Company of Memphis. Falstaff also produced its own Dublin Stout and Special Pale near beers, the former patterned after the famous Guinness brand. While such activities kept the plant busy, by 1930 Papa Joe was forced to get friends to loan him more money in order to stave off bankruptcy of the Falstaff Corporation. He did so with a sense that the company would just have to hang on for a while longer, as in his mind the repeal of Prohibition was nearing.

Two years later, legal beer was looking like a sure thing. In a complex reorganization of their company, and after many dealings with brokers, bankers, and lawyers, the Griesediecks formed the Falstaff Brewing Corporation, chartered in Delaware on January 16, 1933. A stock swap was okayed by the old stockholders, and the sale of new stock began. With the legalization of 3.2 percent beer set for April 7, Falstaff began preparations for brewing real beer in the old Forest Park plant.

In March, corporate Vice President Alvin Griesedieck announced that eight hundred thousand dollars was being spent on buildings, equipment, and materials in preparation for selling real beer. In St. Louis, only Falstaff and Anheuser-Busch had beer ready for the hectic opening night, and demand greatly exceeded supply. The breweries that opened quickly could literally sell beer as fast as they could make it. The first 3.2 percent beer brewed by Falstaff was an all-malt product, although rice was soon added to the formula. The company had kept its yeast culture alive during Prohibition.

After years of losing money, Falstaff earned more than one hundred thousand dollars in the first three weeks following April 7. From the start it became obvious that the capacity of the company's small brewery was insufficient. An agreement was quickly reached to lease the former Otto F. Stifel's Union Brewery in St. Louis, where brewing recommenced on July 1. The

Above: Prohibition-era labels from the Falstaff Corporation.

new Plant #2 was used to produce draft beer. Over at Plant #1, on May 15 Falstaff took out a permit to build a new three-story, $250,000 bottling shop.

By September the company was producing twenty-five thousand barrels a month. Falstaff declared its first stockholder dividend of 25 cents a share, and Papa Joe was well on his way to paying back the friends who had kept him afloat before Repeal. By the end of 1933, more than 150,000 barrels had been produced. Such strong sales continued, with the company announcing a net income of $118,448 for the first six months of 1934.

The next few years marked an incredible period of growth and expansion for Falstaff. Before Prohibition, the Lemp Brewing Company had sold Falstaff brand beer throughout the country, and Joe and Alvin Griesdieck were determined to do the same afterwards. In addition to expanding the two St. Louis plants, they ended up adopting a strategy of buying existing breweries elsewhere. In Omaha, Nebraska, the newly reopened Krug Brewing Company was having financial problems. Albert Krug, president of the company, had married into the Griesedieck family. He had also helped Papa Joe out financially during the 1920s. This greased the skids for Falstaff's leasing of the Krug plant effective April 5, 1935. Falstaff later bought this new Plant #3 outright.

To boost sales, Falstaff became a heavy local radio advertiser. In 1936, it advertised its stronger seasonal brew by sponsoring a show called *Falstaff Winter Beer Frolic*. This promotion was followed up by a new show called *The Falstaff Tenth Inning*, a three-day-a-week program featuring "breezy advertising" that audiences reportedly didn't mind hearing.

Oil portrait of Alvin Griesedieck, painted by George Leonard Shultz in the early 1950s.

In early 1937, Falstaff acquired its Plant #4, the National Brewing Company of New Orleans. The plant was quickly expanded and improved. Papa Joe Griesedieck and his wife, Mathilde, celebrated their fiftieth wedding anniversary in November of 1937. The family had more to celebrate than just a long marriage—production at Falstaff's four breweries for the year totaled 690,291 barrels, making the company the tenth-largest U.S. brewer.

Alvin Takes Over

Joe Griesedieck suffered a heart attack early in 1938. While he recovered, on July 11, the day of his seventy-fifth birthday, he fell at home and fractured his hip. Three days later he was dead. Papa Joe had bought a bankrupt brewery as the clouds of Prohibition were on the horizon, and had bought the Falstaff brand name as the storm began. But his faith that beer would eventually come back had been vindicated, and Falstaff was thriving. Griesedieck had a reputation for considering his employees part of his family. He held an annual picnic for them on his farm, and Falstaff was one of the first breweries to produce a company newsletter. Called *The Shield*, it was an impressive publication and a morale booster. *The Shield* still exists, as the official newsletter of the Falstaff chapter of the Brewery Collectibles Club of America. In addition, the still-active Falstaff alumni club puts out a newsletter called *The Mini-Shield*.

Papa Joe was gone, but when it came to Falstaff's future, the remaining family was in for quite a ride. In August of 1938, the board of directors selected Alvin Griesedieck to succeed his late father as Falstaff Brewing Corporation president. The company had earned $250,000 for the first six months of the year, and the usual annual stock dividend was declared.

Sales were stagnant for the next few years as the company plowed profits back into the business and contemplated a semi-national or even national expansion. In 1939, the brewery temporarily dropped its radio advertising in favor of a billboard and newspaper campaign featuring the Sir John Falstaff character. The year ended with a corporate profit of nearly $595,000. Falstaff returned to radio ads in 1940 by sponsoring all Browns and Cardinals baseball home-game broadcasts. The company had a huge year in 1941, producing over 1 million barrels for the first time (seventh in the country) and earning over $780,000.

World War II put further expansion plans on hold. Alvin Griesedieck's son Joseph, a 1940 graduate of the Cornell University engineering school, started his Falstaff career on July 1 of that year as a brewer's apprentice and member of the local union. That same summer, Falstaff introduced its first canned beer, in cone-top containers designed to mimic old-world steins. But international events quickly interrupted Falstaff's plans; Joe Griesedieck was soon in the Navy, and beer cans were banned in order to conserve metal for the war effort. The rationing of bottle crowns, and later grains, further hindered Falstaff's growth during the war years. But the management team that would oversee the company's postwar boom was in place. In addition to Alvin and Joe Griesedieck, it included vice presidents Oscar Fischer and Harvey Beffa. Fischer was a longtime employee and former city sales manager. Beffa had served as production manager and advertising manager. Stricken by polio in 1932 but undeterred, Beffa went to work for Falstaff the next year. His father Anton, an immigrant carpenter who ran a successful wrecking company, was part of the Falstaff family, too. Anton supervised the expansion of the Falstaff plant and had loaned Papa Joe money during the dark days. The Beffa family ended up being major Falstaff stockholders.

Other key employees were Jere Newton and Louis Walther. Newton had come to work for Falstaff as a salesman for the Oklahoma

Left: Mash tub, Plant #1 brewhouse, early 1950s.

Bottom: Bottling line at Plant #1, early 1950s.

Facing page: Canned Falstaff draft beer, 1960s (the lion's head logo was used from 1964 to 1969).

and Kansas region in 1924. He came back to St. Louis in the 1930s from a Des Moines distributorship and later served as Falstaff's vice president in charge of industrial relations. Walther was the company's head brewmaster. The son of veteran St. Louis brewer Adolph Walther, he was a 1917 graduate of the U.S. Brewers Academy and then worked for the Griesedieck Beverage Company. The younger Walther also served as president of the local chapter of the Master Brewers Association of America and was later elevated to the job of technical director at Falstaff.

In 1948, Falstaff's production skyrocketed to 2,303,628 barrels. This ranked the company fifth in the nation. The increases were buoyed by expansion of the Omaha and New Orleans plants, and the acquisition of Plant #5—the Columbia Brewing Company plant in St. Louis, which was merged into Falstaff. Profits for the year came to $2.4 million, and the company was listed on the New York Stock Exchange for the first time.

By 1951, Falstaff's market had expanded to twenty states. In a message to employees, Alvin Griesedieck stated that he was proud that his two oldest sons had been accepted into the "Falstaff Family" and that he was confident Falstaff would "go on forever."

Falstaff Plant #6 was created in 1952 when the company purchased the Pacific Brewing and Malting Company plant in San Jose, California. The brew kettles in the San Jose brewery were in poor condition, so Falstaff removed the two in Plant #2, had them enlarged in St. Louis by the Nooter Corporation, and shipped them to California for installation. Production of Falstaff began in San Jose the next year, thus opening up the lucrative West Coast market. That year the company also launched an $18.5 million expansion and modernization program. Three more breweries were acquired in the mid-1950s: the Berghoff plant in Fort Wayne, Indiana (1954), the Galveston-Houston Breweries plant in Galveston, Texas, and the Harry Mitchell facility in El Paso (both in 1956).

In 1953, Falstaff launched a campaign hailing its golden anniversary. While the math was a bit off (the brand was actually launched in 1899 and registered in 1902, not 1903) it did make for good advertising. The company later had similar historical problems when it began boasting of brewing "Since 1870." While Falstaff claimed that Anton Griesedieck started a brewery in St. Louis that year, unless he was secretly brewing at an undisclosed location in his malt house, a December 1878 date appears to be the correct one for his first beer-making venture.

Alvin Griesedieck had not only overseen Falstaff's tremendous growth, he had also been a goodwill ambassador for the company and served his industry as chairman of the Brewing Industry Foundation. But by 1953 he was ready to step aside from day-to-day management of the company. Alvin was elevated to chairman of the board, and his thirty-four-year-old son Joseph replaced him as corporate president and chief executive officer. Under Joseph's leadership the company continued to thrive. Net earnings for 1955 were over $4.3 million, allowing Falstaff to spend over $5 million on plant improvements the next year.

The growth of Falstaff and its youthful president Joe Griesedieck began attracting national attention. The brewery was featured in a 1956 article in *Forbes Magazine*. Noting Falstaff's all-time high sales and profits the previous year, the magazine stated, "One of the keys to Falstaff's success has

been a deliberate policy of limiting its horizons" by only marketing beer within 250 miles of its breweries. This enabled the company to keep prices below that of its chief rivals and near the prices of any smaller local competitors. Of Joe Griesedieck, *Forbes* said he "proved beyond all doubt that he possessed in ample measure the ingredients that make for good management," and the magazine called the corporate strategy of buying old breweries instead of building new ones a "thrifty expansion" that has "looked well on the balance sheet."

The year 1957 was a busy one for the Falstaff Brewing Corporation. Its eight breweries were marketing beer in twenty-eight states, and the Los Angeles and San Diego markets were first entered. A new executive headquarters was built that year in St. Louis. In its early years Falstaff's offices were located in a crude building near its first brewery. They had moved into the Continental Building at Olive and Grand in 1947. The new office building, located at 5050 Oakland Avenue, featured colorful rectangular outdoor panels, four stories, and a basement with a cafeteria. Overlooking Forest Park, the new offices provided for all 350 of Falstaff's local office employees to be unified in a single location. Falstaff paid for a special section in the *St. Louis Globe-Democrat* to celebrate the office's grand opening, with a bronze statue of Papa Joe Griesedieck unveiled at the event. The company boasted about being a pioneer with its "multiple-plant" system that ensured uniform flavor at whatever brewery Falstaff beer was produced. The new building was said to stand "as a symbol of Falstaff's progress," which included 3,700 employees nationwide.

Equally big news came to St. Louis in 1957 when Falstaff took over the Griesedieck Brothers Brewery Company plant. Falstaff needed more local capacity, and in a merger agreement signed on October 7 agreed to give Griesedieck Brothers stockholders nearly $5.3 million of new preferred stock in exchange for control of the business.

Joe Griesedieck was again frequently in the news in 1957. Seen as something of a wunderkind in the U.S. brewing business, Griesedieck told *American Brewer* that a price increase in beer was desperately needed in order for breweries to offset rising costs, but that "conditions make it almost impossible to increase prices at this time." In *Forbes Magazine*, Griesedieck noted that the ever-increasing popularity of package sales was helping the national and large regional brewers, and discussed Falstaff's continued desire for expansion. He admitted it would be tough to move

into the populous eastern market that Falstaff was seeking and said, "In this business, you buy breweries where and when they are available, not when you want them."

Falstaff produced 3,652,821 barrels in 1955 to climb into fourth place among U.S. breweries. The company reached the 4 million-barrel mark in 1957 and moved into third position behind only home-town Anheuser-Busch and Milwaukee's Schlitz. Net income for the year was $4.26 million, and it was again over $4 million in 1958. Sales were still increasing, but spiraling costs were beginning to eat into profits.

In 1958, Edward J. Griesedieck Jr. was elected to Falstaff's board of directors. He had come to the company from Griesedieck Brothers, where he was vice president, and was serving as resident plant manager in Fort Wayne. December 1958 marked the death of Director and Vice President Oscar Fischer, who had been with Falstaff for thirty-eight years.

Forbes Magazine continued to devote attention to Falstaff. A 1959 article still touted the company's policy of buying old breweries instead of building new ones, which Falstaff lacked the capital to do anyhow. The magazine noted the greater sales per dollar invested that Falstaff was enjoying over its rivals. The story concluded, however, that "even Falstaff's admirers were wondering whether the Griesediecks might not need new tactics now that they have apparently run out of bargains."

The year 1961 brought the death of Alvin Griesedieck. He had been with Falstaff since his father had started the company. The next year, longtime employee Harvey Beffa was named chairman of the board. Sales went over the 5 million-barrel mark, although Falstaff had dropped back to the number-four position among U.S. brewers.

In 1965, Falstaff established a feed division. Products included feed for horses and other live-stock, and later Sir John's Choice brand dog food. Joseph Griesedieck Jr. joined the company in 1966, the fourth generation of his family to work for Falstaff. That same year marked the company's all-time high in production at 7,010,218 barrels. This resulted in net income of $4.36 million. Falstaff also entered the lucrative New York market at this time, following the 1965 purchase (for $17.5 million) of Rhode Island's Narragansett Brewing Company. While this brought more brands to the Falstaff fold, it also resulted in an expensive antitrust lawsuit.

In a 1966 *New York Times* article, Falstaff President and Chief Executive Officer Joe Griesedieck stated that the spearhead of the company's efforts in New York was going to be a new package called "the Tapper." This was a 2 ¼-gallon aluminum keg (holding the equivalent of a case of beer) specially designed by Reynolds Metals. The story also noted Griesedieck's many community activities and mentioned that Falstaff had recently signed on as a sponsor of NBC's baseball game of the week, "believed to be the largest single TV sports package ever sponsored by a brewer."

An article the same year in *Dun's Review and Modern Industry* noted that Falstaff was still the top-selling beer in the St. Louis market, with a 40 percent share compared to Anheuser-Busch's 30 percent. Regarding the Tapper and other packaging, Joe Griesedieck joked that, "If people want to drink Falstaff in a paper bag, we'll sell it to them that way."

Above: Tin-over-cardboard, dating from the early 1950s.

Right: Cloth banner, circa 1934.

A Downhill Slide

Two new directors were named to the Falstaff board in 1967—Alvin "Buddy" Griesedieck Jr., vice president and director of marketing, and Harvey Beffa Jr., vice president of the malting and feed division. They replaced longtime employees Jere Newton, who had recently passed away, and Karl Vollmer, who had retired. Vollmer had joined Falstaff in 1948, coming over from the merged Columbia Brewing Company. Ferd Gutting, a finance man, and longtime employee H. J. Colton, former general sales manager, were moved up the corporate ladder at this time.

The end of 1967 brought bad news for the Falstaff Brewing Corporation. For the first time since 1946, production had decreased, and the bottom line showed a net loss of $638,525. Non-recurring expenses were cited as part of the problem, but clearly some cracks were beginning to show in the corporate foundation.

Falstaff again lost money in 1968, but things turned around a bit the next three years, with income topping $1 million each year. The company noted in 1970 that the Falstaff and Narragansett brands were available to 74 percent of the U.S. population, and Falstaff was being sold in forty countries and forty-one states. That year Harvey Beffa turned seventy and stepped down as chairman of the board. At a spring shareholders meeting, company officials assured the assembly that, despite sales problems, Falstaff was on the right track. But by 1971 production had shrunk to 5.1 million barrels, dropping the company to seventh place among U.S. brewers. Joe Griesedieck tried to be upbeat when addressing shareholders in 1972:

"Falstaff today is engaged in a fiercely competitive battle for the beer consumer's favor. We believe we have all the key elements to successfully meet the challenge and secure a larger share of the beer market."

Falstaff had long considered building a new brewery in the St. Louis area. It was felt that a large new plant would drive production costs down, and allow for the remaining St. Louis brewery and the ones in Omaha and Fort Wayne to be closed. A 1970 study on the building of this brewery had to be shelved, however—Falstaff simply didn't have enough money to construct it.

The company made a bold business move in 1972, buying the venerable Ballantine label. While nowhere near as dominant in the New York market as it had once been, Ballantine sales were still over 2 million barrels annually. Terms called for Falstaff to pay $4 million plus a 50 cents per barrel royalty. Falstaff's strategy called for penetrating the New York market by utilizing its excess capacity at the brewery in Rhode Island to brew both Falstaff and Ballantine. Although Falstaff was priced as a premium brand and Ballantine as a low-price brand, Falstaff apparently packaged the same beer under both labels. Unfortunately, Ballantine sales kept falling, and the deal resulted in another costly lawsuit alleging Falstaff had failed to follow a "best efforts covenant" inserted in the contract calling for promotion of Ballantine. The balance sheet for 1972 ended up a disaster—Falstaff had lost $8.9 million. Soon, Alvin Griesedieck Jr. was gone from the Oakland Avenue office. He was listed in the next annual report as an agent for Aetna Life Insurance Company.

While the Ballantine purchase served to increase Falstaff's 1973 production to 6.9 million barrels (its second largest ever), production shrank by over a million barrels the next year. The 1973 balance sheet showed a loss of $5.8 million, which "improved" the next year to a loss of $3.9 million. Into this mess stepped a reclusive California millionaire named Paul Kalmanovitz.

Good-Bye, St. Louis

As Falstaff's April 28, 1975, corporate shareholders meeting approached, St. Louis newspapers began mentioning a proposed recapitalization plan being put forth to Falstaff by Paul Kalmanovitz, the chairman of San Francisco–based General Brewing. Kalmanovitz had previous dealings with Falstaff, having in 1974 acquired the San Francisco plant it briefly owned, shutting it down and then contract-brewing Falstaff at a different brewery.

Kalmanovitz was a native of Poland, who came to the United States as a young man in 1926. He began his American business career running gas stations in New York and then Los Angeles. By the early 1930s he owned numerous garages and later entered the nightclub business. After World War II he entered the commercial real estate business. He first got involved in brewing in the 1950s with California's Maier Brewing Company.

On April 28, shareholders assembled at the Loretto-Hilton Center in Webster Groves for what was described as a "highly charged meeting." They had not been paid a dividend since 1972 and were told that Falstaff's biggest problem was its lack of working capital. While able to make payments on a bank loan, contractual provisions of the loan were being violated due to lack of cash. Something needed to be done. Paul Kalmanovitz was offering $10 million in cash, which would provide $1.5 million to pay off notes, $4 million to pay short-term debt, and $4.5 million in working capital. In addition, he was set to guarantee another $10 million in loans. Stockholders followed management's recommendation and approved the plan. Paul Kalmanovitz was elected chairman of the board. His crony John Miller was elected vice chairman. Joe Griesedieck, Harvey Beffa, and Edward Griesedieck Jr. were all re-elected to the board, but they wouldn't be around for long.

A March 1975 article in the *St. Louis Post-Dispatch* noted Kalmanovitz's "reputation as a sharp cost cutter." Other industry observers noted that a day after Kalmanovitz purchased the Lucky Brewery in California, he fired two-thirds of the employees. This did not seem to bode well for the future of Falstaff in St. Louis.

The fateful board meeting was held on a Monday. Before the week was over, Joe Griesedieck (former president and chairman of the board), Harvey Beffa Jr. (vice president of the malting and feed division), and Charles Dependahl Jr. (vice president and director of marketing) were dismissed from the company. Ferd Gutting was retained and insisted to reporters that Kalmanovitz "plans to make the company a solid organization." The next month it became obvious that Falstaff was preparing to move its corporate headquarters from St. Louis to San Francisco and layoffs would be forthcoming. In an about-face, Gutting was demoted, dropped from the board of directors, and said to be set to retire at the end of the year.

In response to the institution of new severance pay rules, on June 27, 1975, the flag at Falstaff headquarters was briefly flown upside down at half-staff, the universal signal of distress. Instead of dismissed employees receiving their expected one week of severance pay for every year of service (up to twenty-six weeks), the new policies called for employees with one to fifteen years of service to receive nothing, those with fifteen to twenty-four years of service to receive four weeks' severance, and those with twenty-five or more years of service to receive six weeks' pay. Layoffs began in July. By the end of September, Falstaff headquarters were in San Francisco and hundreds of St. Louisans had lost their jobs.

All that remained of Falstaff in St. Louis was the still-functioning Plant #10, the old Griesedieck Brothers facility. Plant #2 had closed in 1952, the original plant in 1958, and the former Columbia plant in 1967. Kalmanovitz denied that he already had plans for closing the St. Louis brewery, telling local newspaper reporters, "The question is how to save it. How long can we keep going like this?"

The answer was not very long, as the brewery on Shenandoah Avenue was closed on November 4, 1977. Company officers said the location was unprofitable because of its age, high maintenance and utility costs, and lack of railroad access, as well as the state's rejection of a proposed self-insurance plan for workman's compensation. The buildings sat empty for years and are still around today. The older portions, the former Consumers Brewing Company buildings erected in the 1890s, are among the most interesting existing examples of pre-Prohibition brewery buildings left in St. Louis.

The corporate headquarters are long gone. The building was torn down in 1989 to make way for today's St. Louis Science Center complex. When plans were first made for the new science center, developers considered using the Falstaff building, but it was decided the design was not appropriate and it would be cheaper to tear it down. All that's left is the elevated walkway across Highway 40 (Interstate 64) connecting the site to Forest Park.

As for the Falstaff brand, it lingered under the Kalmanovitz reign. Production in 1980 amounted to 3,901,000 barrels, still number nine in the

Falstaff delivery drivers assembled at Plant #10 loading dock, early 1960s.

country. Sales dropped 15 percent in 1982, yet the company had cut expenses so much it was able to generate a $2.9 million profit. Critics called Kalmanovitz's methods "shortsighted." But in a 1983 *Wall Street Journal* article, Robert Wineburg, a St. Louis–based brewing industry analyst, noting that Kalmanovitz had slashed annual marketing expenses from $30 million to $7 million, commented, "Sure, his market share is falling, but the rate of decay is about the same as before he took over. There is no doubt in my mind that without Kalmanovitz, Falstaff would be dead today."

Falstaff may have been alive, but it was soon on life support. In 1984, production amounted to 900,000 barrels, the lowest since 1941. On January 14, 1990, the Falstaff Brewing Corporation was effectively defunct when its last remaining brewery, in Fort Wayne, was closed. While the brand continued to be produced at other breweries, including Pearl, Pabst, and the City Brewery of LaCrosse, Wisconsin, sales quickly dwindled. Production amounted to a mere 27,947 barrels in 2000. Brewing of the once-mighty Falstaff brand ceased in 2005. The year before, just 1,468 barrels had been produced.

Considerable ink has been spilled in attempts to explain the meteoric plunge of Falstaff's fortunes. Why did Falstaff fail? In retrospect there were a number of factors, including but not limited to the following:

Above: Falstaff quart bottle label, 1940s.

Right: Falstaff corporate headquarters, 5050 Oakland Avenue, 1957–75.

- The Narragansett purchase, which resulted in a lingering federal lawsuit.
- The Ballantine purchase and the inability to get production and distribution straightened out there.
- A change of formula for the Falstaff brand, which proved to be less popular.
- The Tapper. These miniature aluminum barrels, which held the equivalent of a case of beer, cost Falstaff $48 apiece. With a deposit of only $1, many went unreturned, thus costing Falstaff $47 for every one sold, resulting in a loss of over $12 million.
- All Falstaff breweries were old and less efficient than competitors'.

The fact was that the Falstaff Brewing Corporation, in its efforts to grow, had purchased older breweries. Such plants were less expensive to buy, but more expensive to operate because of inefficiencies. Also, many of these breweries were in landlocked locations, with no existing rail facilities. Falstaff was the only major U.S. brewer that never constructed a new brewery—all of its expansion was done by purchasing older facilities. Whether or not that was what finally sealed its fate, the bottom line is that Falstaff simply could not sell enough beer or limit production costs sufficiently to survive the beer wars that took place in the 1970s and beyond.

Forest Park Brewing Company

3662 Forest Park Boulevard

Forest Park Brewing Company	1910–1917
Griesedieck Beverage Company	
(a.k.a. Griesedieck Brothers Plant #2)	1917–1920
Falstaff Corporation	1920–1933
Falstaff Brewing Corporation, Plant #1	1933–1958

Top: Forest Park Brewery photo taken in 1917.

Bottom: Caricature drawing of Ed Wagner Jr. and his first brewery, from the *Granite City Press-Record*, which shows little Ed astride the brewery in that town.

Facing page: Packaging area, Griesedieck Beverage Company, 1917–1920.

The Forest Park Brewing Company was one of the last additions to the St. Louis brewery business prior to Prohibition, incorporated in 1910 with a capital stock of $100,000. Initial plans called for the erection of a fireproof building that measured 150′ × 120′, at a cost of $35,000 plus installation of about $60,000 worth of brewing and refrigerating equipment. The business was the culmination of the brewing careers of the father and son team of Ed Wagner Sr. and Ed Wagner Jr. They were well known locally for their previous association with the American Brewing Company of St. Louis and their namesake Wagner Brewing Company in nearby Granite City, Illinois.

Ed Wagner Sr. had quite an illustrious brewing background. Born in 1857 in Frankenstein, Prussia, he served the traditional three-year brewing apprenticeship in Breslau, then went on a three-and-a-half-year "wanderjahr" working at breweries in Germany, Holland, and Belgium. In early 1877, Wagner came to the United States, working briefly in Pittsburgh before moving to Chicago. In the Windy City he worked first at the Hoerber Brewery, then moved over to the Schoenhofen plant. He headed west to Denver in 1881, then to San Francisco to work for Wieland's, and then to Boulder, Colorado, to become foreman at the Weisenhorn and Voegtle Brewery. Wagner returned to Chicago in the summer of 1884. The next year he and Charles Duer purchased the Gehring Brewery. A partner named O'Donnell came aboard the next year, and the business was renamed the Bavarian Brewing Company, where Wagner continued serving as superintendent.

Wagner was well known in brewing industry circles and served for many years as secretary of the United States Brewmasters' Association. He was lured to St. Louis in 1890 to become head brewer at the newly formed American Brewing Company (ABC), later becoming corporate vice president. In 1893, Wagner organized and became president of the Model Bottling Machinery Company, which operated next door to the American plant. Skillful in the bottling process as well as brewing, he invented the "St. Louis model" pasteurizing and bottle-soaking machine, which was used at breweries throughout the country.

The year 1903 was a big one for Ed Wagner Sr., as he was elected president of the U.S. Brewmasters' Association and together with his son and other ABC officials built the Wagner Brewery in Granite City. After both the Wagner and ABC breweries were absorbed into the Independent Breweries Company (IBC) in 1907, Wagner served as a director and technical manager for IBC. He left to open the Forest Park Brewing Company.

The younger Ed Wagner, a graduate of the Wahl & Henius brewing school, had worked at breweries in Denver and Chicago before joining his father as an assistant brewmaster at ABC. He was manager of the Granite City brewery at the tender age of twenty-four and stayed on there and with the IBC until 1910. Not long after the

Wagners began brewing at Forest Park, they either needed to expand or increase working capital as the amount of stock was doubled to two hundred thousand dollars.

Two brands of beer were produced in the smallish brewhouse, Wagner's Old Time Lager and Forest Park. Both brews were all-malt products, and company advertisements stressed that the beer was as good as the best German imports.

In November 1916, the stockholders re-elected general manager Ed Wagner Sr. as company president, and brewmaster Ed Wagner Jr. as secretary-treasurer. But unfortunately, the business was about to go under. Brewing ended in early December, and later in the month a voluntary petition of bankruptcy was filed in U.S. District Court showing liabilities outnumbering assets by about $19,000. The primary debt was a $200,000 first mortgage held by the German Savings Institution of St. Louis. Forest Park had more than $40,000 in unsecured claims against it and a grand total of $140.13 in the bank.

Ed Wagner Jr. was appointed receiver of the company as it struggled to get out of hock. They continued distributing beer already on hand, but in February the Wagners turned equity in the brewery over to the debt holders. Operations were supposed to continue, but Forest Park closed shortly thereafter, unable to generate any profit.

Into this void stepped veteran St. Louis brewer Joe Griesedieck. The bank persuaded an initially reluctant Griesedieck to take the Forest Park brewery off its hands for $125,000, of which "Papa Joe" put up $5,000 cash. Beer was brewed at the site until late 1918, with the facility serving as the Griesedieck Brothers Plant #2.

During Prohibition the plant was renamed Griesedieck Beverage Company as Papa Joe scrambled to keep the business afloat. Ultimately, the former Forest Park Brewing Company proved to be the plant from which the Falstaff Brewing Corporation dynasty would begin after Repeal. Several of the buildings remain, with a newer Falstaff addition serving as a Jimmy John's franchise, enabling current visitors to have a sandwich while checking out the buildings put up a century earlier by the Wagners.

Ed Wagner Jr. got in trouble during the 1920s while serving as brewmaster at the Griesedieck Brothers Brewing Company, where part of his job included supervising the bottling of illegal full-strength beer. After that, he and his father faded from the brewing industry. Their Forest Park venture marked an inglorious ending to previously stellar careers. It would appear they were primarily victims of bad timing, entering a market that was shrinking due to dry ordinances and full of established (and fierce) competitors.

Gast
Brewing Company

8541 North Broadway

Gast Brewing Company	1900–1907
Gast branch, IBC	1907–1921
Gast Brewery, Inc.	1933–1946
Gast St. Louis Brewing Company	1946–1947
Gast St. Louis Brewing Company, Plant 1	1947–1948

Top: Photo of the Gast Brewery, taken in 1933.

Middle: Early 1940s label, shortly after the brewery opened a bottling shop.

Bottom: Foam scraper, sometimes called a foam comb, distributed by Gast.

Facing page: Paulus Gast as he appeared around 1900.

The name Gast was first associated with St. Louis brewing way back in 1844, when John Gast made beer in a one-room plant. This first Gast brewery was still functioning in 1850, when it made that year's U.S. Census of Industry. It was the smallest of seventeen St. Louis breweries listed, producing a mere 150 barrels a year, with a single employee (presumably John Gast). This early "microbrewery" would soon fade away.

While it would be another fifty years before the Gast name was again associated with St. Louis brewing, family members were in the meantime busy making their mark on the city. Brothers Leopold and August Gast came to the United States from Germany around 1848. They had learned the art of lithography in their native land, and brought a small press along when they immigrated. After spending some time in New York and Pittsburgh, in 1852 they set up shop in St. Louis and became quite successful. According to historian Ernst Kargau, the business (which became known as the August Gast Bank Note and Lithographing Company) stood "without a rival in regard to the superiority, accuracy and beauty of all its productions." August Gast retired as company president in 1885, but the business continued under his name. A new plant was built at Twenty-first and Morgan streets in 1889, which at one point had more than 250 employees.

Leopold Gast's son Paulus, born in Berlin in 1841, came to the United States as a young boy with his parents. Paulus attended the St. Louis public schools and Washington University. After serving as a Union soldier during the Civil War (service which would have an influence upon the selection of his children's names), including in the battle for Atlanta, he returned home in 1864. Paulus spent the next couple of years in Hermann, Missouri, learning about growing grapes and making wine.

After Leopold Gast sold his portion of the lithography business to brother August in 1866, he and son Paulus formed the Gast Wine Company. The Gasts began growing grapes on a fifty-acre plot in the Baden community in north St. Louis. Various brands of wine and champagne were produced, and the business flourished. Years later, Paulus was joined in the wine business by his son Alexander Tecumseh Gast. Born in 1869, Alex Gast started working at the wine company in 1886, and by 1890 he was corporate secretary-treasurer. His nephew Ferdinand, two years his junior, worked in the family lithography business before joining Gast Wine Company as a bookkeeper in 1892. In addition to the winery, vineyard, and wine garden, the family also ran a restaurant called the Gast Viticultural Café, which like the family home was located at 8541 North Broadway.

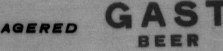

GRAPES OUT, GRAIN IN

By the late 1890s the Gasts' wine sales were being hurt by an onslaught of cheaper brands. The family then decided to phase out the wine business and, in a rather unusual move, go into the brewing business. The Gast Brewing Company was formed in 1899. Construction of a new brewery on the family property began on March 1. Company leaders included Paulus Gast as president, Bernard Felker as vice president, Alex Gast as secretary and general manager, and Ferdinand Gast as secretary-treasurer. Ulysses Gast, another son of Paulus, would serve as plant superintendent.

The Gasts spent three hundred thousand dollars constructing their new brewery. It featured a five-story brewhouse with a seventy-five-thousand-barrel annual capacity. The company's first delivery of its lager beer was made on April Fool's Day 1900. The Gasts' switch to beer must have worked, as in 1905 they spent eighty thousand dollars building a new central depot and office building (which still stands at 1512 North Broadway), and the next year put up a new wash house.

An important figure in the success of the Gast Brewing Company was its longtime brewmaster, Max Rother. He had quite a dynamic career in brewing, beginning with his birth on the grounds of his father's brewery in Germany. Rother apprenticed at an uncle's brewery in Russia, then worked at large and small German breweries and at others in Poland, England, and Belgium. He came to the United States in 1891 to become chief maltster at the McAvoy Brewery in Chicago, then worked at the Brand and West Side plants in that city. After supervising the construction of a brewery in Arcadia, Wisconsin, Rother came to St. Louis in 1902 to take over the Gast brew kettle.

Paulus Gast, who had also served as a St. Louis city councilman, passed away in 1906. The next year Felix Gast, yet another of his sons, was seriously injured in the brewery. He lit a match in a gas-filled room in the bottling department, creating an explosion that caused considerable damage to the building and landed him in the hospital, although he quickly recovered.

The Gast Brewing Company did not remain an independent business for long; in 1907 it joined numerous other area breweries in forming the Independent Breweries Company (IBC). Alex Gast helped organize the merger and profited nicely as he owned 80 percent of the Gast company stock. He also continued to serve as plant manager while Ferdinand was named IBC corporate secretary. Max Rother not only continued as master brewer at the Gast plant, but he also took over similar duties at the IBC's Columbia facility.

Most of the IBC breweries, including the Gast branch, continued making beer until the advent of Prohibition. In 1919, IBC started making its famous root beer, but its American Brewing Company facility was sufficient for producing its soda and legal malt products, and the Gast plant was mothballed in May of 1921.

Ferdinand Gast died during the "dark days" in 1927, in the same house where he had been born fifty-six years previously. At the time of his passing, he was still serving as secretary of the IBC.

"BEST BEER BREWED" BOUNCES BACK

When the country came to its senses and dumped Prohibition in 1933, the Gast brewery was suddenly valuable again. It was taken over by a syndicate of men largely connected with the Love & Co. brokerage firm, including J. A. Love, William Healy, J. Leo Phelan, and Gilbert Strelinger. Alex Gast came back to serve as figurehead president of the new Gast Brewery, Inc. Production started in July of 1933, with Max Rother back in his old role as brewmaster. Gast beer hit the market in September, and like the early products of many reopened breweries, was initially offered in draft form only.

Unfortunately, the brewery started suffering financial problems almost from the start. Although it may have been owned by brokers, it was soon broke. In January of 1935, former St. Louis circuit clerk John Schmoll was named bankruptcy trustee, beginning an association with the brewery that would last the rest of his life. John Schmoll was born in Holland but came to St. Louis at the age of three. He had a career in politics prior to getting involved with Gast Brewery, Inc. In 1937, Schmoll reported to the court that the brewery had made a forty thousand dollar profit the previous year on sales of nearly $1 million. This led to a company reorganization that resulted in Schmoll becoming corporate president.

The brewery then enjoyed a couple more profitable years. It could afford to buy some new delivery trucks in 1937, and in the summer of 1938 a separate Gast Bottling Company was formed in order to build a new bottling plant. By October the addition was up and running, and customers could begin popping the crowns off bottles of Gast Golden Lager.

But by the time John Schmoll passed away on New Year's Eve 1939, the company was again having money problems. Oliver Remmers was brought in to replace Schmoll as court trustee, and another reorganization plan was filed in March. To raise desperately needed cash, the new bottling shop was sold in July 1940 for eleven thousand dollars. A week later Remmers was encouraging the brewery's creditors to buy and operate the plant, as he felt that was the only way they could ever hope to get any of their money back. This plan must have been rejected, as on November 1, 1940, it was announced that the assets of Gast Brewery, Inc., would be offered for sale at public auction. Any bids made must not have been accepted, and soon the brewery was back making beer under the old trusteeship.

America's entry into World War II was beneficial to many small brewers

and may have helped to save Gast. Brewing ingredients were being rationed, and because many of the larger breweries had government military contracts to fulfill, a scarcity of brew resulted, giving breweries like Gast a brief niche. The year 1944 saw sales of 33,235 barrels, which increased the next year by a few hundred barrels. But while Gast was still surviving, it was by far the smallest brewery in St. Louis—the next smallest, Columbia, was selling more than 250,000 barrels a year. Still, Oliver Remmers felt that the plant could operate profitably, and in early 1946 he filed yet another reorganization plan in an attempt to end the company's twelve-year receivership.

Gast received a small windfall in January 1946 when it was awarded $7,500 as settlement from an old bond taken out on John Schmoll. Remmers charged that Schmoll had "misappropriated" beer made by Gast for his own use through a dummy corporation, and the bond company was willing to settle for that amount.

The court finally approved a new reorganization plan in June of 1946. The plant began doing business as Gast St. Louis Brewing Company. The next year there was a management shuffle when Oliver Remmers resigned as director and chairman of the board. Walter W. Fox took over as corporate president, with J. F. Corkery vice president. Former vice president J. W. Brady replaced Remmers as board chairman.

In November 1947, the officers made a bold move, deciding to lease the idle Schott brewery in nearby Highland, Illinois, and renaming it Gast Plant Number 2. The first Gast draft made in Illinois hit the market two months later. By April, Gast bottled beer was flowing out of the Highland brewery as well. The company even built a new cinder-block stockhouse on the Highland grounds.

In 1948, after a fire caused twenty-five thousand dollars worth of damage to the St. Louis Gast

Top: Alex T. Gast, photo circa 1934.

Left: Gast Golden Lager crown, companion to the label on page 104.

Facing page, far right: Two matchbooks emphasizing Gast's wooden-barrel aging.

Facing page: A corner tavern selling Gast beer.

plant, the company moved all of its operations to Highland. Ironically, the newly acquired Plant Number 2 had outlived the home facility. Production for the year was thirty-eight thousand barrels, down from the sixty thousand put out in 1947.

It soon became obvious that the company was again financially strapped, and on October 8, 1949, the last Gast brew rolled down the line in Highland. Ten days later, Gast St. Louis Brewing Company filed court papers seeking to liquidate the company. The final balance sheet showed four times as many liabilities as assets.

While the brewery in Highland has been well preserved and part of it is used as a local history museum, the same cannot be said for the original Gast brewery. Most of the buildings were torn down in 1956. All that remains is the former bottling house, which for many years was home to a pizza factory. While it's too late to get a Gast beer to go with your pizza, one need go no farther than the local liquor store to get a reasonable facsimile, as numerous "old-timers" have equated the taste of Gast draft to today's Miller Genuine Draft. Many of these same beer drinkers also disparaged the taste of Gast in bottles, which one described as having a "burnt" taste.

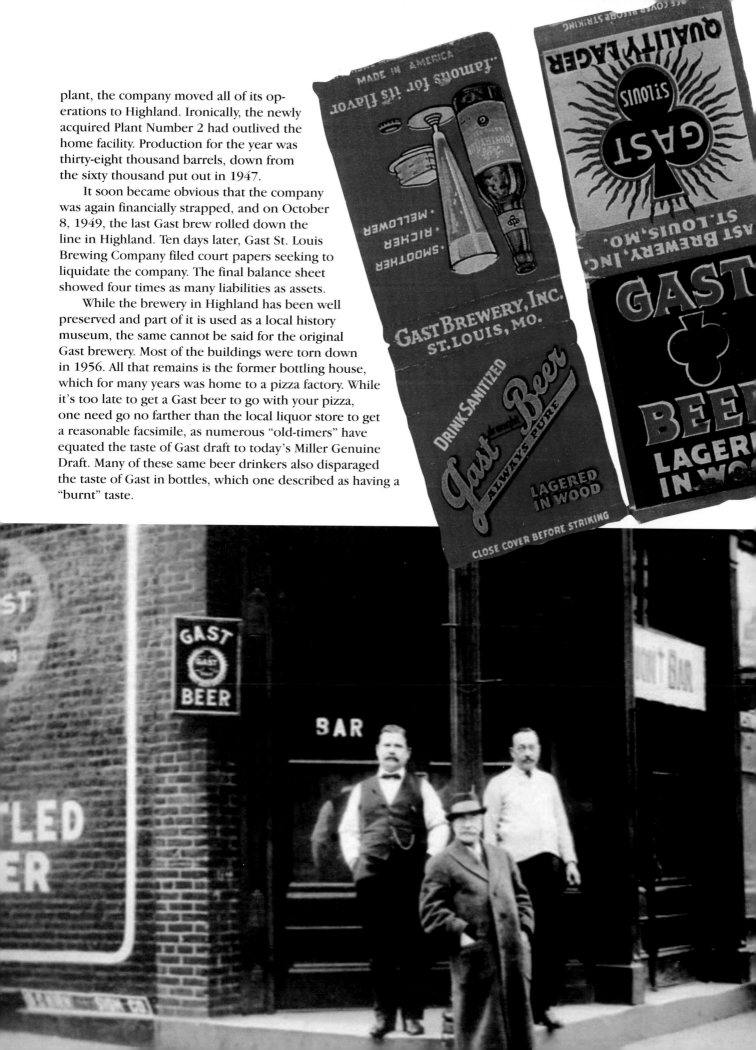

Green Tree Brewery

135-37 S. 2nd Street

Green Tree Brewery, Joseph Schnaider & Co.
(Schnaider & Feuerbacher)   1855–1863

906 Sidney Street (new site)

Green Tree Brewery, Joseph Schnaider & Co.
(Schnaider & Feuerbacher)   1863–1865
Green Tree Brewery, Feuerbacher & McHose 1865–1865
Green Tree Brewery,
Feuerbacher & Schlossstein   1865–1880
Green Tree Brewery Company   1880–1889
Green Tree branch, SLBA   1889–1919

Top: Green Tree stock house and wagon shed, circa 1895.

Bottom: Pre-Prohibition Green Tree buck (bock) beer label.

Facing page: Portrait of Max Feuerbacher, date unknown.

In St. Louis history, the Green Tree name goes back to at least the late 1830s, when the Green Tree Hotel and Tavern was operated on Second Street by B. W. Ayres. The Green Tree Brewery was formed two decades later by a pair of German immigrants named Joseph Maximilian Schnaider and Max Feuerbacher.

Schnaider was born in Zell am Hammersbach, Duchy of Baden, in 1832. At age fifteen he began the traditional three-year brewing apprenticeship in the town of Rastatt, following which he worked at a brewery in Strasbourg. He then traveled around France and Germany for a while, taking in the sights and working at various breweries. In 1854, Schnaider followed the path of many of his countrymen and migrated to St. Louis, finding work at the Philadelphia Brewery, where he was soon made foreman.

Max Feuerbacher had a background similar to his partner. Born in 1835 in Muehlhausen, Germany, the son of a brewer, he served an apprenticeship at his father's brewery. At age seventeen he immigrated to the United States and St. Louis, finding a job at the Uhrig Brewery prior to moving over to the Philadelphia Brewery, where he met Joseph Schnaider.

The two young men decided to go out on their own around 1855, opening the Green Tree Brewery a block up the street from the Green Tree (or Gruene Baum) Hotel and Tavern, which was then owned by George Diesz. Their neighbors included the National Brewery and Lemp's Western Brewery.

Schnaider and Feuerbacher carried away from the tavern more than its name, as the men also married two of Diesz's daughters. They would eventually end up running the motel/tavern as well. Schnaider was the senior partner and Feuerbacher the junior partner in the brewery, which operated under the firm name of Joseph Schnaider and Company. Typical of the many small breweries operating in St. Louis during this time, the new concern began operations in a three-story brick structure with a relatively modest daily brew rate of twenty-five barrels. The beer was aged in a cave on Lafayette Avenue.

The Green Tree Brewery survived a serious fire in 1857, which caused ten thousand dollars in damages to a plant valued at eighteen thousand dollars. This did not deter the partners, for they immediately rebuilt and the company continued to prosper. Outgrowing the old facility, a bigger and better brewery was built on Sidney Street in the Soulard neighborhood in 1863. The new site was no doubt chosen at least in part because of the natural cave found below the property, large enough to store six thousand barrels of beer.

Joseph Schnaider didn't stay at the new location long, selling out to partner Feuerbacher in 1865 in order to build his own brewery on Chouteau Avenue. Feuerbacher was briefly joined as a Green Tree partner by Abe McHose, formerly of the St. Louis Brewery, and then by Louis Schlossstein, yet another German immigrant with a remarkably similar background. Schlossstein was born in Bavaria in 1834 and served the usual three-year brewer's apprenticeship. He then set off on his so-called *Wanderjahr*, traveling about the country both to learn about the world and to gain experience at various breweries. Schlossstein must have been enjoying himself, as he spent five years on his brewing odyssey through both Germany and France.

His brother George had previously moved to St. Louis, and in 1858 Louis joined him there. Again he bounced around at jobs in several breweries before landing the foreman's position at the Uhrig Brewery, where he stayed for four years. While there, he married Josephine Uhrig, the widow of Ignatz Uhrig, one of the brothers who had operated the plant.

In 1865, Schlossstein joined Max Feuerbacher at Green Tree by buying into the brewery, with the firm name changed to Feuerbacher and Schlossstein. It was to become quite a successful partnership, with sales expanding greatly starting in the 1870s. To support growing production, a new stock house with a capacity of forty thousand barrels was built. The beer was cooled with natural ice cut every winter (weather permitting) from the Mississippi River. By 1874, annual production reached 21,079 barrels, ranking Green Tree sixth out of twenty-nine local breweries.

Sadly, just like his former partner Joseph Schnaider, Max Feuerbacher began to suffer from ill health at an early age. He was already ailing when in 1880 his business was incorporated as the Green Tree Brewery Company, with Feuerbacher as company president. Brewery employment had grown to about thirty, with eighteen horses required to pull the delivery wagons used to deliver the brew locally.

The early 1880s marked another period of expansion for Green Tree, as in quick order a new malt house, malt kiln, and mash tub were installed, and in 1882 a new icehouse, remodeled stables, and two new refrigerating machines were added. These projects completed, in 1884 Max Feuerbacher handed the reins of the business over to his son Frank and partner Schlossstein, returning to Germany in an effort to regain his health. However, he passed away just ten days after arriving in his native town, in the same house in which he had been born not quite fifty years earlier.

Frank Feuerbacher was an adopted stepson of Max Feuerbacher. Born in 1850, he received his primary education in St. Louis before moving to Cincinnati to serve an apprenticeship in the brewing industry. Frank returned to St. Louis in 1880 and four years later married Caroline Krauss, daughter of John Krauss, a major figure at the Klausmann Brewery in south St. Louis.

Louis Schlossstein, a new partner named E. H. Vordtriede, and Frank Feuerbacher continued to run the thriving Green Tree Brewery, and were joined in its management by Henry Nicolaus, a veteran beer maker who was hired as brewmaster in 1880 and bought into the company shortly thereafter. Nicolaus further solidified his position within the company by marrying Schlossstein's stepdaughter, Mary Uhrig, in 1883.

Among the brands produced by the brewery were its namesake beer Green Tree, Standard, Select, Salvator, and Culmbacher. The company became a notable shipping brewery, establishing depots in various parts of the country and building a bottling shop across the street from the main brewery and directly behind the Frank W. Feuerbacher and Company malt house.

In June 1889, Green Tree was consolidated with numerous other local breweries into the

St. Louis Brewing Association (SLBA), which five months later was sold to an English syndicate. Partners Schlossstein, Feuerbacher, and Nicolaus stayed on in their Green Tree management positions for the new owners.

Louis Schlossstein stepped down from the brewery's helm in 1892 to devote his attention to his many real estate investments. He passed away in September of 1901 in Glenwood Springs, Colorado. Apparently being a beer baron with a major interest in a successful brewery had been a decent occupation, for he left an estate valued at over $2 million. When an inventory of Schlossstein's estate was filed in probate court, it included substantial stock in the SLBA, Boatmen's Bank, South Side Bank, and Northwestern Bank, as well as twenty-two parcels of land in St. Louis and twenty thousand acres in Tennessee.

The Green Tree Brewery's future seemed bright as a branch of the SLBA. The plant was extensively remodeled beginning in 1892. Following the purchase of the nearby Schilling & Schneider brewery two years later, a new boiler house was built, and the improvement program culminated in a new six-story, one hundred thousand dollar brewhouse designed in 1895.

Frank Feuerbacher and Henry Nicolaus both stayed at Green Tree, with the latter named local SLBA president in 1903. The brewery continued as one of the conglomerate's major facilities and the Green Tree brand remained in production. Adolph Walther (who would continue his brewing career after Prohibition at the Griesedieck-Western Brewery in Belleville, Illinois) was brought aboard as brewmaster. But despite some false optimism that saw the 1916 installation of a complete new Barry-Wehmiller bottling unit (capable of filling six thousand bottles an hour), the prohibitionists finally won their war against beer, and in 1919 the Green Tree Brewery was forced to close its doors— as it turned out, forever.

The remaining buildings were demolished in 1965. Years after they were torn down and forgotten, a subterranean reminder of the old brewery was unearthed. On June 15, 1982, while an Anheuser-Busch parking lot was being paved,

a workman uncovered part of the original Green Tree brewery cellars. A stone entrance was visible, providing access to the large cave system.

After pumping water out of the cellars, adventurers were able to explore them extensively. While no barrels or brewing equipment were found, the few artifacts discovered were placed in the A-B archives. In honor of the occasion, a time capsule was placed in a half-barrel and buried in the caves, and work on the parking lot recommenced.

THE BRAND LIVED ON

One of the authors of this book once asked his paternal grandfather which of the beers brewed in Missouri before Prohibition had the best taste, to which Grandpa Cecil responded, "Why, Green Tree in bottles." The conversation continued, with another inquiry being made as to which was the worst tasting beer available locally after Repeal. Without missing a beat, Grandpa responded, "Why, Green Tree in bottles. Just not the same as the original, worse than the worst home brew after beer came back."

The tale of post-Prohibition Green Tree began in July 1933 when a group of St. Louis investors formed a new corporation, the Green Tree Breweries, Incorporated. The sterling reputation of Green Tree beer was no doubt a factor behind the attempted resurrection of the brand. The SLBA had let its registration of the trademark expire, giving the start-up company a chance to snap up (for free) a brand name that still carried favorable local recognition.

At the Green Tree Breweries' first board of directors meeting, Christian Buehner was elected president, Fred A. Bierman vice president, Leroy Lind secretary-treasurer, and August Posdorf general manager. Buehner's election to the top spot was a foregone conclusion, as he owned 85 percent of the company's stock, with the minority interest divided up among the other officers. While it is not known if any of the management team had any brewing experience, they did hire someone who presumably did, as Martin J. Howard soon joined them as brewmaster. The company's only capital asset at the time of its formation was a

Facing page: Louis Schlossstein, from Scharf's 1883 *History of Saint Louis City and County.*

Below: Pre-Prohibition label.

Right: Post-Prohibition Green Tree "Fully Aged Beer" label, circa 1934.

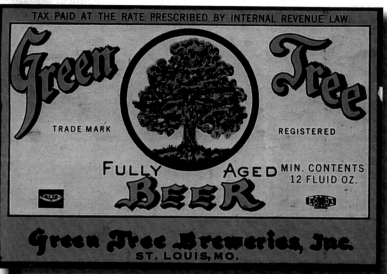

group of industrial buildings located at 135 Russell Avenue, about twenty blocks northeast of the shuttered Green Tree Brewery site on Sidney Street. Valued at seventy thousand dollars after subtracting an outstanding mortgage, the Russell Avenue buildings likely had been built for use as an icehouse or cold storage facility.

Containing two 120-horsepower John O'Brien Company steam boilers and a pair of forty-ton ice machines, the property was viewed as the nucleus around which a brewery would be built. Buehner, who had owned the buildings, swapped his deed of trust in exchange for Green Tree Breweries, Inc., stock when the company was organized. To raise additional capital for building the proposed plant, Green Tree issued a $168,750 stock offering. Alas, the stock sale did not go well. To further complicate matters, in March 1934 the Federal Trade Commission suspended further public sale of the stock. With construction of the new brewery put on hold due to lack of funds, management decided that its best course of business would be to serve as a distributor and wholesaler of 3.2 percent beer. Buehner again dug into his own pockets and advanced the company the required cash to set up this operation, for which he was to receive 50 percent of net earnings.

Buehner was empowered by the Green Tree board of directors to negotiate with local breweries to set up a distribution agreement, which led to the signing of a contract with the fledgling Peerless Brewing Company in nearby Washington, Missouri. By late October 1934, Green Tree bottled beer was back on the streets. Curiously, Green Tree Breweries, Inc., would not bother to file a trademark application to protect the Green Tree

name and logo until a year and a half later.

Distributing its contract brew must not have been as profitable as hoped, as by September 1936 the company was found to be insolvent. The Peerless Brewing Company swooped in and made an offer to purchase some of Green Tree's assets, including exclusive use of the Green Tree trademark west of the Mississippi River (excluding St. Louis). This offer was finally accepted in April of the following year. A few months later a contract was also executed between Green Tree and the Carondelet Brewing Company of St. Louis, allowing the latter to brew and sell Green Tree–brand beer in St. Louis and areas east of the Mississippi.

Unfortunately the Peerless Brewing Company would soon find itself in financial straits and declare bankruptcy. In August 1938 the Carondelet Brewing Company purchased the remaining assets of Green Tree Breweries, Inc. When Carondelet folded in 1941, Green Tree beer disappeared from retailers' shelves.

THE FEUERBACHER MANSION

While the buildings of his Green Tree Brewery Company have disappeared without a trace, one building that can provide a glimpse of the glory years of the company still stands a short block away: the former Max Feuerbacher mansion, at the southeast corner of Sidney and Twelfth streets. The home is commonly called the Lion House because at the top of the outdoor stairs leading to the entrance sit two imposing carved limestone lions, their snarling stares frozen in time.

It is perhaps fortunate that Feuerbacher

decided to build his mansion away from the immediate vicinity of his brewery. The nearby Anheuser-Busch complex continues to grow outward like a giant banyan tree, seemingly ever-expanding onto property where competing breweries once stood. These days, few visitors driving onto A-B InBev's parking lot at the southwest corner of Ninth and Sidney realize it was once the location of the Green Tree brewhouse.

Elmer Mick and his wife, Lee, two stalwarts of the St. Louis breweriana collecting community, now own the Feuerbacher mansion. They first noticed that the property was for sale during a Soulard neighborhood historic house tour in 1982. Two of their sons have lived in the mansion, while another son later purchased the former home of Cherokee Brewery proprietor Ferdinand Herold.

Construction of the Feuerbacher mansion began in 1865 and continued for five years. The master plan was patterned after a castle that Max Feuerbacher had seen as a boy in Germany. The house was furnished with solid brass door handles adorned with the brewer's six-pointed Star of David, which matched those installed in the Green Tree Brewery. The residence also featured what is said to be the first home security alarm system installed in St. Louis. The view from the mansion's roof can only be described as breathtaking. A realtor once described it as "probably the greatest view in all St. Louis." No doubt anyone standing there in 1890 would have seen major portions of the Green Tree, Obert, Schilling and Schneider, Anheuser-Busch, Anthony & Kuhn, and American breweries in all of their beery industrial splendor.

The Mick family enjoys treating visitors to tours of the Feuerbacher mansion, which features fourteen rooms, six marble fireplaces, and a one-hundred-year-old pipe organ. Below the mansion's basement was constructed a large, vaulted, and brick-lined beer cellar. Like just about every mansion in Soulard that was ever connected with a brewery owner, the basement is rumored to have had a connection into the local cave system and/or the brewery—a portal that none of the Micks have ever found despite extensive searching. Anyone interested in St. Louis brewing history owes Elmer Mick and his family a round of applause for all their hard work restoring and preserving the Feuerbacher mansion—today and for generations to come.

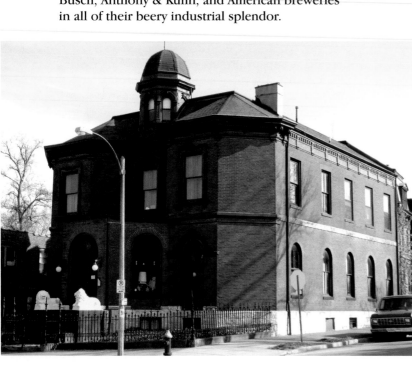

Left: Late 1880s lithograph of girl with serving tray, standing next to a corked bottle of Green Tree Select bottled beer.

Below: Lithograph showing tavern scene.

Facing page: Spring 2009 photo of the Feuerbacher mansion, or "lion house," at 1126 Sidney Street, so nicknamed because of the two large statues astride its steps.

Griesedieck Brothers Brewery Company/ National Brewery Company

National Brewery Company
Northwest corner Eighteenth and Gratiot streets

National Brewery Company	1892–1907
National branch, IBC	1907–1920

Griesedieck Brothers
1900 Shenandoah Avenue

Griesedieck Brothers Brewing Company	1911–1924
Griesedieck Brothers Brewery Company	1933–1957
Falstaff Brewing Corporation Plant #10	1957–1977

Griesedieck Brothers Brewing Company brewhouse, circa 1940s.

The history of the brewing industry in St. Louis is largely a tale of families. From humble beginnings, families such as the Busches, Lemps, Koehlers, and Stifels got rich by making beer. In addition, frequent intermarriage between members of brewing families made the business even more of a family affair. Perhaps no other family had a more significant impact on St. Louis–area brewing than the Griesediecks. The last president of the Griesedieck Brothers Brewery Company, Henry A. Griesedieck, once said in an interview with one of the authors: "It is easier to discuss the breweries in St. Louis that we were not involved in, than the ones we were!"

While Henry's statement was an exaggeration, various branches of the Griesedieck clan were indeed involved in over a dozen area breweries at one time or another. When the industry shakeout of the 1940s and 1950s left just four major local players still operating (Anheuser-Busch, Falstaff, Stag, and Griesedieck Brothers), the latter three were still largely controlled by members of the Griesedieck family.

The brewing lineage of the Griesediecks traces back to Germany in 1766, when Johann Griesedieck began making beer in Stromberg, Westphalia. The building that once housed the Stromberg brewery still stands, now serving appropriately enough as a tavern. More than one hundred years later, some of Johann's descendants made their way to the United States. Anton Griesedieck moved his family across the Atlantic in 1870. They ended up in St. Louis a couple years later, where Anton became involved in the malting business. He branched out into brewing in 1878, joining with August Koehler and Robert Miller to purchase the Thamer Brewing Company, which was then operating out of the former Stumpf Brewery. Doing business as A. Griesedieck & Company, Anton and his partners, along with sons Bernard and Henry Jr. (there's no clue why a man named Anton would have a son named Henry Jr.) enlarged and remodeled the old brewery at Shenandoah Avenue and Buena Vista Street. A new icehouse was also built. The business was incorporated as the A. Griesedieck Brewing Company in 1880.

The Griesediecks were not at their new brewery site for long, however. They sold out for $18,165 at the end of 1881 to the Miller brothers and Henry Wagenhauser. The Griesediecks then turned around and purchased the Phoenix Brewery in St. Louis, marketing their Pearl brand of beer from there until 1889. That year they sold out to the group of British investors known as the St. Louis Brewing Association (SLBA).

National Brewery Opens

The SLBA purchased eighteen local breweries. In the opinion of some, they paid too high a price for many of them. While most of the former brewery operators continued working at their old plants, not so the Griesediecks. They decided to go into competition against the Brits, resigning from the SLBA en masse on June 6, 1891.

The Griesediecks were savvy businessmen who realized that while the SLBA had bought their brewery, longtime retail customers might still be persuaded to buy beer from their old hometown associates. So three sons of Anton Griesedieck (Henry, Bernard, and Joseph) organized the National Brewery Company, building a brand new brewery at Eighteenth and Gratiot streets. While most local brewers used St. Louis architect E. Jungenfeld, the Griesedieck brothers chose August Maritzen of Chicago to design their plant. Corporate officers at National were Henry Griesedieck Jr. as president, Bernard Griesedieck as secretary-treasurer, Joseph "Papa Joe" Griesedieck as superintendent, and youngest brother Frank Griesedieck as assistant superintendent. Beer started moving out the door in the spring of 1892.

Thus began a period of great success for the brothers' brewery. In addition to selling the Standard, Extra Pale, and Pilsner Export draft brands, White Seal and Muenchener were also available in bottles. The jokingly named Willuhafa bottled beer was added at the turn of the century. Known as "The Chief of All Bottled Beers" (likely a play on the local American Brewing Company's slogan "King of All Bottled Beers"), the brand's label featured an odd-looking Indian chief as a logo.

Another wave of brewery consolidation hit St. Louis in 1907, and once again the Griesediecks were in the middle of it. When nine area breweries combined forces to form the Independent Breweries Company (IBC), Henry Griesedieck Jr. was named its corporate president. The IBC continued producing Griesedieck Light Lager at the National plant. Under the guidance of brewmaster Joseph Griesedieck, some of the other old brands were also still made there. According to period ads, Griesedieck Light Lager was "a highly palatable and nourishing beverage, which helps to supply, in a mild form, that energy essential to the human system."

By this time the Griesedieck family had become quite well to do. In 1910, Joseph took time from his brewing duties to take a two-month automobile tour through New England. While motoring to Atlantic City, he stopped by the United States Brewers Academy, from which he had been just the third student to graduate back in 1882. His brother Henry Jr. was suffering from ill health around this time, and in January 1911 resigned from the IBC helm.

Another New Brewery

Once again some of the Griesediecks grew restless working for a conglomerate. In December of 1911, Henry Griesedieck Jr. and his sons bolted from the IBC (which would operate their old National Brewery until 1920) to form the Griesedieck Brothers Brewing Company. Although he owned a majority of the new company's stock, Henry named his son Anton corporate president. This new set of Griesedieck brothers can truly be said to have had brewing in their blood, since their mother was the former Rosa Grone, whose family's Grone Brewery was still operating under the auspices of the SLBA. In addition to Anton, brothers Henry E. and Robert were also stockholders in the new venture. Joining them were brother-in-law Robert Baur, who had married their only sister, Rosa, and E. R. Rombauer.

Rather than building another new plant, the brothers turned to a familiar location for their namesake brewery. For $115,000 they purchased the Consumers Brewery, which had been built in 1896 at the site of the old Stumpf/Thamer facility (and where the Griesediecks had briefly operated their first brewery some thirty years earlier). Consumers had been purchased by the IBC but closed shortly thereafter. The brothers set about rehabbing the plant and were quickly into production. Further construction was begun in 1913, when capital stock was increased from $150,000 to $250,000. Once again the Griesediecks were off and running.

The timing of this new Griesedieck Brothers Brewing Company (GB) could not have been much worse. While the company invested in a new bottle washer and pasteurizer in 1916, the brewing industry was soon plagued by the shortages and rationing of World War I. The thought of Prohibition was clearly on brewers' minds as well, for in 1917 many of them started manufacturing malt beverages with little or no alcohol in them.

By this time Papa Joe Griesedieck had branched out on his own under the banner of Griesedieck Beverage Company. He set up shop in the former Forest Park Brewing Company and introduced a near beer named Hek. While ostensibly a separate company, Griesedieck Beverage was actually closely tied to the Griesedieck Brothers. Papa Joe served as superintendent at both breweries, and some existing Griesedieck Beverage Company records are stamped "Griesedieck Plant #2."

It was a cruel twist of fate that, just prior to the enactment of national Prohibition, Griesedieck's Light Lager brand was the leading seller in the St. Louis beer market. Another twist of fate later found

Papa Joe's Plant #2 evolve into the Falstaff Brewing Corporation, which decades later came back to buy out Griesedieck Brothers.

A Cheating Brewery

When Prohibition became the law of the land, the GB brewery started making root beer, grape fizz, and the non-alcoholic Griesedieck Light Beverage. Real beer continued moving out the door as well, and it was not a very well-kept secret. In her book *Wetter Than the Mississippi*, a study of the Prohibition era, author Robbi Courtaway revealed the content of a June 1921 letter written by Bessie M. Shupp to the governor of Missouri. Shupp, secretary of the state Anti-Saloon League and the daughter of its director, wrote Governor Arthur Hyde:

> Father is out of town today, but asked me to write you giving you the names of the breweries down here that are breaking the law. They are the Louis Obert Brewing Co., 12th and McGirk Sts., the Griesedieck Bros. Brewing Co., 19th and Shenandoah Sts., and the Hyde Park Brewing Co. Most every saloon here is now selling the products of one or more of these breweries.

GB was first nabbed in a raid on June 11, 1921. The company was fined a mere $250. In February 1924, state agents again raided the brewery, seizing more than seven hundred cases of beer and taking into custody corporate Secretary Raymond Griesedieck, Superintendent J. Edward Griesedieck, and forty-three employees. A few months earlier it had been leaked to the *St. Louis Post-Dispatch* that not only was the Griesedieck Brothers Brewing Company still manufacturing real beer, it was doing so under the protection of two crooked state officials.

Brewery officials later became star witnesses at the trial of Prohibition agent Heber Nations, which resulted in the so-called "bright and shining light" of dry law enforcement being convicted of taking bribes in exchange for protecting the brewery. Chief witness Raymond Griesedieck stated that he had been approached by Nations's associate Charles Prather with a protection offer. "I told him I thought one dollar a case was a high price, but that I was going to run and try it," Griesedieck testified. He detailed making numerous cash payments of more than one thousand dollars at both the Jefferson and Claridge hotels. GB brewmaster Ed Wagner, whose confiscated red leather notebook documented seventeen thousand cases of real beer leaving the brewery, testified that 5 percent alcohol beer was bottled at the brewery on seventeen different occasions.

Presumably the brewery remained closed for the balance of the Prohibition years following the 1924 raid. Criminal charges were still pending against Raymond Griesedieck when he died at the age of forty-two in 1930.

Happy Days Again

When the United States finally gave up on Prohibition in 1933, the Griesedieck brothers were anxious to get back in the business. They reorganized under the name Griesedieck Brothers Brewery Company. While not quite prepared to have beer ready in April when it again became legal, they were not far behind, with their product hitting the market in July.

The three remaining Griesedieck brothers headed the revived business, with Anton as president, Robert as vice president, and Edward as corporate secretary. Joining them as officers and investors were Edgar and Raymond Peters, sons of a local shoe magnate. The Peters Shoe Company, formed in 1892, had merged with others into the International Shoe Company in 1911. International

Left: Tin-over-cardboard sign, circa 1916. Note the "Save The Coupons" notation.

Facing page: Cardboard displaying the racehorse Man O' War and four of his sons.

would later end up buying and operating in the former Lemp brewery complex.

It didn't take long for the Griesediecks to once more succeed in the beer business. The new GB had the clever idea of pricing its Light Lager beer cheaper than local competitors Anheuser-Busch and Falstaff. Before these rivals could respond, in the words of Falstaff executive (and relative) Alvin Griesedieck in his book *The Falstaff Story*, "it wasn't long before Griesedieck Brothers had literally taken over the town."

By 1936, sales were double the largest of any pre-Prohibition production year, and about 75 percent above those of 1935. In fact, GB had to terminate the contracts of some of its distributors because the brewery could not brew beer fast enough to fill all the orders that were pouring in. Buoyed by this success, GB immediately began to further modernize and expand its plant, including the installation of two new three-hundred-barrel brew kettles. From 1933 to 1939, around $2 million was spent on improvements, leading to a doubling of brewing capacity.

According to a 1935 article in *American Brewer*, Griesedieck Brothers was among the industry leaders in the marketing of beer to women. It was a logical sales strategy for two reasons. First, ladies were seen as potential customers in their own right.

Second, as they were typically the family grocery shoppers, housewives could influence which beers were purchased for home consumption. One GB newspaper ad of the time featured a stylishly dressed young lady on the telephone to her local grocery with the tag lines "Griesedieck Bros Beer on your grocery list? Party tonight? Is there enough in the ice box?"

Griesedieck Brothers was also one of the first breweries to use cartoons in its advertising. Many such ads were patterned after Robert L. Ripley's "Believe It or Not" newspaper features. In this campaign, the brewery set about providing facts about beer, the brewing process, and the importance of quality—all the while working in pitches touting the merits of its particular brand of brew. One cartoon read: "Only perfectly healthy yeast makes perfect beer. The yeast in [GB beer] is scientifically tested. That's why GB is of such high uniform quality—Drink all you want—it's good for you!" Another of these cartoons invoked the medical profession as a sales tool: "Reasons Why Doctors Prescribe Beer—1. As a nerve stimulant. 2. For vitamin B content. 3. As an aid to digestion. Fill the prescription with perfectly balanced Griesedieck Bros. Beer—You'll feel better."

Unfortunately, GB President Anton Griesedieck would not be around much longer to enjoy the success this clever advertising was bringing to his brewery. He passed away on December 4, 1935, at age fifty-five. He was succeeded as brewery chief by his brother Robert.

GB—GOOD BUSINESSMEN

Griesedieck Brothers was not afraid to try new things to sell beer. In 1936, the brewery became one of the first to use the so-called Handy bottle for its Light Lager. A case of these squat containers was said to weigh sixteen pounds less than regular bottles. While many competitors sold this bottle as a throwaway, GB marketed them as returnables.

By 1941, production was up to four hundred thousand barrels per year, and that spring the brewery became the first in St. Louis to start utilizing the Crowntainer can. The brewery's decision to start putting the Double Mellow brand in cans prompted Crowntainer maker Crown Cork and Seal to take out a full-page ad in *American Brewer*. In the ad GB purchasing agent J. P. Huelsing crowed, "Crowntainers are just the thing for beer. These seamless Crowntainers certainly keep out all foreign tastes."

A huge factor in the success of Griesedieck Brothers had been brewmaster Harry Birsner, a well-traveled veteran brewer and a native of St. Louis. When Birsner left for the Atlas Brewing Company of Chicago in 1941, he was replaced by young Edward Vogel Jr., who would likewise enjoy a long and illustrious career in the industry. Vogel's accomplishments included co-authoring the well-known book *The Practical Brewer*, writing magazine articles on brewing, and later becoming GB vice president. Following his career at Griesedieck Brothers, he went on to hold numerous lofty positions at Anheuser-Busch.

Griesedieck Brothers continued to expand during the 1940s, and for a time the brand was the best-selling beer in St. Louis. Disaster struck the company in 1942, however, when President Robert Griesedieck died following a car wreck. Succeeding him was youngest brother Edward. The Peters brothers likewise moved up the corporate ladder at this time. The 1940s also saw the brewery gain radio sponsorship rights to St. Louis Cardinals baseball games and Saint Louis University basketball contests. During games broadcast over the Griesedieck Brothers Cardinal Baseball Network, announcer Harry Caray urged listeners to drink GB. At its zenith, the network boasted more than ninety radio stations scattered across ten states.

In November 1947, the company began another $2 million expansion program, including a new boiler house, a $750,000 fermentation house, a stockhouse, and another bottling shop. By 1950, yearly production was close to a million barrels, and GB beer could be found on shelves in twelve midwestern states. Griesedieck Brothers was always quick to take on local competitors. When the brewers of Alpen Brau began a sales promotion urging customers to turn in their used bottle caps for Eagle Stamps, GB tried to trump the scheme by instead handing out cash for its crowns.

GB certainly didn't scrimp when it came to spending on advertising. By the late 1940s, it was spending $2 million a year on billboard, radio, television, and newspaper ads. Ever searching for new markets on which to spend its advertising budget, Griesedieck Brothers went after African American consumers in a big way. The brewery initially employed black disc jockeys in East St. Louis and Memphis, later expanding the practice into a list of locations that one period source described as "much too long to enumerate."

FINAL DECADE

The early 1950s proved to be the high-water mark for the Griesedieck Brothers Brewing Company. Sales were up, and the plant was continuously being updated. In its best production years the brewery was running two ten-hour shifts. Around this time GB introduced a new advertising slogan, "It's De-Bitterized," backed by a patented brewing technique initiated at the brewery in 1949. According to inventor Rudolph

Brewed the Old World Way for the Taste of Today

The Original Griesedieck Bros.

take home 6

Gull, the customized de-bittering method allowed the brewery to "brew beer free from a coarse and bitter taste, in a closed fermenter, due to the fact that the bitter sediment contained in the foam is separated from the other foam at this stage and is of such construction that it can be collected and carried back into the fermentation chamber." Gull had developed his process back in the late 1930s when he was a brewmaster at Anheuser-Busch. Whether the general public really understood what Dr. Gull was talking about is doubtful, but sales did increase during the years of the "It's De-Bitterized" marketing campaign.

The fact that the GB plant was one of the most modern and efficient in the country did not go unnoticed. In 1952, the Theodore Hamm Brewing Company of St. Paul, Minnesota, looking to expand production, made a serious attempt to buy the GB facility, with the intent of killing the GB brand and producing Hamm's in St. Louis. While it came close, the deal did not go through. The Griesediecks wanted more money than Hamm was willing to cough up, and were not overly motivated to sell as the business was still profitable. After this proposed sale collapsed, GB brewmaster Edward Vogel advised that if the company was not going to sell out, it had better expand in order to remain competitive. Vogel proposed building a branch brewery in Memphis, Tennessee. The idea made business sense, as GB sales were booming in that section of the country. But while extensive plans were drawn up, the new plant was never built. According to one source, the Griesedieck family felt it was making all the money it needed and didn't want to borrow any, which would have been required for financing the Memphis expansion.

The St. Louis Cardinals baseball team, long a focus for GB's advertising efforts, was put up for sale in 1952. The brewery was given first option to buy the team but passed, a decision it would soon regret.

Crosstown rival Anheuser-Busch would not make the same mistake, purchasing the ball club the following March after it seemed likely that it would be sold to a group from Milwaukee. Ironically, while A-B owned the Cardinals for the 1953 baseball season, Griesedieck Brothers was still sponsoring the team's radio and television broadcasts due to a pre-existing ironclad contract. After losing sponsorship of the Redbirds, GB sales would begin sliding downwards while A-B's would climb.

Anheuser-Busch added insult to injury by hiring away longtime GB pitchman Harry Caray to announce Cardinals broadcasts. Millions of listeners who used to hear Caray touting the merits of "GB—Good Beer" between innings would now be told about the merits of Budweiser (years later Caray would have a falling out with the Cardinals, publicly snub Budweiser, and proclaim Schlitz a better beer).

In November 1953, Griesedieck Brothers introduced its Jubilee series of flat-top cans. While the colorful can sets produced by a number of breweries in the 1950s are today frequently (and often erroneously) tagged by collectors as "Christmas can sets," the GB series was the real deal, specifically marketed during the December holiday season. Produced in at least six colors, the 1953 Jubilee cans

Facing page: A "3-D" cardboard sign, advertising GB's 1955 series of "Jubilee" multi-colored cans.

Right: Tin-over-cardboard sign, highlighting the new "Handy" bottle.

Far right: Menu cover showcasing the Griesedieck Brothers Crowntainer can design.

feature a pilsner glass on the label. The redesigned sets marketed in 1954 and 1955 were produced in at least a dozen background colors. They can be dated by design, with the 1954 series featuring "Griesedieck Brothers" in block letters whereas the later cans used script writing.

Even though it had passed on buying the Cardinals, GB management was still well aware that good relations with the local community could translate directly into sales. In 1954, the company spent $140,000 to build a unique hospitality house, designed in the tradition of a seventeenth-century European tavern. GB Stein Hall, as it came to be called, was designed as a site for entertaining guests and where civic, religious, and social organizations could meet; it even had air conditioning. "It will reflect the good cheer and good fellowship that have been associated with good beer through the centuries," announced Edward Griesedieck. In addition to parties for tavern owners and distributors hosted by the brewery, the public could also arrange to have meetings in Stein Hall. The brewery provided visitors with free beer and snacks and gave away advertising ashtrays. Guests could admire Edward Griesedieck's impressive collection of steins, many of which were more than one hundred years old and on permanent display at the hall. Around this same time, the brewery made a cash grant to the Missouri Historical Society to establish a brewing industry historical collection, perhaps the first of its kind in the country.

Also in 1954 rival Anheuser-Busch decided to bring a "budget" beer to market. With its St. Louis facility running at full capacity, A-B tried to buy the Griesedieck Brothers plant to produce its planned Busch brand beer. Anheuser-Busch even sent informal proposals to Falstaff, suggesting the bizarre plan that the two brewing giants jointly buy out GB and share split production there. In the end, A-B's offer was rebuffed by GB ownership.

Although A-B wasn't allowed to buy the Griesedieck Brothers brewery, it did manage to hire away brewmaster Vogel two years later. The blow to GB was more than just the loss of a talented employee. Henry A. Griesedieck, the last president of the company, went to his grave claiming that after Vogel jumped ship, Busch Bavarian began tasting exactly like GB-formula beer masquerading in an A-B-filled can. Also according to Henry, the cheaper-selling Busch brand cut heavily into sales of GB.

Griesedieck Brothers soon realized it needed to market its own "budget beer" to keep up with the competition, and decided to do so in a way it hoped would not tarnish its flagship brand. So when it launched Old St. Louis Select in the fall of

1956, the cans listed Lami Brewery as producer. The Lami name was derived from the name of a city street that bisected the brewery property (and later disappeared, swallowed up by a plant expansion).

Around this same time, advertising started emphasizing that Griesedieck beer was now being krausened. In a publicity stunt, cases of the new beer were shipped via air express to folks described as leading brewmasters in nine European countries. It is unknown whether or not these international brewers liked the naturally bubbly GB brew.

FALSTAFF GRIESEDIECKS BUY GB

On 1955, Edward Griesedieck, the last of the second set of Griesedieck brothers, died at age fifty-nine. His place atop the company was taken by nephew Henry A. "Hank" Griesedieck, who was only thirty-nine at the time. Other youthful family members serving as corporate officers were Edward J. Griesedieck, executive vice president, Robert Anton "Bubby" Griesedieck (like brother Edward J. a graduate of Notre Dame), and William H. Griesedieck, who supervised the firm's public relations department.

Edward Griesedieck's passing created a crisis for the owners of the brewery. The company was still a closed corporation, with all of the stock belonging to Griesedieck family members. Because the stock was so closely held, the Internal Revenue Service slammed the estate with a mammoth tax bill. To maintain control of the business, the family would have had to stretch itself financially to scrape up the cash needed to pay the tax man. This problem, combined with a recent downward trend in sales and the fact that the brewery was actually losing money, convinced the family that it was finally time to sell. Company President Hank Griesedieck entered into negotiations to sell the plant to the Griesediecks—the Falstaff branch of the Griesediecks, that is.

While Falstaff had purchased the Columbia Brewing Company of St. Louis in 1948, it was still looking for additional local brewing capacity due to ever-burgeoning sales. When it became known that GB was up for grabs, Falstaff jumped at the opportunity. The sale was closed in 1957, with the GB brewery renamed Falstaff Plant #10.

After taking possession of its former rival, Falstaff immediately killed the Griesedieck Brothers brand, and after some minor plant modifications began brewing "premium quality" Falstaff there. It was a great deal for Falstaff, as it picked up a state-of-the-art brewery where $7 million had been spent on expansion and equipment upgrades since the end World War II. In 1964, Falstaff converted the former GB Stein Hall into the Falstaff International Museum of Brewing, featuring the brewing history of all St. Louis breweries.

By the late 1960s, Falstaff had grown into one of the largest brewers in the country, with a portion of the success attributable to the takeover of the efficient GB plant. But by the mid-1970s, Falstaff found itself in financial trouble. Perhaps hopeful that St. Louis beer drinkers had forgotten the cursory manner in which the Griesedieck Brothers brand had been killed off, Falstaff resurrected GB beer in 1976. According to Falstaff advertising at the time, the revised GB, available in both cans and bottles, was being brewed using the original formula. While claiming the move was being made out of nostalgia, the truth was that Falstaff was bringing GB back to market as part of a desperation move to save itself. It didn't work. While initial sales of the revived GB were promising, demand soon collapsed. Falstaff's corporate performance continued to slide, too. Soon the company would cease being a major player in the U.S. beer industry.

In 1977, Falstaff closed both Plant #10 and the brewing museum for good. Thus ended the brewing of the original Griesedieck beer at the former GB brewery location. The majority of the plant built as the Consumers Brewery still stands, with most of the space converted into warehouse and light industrial use. An attempt by the Meramec Brewing Company to open a microbrewery in a former stockhouse failed because of higher-than-expected construction costs.

GB BACK AGAIN & AGAIN

The second rebirth of Griesedieck Brothers beer occurred a decade later. In July of 1987, the newly formed Griesedieck Bros. Brewery Co., Inc., of St. Louis announced the brand would again return to local retailers' shelves. Entrepreneur Steve DeBellis masterminded this return of GB by contracting with the Hibernia Brewery of Eau Claire, Wisconsin, to brew and package his version of the beer. The new GB cans featured designs reminiscent of earlier Griesedieck Brothers packaging.

Today, ownership of the Griesedieck Brothers brand trademark is back in the hands of the "GB" branch of the family. Griesedieck Brothers beer is back on tap and in bottles at various St. Louis–area locations. The brand is currently being brewed in Black River Falls, Wisconsin. The backers of this fuller-flavored GB stated on their website that their goal was to build a local microbrewery when sales justified the expenditure. If it ever gets built, the brewers at the new plant will certainly be able to point back to the illustrious history of Griesedieck Brothers beer in St. Louis.

1940s vintage photo of the GB brewery smokestack.

H. Grone Brewery Company
(a.k.a. Clark Avenue Brewery)

2219 Clark Avenue

H. Grone & Company	c. 1864–c. 1882
H. Grone Brewery Company	c. 1882-1889
Grone branch, SLBA	1889–1918

Top: Grone Brewery workers photo, dating to after the SLBA merger.

Middle: Brewery scene, circa 1895.

Bottom: John Kunz's tavern with Grone signs.

According to the 1903 tome *100 Years of Brewing*, the H. Grone Brewery Company "originated in the crude brewhouse for the making of lager beer which was erected by Henry Grone, Herman Damhorst and John Whelan, in 1861." Prior to 1860 the same three men had started a soda business at Eleventh and Market streets. The soda plant continued there for a number of years, with the location also serving as the brewery office. It is unclear if the original brewery was at the same location as the soda business, or at the Clark Avenue location where it was destined to operate for six decades. An 1864 city directory lists the brewery of Henry "Crone" and Company on the east side of Menard between Victor and Sidney. This was the site of the Gambrinus/Jaeger brewery (later Anthony & Kuhn), so either a misprint or a clue that Grone, Damhorst, and Whelan had temporarily set up shop in the Soulard neighborhood.

Henry Grone was born in Westphalia, Germany, in 1826. How he came to end up in St. Louis and what his brewing background was are mysteries. The establishment of his namesake brewery on Clark Avenue is first documented locally by its appearance in an 1865 city directory. Like many of its contemporaries, the Grone family residence and a brewery-owned saloon were also located on the site.

The business was known as the Clark Avenue Brewery during its early life, but by the 1880s the H. Grone Brewery Company tag was adopted. The brewery was quite successful. Production reached nearly 20,000 barrels annually (ranking ninth of twenty-nine local breweries) in the early 1870s, which increased to 27,532 barrels in 1878. That year a new icehouse was built and other improvements made to the facility. According to *The Western Brewer*, at the time the Grone Brewery was "doing a local trade exclusively."

Herman Damhorst died in 1877 and was succeeded by Ernst Link. Grone's 1884 production figure was between thirty-five thousand and forty thousand barrels. This enabled it to check in at number eight on the list of twenty-two St. Louis breweries. Growing sales demanded greater production, so numerous additions and improvements were made to the plant in the mid-1880s. This helped make it attractive to potential suitors, as a wave of consolidation began to hit the national and St. Louis brewing scenes. In 1889, the Grone plant was one of eighteen merged into the St. Louis Brewing Association (SLBA). Within a few months the syndicate was sold to English investors, capitalized at a whopping $14 million. The new owners retained Henry Grone as brewery manager, and he stayed until his retirement in 1898.

Two of Grone's sons had stayed active in the former family brewery as well. John G. Grone, who was born in St. Louis in 1864 and grew up in the business, succeeded his father as branch manager. In addition, he was active in the continuing Grone and Company soda water business and a longtime second vice president of the SLBA. His brother Herman Grone joined him as the brewery's assistant manager.

Brewery founder Henry Grone passed away in 1903. Herman Grone died in 1916 at the rather young age of forty-five. In June of 1916, John Grone announced that he was resigning as manager of the Grone branch, though retaining his financial interest in the SLBA.

The Western Brewer further reported that John Grone was leaving the beer business in order to devote his entire time to managing the Grone estate. The very next day Frank Forster, who had resigned as SLBA vice president two weeks earlier (supposedly to devote his attention to the Frank J. Forster Baking Company), withdrew his resignation. SLBA President Henry Nicolaus assured *American Brewer* that "there had been no friction between board members" and that John Grone would continue with the association as a consultant.

Whether or not this shows that there was some undisclosed corporate monkey business going on within the SLBA, it became a moot point. The brewing industry was soon hobbled by wartime restrictions and within a few years shut down completely by national Prohibition. While the SLBA had closed a number of its original eighteen breweries over the years, the Grone branch remained open longer than many, operating until September 1918.

When the Eighteenth Amendment was repealed fifteen years later, the Grone plant was never mentioned as a candidate for reopening. Among the SLBA plants, only the Hyde Park facility

would have a second life. The four-story Grone brewhouse was torn down in 1941. The Clark Avenue/Grone Brewery was briefly back in the news in a 1979 *St. Louis Post-Dispatch* article. On December 5, 1978, a bulldozer operator discovered several underground openings while preparing a building site at Twenty-second Street and Clark Avenue. George Hensley, president of Schneider-Hensley Construction Company, went down a forty-foot ladder and encountered a flooded room. After about ninety thousand gallons of water were pumped out, Hensley and architect Donald Wilson entered the chamber and found two brick and stone vaults 18′ × 78′ across and 18′ high. Some strange items turned up in these old brewery cellars, including unused stacks of post-Prohibition beer bottle label sheets from various breweries in Minnesota, Ohio, Kansas, and California. What they were doing in the Grone caves was a baffling mystery.

Since the old beer vaults were found to be structurally sound, the entrances were sealed and it was declared they would present no danger to the one-story office and warehouse which were to be built above them. They are undoubtedly still down there, all that remains of the H. Grone Brewery Company.

While the Grones disappeared from the St. Louis brewing industry, the family remained active in other local businesses. One was Grone Construction, a building company that among other projects worked on the Bevo Mill for Anheuser-Busch. According to family members, if a St. Louis building included a stork in the design, it was built by the Grones, who used the bird as their symbol. The well-known Grone Cafeteria, opened in 1931, was another of the family's ventures. A second restaurant was later started. Both remained in business until 2004.

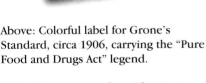

Above: Colorful label for Grone's Standard, circa 1906, carrying the "Pure Food and Drugs Act" legend.

Right: Factory scene from *The Western Brewer*, June 1879.

Home Brewing Company
(and predecessors)

Pfund/German Brewery
1710-12 Carondelet Avenue

Frederick Pfund	1857–c. 1858
Eckerle & Weiss	c. 1858–1864
German Brewery, Eckerle & Siemon	1864–1867
German Brewery, Theobald Eckerle	1867–1870

Southeast corner of Miami Street and Capitol Avenue
(new brewery)

German Brewery, Theobald Eckerle	1869–1871
Bavarian Branch, E. Anheuser & Co.	1871–1875
Bavarian Branch, E. Anheuser Co.'s Brewing Association	1875–1879

3601 Salena Street (address change)

Home Brewing Company	1892–1907
Home branch, IBC	1907–1909

Top: Circa 1895 factory scene, first published in E. Jungenfeld & Co.'s *Portfolio*.

Bottom: Heidelberg label boasting "Genuine German Beer."

The site of the Home Brewing Company, which opened in 1892 at 3601 Salena Street, has one of the most fascinating histories of any brewground in St. Louis. It was known as the German Brewery in its early years, served as a branch of the E. Anheuser Co.'s Brewing Association in the 1870s, then years later became the location of the Home Brewing Company, a completely new brewery. More recently it has hosted the new Gambrinus Hall, a meeting place and the main offices for the Brewers and Maltsters Local #6 Union, today known as Teamsters Local #6.

What eventually evolved into the Home Brewing Company started with a brewery opened by Frederick Pfund around 1857 at 155 Carondelet Avenue (now South Broadway). Within a couple of years the concern was taken over by brewing partners Theobald (sometimes called Theodore) Eckerle and Mathias Weiss.

When Weiss left in 1864 to head over to the nearby Arsenal Brewery, he was replaced by Frederick Siemon. From a well-to-do German family (his father was once superintendent of the German mail system), Siemon had nonetheless learned coopering and brewing at an early age, serving a three-and-a-half-year apprenticeship at those trades in his native land. In 1834, at age seventeen, Siemon arrived in St. Louis. He first got a job in Stephen Stock's Oregon Brewery. His biography in the 1906 *Book of St. Louisans* says that from 1836 to 1847 he was "foreman of a brewery located at the corner of Seventh and Sidney Streets" that went unnamed. The Oregon Brewery was on Seventh Street (though not at Sidney) so it is unclear if this is a reference to it or a different brewery. Siemon then went back to Germany for some time before returning to St. Louis to team with Eckerle.

By the mid-1860s the partners were calling their business the German Brewery. During this period Eckerle also operated a malting company at 607 Geyer Street, not far from Tony Faust's famous restaurant. In addition to their brewery at the renumbered 1710–12 Carondelet, Eckerle and Siemon had built large beer storage vaults many blocks up the street at the corner of Miami Street and Capitol Avenue, just off Carondelet.

Fred Siemon retired in 1867, although by the next year he had become a partner in the Lincoln Brewery in East St. Louis. This left Eckerle as the German Brewery's sole proprietor. He began construction of a new brewery over the site of the cellars in the late 1860s. Both sites apparently operated concurrently for a couple of years, but by 1871 the old brewery was closed and beer making moved to the new location exclusively.

Eckerle was not long for his new venture. A mile or so down the road, a rapidly growing brewing concern owned by Eberhard Anheuser and his partner and son-in-law Adolphus Busch found itself needing more production and storage capacity because of its ever-increasing sales. E. Anheuser & Co. (Anheuser and Busch) decided to purchase the German Brewery from Eckerle. As Anheuser and Busch's plant was then known as the Bavarian Brewery, the newly purchased facility operated as the Bavarian Branch Brewery for nearly a decade. So, contrary to popular belief, A-B's first satellite brewery was not the one opened in Newark, New Jersey, in 1951, but rather the former German Brewery in its hometown.

The Bavarian branch continued operating under that name even after Anheuser and Busch dropped the "Bavarian" moniker from their main brewery in favor of E. Anheuser Co.'s Brewing Association. In 1879, when the U.S. Brewers Convention was held in St. Louis, an account in *The Western Brewer* mentioned that the branch was still open. Soon thereafter, though, it was closed, as it no longer appears in city directories after 1879. While the again renamed Anheuser-Busch Brewing Association continued its staggering growth, expansions and improvements at the main plant had rendered a branch brewery unnecessary.

The local beer market continued to grow through the next decade, and the buyout of many area breweries by the St. Louis Brewing Association (SLBA) conglomerate in 1889 left numerous former brewers with an itch to get back into the business. Thus would the old German/Bavarian location once more rise up to serve the industry.

In 1891, Theodore Herold, who had worked at his father's Cherokee Brewery in St. Louis, organized and became president of a concern calling itself the Home Brewing Company. While the new investors considered adopting the name Kaiser Hill Brewery, they ended up choosing the Home name likely for two reasons: first as a ploy to sell the company's bottled product to home consumers, and second as a reminder that its owners were local men, not British investors like the owners of the SLBA breweries.

Home was incorporated on December 16, 1891, with $250,000 of stock equally divided between Theodore Herold, who was named company president; his brother Robert F. Herold, who would serve as plant superintendent; William Stutz, who was named vice president; and Anton C. (Tony) Steuver, who with his father Charles (Carl) would go on to play a prominent role in the business. The partners proceeded to construct an all-new brewery, designed by E. Jungenfeld and Company, on the site of the old German/Bavarian plant. Home beer first hit the market on March 10, 1892. Built with an annual capacity of seventy-five thousand barrels, the brewery employed more than forty men, thirty horses, and ten wagons. Among the brands produced were Standard Lager, Genuine

German Beer, and Imperial Pale. Many of Home's advertisements stressed its product as "genuine German beer," suggesting that only water, barley, hops, and yeast were used in the brewing process. It was also a fitting motto for a plant that traced its roots to the former German Brewery.

In 1895, the Herold brothers transferred their stock in the Home Brewing Company to Carl and Tony Steuver in exchange for $87,500 cash. Carl took over as company president. The Herolds soon started the rival Consumers Brewing Company.

A native of Germany and a '49er during the California gold rush, Carl Steuver led the Home Brewing Company until his death in 1900. He was also instrumental in developing the Forest Park Highlands both as an entertainment venue and as a sales outlet for Home-brewed beer. The brewery had helped finance the 1896 opening of the Highlands Cottage Restaurant, a beer garden in Forest Park. When the original owners failed, the Steuvers took over operations and added an amusement park. New rides and attractions were added yearly. John Philip Sousa was among the performers on the bandstand, which had been adapted from the Japanese pagoda at the 1904 World's Fair.

Tony Steuver, who was born in Clinton County, Illinois, in 1866, succeeded his father as corporate president and treasurer. He had come to St. Louis as a boy with his parents and was a graduate of Saint Louis University. While spending his working career in brewing, he would also find time to be a prominent Democratic politician and a St. Louis police commissioner. Steuver had worked for the Green Tree Brewery early in his beer career. Steuver flirted with disaster in December 1906 when he was involved in a car wreck, ramming into a streetcar at the intersection of Kingshighway and Delmar. While "severely bruised," Steuver and his passenger were not seriously hurt, but *The Western Brewer* said that "the auto, which is one of the finest in St. Louis, was damaged to the extent of $500."

Robert Hafferkamp, longtime brewery manager, was another prominent player in the Home Brewing Company. When he retired in 1908, after spending more than fifteen years on the job, company employees pooled their resources and presented him with a silver-handled umbrella.

Perhaps Hafferkamp had seen storm clouds on the horizon. One of numerous plants that had been purchased by the Independent Breweries Company syndicate in 1907, the Home Brewery branch was closed in early spring of 1909. An insurance map published that year indicates the brewery was "Not in Operation, To Be Removed." This same map also shows the nearby fireman's engine house #3, a wonderful building that stands in the neighborhood to this day. Steuver's Cottage Restaurant closed in 1920, and two years later, with his health failing, Tony Steuver sold the Forest Park Highlands.

The old Home brewery neighborhood wound up serving the industry once more in 1911, when the Brewers and Maltsters Local #6 established its Gambrinus Hall in the vacant Shepard School. The three-story main building was literally in the shadow of the old Home brewhouse and served as the union's business office. It included a large assembly hall for meetings and a long basement bar. A bowling alley was also added. In January 1964, the remaining brewery buildings and Gambrinus Hall were scheduled to be torn down to make room for a parking lot and a new union hall. Portions of the underground cellars were to be filled with bricks taken from the nearby General Conveyor Manufacturing Building, which was also being demolished.

The impending destruction/construction came to the attention of local spelunkers Hubert and Charlotte Rother. Their underground explorations revealed a remarkable series of storage caves and a number of well-preserved large wooden beer vats. According to their book *Lost Caves of St. Louis*, "the Home Brewery Cave was one of the most interesting caves we had ever explored . . . it had a vast network of cellars built on three levels. It was also the only brewery cave we ever visited that still had intact beer vats."

Today all above-ground traces of the Home Brewing Company have disappeared. Underground, the partially filled caverns and moldering vats are hidden reminders of the site's interesting history. Nearby, the new Gambrinus Hall continues to serve Teamsters Local #6, even surviving the 1966 wedding reception of one of the authors.

Brewery workers wearing Brewers and Maltsters Local #6 ribbons, drinking dark beer, and surrounded by great breweriana.

Only a handful of the breweries in St. Louis were located in the northern part of town. The longest-lived of these was the Hyde Park brewery at 3607 N. Florissant Avenue, where brewing took place under a variety of regimes for nearly a century.

The neighborhood where the brewery was built was originally a part of the town of Bremen. German immigrants were enticed to Bremen by Emil Mallinckrodt, who promised them cheap land and a predominantly German local culture. His strategy worked, as the new settlement reminded him so much of the fatherland that he noted, "One [in Bremen] believes he is in Germany when he hears *Plattdeutsch* [low German] and the clatter of wooden shoes in the street." Bremen would eventually lose its autonomy, swallowed up in 1855 by the expanding city of St. Louis.

William Moran began brewing at what became the Hyde Park brewery in 1862. An 1864 city directory refers to Moran's establishment as the Heckar Brewery. This is likely a misspelling of Hecker, indicating that the brewery was named after German revolutionary Frederick Hecker, who had launched a failed war in an attempt to form a German republic. In 1848, he moved to a farm in Summerfield, Illinois, about thirty miles from St. Louis. Hecker had fought in the U.S. Civil War as a colonel in his own regiment from 1861 to 1864. Though it is not known if Hecker had any connection with the brewery, the name would certainly have been popular among the local Germans.

While Hecker became one of the most beloved of all German democrats, the brewery name didn't last, as by 1868 William Moran's brewery had taken on the Emmet Brewery tag. This is another name obscured by time, but it may have just been Moran using the name of another revolutionary, as Robert Emmet was an Irish rebel hero who inspired an aborted uprising in 1803. At the age of twenty-seven, Emmet was tried for treason and hanged, ensuring his legacy as a romantic hero. With a name like Moran, the brewery owner was likely an Irishman, so it is certainly possible he was moved to name his brewery after the Irish martyr. Unfortunately, Moran himself is an obscure figure in St. Louis brewing, leaving both him and his brewery names a bit mysterious.

William Moran's Emmet Brewery produced 4,724 barrels of beer during the 1873–74 brewing year. That total ranked it twenty-first out of twenty-nine breweries operating in St. Louis. Moran continued running the business until 1876, when it was sold to veteran St. Louis brewer Robert Jacob, who had recently sold his one-quarter interest in the Wainwright Brewery to Ellis Wainwright. Joining Jacob as a partner in his new venture was local maltster Marquard Forster.

Early in 1878, Robert Jacob abruptly ended his involvement in the brewery, selling his share to a gentleman named L. Bergen. Jacob soon opened a brewer's supply

Hyde Park Breweries Association

3607 N. Florissant Avenue

William Moran, Hecker Brewery	1862–c. 1868
William Moran, Emmet Brewery	c. 1868–1876
Jacob & Forster	1876–1878
Forster & Bergen	1878–1878
Hyde Park Brewing Company	1878–1889
Hyde Park branch, SLBA	1889–1919
Hyde Park Breweries Association, Inc.	1933–1948
Hyde Park Breweries Association (division Griesedieck-Western)	1948–1954
Carling Brewing Company	1954–1957

Top: Hyde Park as it appeared in the 1930s.

Bottom: Henry Nicolaus from the "Men Whom You Know" column in the April 1938 issue of *Modern Brewer.*

house, which according to *The Western Brewer* "in an incredible short space of time has established a large trade . . . in hops, malt, barley and everything needed in a brewery." Despite such accolades, within two years Jacob's new company had failed and was assigned in bankruptcy court.

His former brewery was to meet quite a different fate, however. The year that Forster had become a partner in the brewery, it had produced just 3,804 barrels. Such small production made the beer from Forster & Bergen's brewery an extremely unlikely candidate to become a St. Louis household word, but that's exactly what Hyde Park was destined to become.

Forster bought out partner Bergen in the fall of 1878, and the business was then incorporated as the Hyde Park Brewing Company, taking its name both from the neighborhood where it was located and also a nearby city park. Marquard Forster was president, and his sons C. Marquard and C. August were secretary and treasurer-superintendent, respectively. Marquard Forster was a native of Bavaria who had immigrated to St. Louis in 1846. He established a vinegar factory and grocery (similar to pioneering brewer Adam Lemp) at Fourteenth and Spruce streets that operated for many years, and later went into the malting business. He eventually purchased the Hunicke malt house at Sixth and Gratiot, a plant that would continue serving his Hyde Park brewery for years to come.

In a strange bit of irony, Julius Hunicke, who had sold his malt house to Forster, was later associated with Robert Jacob's failed brewery supply house. This left Forster successfully carrying on both of the businesses that the two partners in the failed company had sold to him. As for Robert Jacob, he would go to work for Anheuser-Busch following the bankruptcy, not surprising as he was married to a niece of Adolphus Busch.

August Forster, Marquard's eldest son, was born in 1853. He attended Washington University in St. Louis, then at age nineteen left to attend brewing school in Germany, where he apprenticed at several breweries before returning home in 1876. At a time when mechanization was beginning to drastically change the brewing business, August's experience with the modern methods of European brewing prepared the Forsters to begin

expanding. What had essentially been a neighborhood brewery was about to turn into something much bigger.

New buildings and equipment were soon up and running, with production increasing to nearly ten thousand barrels in 1878 and over fourteen thousand barrels the next year. By 1884, production had skyrocketed to over forty thousand barrels. In less than a decade Hyde Park had grown from one of the smallest to one of the largest St. Louis breweries.

The Forsters sold the Hyde Park Brewing Company to the St. Louis Brewing Association (SLBA) syndicate in 1889. This group bought out most of the breweries in St. Louis, while retaining many of their former operators as managers. August Forster continued managing the Hyde Park branch, and brewmaster Otto Ritter also stayed on. Likewise, brother C. Marquard Forster became an SLBA director and manager of the company's City Brewery branch. Joining the Forsters in the business was their youngest brother Frank, who became assistant manager of the Hyde Park plant.

The British investors financed an expansion of Hyde Park in 1892, building a new brewhouse that featured a five-story malt storage section. Marquard Forster passed away in 1900, the same year son C. Marquard was named an SLBA vice president. The elder Forster had left the beer business to his sons, devoting most of his later years to numerous real estate ventures. Just two years later August Forster died from Bright's disease. He was only forty-nine years old.

The Hyde Park brewery became one of the SLBA's primary facilities and was the site of continuing additions and improvements. In 1907, Hyde Park bottled beer was introduced. It was to become a top local seller and the flagship label of the SLBA facilities. While the brand was still being brewed at the Hyde Park plant, it was at first being bottled only at the SLBA's Lafayette branch. To advertise this new bottled product, the motto "Seldom Equaled—Never Excelled" was used. This pitch was destined to reappear after Prohibition as well. Period ads also emphasized the lengthy aging period ("many months") used to produce Hyde Park beer.

C. Marquard Forster died in 1912. In addition to his brewing activities he had been involved in numerous trust companies and banks, as well as vice president of the Kinloch Telephone Company. Remaining brother Frank Forster replaced his sibling as first vice president of the SLBA, and also served as Hyde Park plant manager from 1911 to 1918. In 1916, he an-

Above: Hyde Park brewery workers photo before Prohibition. Note "Hyde Park Beer" flag above the workers' heads.

Facing page: Pre-Prohibition portrait of Marquard Forster.

nounced he was resigning from the office of SLBA vice president, but his associates soon talked him into staying. Whatever politics were being played on the corporate level, before long the brewing business would be history. Frank Forster would later serve the industry as vice president and sales manager of the post-Prohibition revival of the Columbia Brewing Company in St. Louis. He was diversified as well, being principal owner of the Frank J. Forster Baking Company before passing away at age sixty-four in 1936.

While the clouds of national Prohibition were forming on the horizon, some brewers remained optimistic and continued to upgrade their plants. The early years of the twentieth century were seeing constant innovations in bottling processes, and in 1916 three bottling units, each capable of filling six thousand bottles per hour, were installed at the Hyde Park brewery. Within a few years, these state-of-the-art machines would fall silent as the Eighteenth Amendment became the law of the United States.

Strange stories concerning the Hyde Park brewery appeared in St. Louis newspapers in early July 1919. They told the tale of Spot the dog, with the *St. Louis Post* carrying the headline "Dog Spot Is Dead!" For ten years Spot had been the faithful pet of Joe Biersinger, stable foreman for Hyde Park. It was said of the dog that he was almost human in some ways. For one thing, the canine traveled daily from his home in the stable to the brewery's taproom for a glass of beer. After refreshing

himself, Spot was said to be ready for a bout with anything on four legs or two, whichever happened to wander across his path. Alas, with the enactment of Prohibition, good dog Spot was forced to forego his daily sip of the suds. Spot's suffering was short-lived, however, as he was run over by an automobile at Eleventh and Gratiot streets shortly after his beer supply was cut off by the law. Hyde Park employees who saw the dog killed declared that Spot ended his life rather than face an existence without beer. Spot's death was followed by thirteen long years of Prohibition and the lawlessness it spawned. Perhaps it all could have been avoided if the country had just paid a little more attention to the suicide of Spot, the Hyde Park dog.

During its thirty years of doing business in St. Louis, the SLBA had closed some breweries and sold others, but by the arrival of Prohibition it was still operating eight breweries and countless saloons. The company had brought out Colda as its non-intoxicating beverage in 1917, but like most near beers it was a flop. While the association's Chouteau Avenue branch would continue as a cold storage and ice plant as well as SLBA corporate headquarters, most of the plants were mothballed. Only Hyde Park was destined to reopen after Repeal.

Henry Nicolaus and the
Revival of Hyde Park

Though some of the Forsters died young, the same cannot be said of Henry Nicolaus, who would become the major figure in the early post-Prohibition revival of the Hyde Park brewery. Born in 1850, Nicolaus was the son of a German brewer. His father was said to have told the youth, "Henry, when you grow up you are going to be a brewer; a good one, too." This prophecy was more than fulfilled over the course of Nicolaus's long career. Following the urging of friends who had already immigrated, Nicolaus arrived in St. Louis in 1867, where at the age of seventeen he began his American beer career at the Becker and Hoppe malt house, going to work the day after his arrival. He later worked as a brewer at the National Brewery of Zepp and Hartman, then the Cherokee Brewery, and next at E. Anheuser and Company until 1872.

Nicolaus then returned to his native land, spending ten months at breweries in Munich and Vienna to learn the latest in brewing techniques. Returning stateside, he gained additional experience at the Windisch-Muhlhauser (Lion) Brewery in Cincinnati from 1873 to 1875, and as superintendent at the Leisy Union Brewery in Keokuk, Iowa, from 1875 to 1879. After four years at Leisy's, Henry was offered a partnership in the brewery, but he declined. As he would later comment on this period in his life, "I had visions of better things in a bigger city."

He returned to St. Louis to find these "better things," accepting the position of brewmaster at the Green Tree Brewery. After only nine months there he became a partner in the business. When Green Tree was absorbed by the SLBA in 1889, Henry became a company director while continuing to manage the brewery. He was part of the Green Tree family in more ways than one, having married Mary Uhrig (of the St. Louis brewing family), who was the stepdaughter of Green Tree co-owner Louis Schlossstein.

On New Year's Day, 1903, Henry Nicolaus was named president of the local operations of the SLBA. It was a good year for him, as a few months later he also beat the rap on a bribery charge involving the Suburban Street Railway Company.

Fellow brewer and railway director Charles Denny was not so fortunate, being found guilty of perjury as part of the same case and sentenced to two years in prison. Legendary St. Louis brewer Ellis Wainwright spent the next eight years in France rather than face similar charges.

The first decade of the 1900s was also a good one for the SLBA. While the purchase and expansion of so many facilities had cost the British owners dearly, and some of the plants had been closed due to over-capacity, beer sales continued to grow.

Henry Nicolaus had become involved with the Forster family not just through their mutual affiliation with the SLBA, but as was typical with St. Louis brewing families, they became relatives. Katie Nicolaus, Henry's daughter from his second marriage (to Mathilda Griesedieck, also from a brewing family, after his first wife had passed away) married C. Marquard Forster. Another daughter, Stella, became the wife of an Adolphus Busch nephew. Henry Nicolaus stayed at the helm of the SLBA as its president until the advent of Prohibition. He then resigned, and as he thought at the time was retired for good to his summer home in Battle Lake, Minnesota.

Beer became legal again in the spring of 1933, making the shuttered facilities of the SLBA of interest to investors. In June, three of these breweries—Hyde Park, Lafayette, and Wainwright—were purchased for $650,000 by the investment house of Stifel, Nicolaus and Company.

This company, which exists to this day, illustrates how some beer barons were able to maintain their wealth during the dark days of Prohibition by diversifying into real estate and other investments. The breweries owned considerable prime real estate with their large number of tied saloons, so it was a natural sideline. The Stifel family, like the Nicolauses, came from a long line of brewers. Stifel, Nicolaus and Co. had been started in St. Louis in 1890 as Altheimer & Rawlings, adopting the Stifel Nicolaus name in 1923.

The 1933 breweries purchase ultimately landed the SLBA in court, when L. M. Gaines sued it for $32,500. He alleged that he was owed that amount as a sales commission. Why the SLBA and Stifel Nicolaus, which were being run by some of the same people, would have needed such an agent was not explained. It is unclear exactly what the company's intentions were regarding the other two plants, but brewing would quickly recommence at the Hyde Park location.

After the purchase, Louis J. Nicolaus, a partner in the investment firm, called his father, Henry, and asked him to run the newly purchased breweries. Henry at first declined, but then changed his mind and accepted. The Forster family remained involved in the business as well, with L. Marquard Forster named vice president of the newly formed Hyde Park Breweries Association, Inc. Henry Nicolaus was elected corporate president, with C. Norman Jones, another former SLBA executive, named secretary-treasurer. The corporation had authorized capital stock of $2 million, of which $675,000 was quickly subscribed. Unlike many other reopened breweries, operating cash would not be a problem. Selected to man the brew kettle was August Ritter, son of longtime Hyde Park brewmaster Otto Ritter.

Despite his initial reluctance, after accepting the top post at Hyde Park, Henry Nicolaus blew out of retirement in a whirlwind of activity. Within twenty-four days of his being chosen president, all of the contracts had been awarded for purchasing the new fixtures and equipment required to rehabilitate the plant. When brewing operations were about ready to start, Nicolaus came to the brewery one Sunday, donned a pair of overalls, and inspected the brewery from top to bottom. The very next day he gave the order to begin brewing.

On December 14, 1933, Hyde Park draft beer returned to the market. It was to become the

Facing page: Hyde Park coaster from the 1940s, featuring the company's shield logo.

Left: Deliveryman's hat, sporting "Hyde Park 75" emblem, from the 1950s.

Below: Delivery truck from the 1930s.

top-selling draft product in the city of St. Louis throughout the mid-1930s. Hyde Park continued with a couple of unusual brewing techniques during its post-Prohibition revival. One was the use of a square brew kettle. Built out of iron in 1892 and still performing admirably after World War II, the oddly shaped kettle had a capacity of 425 barrels. It was a sturdy brewhorse, as four times a day a brew was completed in the vessel; since each batch required six hours it was literally used around the clock for weeks on end. Master brewer August Ritter once said of the square brew kettle that he would match his "old pal" against any other kettle in operation. Old-time Hyde Park brewery workers were often heard to say that the square kettle helped give their favorite lager its crisp, distinctive, and delicious taste.

Another factor in the flavor of Hyde Park beer was the brewery's unusual three-month lagering period, which was frequently emphasized in advertising. "Always aged 3 months" and "There's a difference in taste—because there's a difference in time" were just two phrases used. The brewery had a 105,000-barrel capacity in its cellars to accommodate this lengthy process. All Hyde Park beers were also 100 percent krausened.

Life was not always easy for the brewing industry after Repeal. The country was still mired in economic depression, and despite the pent-up demand for beer it would be many years before sales would reach pre-Prohibition levels. Hyde Park, however, was able to generate modest yearly profits and pay small dividends to stockholders from the start. An impressive 150,000 barrels of beer left the brewery in its first year of operation.

Hyde Park bottled beer was not reintroduced until December 14, 1935, exactly two years after the draft version had become available. A large advertising campaign was undertaken, including full-page newspaper ads with banner-sized type. One read "The Whole Town will turn out for Hyde Park—Now In Bottles" with mammoth illustrations of the brewery and its new bottle. These ads also continued the policy of publicizing the lengthy lagering period of Hyde Park beer. A new shield emblem was designed as the company's symbol. A huge example was erected in left field at Sportsman's Park, home of both the St. Louis Browns and Cardinals baseball clubs. The brewery was located not far from the ballpark.

In the mid-1930s Hyde Park began sponsoring several radio programs. *Hyde Park Serenade* provided music performed by the Hollywood Orchestra. Other programs included *Friendly Bill*, which featured hillbilly music, and *Country Journal*,

which stressed stories deemed to be of interest to rural areas. Seeking to cover all advertising bases, the brewery also became a sponsor of Browns and Cardinals radio broadcasts. Hyde Park's *Dope from the Dugout* was a pregame show, with *Grand Stand Managers* airing after the games. Radio seems to have been a wise choice on which to spend such a big chunk of its advertising budget, as case-lot sales of Hyde Park bottled beer doubled between 1936 and 1937, and then almost doubled again by October 1938.

Business was booming enough that in early 1938 contracts were signed for $250,000 worth of new buildings and improvements. A new bottling house was built, doubling Hyde Park's bottling capacity. An additional story was added over many of the existing buildings, lagering cellars were expanded, and a new government cellar (where beer is stored after going through government meters for tax purposes prior to packaging) was constructed. An optimistic Henry Nicolaus told *American Brewer* that "talk of recession in various fields will not prevent us from going ahead with the expansion."

On June 28, 1938, Henry Nicolaus died at age eighty-seven from a cerebral hemorrhage at his home in Minnesota. Despite failing health, the "oldest brewer in St. Louis," with fifty-nine years of industry experience, had been active in Hyde Park until the end. Only the thirteen years of Prohibition had prevented Nicolaus from establishing the incredible record of seventy-two years in the beer business.

Succeeding Nicolaus as corporate president was L. Marquard Forster, with Fred Snell moving up to vice president. Louis J. Nicolaus succeeded his father on the Hyde Park board of directors and later became chairman of the board.

In January 1939, ground was broken for a five hundred thousand dollar expansion of the brewery, including a four-story storage building at 2110 Salisbury. Hyde Park would soon boast of an annual capacity of four hundred thousand barrels, a 40 percent increase. To make way for all of the construction, the company's office was moved temporarily to the nearby north St. Louis Turner Hall, which is still a local landmark. When office workers moved back to the brewery, it was into a spacious building with modern florescent lighting and even air conditioning. The company's new sternwirthe (hospitality room) was located in the basement of the office. Solid income was enabling all these improvements. Hyde Park had earned a net profit of over $440,000 for the year ending March 1938, which increased to over $660,000 the next fiscal year.

Another member of the Forster family became associated with the brewery, with August F. Forster working his way up the sales force to become sales manager in 1940. His cousin L. Marquard Forster—Hyde Park president, chairman of the board, and general manager—passed away from heart failure in 1943. Likewise a third-generation brewer, he had earlier in the year been chosen a director of the St. Louis Chamber of Commerce and was only forty-eight when he died. Louis S. Dennig, former president and general manager of the St. Louis Independent Packing Company, succeeded Forster as company president. (Dennig's move from meat processing to brewing marked a complete reversal of his father Louis, who had been area sales manager for Anheuser-Busch until 1910, when he became president of the packing company.) August Forster was named one of Hyde Park's vice presidents.

August Ritter, who had commanded the kettle at Hyde Park since Repeal, retired not long after L. Marquard Forster's premature death. It marked the first time since 1880 that a Ritter had not helped manage the Hyde Park brewhouse. Henry Eder, a native of Munich and a graduate of the Wahl-Henius brewing school, succeeded August Ritter as

Right: Brewery executives inspect a newly installed aging tank.

Below: Several Hyde Park deliverymen carrying bottles of beer in string-handled beer bags.

master brewer. Eder had worked at various St. Louis breweries since 1933 and was so respected by his colleagues that he was chosen president of the St. Louis District of the Master Brewers Association of America in 1946.

Hyde Park continued strongly through the World War II years and beyond. In January 1946, the company's stock split with 2 ½ shares exchanged for each of the old. During the war the company had added itself to the list of about ten breweries advertising in publications with a national circulation. While not distributing nationally, it began running "Lucky you, when you live or travel where you can enjoy Hyde Park" ads in magazines such as *Business Week*. Another advertising innovation was company sponsorship of a local TV show called *Meet St. Louis*. This man-on-the-street show, which first aired in early 1947, was said by the trade publication *American Brewer* to be the first television program ever sponsored by a brewery.

The St. Louis brewing scene was rocked by big news in the fall of 1948, when the Hyde Park Brewing Association was merged into the Griesedieck-Western Brewery Company of nearby Belleville, Illinois. The Hyde Park stockholders were paid about $6.5 million for their equity in the business.

While the Hyde Park brands continued flowing out of the St. Louis brewery, Griesedieck-Western later began producing its flagship Stag brand there as well. Rather surprisingly, Hyde Park sales turned up a sharp 18 percent following news of the merger. At the time, Edward D. Jones, Griesedieck-Western president, stated that while the Belleville plant was unable to keep up with demand for Stag, the Hyde Park plant was producing considerably under its yearly capacity of eight hundred thousand barrels. While steadily profitable for many years, for the four months ending in July of 1948 Hyde Park found it had a net loss on the balance sheet of more than seventy thousand dollars. This no doubt helped spark the sale.

The Hyde Park brewery celebrated its seventy-fifth anniversary in 1951. In honor of the occasion a new label, Hyde Park 75, was unveiled. The company also began marketing another new brand, Hyde Park Stout Malt Liquor. Unfortunately these would prove to be the last hurrahs for Hyde Park beer. Griesedieck-Western was itself bought out by the Carling Brewing Company in October 1954. One of Carling's first moves was to kill the Hyde Park brands. The St. Louis brewery began producing Black Label beer and Red Cap ale in addition to Stag.

On April 1, 1957, brewing was halted at the Hyde Park plant, and with it came the loss of about 350 jobs. Carling transferred production to its ever-expanding Belleville facility and to the other breweries it began operating across the country. A fire had damaged part of the former Hyde Park brewery prior to its closing, which hastened the razing of the majestic old brewhouse in October 1958. In announcing the brewery's closing, a Carling spokesman noted that a study of the St. Louis and Belleville plants had been made. It was decided that the larger Belleville plant, with its excellent railroad siding, could best serve the area. The former Hyde Park plant could not be expanded owing to its location and was further hampered by a lack of railroad access. The Carling representative told *American Brewer*, in words that still ring prophetic: "The trend in the brewing industry is toward larger plants. Owners of smaller plants, whether they are single plant companies or firms with several plants, have found it difficult to operate economically and remain competitive."

While some of the later additions to the brewery are still standing and have been occupied by other businesses, notably Krey Packing, many are deteriorating and not much to look at. This is a fate shared by much of the surrounding Hyde Park neighborhood. The variety of Hyde Park breweriana produced during the many years when the brewery was a significant player in the St. Louis beer game is much more attractive and being preserved by collectors.

Four backbar cardboard cutouts of Gay '90s characters drinking Hyde Park beer.

Independent Breweries Company

The formation of the Independent Breweries Company (IBC) marked the second consolidation of the St. Louis brewing industry. It was organized in 1907 and consisted of nine breweries (seven in St. Louis and one each in the Illinois towns of East St. Louis and Granite City), all of which had opened since the first (SLBA) merger in 1889.

Again the Lemp, Anheuser-Busch, and Obert breweries stayed independent, as did the more recently opened Schorr-Kolkschneider Brewing Company.

The Western Brewer first reported on the IBC merger in May 1907, stating that the deal was being completed and mentioning unnamed "financiers" behind it. Two months later it stated that the deal had been "put through" by James S. Brailey Jr. of Toledo, Ohio. A different section of that same publication reported that the IBC had been incorporated at $8 million by Edward F. Otto (who owned twenty-four shares of stock), George K. Fisher (thirty-three shares), and Frank Obenier (also thirty-three shares). Still another report in the same issue listed the following as members of IBC's corporate brass: Henry Griesedieck Jr., of the National Brewing Company, president; a pair of vice presidents in Zach W. Tinker (Columbia) and Louis Haase (Empire); Hugo Koehler (American), treasurer; Henry C. Griesedieck (Consumers), assistant treasurer; and Ferd Gast (Gast), secretary. Additional directors included Edward Wagner (Wagner), Alex Gast (Gast), Henry L. Griesedieck (Central), A. C. Steuver (Home), Herman Stifel, Henry Ziegenhain, A. H. Bauer, and M. C. Harney (the latter of Cleveland).

This announcement also included a disclaimer by company President Henry Griesedieck Jr. in which he stated, "I fear the erroneous impression may have been created that the ownership and control of the new company is in the hands of eastern people. This is not true. St. Louis men and St. Louis money own and control the corporation absolutely." Griesedieck further remarked that the purpose of the merger was not to affect the price of beer, and that the IBC would see to it that the saloons it supplied would follow all regulatory laws and not allow "vicious and immoral persons" to congregate on their premises.

The American Brewing Company, operated by the Koehler family, was the largest brewery involved in the merger. A relative, Casper Koehler, was part the Columbia Brewing Company, while members of the Griesedieck family were involved in the National, Central, and Consumers breweries, all part of the merger. Clues to the exact financial machinations behind the consolidation have been lost to time. Certainly the new company could effect cost-saving measures. The Home and Consumers plants were quickly closed, and bottling lines reduced to two locations (presumably American and National), but even with these economies, the IBC would not prove to be much of a financial success. Part of the problem may have been excessive salaries. As related by Alvin Griesedieck in

Top: 1924 label for Mateo, a beverage prepared from the Yerba Mate, an herb grown in South America.

Middle: Alpen Brau Special, a near beer marketed by IBC during Prohibition.

Bottom: Circa 1910 litho for Alpen Brau Bottled Beer.

The Falstaff Story, "in the case of the Independent Breweries Company, salaries were paid in accordance with the individual's previous position and remuneration. I remember my father telling me, for example, that one of the partners was being paid $15,000 per year [in those days a lot of money] as stable boss."

By 1912, money difficulties forced the IBC to reorganize. The previous year some of the Griesediecks had left to start the independent Griesedieck Brothers Brewing Company at the old Consumers site. Hugo Koehler had replaced Henry Griesedieck Jr. as IBC president. A committee appointed by the corporate board ended up organizing a stock deal agreeable to 90 percent of the involved parties, enabling the IBC to pay its bills, and allowing brewing to march on.

The Columbia Brewing Company had introduced Alpen Brau beer at the 1904 World's Fair, and that became the IBC's flag-

ship bottled brand. The company's home office was at the American Brewing Company branch. As Prohibition neared, Hugo Koehler, Louis Haase, A. C. Steuver, and brothers Alex and Ferd Gast served as corporate officers, with Henry C. Griesedieck overseeing brewing operations. Independent began making its IBC root beer in 1919, apparently at the American location. It was a fair success, but the other IBC breweries saw little activity once beer became illegal. By the 1920s, the IBC was facing bankruptcy, having spun off its only profitable arm into the Independent Realty Company.

Investors became interested in some of the old IBC breweries as Repeal loomed. The company's general mortgage bondholders' protective committee sold the American plant for $275,000, and it reopened. Likewise the Central, Gast, and Wagner breweries were resurrected. Another group that included longtime IBC President Hugo Koehler and a pair of gentlemen who were part of the Independent Realty Company—J. Spencer McCourtney and Mark Steinberg—purchased and reopened the Columbia plant. They took with them the IBC's Alpen Brau label, which lasted until the 1940s, when Columbia was acquired by Falstaff, which continued brewing at the old IBC site until 1967.

In the end, the Independent Breweries Company proved to be a short-lived venture. Despite being owned and operated by veteran St. Louis brewers with modern plants, it met with limited success. More than anything, it was perhaps a victim of timing. Just a few years after its formation, the U.S. brewing industry started heading downhill. Wounded by the dry movement and paralyzed by government restrictions during World War I, it was finally killed by the Eighteenth Amendment.

Above: Celluloid-over-cardboard sign for PEP, marketed to mothers and their children.

Right: Sampson Malt Syrup can, sold during Prohibition, providing one of the main ingredients required to (illegally) brew beer at the consumer's home.

While in later years it became one of the largest breweries in St. Louis, when established in the 1850s what was then called the Great Southern Brewery was not even within the city limits. Rather it was in the separate town of Carondelet, an old village of about three thousand residents. Carondelet was originally settled by French and German immigrants, and by 1860 it was home to three breweries. One, which was operated by Rudolph Brisselbach, produced two thousand barrels in 1860. Another, later called the South St. Louis Brewery, was located on the west side of Second Street, between Market and Grundy. In 1859, it was being operated by Jacob Fritz. The next year twenty-five hundred barrels were produced. This brewery stayed in business until the early 1870s, when it was being run by the Gsell family. Simon Ziegelmeyer also ran a brewery in Carondelet and was likely the town's first brewer. He produced three hundred barrels in 1850, and he was still in business in 1860 when a business directory ad mentioned the "lager beer constantly on hand" at the Carondelet Brewery and adjacent saloon. It is unclear if Ziegelmeyer's plant was the same as either of the two mentioned above, or was at a third site.

Carondelet's largest brewery in 1860 was the Great Southern Brewery, which made three thousand barrels that year. Located at the corner of Main and Steins, the owners were the estate of Carl Klausmann and a man named Decker. The Klausmann name later became synonymous with Carondelet brewing, but Carl Klausmann had actually been trained as a painter. Born in 1810 in Baden, Germany, he worked there as a sign painter prior to immigrating to the United States in 1839.

Klausmann headed to Louisville, Kentucky, and while there met his future wife, Maria Uhrig. When she moved to St. Louis to join other family members (including brothers Ignatz and Joseph, who would later run the Camp Spring Brewery), Carl Klausmann followed her there. They were married in 1841 and together would go on to run a restaurant called Our House in St. Louis at the corner of Main and Walnut. Their restaurant was a success, and with money they had saved the couple moved to Carondelet in 1857 to run a brewery. The historical record is unclear as to whether or not this was a pre-existing brewery, or if Klausmann's partner Decker was involved at the start. Nor is it known if he was the same fellow Jacob Decker, who briefly operated the Jackson Brewery in St. Louis in the late 1860s.

Carl Klausmann proved to be a capable brewery operator, but he did not get to enjoy his new vocation for long, passing away in 1859. Despite having six children to rear, Maria Klausmann bucked the sexual mores of her time and opted to take over her late husband's role in running the business. She was an able businesswoman, too, with sales gradually growing to the point where a bigger brewery was needed. In 1873, a new plant was constructed near the River des Peres at Main Street near

Klausmann Brewery Company

Northwest corner Main and Steins, Carondolet

Great Southern Brewery,
Klausmann & Decker   c. 1857–c1860
Southern Brewery, Klausmann & Co.   c. 1860–1873

8639 S. Broadway (new site)

Southern Brewery, Klausmann & Co.   1873–1878
Klausmann Brewery Company   1878–1889
Klausmann branch, SLBA   1889–1918

Top: Bottling shop brewery workers photo, August 14, 1893. Note child laborers perched atop the huge stack of empty bottles.

Bottom: Another Klausmann photo, this one featuring two different corner signs.

Catalan. Mrs. Klausmann continued operating the brewery in her name with partners William Buchholz and Louis Will until 1878, when the Klausmann Brewery Company was organized.

The 1870s marked something of a turning point in the brewing industry. Increased mechanization and improved transportation were starting to make the neighborhood brewery a thing of the past. Brewery owners were increasingly faced with the choice of either expanding or quitting.

The four stockholders of the new Klausmann Brewery Company started fairly small. Three partners—Maria Klausmann, Nicholas Eckerle, and John Krauss—each held one hundred shares of stock worth ten thousand dollars, while corporate Secretary Fred Rathgeber owned just fifteen shares. Krauss was named company president and treasurer. In 1880, the brewery remodeled its icehouse and began building a new malt house. Further improvements were on the way in 1883, when company stock was raised from $31,500 to $126,000. Krauss, Eckerle, and Klausmann each purchased three hundred extra shares, while Rathgeber took

forty-five more. A bottling shop was among the improvements financed by the deal.

Like Carl Klausmann, John Krauss did not have a brewing background. Born in Bavaria in 1833, he apprenticed as a blacksmith and came to the United States in 1850, moved to St. Louis in 1855, and then moved to Carondelet in 1857, when he was appointed head blacksmith in the shops of the Iron Mountain Railroad. Krauss served in the Union army during the Civil War, managed his own blacksmith shop, "bored the celebrated artesian well at the insane asylum," and also became involved in the Carondelet zinc works, Carondelet Electric Light and Power, and the Southern Commercial Bank. According to NiNi Harris in her book *History of Carondelet*, Krauss became known as the town's "financial tower." Claims in *Commercial and Architectural St. Louis* that Krauss "lifted [the] brewery from the creditor's grasp," are possibly a bit overblown, however, as he did have two equal stockholders along with him, one of whom was the brewery's former proprietress. Krauss certainly threw himself right into his new venture, taking an active role as brewery manager. In 1882, the company began operating the former Gundlach Brewery in Columbia, Illinois, as a branch. Since a ferry ran from Carondelet across the Mississippi to near Columbia, it was a convenient merger.

Instrumental to the St. Louis brewery's success was its large beer garden, which included an underground cave. It became a site of regular concerts and featured a platform for dancing. Klausmann also became a shipping brewery, bottling its beers for export to points far and wide. In early 1889, the company announced that it was building a cold storage house in Tuscaloosa, Alabama. That same year the Klausmann Brewery Company was one of eighteen local breweries combined into the St. Louis Brewing Association (SLBA), a concern controlled largely by British investors. As at many of the other SLBA plants, the American management stayed on the job at Klausmann, with John Krauss continuing as manager. He was joined by his son Christopher as assistant manager.

The next years brought considerable bad news to the Klausmann brewery fold. Chris Krauss caught cholera and died in 1895 at just twenty-eight years of age. He was described in an obituary in *The Western Brewer* as "a liberal patron of charitable and public enterprises of all sorts, and took a lively interest in all sporting matters." His

Left: A Klausmann corner sign, similar to one seen in the brewery workers photo on the previous page.

father died just two years later, and 1898 marked the death of Maria Klausmann, who passed away at age eighty-three in her residence at 8605 South Broadway. As unconventional in death as she had been in life, she instructed her survivors to have her body cremated. Mrs. Klausmann had been the last survivor of the original partners in the Klausmann Brewery Company. Upon her death the SLBA took control of her brick home, which had been built at the same time as a new brewhouse, with the understanding that she could live in it as long as she wanted.

More unhappy news came in 1899, when a stable fire at the brewery caused four thousand dollars in damages, but luckily all but one of the forty horses and mules kept there escaped. Then in 1903 Klausmann brewmaster Rudolph Elschepp died. The forty-six-year-old had been manning the brew

Right: Newspaper ad for Klausmann Standard Pale and Export beers, circa 1912. Used with permission of Missouri State Historical Society.

Below: A Klausmann-tied tavern. Note several different trays on the walls, and a factory scene lithograph in the back of the room.

kettle for a decade.

News at the brewery itself was much better. While the SLBA gradually closed some of its breweries, it had a fondness for the Klausmann plant. In January 1898, a permit was taken out to build a four-story brewhouse and a three-story bottling shop.

Turn-of-the-century newspaper ads indicate that the Klausmann branch was producing draft brands called Standard and Extra Pale Lager. One of its bottled brands was given the odd name of Pale Minstrel, and another was named Eureka.

After the death of John Krauss, William Huppert took over as brewery manager. He would oversee continued growth at the brewery. With the Prohibition movement gaining steam in certain parts of the country, in 1908 *The Western Brewer* announced that Klausmann was building a new bottling plant in Jackson, Tennessee, in order to supply the trade with Klausmann Temperance Brew. Another new label brought out around this time was called Hop Brand. The local paper announced in the fall of 1907 that the brewery had received forty thousand pounds of hops for flavoring the brand and was making arrangements to extend sales to Cuba and South America.

The March 1908 issue of *The Western Brewer* featured photos of some of the twenty large storage tanks the brewery had installed to age Hop Brand. The magazine stated that the brew "has gained a wide popularity and has been instrumental in adding" to company sales. The wooden tanks were manufactured by Mangold Stave and Cooperage Company of St. Louis, with installation supervised by Ed Schenk, that company's vice president and manager.

By the 1910s, the SLBA had decided to emphasize the Hyde Park label, with several of its remaining plants devoted to brewing that brand. It is unclear if the Klausmann branch continued making its unique brands after this time or not, but the SLBA did operate the Klausmann facility until 1918.

While the Eighteenth Amendment would not be repealed until 1933, three years earlier the Klausmann Brewery had been back in the news. In October 1930, a bootlegger's still exploded in a section of the brewery's refrigerating plant, causing fifteen hundred dollars in damages to the building and an adjacent trucking company. Conveniently, nobody had been around at the time of the explosion, and the SLBA was quick to explain that it had recently rented the buildings.

When beer finally became legal again, many investors were interested in former breweries. In July 1933, it was reported that the Klausmann facility had been sold for one hundred thousand dollars to a local syndicate. Attorney Lowell Sparling negotiated and announced the deal, stating that several of the investors were veteran brewing men, but that he was unsure if they were going to rehab the plant or just try to resell it. The property included a 320-foot frontage on two streets and thirty buildings with over 100,000 square feet of floor space. This deal ended up falling through, but in March 1934 it was again announced that the brewery had been sold. Lynn Barnes of Tulsa, Oklahoma, took hold of the title and said he represented a syndicate of Chicago and Oklahoma men who intended to invest between $1.5 and $2 million dollars to build a two hundred thousand-barrel brewery.

Three months later the empty brewery was again in the news when *American Brewer* reported on an unusual situation involving the arrest of two gentlemen named Adolph Busch and Henry Schuerman, partners in the company Adolph Busch, Inc. Busch insisted that they were intending to build a brewery on a tract of land that had formerly been the location of Klausmann's beer garden and clubhouse. He said he was a cousin of August Busch Sr. and formerly had been connected with Anheuser-Busch. The latter company recently had filed suit against Adolph Busch, Inc., to restrain it from using the Adolph Busch name.

Adolph Busch and Schuerman were accused of mail fraud after they attempted to sell stock in their proposed brewery by sending out ads soliciting one thousand dollar investments. How things proceeded after their arrest is unclear, but their brewery project never got off the ground.

In early 1935, it was reported that the previous buyers of the Klausmann property were in default on the first of two thirty thousand dollar mortgage payments, and that a foreclosure sale would be held on February 11. However, the property continued to be owned by the SLBA. In April 1937, SLBA President C. Norman Jones announced that the brewery buildings would be torn down in order to save on real estate taxes. A permit was issued to Atlas Wrecking and Supply to do the job. As all of the brewing equipment had previously been removed and scrapped, all that remained were the floors and walls.

Today the old brewery grounds are home to various businesses, including a moving and storage company. But a fragment of the old brewery exists on the north end of the property just off Catalan Street— the Club House building, which was once adjacent to the beer garden. Also, a number of blocks up the street are portions of the original Southern Brewery, closed in the 1870s but used as an office, saloon, and malting plant for some years after.

Though by now long forgotten, the Lafayette Brewery, which for many years operated as the Brinckwirth-Nolker Brewing Company, had a long and interesting history. Michael Kuntz founded the Lafayette Brewery around 1842. It was then located on the south side of Carr Street between Seventh and Eighth streets. Around 1850 the plant was purchased by Theodore Brinckwirth and a partner named Bergesch. Theodore Brinckwirth had trained to be a brewer in his native Germany. In 1846, at age twenty-nine, he immigrated to the United States, where he partnered with Casper Ruff at a brewery in Quincy, Illinois. He stayed a few years before heading down the Mississippi to St. Louis.

The Lafayette Brewery did well under its new owners. Brinckwirth was able to purchase some property at Eighteenth and Cass streets in 1857, and the next year he bought out his partner. Brinckwirth first had storage cellars built on the Cass Street site then began construction there of a new brewery, which opened in 1864.

Theodore Brinckwirth didn't get to enjoy his new digs for long, however, passing away in 1866. Frank Griesedieck, a member of the famous St. Louis brewing family, had first met Brinckwirth in Quincy and was a longtime employee at Lafayette. He had purchased a share of the brewery when Brinckwirth's health began to fail, and he continued running the new plant along with Brinckwirth's widow. Griesedieck also helped establish a malt house at the site of the original Lafayette Brewery, which was later moved to 1130 Eleventh Street.

A ST. LOUIS BREWSTER

In the nineteenth century it was unusual for women to take part in the operation of a brewery, although no doubt they pitched in when needed. The diminutive term *brewster*, first coined in England back when it was common for women to make beer as part of their household duties, was sometimes used to describe female brewers. One of the earliest brewsters in St. Louis was Fredericka Lanvers Brinckwirth, who married her brewer husband in 1846. She had helped in the business prior to her husband's death, both by keeping books and assisting in management. According to Hyde and Conard, Mrs. Brinckwirth "was to her husband a helpmate in the full sense of the term. Nature endowed her with a practical mind and much business sagacity, and her wise counsels contributed much to his success as a business man."

In addition to continuing her role at the brewery, Fredericka also raised eight children, only two of whom would survive to adulthood—Louis and Louisa. The latter married William Nolker in 1873, and he would soon go to work in the family brewery.

Lafayette Brewery
(Brinckwirth-Nolker Brewing Company)

Carr Street between Seventh and Eighth

Lafayette Brewery, Michael Kuntz	c. 1842–c. 1850
Lafayette Brewery, Brinckwirth & Bergesch	c. 1850–1858
Lafayette Brewery, Theodore Brinckwirth	1858–1864

1714 Cass Street (new site)

Lafayette Brewery, Theodore Brinckwirth	1864–1865
Lafayette Brewery, Brinckwirth & Griesedieck	1865–1873
Lafayette Brewery, Brinckwirth, Griesedieck & Nolker	1873–1879
Lafayette Brewery, Brinckwirth & Nolker	1879–c. 1881
Brinckwirth-Nolker Brewing Company	c. 1881–1889
Brinckwirth-Nolker branch, SLBA	1889–1905
Lafayette branch, SLBA (became bottling plant only)	1905–c. 1909

Photo of William F. Nolker, taken from Scharf's *History of Saint Louis City and County.*

He found success as the general manager of the Vulcan Manufacturing Company. Nolker sold his interest in that business and came to St. Louis in 1873 in order to marry Louisa Brinckwirth. Following the couple's six-month European honeymoon, Nolker settled into the brewing industry. While at most a middle-size brewery in its early years, by this time Lafayette was producing twenty thousand barrels a year, ranking it eighth out of twenty-nine St. Louis breweries.

Brewery partner Frank Griesedieck died in 1879. A few years later the business was formally incorporated as the Brinckwirth-Nolker Brewing Company. On the board of directors were corporate President William F. Nolker, Secretary-Treasurer Louis Brinckwirth, and his mother Fredericka Brinckwirth. Louis Brinckwirth was born in 1855 and grew up in the beer business. As a young man he worked in the family brewery, then left for a year to work at the Blatz Brewery in Milwaukee. After a year at the Reymann plant in Wheeling, West Virginia, he came back to St. Louis in 1878 as the junior member of the family firm. Annual production had climbed to thirty-five thousand barrels, still eighth largest in the city.

In 1880, a large fire caused some fifteen thousand dollars worth of damage at Brinckwirth-Nolker. This became the catalyst for a huge improvement project at the brewery, including a new malt house. In 1882, a new brewhouse and other buildings, including an employee dormitory, were put up. Amidst all this good news came the death of Louisa Brinckwirth Nolker in 1883.

THE SECOND GENERATION

William Nolker had an interesting background, although it wasn't in brewing. Born in 1840 in Hanover, Germany, he came to Baltimore in 1857 and then went to Cincinnati, where he worked at a hotel owned by his brother. He next took a job in a restaurant, then was a streetcar conductor. Nolker continued bouncing around, toiling at a bank and a hardware store before serving as a Civil War soldier for three months.

TO THE SLBA

The St. Louis Brewing Association (SLBA) merger of 1889 brought Lafayette and many other local breweries under the umbrella of an English syndicate. With its modern facilities, what was called the Brinckwirth-Nolker branch became one of the SLBA's primary plants. Louis Brinckwirth continued as assistant manager of the brewery until 1902. After retiring from the beer business he was active as vice president of the German American Bank, where his brother-in-law William Nolker was also a director. Nolker had

Top: The stylized "B-N-B" on the left side of the label stands for "Brinckwirth-Nolker Brewery."

Left: The "D & J.E. Morische" on this glass mug was probably an area restaurant serving Lafayette beer.

Facing page: Lafayette (Brinckwrith and Griesedieck) brewery workers.

likewise stuck with the SLBA, serving many years as treasurer of the local management contingent. Once he left the company, the SLBA was prompted to go back to calling the brewery the Lafayette branch.

Although beer production apparently ended around 1909, the brewery remained open until Prohibition and beyond. It became the exclusive bottling facility for the SLBA's flagship Hyde Park brand, and bottling of non-alcoholic beverages continued there until 1928.

The decade before the passage of the Eighteenth Amendment was not a kind one to the former Brinckwirth-Nolker principals. The deaths of both Fred Nolker (son of William and Louisa) at age twenty-nine, and Frank Hartung, who had spent eighteen years at the brewery, the last ten of them as master brewer, occurred in 1904. More bad news came on May 19, 1906, when William Nolker was killed in an auto accident near Paris, Illinois. Five years later Louis Brinckwirth passed

away. He was survived by three children and his wife, the former Josephine Grone.

THE END COMES

Some of the SLBA breweries fell back into the hands of local investors during Prohibition, and in 1933 these investors still owned the Lafayette, Wainwright, and Hyde Park breweries. As Repeal loomed, the reopening of all three plants was considered. In the end, though, only Hyde Park would be resurrected. A 1936 newspaper article reported that plans were underway to tear down the former Lafayette/Brinckwirth-Nolker facility. The next year all the buildings came down, with the given reason "to save taxes." Today the former brewery site is home to public housing projects. While the buildings have disappeared without a trace, the lagering caverns are undoubtedly still down there somewhere.

Lemp
Brewing Company

Sixth and Morgan streets

Adam Lemp brewing in small quantities
at his family grocery   c. 1840

Western Brewery, 37 South Second Street

Lemp & Company	c. 1841–c. 1851
Adam Lemp	c. 1851–1862
William J. Lemp & Company	1862–1864
William J. Lemp	1864–1865

Western Brewery, southwest corner of Thirteenth and
Cherokee streets

William J. Lemp	1865–1892
William J. Lemp Brewing Company	1892–1919

Top: As noted on the photo, coopers at the Lemp
brewery. Used with permission of Lee Stertz.

Bottom: Several delivery wagons can be seen in
this photo taken next to the Lemp brewery, a block
south of Cherokee Street.

Facing page: Oil portrait of brewery founder Adam
Lemp. Used with permission of Missouri Historical
Society.

The Gateway Arch in St. Louis, Missouri, was dedicated as a memorial to the pioneers who opened the American West through the St. Louis gateway. In a sense, it could also be seen as a memorial to the introduction of the beverage known as lager beer, which launched a brewing revolution in the middle of America. This fostered a national industry that now sells millions of barrels of its golden product every year. The Gateway Arch now stands on ground once occupied by Adam Lemp's original brewery, where long ago he brewed the first lager beer in St. Louis.

The Lemp family and brewery story is one of phenomenal success, wealth, and fame. It is also a tale of sadness, scandals, and suicides.

DAWN OF THE LEMP DYNASTY

The Lemp saga began with the birth of Johann Adam Lemp on May 25, 1793, in the province of Hessen, presently a part of central Germany. Adam Lemp, as he preferred to be called, had learned the brewer's trade as a youth in Eschwege, Hessen. He went on to become a master brewer in the cities of Gruningen and Eschwege. His father, Wilhelm Christoph Lemp, had been a master cooper and church warden.

Following many of his countrymen, Adam Lemp sailed to America in 1836. After spending time in Cincinnati, Adam moved to St. Louis in 1838, where he established a small mercantile or grocery store at Sixth and Morgan streets. In addition to the general merchandise that was sold in mercantile stores of this era, he also sold in small quantities two items he manufactured himself: vinegar and beer.

Apparently, Adam saw a greater future in manufacturing, because after a couple years he established a new factory at 112 South Second Street between Walnut and Elm streets. The new plant was built to produce both beer and vinegar, a common manufacturing practice at the time. For the first few years, Adam sold his beer in a public house, or to use the more popular term, pub, that was attached to the brewery. By the mid-1840s, the growing popularity of Adam's beer allowed him to discontinue vinegar production and concentrate on beer brewing.

While 1840 was the date usually given by the William J. Lemp Brewing Company for the founding of the enterprise, the actual date that Adam Lemp began brewing beer in commercial quantities, and in particular lager beer, is in doubt. One source on the industrial history of the area gives the date as 1838. It is certainly possible that he carried the lager yeast with him, since he arrived in 1836 from Germany having been most recently employed in a brewery. Gregg Smith, in his *Beer: A History of Suds and Civilization*, states that strong evidence exists that Adam Lemp made a lager as early as 1838, beating the otherwise widely acknowledged lager pioneer, Philadelphia brewer John Wagner, by two years. If Adam Lemp did indeed bring the lager yeast with him upon his immigration, and used it while brewing in his mercantile store in 1838, then he deserves the crown as the first lager brewer in America.

Other sources however, seem to point to a date as late as 1842 for the start of his lager beer brewing. For example, *The (St. Louis) City Directory of 1840–41* lists Adam Lemp as still in the grocery business, with no mention of the brewery on Second Street. Brewery historian James Lindhurst indicated that 1841 was the year Adam purchased (for eight thousand dollars) the lot where his brewery was built. James Neal Primm, in his *Lion of the Valley: St. Louis, Missouri*, gives 1842 as the date that Adam Lemp "revolutionized the city's brewing industry by introducing lager beer at his new plant on south Second Street." The May 30, 1857, edition of the *Daily Missouri Republican* newspaper states that his Western Brewery was established "15 years ago," which would again point to an 1842 establishment date for the brewery.

The fact that the brewery itself never made a point of mentioning how early it began brewing lager beer would also point to the later date. But whatever the exact date that Adam Lemp introduced his lager beer, few dispute that his was one of the first produced in America, and without question the first brewed in St. Louis.

The term *lager* comes from the German verb *lagern*, meaning to stock or to store. Early German brewers, like their later American counterparts, stored their product in cooling caves during the summer, hence the use of the term. The lagering, or aging, process does several things to beer that only time can do—allowing unremoved yeast a chance to settle, improving the beer flavor and enabling the beer to store longer. The end result is a sparkling, effervescent beverage called a lager. This style of beer is also different in that it uses bottom-fermenting yeast, while "true" ales use top-fermenting varieties; lager beer is more stable than top-fermented malt beverages. Thus lager beer became commercially important to brewers in the years before artificial refrigeration, because it gave them a product that did not have to be consumed quickly before it went bad.

Lager beer was quick to catch on in St. Louis,

eventually almost to the exclusion of other styles. Reasons included the many natural lagering caves in the area and the huge influx of German immigrants soon arriving on the scene.

Adam Lemp helped start a revolution in the industry, and for that reason is rightly called the "Father of Lager Beer in St. Louis." Like most early brewers, Adam Lemp had business partners; Louis Bach was his first. An 1842 city directory lists A. Lemp & Co. (Lemp and Bach) as a brewery and vinegar maker in the basement of 32 S. Second Street (subsequent city directories listed the address as 37 S. Second). That year the partners advertised their vinegar for sale in a January 4 newspaper ad. Beer was not mentioned, but since beer was normally brewed in the cold winter months, it may have already been brewed but just not ready for sale.

By 1845, the Western Brewery, as the A. Lemp & Co. plant became known, took on an additional partner in John Koechel. In the late 1840s, Louis Bach was running the brewery's distribution center on Fourth Street but later left the company. Koechel stuck around until 1851.

ADAM LEMP'S NEW CAVE

The expansion of Adam Lemp's new enterprise was relatively rapid, due to the great public acceptance of his new beer, and his brewery was soon too small to meet demand. The main problem was a lack of space available to store or lager the beer. The solution, Lemp believed, would be found in a newly discovered natural limestone cave, located just south of the St. Louis city limits, at what is now the northwest corner of Cherokee Street and DeMenil Place. By utilizing ice chopped from the nearby Mississippi River, the temperature in the cave could be controlled during the lagering process.

Adam Lemp purchased a lot over the entrance of this cave, then began the task of excavating it. Early in 1845, the remodeling activity was completed. Apparently this underground digging caused something of a local stir, as the editor of the *Daily Missouri Republican* visited the cave and wrote about what he found in the April 10, 1845, edition of that newspaper. The editor described the cellar as extending to a depth of over fifty feet, about one hundred yards long, and averaging about twenty feet in width. Inside were several oak casks, each holding twenty or thirty barrels of beer, which had been brewed at the Second Street brewery and carted to this cave for the lagering period. By the end of the first year of operation, more than three thousand barrels of beer had been stored in the cave.

Lemp's Western Brewery continued to grow during the 1840s. By 1850, it was already one of the larger breweries in St. Louis, with an annual production of four thousand barrels, ranking it sixth out of seventeen local competitors. Manned by a crew of six, the plant was valued at forty thousand dollars. The following decade continued to see the brewery gradually grow.

While Lemp's lager beer led to financial success for the brewery early on, surprisingly, as late as 1857, only about 57 percent of production (four thousand barrels versus three thousand of *schlenk*, or common beer) was lager. The seven thousand barrels produced that year ranked the Western Brewery ninth out of twenty-nine St. Louis brewers. In 1858, Lemp's beer captured first prize at the annual St. Louis Fair. That same year, Adam Lemp was listed in *R. G. Dun Credit Reports* as "The most substantial brewer in the city—has made sufficient money to make him independent—owns valuable real estate." Production rose to 8,300 barrels in 1860, ranking the company seventh out of forty local breweries.

Lemp's saloon was a major factor in the early growth of the brewery. Located at 112 S. Second Street, the tavern was improved throughout the 1850s, becoming the largest in the city. The popular hot spot served only Lemp's beer and no hard liquor. This policy served a dual purpose, as not only were beer sales enhanced, but the saloon's reputation improved as well, with beer seen by many as a beverage of moderation that served to keep drunks off the premises. The saloon would stay in business into the twentieth century.

On August 25, 1862, Adam Lemp died a rich man (but nowhere near a millionaire, as has been falsely reported), having built and managed his Western Brewery to a good competitive position in the St. Louis industry. Lemp must have been a popular citizen of his community, as his funeral procession consisted of over thirty horse-drawn carriages.

In his will, Adam Lemp bequeathed the Western Brewery, along with "all of the equipment and stock" in common to both his twenty-six-year-old son (and brewery superintendent) William Jacob Lemp and grandson Charles Brauneck. There may have been friction between the two inheritors of the brewery, as the will contained the condition that if either contested the will, the other would receive the property. Brauneck and William Lemp

Above: Lemp table tent from around 1906.

Right: "Crowned Wherever Exhibited" Lemp corner sign.

formed a partnership in October 1862 and agreed to run the business under the banner of William J. Lemp & Company. This partnership, however, was destined to be short-lived, as it was dissolved in February 1864 when William bought out Brauneck's share for three thousand dollars.

Unlike many businesses that wilt when a strong leader dies, Lemp's brewery actually grew and blossomed after William Lemp took control. The Western Brewery was then producing twelve thousand barrels of beer annually, virtually all of the lager type. William Lemp was born in Germany in 1836 and spent his childhood there until his father brought him to St. Louis at age twelve. William had struck out on his own as a brewer in addition to working for his father, partnering with William Stumpf for a time in a St. Louis brewery established by the latter. At the outbreak of the Civil War, Lemp enlisted in the Union army, but he was mustered out within a year. A short man at just over five feet tall, he and his brewery would nonetheless both become giants in the brewing industry.

MOVING TO CHEROKEE STREET

*O*n 1864, William Lemp purchased a five-block area around the storage cellar on Cherokee Street and began construction of a completely new brewery. By putting the new facility over the storage caves, it would no longer be necessary to move all of the kegs by wagon from the Second Street brewery. The original brewery was eventually abandoned but remained standing until 1939.

By the early 1870s, Lemp's Western Brewery was the largest in St. Louis out of a field of thirty, with E. Anheuser & Company's Bavarian Brewery coming in second. Lemp produced 34,107 barrels in 1874. In 1877 the brewery was the nineteenth largest in the country, producing 61,229 barrels. Construction of a bottling plant was started the following year. It opened the next fall, with much of its new machinery provided by the Conrad Seibel Works of St. Louis.

The Lemp brewery owned four icehouses on the Mississippi River levee in south St. Louis, each having a storage capacity of five thousand tons. These icehouses were cleverly built so as to be able to directly receive supplies via river barges, also owned by the Lemp brewery. The year 1878 marked the addition of the first artificial refrigeration machinery installed in the brewery, which lessened the company's dependence on ice. A new three-story, two hundred thousand dollar refrigerator building was completed in 1881 to house the brewery's growing menagerie of refrigeration equipment.

As befitting the increasingly competitive nature of the beer business, breweries throughout the nation began competing for prizes at large fairs. Lemp beer had the distinction of winning top prizes at the 1876 American Centennial Exposition in Philadelphia and the 1878 Paris Exposition. By the end of the decade, William Lemp had risen to vice president of the United States Brewers Association.

Production figures from 1879 show Lemp churning out 88,714 barrels, with Anheuser-Busch right behind at 83,160 barrels. By 1884, production at Lemp had doubled, but the brewery had been left in the dust by Anheuser-Busch, which topped the 300,000-barrel mark that year. Nonetheless, Lemp was one of the leading brewers in the country and helping to spread the fame of St. Louis beer around the world.

FIRST BEER COAST TO COAST

*N*ovember 1, 1892, William J. Lemp's Western Brewery was incorporated under the name William J. Lemp Brewing Company and capitalized at $2.5 million. The stockholders elected the following officers: William J. Lemp Sr., president (23,000 shares); William J. Lemp Jr., vice president (1,501 shares); Charles Lemp, treasurer; Louis F. Lemp, superintendent (500 shares); and Henry Vahlkamp, secretary. In addition to learning the business at their family's brewery, all of the Lemp sons attended the U.S. Brewers Academy in New York City.

By then Lemp was a nationally known shipping brewery. Depots had been established throughout the country. In fact, Lemp was the first brewery to establish coast-to-coast distribution of its beers. Lemp beer was being transported in some five hundred refrigerated railroad cars, averaging ten thousand shipments per year. The brewery proper employed seven hundred men. More than one hundred horses were required to pull the forty delivery wagons to make St. Louis city deliveries. The twenty-five beer cellars went down to a depth of fifty feet, and could store fifty thousand barrels at one time. The rated production capacity of the brewery was five hundred thousand barrels a year.

Lemp was one of the first shipping breweries to establish a national exporting strategy. It operated its own railroad, the Western Cable Railway Company, which connected all of the plant's main buildings to its shipping yards near the Mississippi River, and then to the other major area railroads. In the years before artificially refrigerated railroad cars, the large shipping breweries of this time frequently formed their own trunk railroads to make shipments from their plants. Encouraging this were battles with the railroads over the way the brewers shipped their beer. The breweries would cram the rail cars with as much ice as possible (overload them, according to many rail lines) to protect the unpasteurized beer from spoiling during transport. By running their own trunk lines, the major shipping breweries could gain more control over the conditions under which their product was transported to other markets.

Construction of new buildings and the updating of old ones were virtually continuous at the Lemp brewery. The entire complex was built (or remodeled) in the Italian Renaissance style, featuring arched windows, pilaster strips, and corbeled brick cornices (projecting architectural details, such as the rolling Lemp shields). Ultimately the giant facility covered the equivalent of five city blocks. By 1895, all these efforts resulted in Lemp checking in at number eight on the list of leading United States breweries, with production of more than three hundred thousand barrels.

Having expanded its distribution network throughout the United States, Lemp continued to expand overseas. By the late 1890s, Lemp beers were being shipped in large quantities to Canada, British Columbia, Mexico, Central and South America, the West Indies, the Hawaiian Islands, Australia, Japan, and Hong Kong. Lemp beer was even available in the cities of London and Berlin, both well known for their own local brews.

Lemp produced a huge variety of brands over the years, including Extra Pale, Standard, Culmbacher, and a bock it labeled Buck. The Tip-Top brand was introduced in 1892. What proved an even bigger name was introduced in June 1899. Falstaff beer took its name from the Shakespearean character who was also the subject of an 1893 Verdi opera. The Falstaff label soon became Lemp's flagship brand. Lemp began using the shield logo that became synonymous with Falstaff for all of its brands in 1896.

AFTER THE FIRST SUICIDE

William J. Lemp Sr.'s death by suicide occurred on February 13, 1904. The responsibility for leadership of the business fell on his son William J. Lemp Jr., who was subsequently elected corporate president on November 7, 1904. The younger Lemp was born in St. Louis in 1867 and attended the public schools and Washington University. He was aided in the management of the business by his brother Louis F. Lemp. Louis, who was born in 1869, took advantage of the family fortune in his youth to explore his passion for sports. At age eighteen, he admired the boxer John L. Sullivan to such a degree that he went to New Orleans to bet five thousand dollars on one of his fights. Louis also said that if Sullivan didn't win, he would ride all the way home in a hearse. Sullivan lost, but Louis reneged and took the train home. In his later years, Louis continued his love of sports by becoming a pioneer supporter of automobile and airplane events. William Lemp Sr.'s widow, Julia, passed away in 1906. She left an estate valued at approximately $10 million.

The Lemp brewery was soon facing a much altered St. Louis landscape, when in 1907 nine large area breweries combined to form the Independent Breweries Company (IBC). This was the second huge merger in the local beer business, following the 1889 formation of the St. Louis Brewing Association (SLBA). The SLBA absorbed eighteen breweries and like the IBC continued operating many of them up to Prohibition. The formation of these two conglomerates left only Lemp, Anheuser-Busch, the Louis Obert Brewing Company, Schorr-Kolkschneider, and a handful of small neighborhood breweries as independent St. Louis beermakers.

Lemp continued on. *The Western Brewer* reported in 1908 that the brewery had installed the largest bottle soaker in the world, capable of cleaning one hundred thousand bottles a day. At the time of the article a second such soaker was already being installed. Two Lemps made industry news in 1913. It was reported that Charles Lemp had visited all of the Lemp depots in Texas and also journeyed to Mexico. He had been unfazed by the revolutionary violence happening south of the border. Edwin Lemp was reported to have left the brewing industry to take up farming. He was requesting that his friends forsake the golf links to help him on the farm and thus get a "real" tan.

These humorous stories may have been intended to take the brewers' minds away from the clamor of the temperance movement, which was of growing concern to the whole industry, especially shipping breweries like Lemp. Localities throughout the country were beginning to vote themselves dry. The first heyday of United States brewing was about to draw to an abrupt halt.

Facing page: Rarely seen Lemp self-framed tin sign, advertising Lemp's Extra Pale beer.

Below: A young woman pours a bottle of Falstaff to three gentlemen at a table. This young lady can also be seen on more than one of the Lemp postcards.

CERVA, THE LAST HOPE

*I*n 1914, the Lemp Brewing Company registered the advertising print "Falstaff and Happiness." Subsequent events would render the title a bit ironic. Like most of its competitors, the brewery limped on through the years of World War I. According to numerous accounts, some of the company's equipment was allowed to deteriorate during this time as the Lemp family, its vast fortune already made, began to lose interest in the business. The last major capital improvements to the plant were the erection of a stockhouse addition and the installation of the giant grain elevators on the south side of the complex in 1911.

With the shadow of Prohibition falling across the land, Lemp, like many other breweries, introduced a pair of non-intoxicating malt beverages. Tally was introduced in the spring of 1915. It must not have been much of a seller as Cerva was added two years later. While Cerva did sell moderately well, revenues were nowhere near enough to cover

the company's overhead. The giant plant closed without notice on May 3, 1919. Employees learned of the brewery's closing when they arrived for work only to find the plant's doors and gates locked shut.

William Lemp was convinced that there was no future in the beer business. When his friend Joe Griesedieck offered to buy the Falstaff trademark in 1920, Lemp accepted the offer.

International Shoe Company purchased almost the entire brewery at auction on June 28, 1922, for $588,000, a small fraction of its estimated pre-Prohibition value of $7 million. Unfortunately for brewery historians, virtually all of the Lemp company records were pitched shortly after International Shoe moved into the complex. International Shoe used the larger buildings, and even portions of the caves, as a warehouse.

Six months after the brewery was auctioned, a depressed William Lemp Jr. shot himself to death in his Lemp mansion office.

A NEW BEGINNING

*I*n 1992, International Shoe (renamed Interco) sold the Lemp complex to LB Redevelopment for two hundred thousand dollars, about a third of the price it had brought three-quarters of a century before, and considerably less than its one-time $3 million-plus asking price.

In February 1997, the St. Louis Board of Aldermen approved a redevelopment plan that gave LB Redevelopment tax abatements for up to twenty-five years. Published plans called for turning some of the larger buildings into a dining and entertainment destination. Tentative plans for the complex included a thirty-five hundred–seat event center, a courtyard festival location, and an eighty-room hotel. A spokesman for LB Redevelopment projected twenty years of development. LB made little progress in fulfilling its plans. In 1999, the Lemp complex was sold to four new owners: Vernon Gross (a sculptor with a studio on the site),

There are around a dozen advertising pieces in this Lemp Brewery workers' photo.

Paul Pointer (owner of the Lemp Mansion and a banquet facility in the former Lemp stables), and the father/son team of Shashi and Rao Palamand. The latter was a former executive at Anheuser-Busch. The Palamands were then operating four brewpubs, including the Old 66 Brewery and Restaurant in suburban St. Louis.

The new owners did considerable restoration and preservation work throughout the complex. Plans for a microbrewery and a brewery museum were discussed. But while some of the buildings were occupied, many of them remained empty. The property was put back on the market in 2006.

Early in 2007 it was announced that Jacob Development of St. Louis had placed the property under contract. That company's plans quickly went nowhere, and in May it was reported that a new group, Garrison Development of Kansas City, was taking over the project.

In 2008, a Garrison spokesman told the *Post-Dispatch* that its $140 million redevelopment project was a "go," and that the company felt "confident we can get to the finish line." Plans called for an apartment complex of 439 units and 85,000 square feet of stores and offices. As with other recent efforts at redeveloping the old Lemp brewery, Garrison's work appears to be proceeding slowly.

One bright spot in the neighborhood is The Stable, a brewpub across the street from the main Lemp complex. Opened in 2008, the business began serving its own beer on site in May 2009. The brewpub/distillery takes its name from its location, in what before Prohibition was the William J. Lemp Brewing Company stable and wagon house.

Aerial photo of the Lemp brewery complex, circa 2004.

THE FIRST BEER TO BE DELIVERED BY AIR

The William J. Lemp Brewing Company issued more than 130 different postcards in the years preceding Prohibition. These postcards—some humorous, others featuring real photos—are avidly sought by many collectors. One of the rarer Lemp photo postcards shows a crowd of people standing in the brewery loading yard off Cherokee Street. They are grouped around an early glider-type aircraft, not much advanced from the Wright brothers' machine that had made its maiden flight at Kitty Hawk less than a decade prior. A wooden beer bottle case marked "Brewed in the Brewery of Lemp" can be seen being loaded onto the airplane. The postcard carries the caption, "Falstaff is the first Bottled Beer to be delivered by aeroplane."

The air deliveries were also the subject of a full-page ad the brewery took out in the October 8, 1912, *St. Louis Times*. This ad noted that the "aeroplane" circled the Lemp smokestack as it left the neighborhood but doesn't mention the beer's destination.

Another seldom-seen Lemp photo postcard shows the same airplane, now airborne, flying above the Lemp brewery's engine house. This postcard carries the same caption as the other and also is marked "Circling the Lemp Smoke Stack."

Neither of these two postcards carries a date; no "from" or "to" information, or other details of the flight. However, there is a story behind the "first bottled beer to be delivered by aeroplane" Lemp postcards. William J. Lemp Jr. was an early supporter of aviation, and used its novelty value for advertisements, as well as for promotions of flying events he sponsored. These postcards were issued to celebrate the first air delivery of beer in 1912. The following is an excerpt from a letter dated September 22, 1967, addressed to "Advertising Manager, Falstaff Brewing Corporation," from John G.

Shea, which tells, as they say, "the rest of the story:"

"Your advertising of Falstaff beer in the New York newspapers rings an ancient bell, which, I thought had long since been silenced by the years. Several years ago, as a professional writer on aviation history, I had an opportunity to chronicle the start of scheduled airplane transportation—which originated between St. Petersburg and Tampa, Florida, in 1914. Visiting St. Pete, I had the pleasure of meeting with Jay Dee Smith—an 'early bird' airplane pilot, and mechanic to the Benoist aircraft used in the world's first scheduled airline operations.

A chap by the name of Tony Jannus was the pilot of the first airline operation. Jannus was the Lindbergh of that era. He had established several altitude and long distance flying records prior to 'settling down' to pilot the first Benoist 'airliners.' Now among his records was a flight in 1912, in a Benoist-type aircraft from St. Louis to New Orleans. And who sponsored this flight? The Lemp Brewery!

Here's the rest of the story that you should be told before it gets lost in the labyrinths of time:

Smith, who serviced the Benoist aircraft, followed Jannus down the rivers by land. The epic flight started at St. Louis with the Mayor, and various officers of the Lemp Brewery strapping a case of Falstaff bottled beer to the wing, behind the pilot's perch. Jannus was instructed to deliver the case of Falstaff to the Mayor of New Orleans. The flight was to be made in short, daily hops. First day out, Smith—upon meeting up with Jannus at a predesignated spot along the river—noticed the pilot was feeling no pain. Further observation revealed the case of beer had been broached—and Jannus was joyously engaged with the twelfth bottle.

How about the Mayor of New Orleans? Smith inquired. No Problem, Jannus chortled.—Case flies much better empty!

And that is why the Mayor or New Orleans almost lost his official aplomb while accepting an empty case of Falstaff beer. And now that all the principles are dead, until now, not a person in the Lemp, and later Falstaff Brewing Corporation, knew anything about this!"

Above: Lemp postcard publicizing "Aviator Jannus loading case of Falstaff Bottled Beer onto his Hydro-Aeroplane."

Right: This Lemp postcard photo records the delivery of Falstaff at the St. Louis Fairgrounds.

Facing page: Jannus is seen circling the Lemp brewery smokestack in this Lemp postcard.

is the first Bottled Beer delivered by aeroplane.

Lemp Smoke Stack

THE TRAVELS OF ADAM LEMP'S BREW KETTLE

Visitors seeking to use the new outdoor wine garden at the rear of the Hermannhof Winery in Hermann, Missouri, in 1991 found one of the paths blocked by a large metallic kettle, obviously flipped upside down. While the copper mass was not marked, anyone knowledgeable of St. Louis brewing history would probably have recognized the object: Adam Lemp's original brew kettle.

How did this symbol of Adam Lemp's lager legacy travel to the Missouri River town of Hermann? The owner of the winery, James Dierberg (a member of the Dierberg's Markets grocery clan), was a member of the Missouri Historical Society, which owned Lemp's brew kettle. Dierberg had agreed to care for the historic vessel for a year, as the society was renovating the building where it had resided, and was short of storage space.

The location for temporary storage of the brew kettle at Hermannhof seemed appropriate enough since, ironically, the Hermannhof Winery was located in the same building that before Prohibition had been the home of the Hugo Kropp Brewing Company. Hermann was actually the second location in which Lemp's brew kettle had been stored that year. Dierberg had originally placed the kettle in the yard of his house, located in an upscale suburb of St. Louis. However, after neighbors began to complain, he felt compelled to move the kettle again, to the Hermannhof Winery.

A study of the history of Adam Lemp's brew kettle provides details on its travels and also highlights the workings of a mid-nineteenth-century brewery. While it was considered "state of the art" in 1840, the brew kettle seems almost comically small by modern standards. Today's typical brewery operated by any of the large national brewers utilizes several brew kettles of over five hundred barrels (15,500 gallons) capacity, leading to the ability to produce millions of barrels of beer per year, per plant. Using his original twelve-barrel brew kettle, Adam Lemp is thought to have produced just one hundred barrels of beer his first year.

In *100 Years of Brewing*, a volume produced by H. S. Rich and Company in 1903 and devoted to the history of brewing in America, the following quotation appears: "The twelve barrel-kettle [*sic*] in which Mr. Lemp brewed this early beer, as well as the first lager beer in St. Louis, is still preserved as a curio of the industry, by William J. Lemp, to whom the business descended." This statement, with an accompanying photograph of the kettle,

Falstaff Brewing Corporation postcard from the 1960s, highlighting Adam Lemp's original brew kettle, then on display at the Falstaff International Museum.

makes it possible to authenticate Adam Lemp's brew kettle, as the dents visible on it then are still recognizable today.

The kettle, probably produced in St. Louis or Chicago, was essentially handmade and typical of the brewing equipment of the era. Eight copper sheets were beaten into shape with a hammer and riveted together to form seams. As craftsmen could not weld copper at that time, they lapped the seams and put closely spaced rivets, 1/2 inch apart along each seam line, in the plate joints to make it watertight. The kettle has two drain spouts, the upper one for the wort, and lower one for the yeast. The curved plate of copper, used for the bottom of the kettle, was cast in a single piece. Dimension wise, the kettle was built four and a half feet tall, with a circumference of eighteen feet, and a brewing capacity of twelve barrels (372 gallons). The Hermannhof Winery did not have to worry too much about the security of Lemp's brew kettle during its storage there, as its weight is estimated to be between 550 and 600 pounds.

Adam Lemp's original brew kettle probably saw service for only a decade or two at the most. It is doubtful that it was still being used by the time construction began on the Western Brewery on Cherokee Street during the Civil War, because of the kettle's small capacity. Where the kettle traveled and resided while in the custody the Lemp family for the next century is uncertain, although it was obviously moved before the original Lemp brewery on South Second Street was torn down in the 1930s.

Missouri Historical Society records show that the brew kettle resumed its travels when it was delivered as a gift to the society by Edwin Lemp in 1955, with the following note: "This kettle was used by my Great Grandfather in 1840 or 1841 here in St. Louis, when he began his first brewery." The kettle remained at the society for a number of years, until it was placed on "permanent loan" to Falstaff's new museum in 1964. There it remained proudly on display, until Paul Kalmanovitz closed the St. Louis Falstaff Plant #10 brewery, and the adjacent museum, in 1977. With the closing of the Falstaff Museum, the brew kettle was transported back to the Missouri Historical Society in St. Louis, where it remained until its yearlong stay at the Hermannhof. It is now safely back at the Missouri Historical Society, preserved for future generations interested in brewing history to view, study, and enjoy. Hopefully, the travels of Adam Lemp's original brew kettle have ended forever!

GHOSTS IN THE ATTIC: A TOUR OF THE LEMP MANSION

The Lemp Mansion was built by Jacob Feickert in 1868, in the then-fashionable Italianate style. Feickert was William J. Lemp Sr.'s father-in-law. As the 1870 census credits Feickert with real estate and personal assets of only thirty-five hundred dollars, it is certain that Lemp money was used in the construction of the home. In any case, it was purchased outright in 1876 by William J. Lemp Sr. for use as a residence and auxiliary brewery office. Although already an impressive structure when William J. Lemp Sr. moved there, he nonetheless spent opulently, expanding the residence into a thirty-three-room Victorian showplace.

The Lemp Mansion was installed with three room-size, walk-in vaults, each measuring thirteen feet high, fifteen feet wide, and twenty-five feet

as a boardinghouse until being rescued in 1975 by the Pointer family, who have since restored it.

With three suicides in the Lemp Mansion, it is not surprising that the house would have a haunting reputation. But is it really haunted? Well, a few years ago, a part-time tour guide, strolling around the Lemp Mansion Restaurant after closing hours, reported suddenly hearing horses neighing and rustling. The noises seemed to originate from just a few feet outside the north end of the building, down from where William J. Lemp Sr. had kept his office. Running to the window, the tour guide was distressed to find no horses anywhere in sight that night. Perhaps it is only a coincidence, but shortly thereafter, when the parking lot was expanded closer to the north wall of the Lemp Mansion

Drawing of the Lemp Mansion depicting life in the 1890s, from a Lemp brewery tour booklet.

deep. When the Lemps left town for the weekend, they placed their paintings, jewelry, and other valuables into one of the vaults until they returned.

The Lemp Mansion was just as impressive underground as it was above. A tunnel ran between the house and the brewery. Utilizing a portion of the Cherokee cave, the Lemps built an auditorium, ballroom, and swimming pool that could also be reached from another tunnel (now sealed) leading from the basement of the mansion. The swimming pool was heated year round using hot water piped in from the boiler house at the brewery, located a short distance away.

Like the Lemp family, the Lemp Mansion itself suffered a decline in the years after Prohibition. In the mid-1960s, a substantial portion of the mansion grounds and one of the two carriage houses were lost to the construction of the Ozark Expressway, now called Interstate 55. After Charles Lemp's death in 1949, the mansion left the hands of the Lemp family, and it suffered further in the years it served

Restaurant, evidence was unearthed that the area where the ghostly horse cries had originated had once been used as a tethering lot for horses.

Others, from restaurant employees to renovators, have reported unusual phenomena happening in the mansion as well. An annual haunted house is held during Halloween in the Lemp caves, taking advantage of the ghoulish Lemp reputation.

At one time, the Lemp Mansion was thought to have a "zoo" in some of the carriage house buildings. The rumor was started by neighborhood citizens, who frequently heard unearthly howlings at night, especially during full moons. The truth is that the noises were not coming from an exotic animal, but from a relative suffering from schizophrenia, who was in the care of the Lemp family.

Today, the Lemp Mansion is both a restaurant and a bed and breakfast. Patrons can have a leisurely meal and relax in one of the rooms in which William J. Lemp Sr. or William J. Lemp Jr. committed suicide, and await their ghostly appearances.

THE DUTCH ACT

Suicides by prominent St. Louis German Americans, including a number of brewers, became so notorious that they were nicknamed the "Dutch Act," a phrase coined by the St. Louis Police Department. Four members of the Lemp family took their own lives. William Lemp Sr. was the first. Following the deaths of his favorite son, Fred, in 1901 and his close friend, brewer Frederick Pabst, in 1904 (Lemp's daughter Hilda had married Pabst's eldest son, Gustav, in 1877), associates described Lemp as a nervous, changed man, who while still showing up for work at the brewery had become indifferent to its operations. On February 13, 1904, he shot himself in the head with a .38 caliber revolver in an upstairs bedroom of the Lemp Mansion. He was sixty-seven years old.

Lemp's daughter Elsa was the family's second suicide, taking her own life in 1920 at her St. Louis home. She was only thirty-six.

William Lemp Jr. was soon to follow. Doubting that Prohibition would ever end, he had sold his company's famous Falstaff trademark to Papa Joe Griesedieck. Then, after receiving only eight cents on the dollar for his auctioned brewery, Lemp became increasingly morose and depressed. Months later, on December 29, 1922, the fifty-five-year-old Lemp shot himself in the heart in his mansion office.

Charles Lemp was the family's final suicide. William Jr.'s brother had worked at the brewery in his younger days before going on to a successful career in banking and politics. But the old bachelor grew ever more reclusive with age, and in 1949, aged seventy-seven and bothered by arthritis, shot himself in his bed at the Lemp Mansion.

Top right: Portrait of William J. Lemp Jr., from *The Makers of St. Louis: The Mirror, 1906.*

Right: Portrait of William J. Lemp Sr., from *The Makers of St. Louis: The Mirror, 1906.*

THE LAVENDER LADY

Painting of Lillian Lemp, the "Lavender Lady." Used with permission of The Lemp Mansion Restaurant.

The Lemp brewery was rocked in the years before World War I by the very public battles between William Lemp Jr. and Lillian (Handlan) Lemp, the "Lavender Lady," during their scandalous divorce trial and subsequent child custody disputes. The couple had married in 1899. Lillian's nickname was derived from her penchant for dressing in her favorite color, and going so far as to have her carriage horses' harnesses dyed lavender.

For the length of this messy trial, all four St. Louis newspapers devoted extensive front-page coverage to the battling socialites and their lawyers, including huge courtroom drawings. Part of the reason that the Lemps were willing to air their dirty laundry in a public courtroom was that both wanted custody of their son, William III. The trial opened in February 1909, and the crowds that flocked to the courthouse each day to witness the drama were treated to tales of violence, drunkenness, atheism, and cruelty.

Lillian charged that her husband drank to excess and kept company with other women. William countered that among other things his wife had been seen drinking and smoking in public. A divorce was granted in large part based on the testimony of a servant who stated that she had found feminine hairs of various colors in William's bathroom while Mrs. Lemp was absent.

Two years later, William and Lillian were back in court again, battling over the custody agreement of their only child. At the new trial, the Lemp family coachman related that there had been a series of monkey and chicken fights at the Lemp brewery stables, and that young William III had witnessed live birds being fed to the monkeys. According to Lillian's testimony, if the butler moved too slowly, William would take his pistol out and lay it on the tablecloth. Lillian also cited William's habit of slaughtering neighborhood cats as one of the reasons for denying her ex-husband access to their son. William responded that he did not kill cats for pleasure, only shooting those that disturbed his sleep.

William Lemp Jr. finally reacted to all of the publicity by building a country home on the Meramec River to which he increasingly retreated. In 1915, he was married to Ellie Limberg, widowed daughter of the late St. Louis brewer Casper Koehler.

THE LEMP CHARGERS

Today, the term *charger* brings to the minds of most breweriana collectors the concave metal advertising trays that became popular after the lithography onto metal process was perfected over a century ago. The derivation of the term *charger* actually predates the invention of the lithographic technology and was coined in the 1840s to describe a new type of large, mass-produced metal serving tray. The original chargers were used in kitchens and dining rooms as meat platters that, because they were bowed in the middle, could also hold gravy without spilling, which helped to keep the main dish hot until it was consumed. When the company American Art and its competitors starting producing lithographed art on this shape of tray in the 1890s, the new form of advertising was quickly nicknamed a charger by tavern patrons, after the earlier kitchen platters, and the moniker stuck.

The William J. Lemp Brewing Company distributed six different charger designs with a diameter of twenty-four inches and two with a sixteen-inch diameter. The first of the larger size was manufactured in the early 1900s, with new designs added every two or three years over a fifteen-year period. Apparently the production run on every new design to the set was increased, as the newer issues are fairly common, while the oldest ones are rarely seen. The two sixteen-inch chargers, one featuring Sir John Falstaff, the second a buxom young lady toasting with a glass of Lemp beer, were both issued in 1907.

A 1917 Lemp charger titled "Lady Pouring Sir John a Falstaff Beer" continued advertising Falstaff even after the Lemp Brewing Company closed. When Papa Joe Griesedieck purchased the Falstaff trade name from William J. Lemp Jr., as part of the transaction the former also received a quantity of Lemp Falstaff advertising, in the form of sand puzzles, tin signs, and chargers. The Falstaff Corporation "recycled" this trove of Lemp advertising by blocking out the Lemp references with white paint and stenciling in the Falstaff name as space permitted.

Beginning in the late 1960s, the Falstaff Brewing Corporation capitalized on its Lemp Falstaff heritage by creating replicas of several of the Lemp chargers. The Falstaff re-issues were created utilizing new artwork and, though attractive, pale in comparison to the vibrant colors and crisp details found on the Lemp originals.

THE TASTE OF FALSTAFF

Many have commented while viewing turn-of-the-century brewery worker photos, that the beer in the glasses or mugs in the workers' hands invariably resembles murky mud. The question that then comes to mind of many beer lovers is, what did the old brews really taste like? Beer does not improve with age, so one can't just uncork a bottle of Lemp Extra Pale, 1901, and find the answer by taste.

Fortunately, at least in the case of Lemp's Falstaff, we do have a good idea of what it tasted like. A number of "old-timers" who drank Lemp's Falstaff were interviewed in the years after Repeal. Most described it the same general way: medium gold in color, dry, effervescent, with a pronounced hopped tang, and a long, slightly salty finish. Further, all these same men compared the original Falstaff taste to one brand that is still on the market: Heineken, imported from the Netherlands. So, the next time you drink a bottle of Heineken, close your eyes and think of Lemp's Falstaff beer and the glory years of the William J. Lemp Brewing Company.

A bottle still full of Lemp's Falstaff beer.

Liberty
Brewing Company

(later Burton Ale and Porter Brewing Company)

2534 Dodier Street

Charles F. Becker	1865–1867
Becker & Kuester	1867–1868
John H. Kuester	1868–1869
John F. Heidbreder & Co.	1869–1873
Heidbreder & Niemann	1873–1875
John F. Heidbreder	1875–1882
Liberty Brewing Company	1882–1889
Liberty branch, SLBA	1889–1894
Burton Ale and Porter Brewing Company	1899–1901

This photo of the Liberty brewery and a different view of the plant on the next page, are both from E. Jungenfeld & Co.'s *Portfolio*.

A mug manufactured by the renowned Villeroy & Boch Company in Germany for the short-lived Burton Ale & Porter Brewing Company.

The Liberty Brewing Company of St. Louis began just as the Civil War was ending. It was a good time and place to start such a business, as St. Louis had been a safe haven during the war, attracting numerous migrants and poised to draw many more. Charles F. Becker opened the north St. Louis brewery. John Kuester became his partner in 1867, then ran the place himself the next year. A more permanent owner came on the scene by 1869, when the business became known as the Liberty Brewery of John F. Heidbreder and Company.

Production figures for the 1873–74 brewing season show that Liberty produced 4,220 ¾ barrels (it is unclear why the brewery's output wasn't measured in full barrels like most other plants). John Heidbreder became Liberty's sole owner in the mid-1870s after buying out a partner named Niemann. While remaining rather small compared to most other local breweries, Liberty had many successful years under Heidbreder's leadership. By 1877, annual production was over six thousand barrels, which increased more than one thousand barrels per year into the next decade. So much beer was leaving the plant that a huge new stable, designed by E. Jungenfeld, was built in 1880. This was a sign of things to come, as other improvements were begun in 1882, the same year the business was formally incorporated. A new Boyle ice machine was installed inside a new fermenting house, other new machinery was purchased, and a new office building was erected. The brewery had been established at what was then Twenty-first Street, between Dodier and Parnell. When area streets were renumbered, Twenty-first Street became Twenty-fifth Street.

Next to nothing is known about John Heidbreder. He must have died in the mid-1880s, as his wife then became company president. She sold the brewery to the giant St. Louis Brewing Association (SLBA) syndicate in 1889. As it was one of that company's smaller plants, Liberty was closed just a few years later.

The brewery sat idle for several years, but in 1899 a new company leased and reopened it as the Burton Ale and Porter Brewing Company. The corporate president and brewmaster was John Michael Friedrich, with partners A. J. Duffy, James Cavanaugh, and the Van Nort Brothers Electric Company. Capitalized at a mere twenty-five thousand dollars, the company borrowed the Burton name from the famous brewing city in England, whose mineral-rich artesian waters were known for producing excellent ale- and porter-style brews. According to *The Western Brewer*, Friedrich and partners remodeled Liberty into a "modern ale and porter plant."

J. M. Friedrich was not from Burton-on-Trent, but rather had been born in Bavaria in 1860. He came to the United States at age fifteen and spent five years in the far West before returning to Germany to serve his mandatory term in the army. He returned to America in 1884 and moved to Indianapolis. In 1892, he graduated from the U.S. Brewers Academy, then got a job in St. Louis as brewmaster at the

SLBA's Cherokee Brewery branch, from which he resigned to become head man at Burton.

The choice of brewing ale and porter was an interesting one for the company, as lager-style beer had become the local king. Friedrich must have become impressed with the other styles during his time at Cherokee, which was one of the few St. Louis breweries that continued making them throughout its existence. But perhaps Burton was a century before its time, as the venture proved to be short-lived. The brewery was closed again, this time for good, in 1901.

Following the demise of the Burton Ale and Porter Brewing Company, J. M. Friedrich landed on his feet, first working at the Grone Brewery in St. Louis, and then purchasing the City Brewery in Hannibal, Missouri, from the Riedel family in October of 1902. His days there were disastrously short, however, as less than a year after moving up the Mississippi he died at age forty-three of complications from an appendix operation.

The Liberty/Burton brewery stood silent for the next decade. A small portion of it was used for a furniture warehouse. Then in 1914, it was announced that the brewery was being turned into a mushroom-growing facility. Several men connected with the Missouri Botanical Garden (calling themselves the Mushroom Cellar Company) leased the facility in order to raise fungus in the cellars. A trip to the old brewery site today shows it occupied by a few long brick buildings that bear no resemblance to photos of the brewery. They are either of later construction or else altered so much as to be unrecognizable. Also gone from the neighborhood is the nearby Hannemann/Columbia weiss beer plant (now a vacant lot), as well as Sportsman's Park, where the Cardinals and Browns played just a few blocks west of the brewery.

Mutual
Brewing Company

236 S. Boyle Avenue

1913–1916

Above: Part of the former Mutual brewery in the 1960s not long before it was demolished.

Facing page: Mutual embossed and labeled bottle. The "In Golden Bottles" refers to the brewery using a yellowish golden glass, instead of the standard brown.

The short-lived Mutual Brewing Company was the brainchild of members of the St. Louis Retail Liquor Dealers' Association. They incorporated the business in December 1911. Plans called for a $150,000 brewery plant to be operated on a cooperative basis. Similarly organized companies had been opened throughout the country. By running their own plant, retailers could avoid having to deal with brewery middlemen and distribute products designed to suit their own needs. Incorporators of the company included Lorenz F. Padberg, Patrick Henry Nolan, Ignatius J. Bauer, Martin Fellhauer, and H. G. Eberhardt. In early 1912, the company purchased a four hundred by two hundred foot lot at the northeast corner of Boyle and Duncan streets, extending back to the Wabash Railroad tracks.

BEST LAID PLANS

Brewery architect and engineer Wilhelm Griesser drew up the brewery's plans. They included several unusual aspects. In place of the normal stockhouse would be the "Wilhelm Griesser Direct Storage System." In this process, only the beer was cooled and not the storage rooms. This supposedly helped give the brewer absolute control of the product from the time it left the brew kettle. Filtered and sterilized air was used for fermentation, and packaging of the beer was also done in a warm room. The brew was kept in an enclosed apparatus free from air at all times. The company also felt that eliminating work in cold rooms would improve the health and work environment of its employees.

Work commenced on the plant in the spring of 1912. The brewery would feature mosaic floors, white enamel walls and ceilings, a 450-barrel brew kettle, facilities for bottling 100 barrels a day, and an ice plant. At a May board meeting the company chose Lorenz Padberg as president, Ignatius Bauer as secretary, and Charles Autenreith as treasurer. Other officers included P. H. Nolan (first vice president and manager) and Albert Lutz (second vice president). Daniel Sutter was named brewmaster.

Construction continued into the summer. In July it was announced that the brewery would use electric power generated in Keokuk, Iowa. Management stated that it was the first brewery to use such service, which was expected to garner 30 percent savings in energy costs. At a large party in August the cornerstone of the brewery was laid. More than two thousand attendees enjoyed refreshments and an extensive program of entertainment, emceed by M. F. Farley of New York, the president of the National Liquor Dealers' League.

DELAYS

It took a while for Mutual to get up and running. It is unclear if the delay resulted from cash-flow problems, but in October capital stock was raised from $250,000 to $400,000 and a few months later increased again to $600,000. At the annual board meeting held on January 14, 1913, the company announced that the plant was nearing completion and hoped to begin brewing on April Fool's Day. More than seven hundred stockholders attended the meeting, where vice president and general manager P. H. Nolan stated that Mutual's beer would be sold only to licensed liquor dealers. Based on the number of stockholders and the success of such co-op breweries in other parts of the country, Nolan anticipated first-year sales of 150,000 barrels.

Although beer was still not flowing, in March 1913 Mutual bought additional land at the southeast corner of Forest Park Boulevard and Boyle Street. This was to provide space for additional bottling facilities, more storage room, and an enlarged ice plant. A modern apartment house would also be built for employees.

Mutual finally had its opening ceremonies in June. Among the speakers were St. Louis mayor Henry Kiel (who was also a stockholder), Padberg, Nolan, and *The Mirror* editor William Marion Reedy. Following the program, a brewery tour was held and a chicken dinner served.

On August 22, Mutual beer was ready to be tapped. A crowd estimated at ten thousand came to the lavishly decorated plant to sample free beer and enjoy "lively" music. The crowd included many liquor store owners as well as representatives of rival breweries.

According to an account in the October 1913 issue of *The American Brewer*, the new brewery was "located on high ground and almost in the heart of the finest residence section of St. Louis." There were 1,060 stockholders, 935 of whom were retail liquor dealers. These included 760 dealers from St. Louis and the rest from other Missouri and Illinois towns. Nolan was described as "the fighting friend of the retailer from one end of the country to the other." Furthermore, "to Mr. Nolan the success of the new company is mainly due. For sixteen months he has devoted his splendid ability and energy to the work, and today he has the confidence and respect of not only the directors and stockholders of the company, but of the business community of St. Louis as well." At last Mutual beer "in golden bottles" was hitting the retailers' shelves.

OOPS

Contrary to this glowing report, in the fall of 1914, bankruptcy proceedings against Mutual got underway in U.S. district court. Angry creditors included Illinois Glass Company (owed $2,700), Bittel-Leftwich Tire Service Company ($129), Neustadt Automotive Supply Company ($9.42), and Manhattan Electric Supply ($38.38).

Mutual's second vice president, Albert Lutz, expressed dismay during the hearing. According to his testimony, the company was meeting all of its financial obligations, had plenty of operating capital, and was making a profit. The brewery presented a requested schedule of assets and liabilities to the court. It listed assets of over $1.2 million with liabilities of less than half that. A hearing was scheduled for November 24, at which Nolan was supposed to testify.

A BULLET IN THE HEAD

P. H. Nolan had been the general director of the American Brewers' Association and an editor of liquor-interest periodicals. In addition to helping organize the Mutual Brewing Company, he had helped start eleven similar plants around the country. Described as "wealthy," Nolan had nonetheless been feeling the pressure of Mutual's financial woes.

Above: A detail of a Mutual trade card. Not shown here, but printed elsewhere on the card is the note "The Most Modern Brewery in the United States."

Bottom: The square hole in this opener was used to adjust the carbide lights on early automobiles.

Friends later described his recent mental condition as "strange," which they ascribed to three things—the recent loss of his right eye from an accident; the charges against him of mismanagement by the twelve Mutual stockholders who wanted a receiver appointed to run the company; and despondency over old friends disparaging him, acts he felt were being instigated by rival brewers. Nonetheless, friends who had gone out with him the night before the scheduled hearing felt that he appeared more cheerful than he had in weeks. Little could they have guessed that following their outing, Nolan would return to his office at the brewery and kill himself with a bullet through the head.

CALL FOR *Mutual* BEER IN GOLDEN BOTTLES

STRUGGLING TO SURVIVE

Patrick Henry Nolan was gone, but the problems continued for the remaining crew at the Mutual Brewing Company. January 1915 found the company in court trying to satisfy its creditors. Despite the approximately $150,000 owed them, most of the brewery's debt holders expressed a willingness to accept promissory notes payable in two years. A couple of dissident creditors tried to quash this plan. Finally in March an agreement was reached. All parties expressed pleasure with the efforts of new Mutual manager Charles Fisher, and it was felt that the company had been put on a "paying basis."

In early 1916, Wilhelm Griesser took over as manager of the brewery he had designed. In June, the company announced that it could afford to pay off some of its mortgage notes with hopes that by January they would all be paid off. Griesser declared that the financial condition of the company was growing stronger.

Mutual's president, Lorenz Padberg, was in the news in July 1916. He declared that he was in accordance with the plan of August A. Busch to assist the excise commissioner in enforcing dramshop laws and weeding out disreputable saloons. Padberg, former president of the Liquor Dealers' Benevolent Association, was described in *The Brewer & Maltster* as "a public spirited man."

BROKE AGAIN

Soon thereafter Mutual was back in court again, when creditors alleged the company was insolvent and filed a petition for involuntary bankruptcy. The court named Griesser receiver. Padberg filed a petition denying that the brewery was insolvent but agreeing to Griesser's appointment. On November 15, 1916, Mutual was ordered closed by the bankruptcy referee. With dissident stockholders and creditors unable to agree on a plan to save the company, it was felt to be the only logical course. The court declared that the brewery property would be sold at auction. The assets of the Mutual Brewing Company were put up for sale on April 2, 1917. Winning bidders paid $115,000 for the real estate and just under $28,000 for some of the equipment. Later in the year, ads appeared in *The Brewer & Maltster* magazine offering additional Mutual brewing equipment for sale.

Soon the brewing industry was hit by national Prohibition. It appears that nobody was interested in brewing at the Mutual site once beer was re-legalized. The buildings were sold to Harold Dubinsky in 1942, and the next year they were resold to Mr. and Mrs. M. J. Faure. Many of Mutual's old buildings are still present. It is obvious that some of the large brewing equipment was removed from the premises—brick walls were completely torn down, and the shadow of the redone brickwork is plainly visible. At one time the buildings were used by the Comey Processing Company, while more recently other companies have occupied the space. Also in existence is a desk that belonged to Mutual Brewing Company president Lorenz Padberg, currently in the possession of his great-grandson, who reports that the desk is marred by a bullet hole. Whether this is a remnant of the suicide of Patrick Henry Nolan or from a different source is open to speculation.

We can theorize that Mutual's failure, however, stemmed from two factors. First, despite raising huge sums of money, the financial workings of the brewery seem to have been shaky from the start. Second, the timing of the project could not have been worse, with Prohibition laws of the era putting a crimp even in the business of established breweries.

Wooden bottle case that once held twenty-four bottles of Mutual beer.

Louis Obert Brewing Company / Arsenal Brewery

Arsenal Brewery
2701 Carondelet Avenue

Guido and Adelbert Steinkauler	c1850–c1859
Guido Steinkauler	c1859–1864
Hehner & Weiss	1864–1866
Mathias Weiss	1866–1869
Weiss & Lempel	1869–1870
Mathias Weiss	1870–1874

2700 S. Twelfth Street (new site)

Wahl & Leisse	1874–1876
Weiss & Obert	1876–1881
Louis Obert	1881–1901
Louis Obert Brewing Company	1901–1927
	1933–1936

Above: The Park Saloon was one of many taverns serving Obert Beer during the World War I years.

Facing page: Photograph of Louis Obert, provided by a descendent.

Legend holds that Louis Obert and Adolphus Busch sailed from Germany to America in 1866 on the same ship. While Busch had spent most of the previous ten years in St. Louis, twenty-one-year-old Louis Obert was leaving his home country for the first time. In many ways, the two men's lives continued to intertwine in the years that followed. Both headed breweries within sight of each other in the Soulard section of south St. Louis, both featured their own portraits and a similar eagle design in advertising, and both became well-known beer barons. Tannhauser and Budweiser, their respective flagship brands, were both introduced in 1876. The men also shared another career parallel in that the breweries bearing their names had been started by others.

THE ORIGINAL ARSENAL BREWERY

The brewery that would eventually carry the Obert moniker was operated by a number of men, in two different locations, during its first three decades in business. Originally called the Arsenal Brewery, after the nearby U.S. Army's St. Louis Arsenal, it was founded by a pair of Prussians named Guido and Adelbert Steinkauler. The exact date that the brewery was founded is unknown, but it can be no later than 1850 since it appears that year in a U.S. census of industry as the Arsenal Brewery of Steinkauler and Druselbia.

Built on what would become the west side of the twenty-seventh block of Carondelet (now South Broadway) between Sidney and Lynch streets, the new brewery got off to a promising start. In 1857, the German-language newspaper *Handels Zeitung* reported the business was producing eight thousand barrels of beer a year, of which forty-five hundred was lager and the balance "schenck" or common beer ["common" beer is of lower alcoholic content and was a weaker beer, generally the second or third brew made with the mash and not lagered]. While small by later standards, this rate of production was enough to put the company in mid-pack out of thirty local breweries.

Around 1859, Guido Steinkauler became sole owner of the business. The 1860 census listed him as holding seventy thousand dollars worth of real estate and personal property, with four servants in his household. His prosperity was due no doubt in large part to his ownership of the growing Arsenal Brewery.

Like many other St. Louis breweries of the time, the Arsenal Brewery operated a popular beer garden in conjunction with the main business. This beer garden became a favorite with thirsty Union army soldiers stationed at the nearby Arsenal. There were so many German American soldiers stationed in St. Louis that Confederate army major Jeff Thompson would write in 1861, only partly in jest:

> I have . . . a plan . . . to make a speedy and bloodless peace. It is to burn all the [St.

Louis] breweries and declare lager beer to be contraband of war. The [German American Union soldiers] will all desert in a week, and the Yankees will then run from the state.

In 1864, Guido Steinkauler sold the brewery to partners Philip Hehner and Mathias Weiss. The latter had previously been a partner with Theobald Eckerle in the German Brewery. The Hehner-Weiss partnership lasted just a couple of years, when Hehner left to join the Excelsior Brewery just a few blocks away, leaving Weiss as sole proprietor. In 1869, Weiss took Lorenz Lempel on as a partner in the Arsenal Brewery. Lempel had developed a thorough knowledge of brewing over a fourteen-year period, having served as brewmaster or foreman in a number of St. Louis breweries, including Wagner's National Brewery, Lemp, English, and Fritz & Wainwright. Lempel stayed at the Arsenal Brewery for only a year, though he later became a partner at Fritz & Wainwright.

ENTER LOUIS OBERT

Louis Obert had the ideal background for operating his own brewery, being a son of a family of brewers. Just under six feet tall, Obert was described as a robust man, who wore a goatee and mustache and in later life carried an omnipresent gold-handled walking stick. He was said to be mild in temperament, he enjoyed music for recreation, and he was above all a shrewd businessman who valued his independence. His parents, Louis and Theresa Obert, had founded their Obert Brewery at the place of son Louis's birth, the town of Zell am Hermerbach in Baden, Germany. After receiving an education in the public schools, the junior Louis served an apprenticeship in his parents' brewery. He then worked for four years at various breweries in Renchen, Offenbach, and Frankfurt before sailing to America. After his boat landed in New York, Louis traveled directly to St. Louis to settle down, accepting a position as foreman for Mathias Weiss at the Arsenal Brewery. While one source lists Obert as working at the "Peswich Brewery" in St. Louis in 1866–67, it is assumed to be an error as this company is not listed in any city directories. An obituary states that after leaving "Peswich" he worked as foreman for the Louis Koch brewery in St. Louis before moving

over to Arsenal.

In any case, according to Obert family tradition, it was around 1867 that Obert plunked down ten thousand dollars (an enormous amount at the time) to buy into the financially struggling Arsenal Brewery. To finance his portion of the partnership, Louis Obert had to take out a loan. The note was co-signed by Joseph Pulitzer, founder of the *St. Louis Post-Dispatch* newspaper. Even with the infusion of Obert's capital, the Arsenal Brewery continued to falter. Obert's life savings were soon gone and by 1870 he had moved on, leaving Weiss to struggle on by himself.

Despite his personal financial turmoil at this time, twenty-five-year-old Louis wed Elizabeth Kolb on September 20, 1870. The union would eventually produce five children, most of whom would follow their father into the brewing business: Louis Jr., William, Karl, Charles, and Elizabeth. That same year, Obert accepted another foreman position at the nearby Koch & Feldkamp Brewery, where he stayed until 1874. Obert then moved to New Orleans for two years, becoming the first superintendent of the Casper Lusse Brewery, and helping produce what may have been the first lager beer made in that city.

Back in St. Louis, the days of the old Arsenal Brewery at 2701 Carondelet were numbered. Mathias Weiss had gradually reduced the scope of the business until by 1874 brewing had been halted and only malting was taking place. Two years later even the malting operation was stopped and the old plant was shuttered, actions that may have been taken in preparation for Weiss's next business move.

THE SECOND ARSENAL BREWERY

Perhaps Louis Obert felt that his destiny was in St. Louis, for in 1876 he returned to that city, serving for a few months as foreman of the Rueppel & Ehlermann malt house. Later that year, Obert again formed a partnership with Mathias Weiss (apparently with no hard feelings from their previous failure), and the duo purchased the two-year-old Wahl and Leisse Brewery at the northeast corner of Twelfth and Lynch.

Peter Wahl and Hubert Leisse had not been new to the local brewing scene, as prior to setting out on their own both had been employed at the Pittsburgh Brewery, yet another plant located on Carondelet Avenue. Wahl had been foreman and

Leisse the bookkeeper at that facility. For their new plant, the pair had appropriated the Arsenal Brewery name from Weiss's closed plant. With the receipts from the sale to Weiss and Obert, Wahl and Leisse headed downriver to Memphis and opened the Tennessee Brewing Company.

The same year Weiss and Obert bought the Arsenal Brewery, a new flagship brand was introduced. Named after a Wagner opera, Tannhauser would receive the majority of the company's marketing attention for the next half-century.

The second Weiss/Obert partnership must have found success early on, as the old malt house on Carondelet was soon reopened. It stayed open for a number of years, presumably to provide the malt for Tannhauser. Furthermore, *The Western Brewer* trade magazine reported in 1880 that the brewery was going to "make some important changes in their icehouse," perhaps a signal that refrigerating machinery was about to be installed.

Upon the death of Mathias Weiss in 1881, the partnership was dissolved with Obert purchasing his former partner's interest from the estate. The Louis Obert Arsenal Brewery was born. However, with production that year of fifteen thousand barrels, it was still a relatively small enterprise when measured against most of its St. Louis competitors.

The late 1880s were a time of consolidation in the brewing industry, in both St. Louis and other parts of the country. When an English syndicate invaded the local market in 1889, purchasing eighteen breweries and creating the St. Louis Brewing Association (SLBA), Louis Obert turned down what many considered an outrageously high offer to sell his brewery to the Brits. He must not have needed the money, as the brewery soon expanded.

For the most part, during this period the Arsenal Brewery management maintained good

Above: View of how the Louis Obert Brewery looked, in this seldom-seen tin sign dating to around 1900.

Facing page: Photo of Louis Obert Jr., president of the brewery in the mid-1930s.

relations with its workers. One exception occurred during the summer of 1893, when the company's union workers went on strike and declared a boycott of all Obert products. The strike quickly turned ugly; an account at the time stated, "A bitter feeling has existed between the employers and employees of the brewery ever since a boycott was declared." This bitterness may have led to sabotage by the striking workers. On July 11, there was a small explosion at the brewery, badly burning employee Louis Ebel. In this day of wooden kegs, it was Ebel's responsibility to inspect the cleanliness of the kegs after they had been washed. This was accomplished by inserting an open flame through the bunghole, into which the inspector then peered. When Ebel inserted his candle into one of the kegs, something in it exploded. He spent the next few weeks recovering at home from his injuries.

While the Arsenal Brewery could box it out with both local competition and organized labor and stay on its feet, on May 26, 1896, it was almost knocked out by an unanticipated foe. On that day a tremendous tornado (or cyclone as they were called in those days) hit the brewery, causing considerable roof damage to several of the buildings. The cyclone had originally touched down as two small funnel clouds running parallel for a few minutes in Midtown. But east of Forest Park the two clouds combined and cut a swath twenty-five city blocks wide to and over the Mississippi River, continuing many miles into Illinois. In St. Louis the Arsenal, Wainwright, Anthony & Kuhn, Phoenix, and Lemp breweries suffered serious damage. Booklets published shortly thereafter showing the tornado damage (more than eight thousand buildings were destroyed) featured representations of the Grim Reaper on their covers, appropriate as more than 250 people were killed in the storm. This total included 47 people killed in a building at Seventh and Rutger, just a short walk from the Arsenal Brewery. Damage to the brewery was quickly repaired, and during the next few years the business continued to slowly grow. In 1901, the brewery was officially incorporated as the Louis Obert Brewing Company. Capital was listed at four hundred thousand dollars by the three incorporators—Louis Obert, Louis Obert Jr., and William Obert.

When the majority of the remaining non-SLBA breweries banded together in 1907, forming their own syndicate named the Independent Breweries Company, Obert again chose not to participate, valuing his independence over the competitive advantages of joining the new confederation. Of the major local breweries only Obert and Schorr-Kolkschneider, along with the two biggest players in town (Anheuser-Busch and Lemp), stayed independent. Actually, not selling out was a bold business decision on Obert's part, as Lemp was five times bigger than Obert and Anheuser-Busch twice as big as Lemp.

Two additional brands were eventually added to the Obert product list: Gold Band and Culmbacher. A 1908 ad in the *St. Louis Republic* described the company's beers, using the sales language puffery of the day:

The great popularity of Tannhauser, Gold Band and Culmbacher beer. And the steady and enormous increase in its sale are due entirely to its *high quality, purity and delicious flavor.* Good water, good malt and cleanly and scientific methods of brewing are essential requisites of good beer. You cannot buy a purer, more delicious, more healthful or nutritious beer than the above brands anywhere at any price. We invite comparison because of its superior quality. Made in St. Louis by St. Louisans. Louis Obert Brewing Company, St. Louis, Mo.

The "Made in St. Louis by St. Louisans" was a thinly veiled sales jab at the SLBA conglomerate, which was still owned by the British.

CHANGING OF THE GUARD

By all accounts, Louis Obert's greatest joy in life was not his brewery, but his amusement park. Located on eight acres at the intersection of Clayton and McCausland in the west end of town, the property also featured a beer garden. The Obert Brewing Company did its best to leverage its connections to the park. The front entrance was topped by a huge copy of the brewery's "LO and Eagle" symbol. Unfortunately, a disastrous fire burned the amusement park to the ground in 1913, and Obert was rather distraught. According to grandson Harry Obert, "It was grandfather's hobby, and I recall him standing out there the day after the fire saying, 'Gott im Himmel! Vat did I do to deserve this?'"

For a beer baron like Obert, in a sense it was a timely death, occurring just a few years shy of the enactment of Prohibition. Thus he would not have to endure the loss of his lifelong livelihood when beer was outlawed. Sadly, his children would, as they continued management of the Louis Obert Brewing Company after his death. Seeing the rising tide of the dry movement sweeping across the country, the Oberts joined the swelling ranks of beer makers producing near beers. Introduced in 1917, the Obert entry was marketed as Trebo (that's Obert spelled backward). In time, the Tannhauser label was also utilized to sell the company's non-intoxicating malt beverage.

PROHIBITION TAKES ITS TOLL

The Louis Obert Brewing Company stayed afloat during the first few years of Prohibition by manufacturing ice and near beer, and by selling property here and there. Another source of income was at least occasional bootlegging, as the brewery was raided more than once, which led to court citations for selling beer containing more than the tiny allowable percentage of alcohol.

At noon on September 8, 1921, a team of federal Prohibition agents, headed by E. J. Hoover and assisted by local police detectives, raided the Obert plant. They confiscated a truck marked "St. Louis Bakers' Association—All Goods Delivered Promptly." The truck had been loaded with 178 cases of unlabeled full bottles later found to contain a beverage with an illegal 4.1 percent alcohol content. Thirteen more cases of the same brew were also seized right inside the front doors of the company. A man had been standing at Twelfth and McGirk streets when the raiding party roared up to the brewery. He ran into the plant, having apparently been on duty as a lookout. John S. Sand, a foreman at the brewery, at first refused to obey orders given by agent Hoover and engaged in a scuffle with the agents, but he was quickly subdued by the police detectives. By the afternoon of the same day, all

Louis Obert died on April 9, 1914, at the age of sixty, after a three-week illness from a complication of pneumonia and asthma. Some sixty years later, in a special feature in the *St. Louis Post-Dispatch*, his grandsons Harry Obert and Louis Obert III spoke on several topics concerning the family's history. Harry Obert provided some of the circumstances around his grandfather's death:

It was the night of Holy Thursday. Grandfather had been ill for several weeks and the doctor told him to stay in. But he liked to walk up to the tavern at 13th and Lynch and play pinochle in the evening. "Doctor, hell!" he said. "I am going to play cards!" He was back in a few hours, saying he felt dizzy and sick. He died before midnight.

At the time of his death, Obert was widely known in both St. Louis business and social circles. He had been a member of the St. Louis Swiss Sharpshooting Club, the North St. Louis Bundeschor, the Rheinischer-Florsinn and the Concordia Turnverein. He was buried in St. Marcus Cemetery, the likeness of his face preserved for posterity, carved larger than life into the front of his funeral crypt.

of the brewery workers had been sent home, and padlocks were placed on all the buildings' outside doors.

Charles Meine, the driver of the seized truck, told the police that the vehicle's owner had sent him to pick up a load of "beverages." Neither Meine, nor the truck's owner, supposedly knew where to deliver the beer.

The seizure of the Louis Obert Brewing Company was short-lived. J. Vance Higgs, attorney for the Oberts, called the action unconstitutional, as "no law in the United States authorizes such an action." Agent Hoover's supervisors must have agreed, as the government padlocks were stripped from the brewery doors the very next day, with Hoover's boss personally overseeing their removal.

The management of the brewery had apparently not yet learned its lesson. Just three weeks later, another team of federal agents raided the brewery, acting on a complaint filed by the Reverend W. C. Shupp, superintendent of the Missouri Anti-Saloon League. In this second raid, a truck parked in front of the plant loaded with ninety cases of bottled beverage was seized, and samples were again taken to the nearby St. Louis Federal Building for analysis. While this beer tested lower in alcohol than that found in the previous raid, the newly seized brew was still over the legal limit of one-half of 1 percent alcohol.

Whether or not the Obert family directly sanctioned the bootlegging is unknown. However, as the brewery was still tightly held by the family, it is hard to believe that they were not at least indirectly involved with the making of illegal brew. Despite the federal raids, the Obert Brewery managed to keep its manufacturing license in hand, and its doors open, until 1927. That year the financial failure of the company accomplished what federal agent E. J. Hoover could not. The lights in the brewery would be turned off for the next six years.

Though shuttered, in January 1930 the Louis Obert Brewing Company still managed to land back in federal court. Mrs. Stella S. Walsh filed suit for receivership of the dormant company, claiming it was insolvent and owed her forty thousand dollars for back rent and taxes on various properties. Mrs. Walsh asked the court to issue an injunction forbidding the brewery from transferring its assets to Obert family members so as to avoid her claim. How this lawsuit was resolved is not known.

OPENED, BUT TOO LITTLE CAPITAL

*O*nce Prohibition ended, many who had previously been in the beer business were anxious to re-enter the industry, including the Obert family. The brewery was reopened in 1933 by three of the sons of the founder. Louis Obert Jr. sat in the president's chair, managed the business, and was bottling house superintendent; William Obert commanded the brew kettle while serving as corporate vice president; and Charles L. Obert served as secretary, treasurer, and advertising manager. Another Obert sibling chaired a key executive position, as Elizabeth M. Obert served as the brewery's office manager. At the age of seventeen months she had been stricken with polio, which left part of her lower body paralyzed. It was said that her illness was contracted as the Obert family mingled with the crowds attending the opening of

the Eads Bridge. Despite her disability, Elizabeth, using crutches when young and a wheelchair in later years, always lived an active life and played an energetic role in the management of the business.

While the Oberts thought they might have enough cash in their coffers to reopen the brewery by themselves, they knew they lacked the funds necessary to carry out full-scale operations. In June 1933, President Louis Obert Jr. filed a request with the Missouri State Securities Department for a permit to sell up to one hundred thousand shares of preferred stock to the public at three dollars a share. This infusion of new capital into the brewery also brought with it a new officer. W. T. Brookings, former president of the Marshall-Hall Grain Corporation, was appointed brewery vice president, in part to watch over his recent purchase of a significant block of Obert stock.

Brewing finally resumed on October 1, 1933, and after a relatively brief lagering period, the finished product started pouring out of the taps of many St. Louis–area taverns. The Oberts had spent $203,000 rehabilitating their old family brewery.

The Obert Brewing Company reintroduced Tannhauser as its flagship bottled brand, in a plant with a yearly capacity of about one hundred thousand barrels. The draft product was simply marketed as Obert beer. In resurrecting the Tannhauser label, the company emphasized the brand's pre-Prohibition days of glory. A June 1934 newspaper ad read:

> Since 1876 . . . Tannhauser Beer. Fifty-eight years ago St. Louis lovers of good beer smacked their lips over their first draft of Tannhauser. For forty-three years thereafter this delightful brew remained the favorite of men and women who appreciate its full body and satisfying taste. And now Tannhauser Lager Beer is back. Again it is made by the same company that brought it into being back in 1876. If you are old enough to remember before-prohibition days, try Tannhauser tomorrow and your taste will tell you that the same old quality and the same aging process now gives Tannhauser the same zestful tang that it possessed in the old days. Yes sir and madam—there's a real thrill in store for you when you taste Tannhauser.

However, despite the cheerful advertising, early cracks were quick to show in the financial foundation of the Obert Brewing Company. In February 1934, a one-year deed of trust was filed against the company. It was designed to protect 162 creditors having claims of over $150,000 against the brewery, debts generated for rehab work and supplies. Obert attorney James E. Carroll stated that the action was being taken to put all of the creditors on an equal basis in their claims.

The Obert family and the other stockholders in the company were starting to feel the financial pinch of the failing enterprise. By June 1934, controlling interest of the brewery had been sold to Vice President Brookings, who with J. M. Sullivan, a consulting engineer, took over management. Despite the sale, it was agreed that Louis Obert Jr. would continue as company president, William Obert as brewmaster, and Charles Obert as corporate secretary. The change in ownership did little to stop the collapse of the business. On August 1, 1934, the Obert Brewery made its last batch of beer forever, as it had run out of raw materials and could not afford to purchase any more. Even so, the company was kept afloat for a time by selling beer already on hand.

In November, nine Obert brewery workers filed suit, alleging they had not been paid for several weeks. Their petition to the court stated that the company was unable to pay its current debts and expenses, and that certain company assets were being "wasted." The suit also alleged that the brewery was attempting to prefer certain creditors when making payments. This suit was short-lived and dismissed the following month, presumably because the company had ladled out the back wages owed the nine workers.

Not surprisingly, without any new batches of beer being brewed, by the spring of 1935 the company was in serious financial trouble. On March 22, the Obert Brewing Company filed a petition in United States District Court calling for a debtor's reorganization of the business in order to forestall foreclosure proceedings and allow time to search for additional capital to resume operations. In addressing the court, the Obert lawyers pleaded that while the brewery had raised more than $300,000 in stock sales to 380 investors, the money had been used chiefly for modernizing the plant, leaving the company insufficient working capital. Assets were listed as amounting to $353,000 balanced against $190,000 of debt. In accepting the petition, bankruptcy judge C. B. Davis warned the Obert lawyers that he was pessimistic about the future of the brewery and that he had no "mystic method for saving failing businesses."

In April, Louis Obert pledged to the court that he had assurances of more money to operate the brewery should the reorganization be allowed.

Facing page: Eye-catching tin sign, featuring a scene from Richard Wagner's Tannhauser Opera, for which the company's signature brew was named.

Left: Match safe given away by the Obert Brewery.

Facing page: Louis Obert Sr.'s portrait is prominently displayed on this "pie" style tray, one of the more common (but still hard to find in good condition) pieces of St. Louis breweriana.

He also downplayed the notion that a loan might be obtained from the U.S. Reconstruction Finance Corporation, a possibility brought to the court's attention by creditors. Noting that only one brewery, the Star-Peerless Brewery of Belleville, Illinois, had been able to obtain such a loan, Obert said it was his understanding that it was contrary to government policy to grant loans to breweries or distilleries.

While Judge Davis may have been skeptical of the company's future, on April 26 he placed control back into the hands of the existing management team and ordered the company to file a reorganization plan within thirty days. On reporting back to the court in mid-November, the Obert lawyers told Judge Davis that all negotiations to obtain funds had failed, and that the required approval of two-thirds of the creditors to the proposed plan of reorganization had not been met. The court was asked to appoint a trustee for the company so that it could be liquidated. Two weeks later brewery officials were back in court with another plan, stating that they could open again with seventy thousand dollars of capital. This amount would come from twenty-five thousand dollars in trustee's certificates, twenty-five thousand dollars credit from brewery supply companies, and the balance from stockholders and certain note holders.

Again the new funds never materialized, and in February 1936 the Obert Brewing Company was judged bankrupt. A trustee was appointed to liquidate the company, with a final tally of the brewery balance sheet showing liabilities of $257,000 overshadowing assets of $250,000. It was now clear to all that the plant would never be reopened. The real estate was sold for a paltry $15,000 on October 25, 1937, at the St. Louis Civil Courts Building. The buyer was a creditor's committee representing the holders of the 1934 deed of trust notes.

Why had the Obert Brewing Company failed so quickly after reopening? According to Louis Obert III, it was primarily due to the fact it was undercapitalized and further bled dry by the spending habits of the Oberts:

My father and his brothers inherited grandfather's holdings. Prohibition came along three years later, and to keep on going like they were, they began selling this property, that property. My uncle Bill liked to go into taverns, light up a $10 bill and burn it up, just to show he didn't need it. Eventually they sold the West End Heights property (where the Oberts operated their amusement park) for $50,000 because they were in hock so bad. Today the property is worth several million dollars. My father and uncles didn't pay themselves big salaries: $500 a month wasn't much, even in those days. But the salary didn't mean anything. They used to pay all their personal bills, even light and gas bills, with brewery checks, and when the whole thing wound up, every one of them was $50,000 to $75,000 overdrawn. I had to borrow money to bury my father.

Echoing these thoughts, fellow Obert grandson Harry Obert added, "Our grandfather's sons were silver spoon people. When things got rough, they didn't know what to do."

Louis Obert Jr., who went to work as a Falstaff salesman following the demise of the Obert Brewing Company, died in June 1942. His brother Charles passed away that November, followed a few months later by their mother Elizabeth. Meanwhile, third-generation brewer William F. Obert continued in the family tradition. A 1942 graduate of the Siebel Institute, he worked at Anheuser-Busch prior to accepting the position of assistant brewmaster at the Southwestern Brewing Company of Oklahoma City.

The site where the majestic Obert Brewery once stood has joined several other former St. Louis breweries as a part of the sprawling Anheuser-Busch brewing complex. In October 1942, the doors of the long-silent Obert brewery were opened for a short time in a move to support America's World War II efforts and provide some relief to the company's creditors. More than three hundred tons of machinery and equipment were removed and sent to steel mills to be recycled. According to an announcement made by Ley Rexford, regional director of the War Production Board's special projects division, most of the brewery scrap was cast iron, steel, and brass—all essential metals for use in making weapons. The dismantled equipment had been valued at $125,000 at the time of Obert's 1936 bankruptcy hearings. Proceeds of the scrap sale were distributed among the brewery's creditors, who had waited six years for the money. Later the brewery was torn down.

While his brewery and amusement park have disappeared, the Louis Obert mansion at 2631 S. Twelfth Street lives on. Built right across the street from the brewery in 1886, the three-story, ten-room brick mansion is in wonderful shape. The home features its original woodwork and light fixtures. Reminders that the Oberts once lived in the home abound. The letters *LO* are carved into the stone lintel above the main doorway. The front doors contain exquisite frosted windows featuring two peacocks—reminders of the birds raised in the backyard by Louis Obert Sr.

Nicks in the wooden planking of the back stairwell, made by Elizabeth Obert's walker as she labored up and down the steps, can also still be seen.

Fate is fickle. The name Adolphus Busch went on to become a household name, while that of former shipmate Louis Obert is but a footnote in the history of American brewing. But if Louis Obert could come back to visit his old mansion today, he not only would feel right at home due to the careful preservation, but also he could sit on the front steps of the mansion and smell roasting malt in the air, courtesy of the company that still carries the name of his old friend Busch.

Phoenix Brewery

44 S. Front Street

Fleischbein & Ketterer	c. 1835–c. 1839
Gronenbold & Ketterer	c. 1839–1841

1729 Lafayette Avenue (new site)

Staehlin & Ketterer	1841–1852
Christian Staehlin	1852–1859
Staehlin Jr. & Halm	1859–1864
Staehlin Jr. & Briedenbach	1864–c. 1867
Christian Staehlin Jr.	c. 1867–1873
Phoenix Brewing Company	c. 1873–c. 1875
St. Louis Brewery Company	c. 1875–c. 1880
A. Griesedieck Brewing Company	1883–1889
Griesedieck branch, SLBA	1889–1891
Phoenix branch, SLBA	1891–c. 1912

Top: 1890s photograph of the Phoenix Brewery, with delivery wagons on the street, first published in E. Jungenfeld's *Portfolio*.

Bottom: Undated photo of Phoenix Brewery child laborers working in the bottling department. It was a common practice for breweries to hire children in the early years of the twentieth century.

Although it operated for nearly eighty years in the days before Prohibition (and almost made a comeback afterward), the Phoenix Brewery is still one of the most obscure of the larger St. Louis breweries. Some historians have speculated that the brewery had its start with Thomas Biddle's Phoenix Brewery in the mid-1820s. But there is no evidence supporting this, and they were almost certainly separate operations.

It was around 1835 that a second Phoenix Brewery was established downtown at Front and Myrtle streets by partners Jacob Fleischbein and Lorenz Ketterer. When Fleischbein left in the late 1830s to take over a brewery in nearby Belleville, Illinois, brewer Ketterer took on a partner named Gronenbold.

NEW DIGS

In 1841, Ketterer teamed up with Christian Staehlin to build a new Phoenix Brewery at the southeast corner of Lafayette and Second Carondelet (later Eighteenth Street) in south St. Louis. Christian Staehlin had come to the United States from Baden, Germany, in 1833, settling on a farm outside of St. Louis. In 1837, he moved to the city, working at various businesses on the levee prior to entering the brewing industry. The pair was successful, as in 1847 Phoenix produced about 2,500 barrels of beer, which increased to 5,500 barrels by 1850. This ranked third in local production behind only the Winkelmeyer and Uhrig breweries.

Staehlin ran the business alone following Ketterer's departure in the early 1850s. Sales continued to soar for Phoenix through that decade. Production reached seventeen thousand barrels in 1856. The plant was enlarged in 1858, becoming something of a Taj Mahal of St. Louis breweries. A local newspaper described the grounds as surrounded by a high fence and featuring a huge two-story artificial underground cavern. Each story was twelve feet high, with various passageways leading from low doors to storage vats capable of holding five thousand barrels of beer. The cave featured floors, pillars, and arches made of stone.

While it ranked second in St. Louis beer sales behind Winkelmeyer, the Phoenix Brewery was described as having the most modern brewing equipment in town, with the plant valued considerably higher than any of its local rivals.

In the late 1850s, Christian Staehlin retired, handing the reins of the business over to his son Christian Jr. The younger Staehlin was joined by a new partner named Joseph Halm, until 1864, when Halm jumped ship to open his own brewery practically next door. While Halm's brewery didn't last long, it did employ George Staehlin as a clerk, indicating that there may have been some familial connection between the Halms and the Staehlins. Henry Briedenbach, former foreman at the Pittsburgh Brewery in St. Louis, replaced Halm as a partner at Phoenix for a couple of years, but by 1867 Christian Staehlin Jr. was once more sole proprietor.

Left: Spectacular 1850s lithograph of Christian Staehlin's Phoenix Brewery. Courtesy Library of Congress.

Below: A 1906 Pearl brand bottle label, from the days when Phoenix was part of the SLBA.

Although the Phoenix Brewery had been one of the largest in St. Louis in earlier years, production shrank a bit in the post–Civil War era. The 1873 production figures ranked it fifteenth of thirty local breweries, at 10,657 barrels. Around this time the business was incorporated, with I. W. Schaefer named the brewery's corporate president and Staehlin continuing as superintendent. Apparently the Staehlins had once more needed the financial backing of a partner. Despite such help, the brewery was closed around 1875.

A (NON) PHOENIX RISES AGAIN

The Phoenix Brewery was shut down only briefly, however, as a group calling itself the St. Louis Brewery Company bought the facility and brewing commenced once more. City directories listed the company's secretaries, including John Altgeld (1876), Fred Hertel (1877), and George Class (1878–80). Whether these gentlemen were investors, brewers, or just pencil pushers is unclear.

The St. Louis Brewery Company produced 11,091 barrels in 1877, which increased considerably the next year to 15,060. But production dropped to 10,527 barrels in 1879, and by 1881 the plant was once more shuttered.

GRIESEDIECKS TO THE RESCUE

Henry Griesedieck came to St. Louis from Quincy, Illinois, in 1864 to help start a malting plant at 716 Carr Street (the site of the original Lafayette Brewery). He also ran a saloon across the street. His brother Anton Griesedieck became a malt house partner in 1872, having migrated to the United States from Germany in 1870. The two brothers would later operate separate St. Louis malting plants. Anton Griesedieck wanted a more direct role in the brewing business, so in 1878 he and sons Bernard, Henry, and Joseph, together with partners August Koehler and Robert Miller, purchased the old Stumpf/Thamer brewery. They operated under the name A. Griesedieck & Company. The Griesediecks sold their interest in this brewery to some of their partners at the end of 1881.

This sale paved the way for Anton and his boys to purchase the former Phoenix Brewery from

A Phoenix tin-over-cardboard sign, from the early 1900s.

the St. Louis Brewery Company, incorporating the business as the A. Griesedieck Brewing Company. Following some rehab work on the plant, the Griesediecks' Pearl brand beer began flowing out the doors to the public.

By 1884, while ranking only thirteenth of the twenty-three breweries in St. Louis, production had increased to over twenty thousand barrels a year. The business was successful enough that the Griesediecks were able to expand. Their improvements culminated in a giant stockhouse, completed in 1889 and featuring two floors below ground and three above.

Later that year the brewery was sold to the St. Louis Brewing Association (SLBA) syndicate, a group headed by British investors that bought eighteen area breweries. The Griesediecks remained active in the brewery, running it for the Brits as the Griesedieck branch of the SLBA.

PHOENIX ONCE MORE

On June 1891, the Griesedieck brothers resigned from the SLBA in order to build a new plant at Eighteenth and Gratiot—the National Brewing Company. This prompted the conglomerate to dump the Griesedieck name from the branch plant and revert back to the old Phoenix moniker.

Former Phoenix brewery proprietor Christian Staehlin Jr. passed away at age seventy-five in 1903. He had arrived in St. Louis with his family at age four in 1833, and left the Phoenix Brewery while in his late forties. In his younger years he had served as a city councilman and was elected to a two-year term as city treasurer. In a touch of irony, Staehlin lost so much money in various business ventures after selling the Phoenix Brewing Company that he had to go to back to work as a solicitor for the SLBA.

While a number of the SLBA breweries ended up closing within a few years of their purchase, not so with Phoenix, which according to *American Breweries II* stayed in operation until 1912. The plant continued to be listed in city directories until 1916, indicating that at least some type of beer-related activity must have gone on until then. National Prohibition was just around the corner.

FALSE STARTS, DESTRUCTION

The former Phoenix Brewery was no longer owned by the SLBA when beer was re-legalized in 1933, but the plant was still of interest to other prospective brewers. A mysterious group known as the Marth Brewing Corporation took out a federal permit to brew at the old Phoenix plant in 1934, but operations never got off the ground. Phoenix was in the news again in early 1936, when it was purchased by the Carondelet Brewing Company, which since 1933 had been brewing at 2025 Gravois Avenue. Carondelet's plans included spending two hundred thousand dollars to upgrade the facility and purchase new equipment.

Carondelet had dreams of running a one hundred thousand–barrel capacity plant and hiring eighty employees to man the fifty-thousand-square-foot facility. An opening date of mid-1936 was set, but this was another project that never came to fruition. Brewing was destined to never return to the old Phoenix/Staehlin brewery.

In 1964, after learning that the brewery was slated for demolition to make way for interstate highway construction, the spelunking team of Hubert and Charlotte Rother visited the brewery's cellars. The building's owner was operating a used auto parts store next door and allowed them access. They hopped over several piles of old tires at the entrance and found the rest of the cellar empty. The brickwork was still impressive, and hooks that once held aging vats were still in the ceiling. The Rothers could not enter the brewhouse because it was already in the early stages of demolition. Not long afterward, the buildings were torn down. The Phoenix Brewery has disappeared without a trace, the grounds today occupied by vacant lots abutting Interstate 44.

Some brewing history does remain across the street at 1821 Lafayette, where a large brick house was recently for sale. A realtor's flyer grabbed from the front yard revealed that the home had been built by the Griesedieck family in 1890. The $350,000 price tag included original stained glass windows bearing the Griesedieck family crest.

Early in the twenty-first century, brewing finally returned to the Lafayette Square neighborhood with the opening of the Square One Brewery at the corner of Eighteenth and Park. The brewpub is located about halfway between the former sites of the Phoenix Brewery and Joseph Schnaider's Chouteau Avenue Brewery. Farther east on Park Avenue were once a pair of Griesedieck malt houses as well as the old Hoppe Malt House.

The St. Louis Brewing Association (SLBA) was organized in 1889 to effect a merger of eighteen area breweries—seventeen scattered throughout the city of St. Louis and the Heim brewery in East St. Louis. According to the June 15, 1889, edition of *The Western Brewer*, the consolidation (or syndicate as it would become known) represented every brewery in the city producing more than one thousand barrels of beer a year except for three holdouts—Anheuser-Busch, Lemp, and Obert/Arsenal, all located near each other in the Soulard neighborhood.

Chosen as officers of the SLBA were Ellis Wainwright of the Wainwright Brewing Company, president; Charles G. Stifel (City Brewery), vice president; Louis Schlossstein (Green Tree Brewery), second vice president; William F. Nolker (Brinckwirth-Nolker Brewing Company), treasurer; and Philip Stock (Schilling and Schneider Brewing Company), secretary. Capital stock was issued in the amount of $5.25 million, said to be half of the appraised value of the companies.

Six months later, *The Western Brewer* reported that the SLBA's breweries were "likely to be sold to" an English group that a London newspaper said would be capitalized at over $12 million. The British investors took on the name St. Louis Breweries, Limited (SLBL). The American sellers would retain the SLBA name for the local operating division, and most would remain as managers of their respective breweries.

The SLBL was just one of many such British syndicates taking over breweries across the United States, although the SLBA deal was the largest. It represented an effort by English capitalists to invest their money outside of the stagnant British economy. It is unclear if the British transaction was already in the works when the SLBA was first formed, and while it would be fascinating to know the financial underpinnings of these deals, details are sorely lacking.

In its 1890 corporate elections, the SLBA re-elected Ellis Wainwright to the presidency (where he would remain until 1901). Anton Griesedieck (of A. Griesedieck Brewing Company) and Henry Grone (H. Grone Brewery Company) were named vice presidents with the following additional directors:

Henry Anthony (Anthony & Kuhn)
C. Marquard Forster (Hyde Park)
Theodore Herold (Cherokee)
John Krauss (Klausmann)
Louis Schlossstein (Green Tree)
Otto Stifel (City)
J. C. Van Blascum (affiliation unknown)
Christopher Winkelmeyer (Winkelmeyer)

Several of the syndicate's breweries were quickly closed as there was plenty of brewing capacity to go

St. Louis Brewing Association

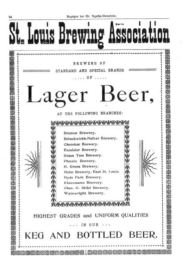

Top: Ad listing all the SLBA breweries in 1900.

Middle: A pressing of the intertwined letters "SLBA" into the back of a wooden tavern chair.

Bottom: A 1906 City Brew bottle from the SLBA.

around, while others fell by the wayside later on. The SLBA's primary branches became Green Tree, Grone, Hyde Park, Klausmann, City, and Wainwright. Brewing ended at the Lafayette Brewery around 1909, but the plant was kept around as the company's primary bottling facility. The Hyde Park bottled brand, introduced in 1907, became the SLBA's flagship label, although Green Tree and others were also retained.

Otto Stifel succeeded Ellis Wainwright as SLBA president in 1901 when the latter went on a ten-year European exile to avoid legal problems. Stifel left a few years later to take over the Union Brewing Company (formed in 1898) and was succeeded by Henry Nicolaus, a brewmaster and former co-owner of the Green Tree Brewery.

Several of the SLBA's branches underwent name changes after various families left the association. A. Griesedieck went back to its old Phoenix name in 1891 when the Griesediecks jumped ship to form their own National Brewing Company, the Excelsior name was moved to the Winkelmeyer plant when the latter was torn down for Union Station, the City name replaced Stifel after Otto Stifel stepped

down from the SLBA, and the Brinckwirth-Nolker plant reverted to its old Lafayette tag in 1905. At that time Henry Nicolaus was corporate president, C. Marquard Forster and John Grone vice presidents, and Stephen Stock still secretary-treasurer. Serving as assistant treasurer was C. Norman Jones, who had come to St. Louis from England in 1896 as a representative of the SLBL and had stuck around at the SLBA. These gentlemen were joined in the boardroom by directors William A. Haren and Frank Forster.

In 1891, the combined output of the SLBA plants was 842,281 barrels. By the mid-1890s sales had shrunk to under 700,000 barrels, with the company barely making a profit. Part of the sales slump may have been caused by labor problems. *American Brewer* reported in 1894 on the fifteen British-owned American brewery syndicates, one of which, the SLBA, was said to be shaking the confidence of investors due to a boycott. In 1895, responding to the previous year's 11 percent decrease in sales, the SLBA's annual report insisted that:

> This decrease has been due to the general depression. . . . Some trouble has been experienced during the year with the labor union, whose exacting demands could not be complied with, and for some time the product of the company has been boycotted by the

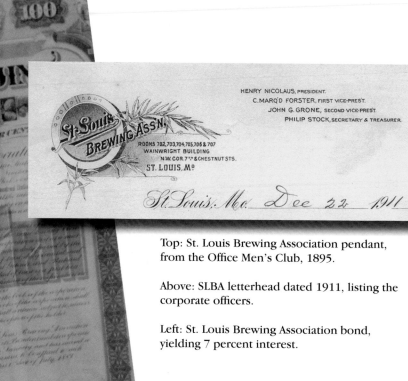

Top: St. Louis Brewing Association pendant, from the Office Men's Club, 1895.

Above: SLBA letterhead dated 1911, listing the corporate officers.

Left: St. Louis Brewing Association bond, yielding 7 percent interest.

Knights of Labor; but no great importance is attached to the action of this body . . .

The problems with the union were eventually resolved, and sales soon began to rise, but they would not exceed the 1891 total until 1911, when 883,608 barrels were sold. The SLBA netted a profit of over $700,000 the next year.

When Prohibition arrived in 1920, most of the SLBA breweries were mothballed. Hyde Park stayed open, producing Hyde Park near beer, sodas, and other items. The bottling shop at the Lafayette branch was also used, and the SLBA continued operating and maintaining its office at the Chouteau Avenue Crystal Ice and Cold Storage Company in a building that was part of the old Joseph Schnaider Brewing Company (closed brewing-wise by the syndicate in 1893).

By the time beer was legal again in 1933, the SLBA owned just three of its old breweries (besides the Schnaider ice plant)—Hyde Park, Wainwright, and Lafayette. Those properties were purchased by the St. Louis investment firm of Stifel, Nicolaus and Company for $650,000. The president of this business was Herman Stifel, whose father Christopher had been a brewer in St. Louis. Herman Stifel was also a cousin of one-time SLBA president Otto Stifel and had married into the brewing Forster family.

Louis Nicolaus, the son of former SLBA president Henry Nicolaus, was likewise part of the investment firm. While they initially entertained grandiose plans of reopening all three breweries, only the Hyde Park facility got back up and running. To get the business going again, Louis Nicolaus talked his father Henry into coming out of retirement. Parts of the Forster family would become involved in the brewery again as well. Hyde Park experienced a fair amount of post-Prohibition success before selling out to the Griesedieck-Western Brewing Company in 1948. The Hyde Park brand would continue until that company was purchased by Carling in 1954. The brewery was shut down a few years later.

A shriveled SLBA, led by C. Norman Jones, Henry Nicolaus, and Joseph Stroer, also continued after Repeal. As late as the 1940s the association still owned local real estate as well as the ice/cold storage plant. Carrying on to this day is the investment company still known as Stifel Nicolaus, the SLBA's longest-lasting corporate descendant.

Photo taken on May 21, 1896, at the sixth annual gathering of the Office Men's Club of the SLBA.

Schilling & Schneider Brewing Company / Louis Koch Brewery

926 Sidney Street

Louis Koch	1859–1874
Koch & Feldkamp	1874–1876
Louis Koch Brewery, Elizabeth Koch proprietor	1876–1879
Koch & Schilling Brewing Company	1879–1882
Schilling & Schneider Brewing Company	1882–1889
Schilling & Schneider branch, SLBA	1889–1891

Top: Employees pose in front of the downtown Schilling & Schneider saloon, beer garden and depot.

Bottom: Louis Koch brewery scene, where the formula for Samuel Adams Boston Lager originated.

While it operated for more than thirty years, the Louis Koch Brewery (which was later taken over by the Schilling & Schneider Brewing Company) is one of St. Louis's most obscure late nineteenth century breweries. Nonetheless, it has a current claim to fame that would makes its old rivals jealous—the formula Louis Koch used for his lager beer is the basis for today's popular Samuel Adams Boston Lager brand. Jim Koch, the founder of the Boston Beer Company, which makes the Samuel Adams brands, borrowed the recipe from his great-great-grandfather.

THE EARLY YEARS

Louis Koch was the son of a German brewer and established his own brewery in 1859 in the Soulard neighborhood of south St. Louis. A large number of breweries were already located there. One reason was proximity to the river, which was a source of water and ice; another was the natural underground caves in the area. Both ice and cool storage space were very important to brewers in the days before artificial refrigeration.

If Anheuser-Busch had been big enough at the time (it was not even owned by Anheuser or Busch yet), it would have been close enough to cast a shadow on Louis Koch's brewery. Other neighbors included the Excelsior, Arsenal, Pittsburgh, and Lion breweries. Jaeger's Gambrinus brewery (later Anthony & Kuhn) was right across the street, and the second plant of the Green Tree Brewery would be right next door.

An early city directory refers to Koch's as the Schlop Brewery, a term which remains a mystery. While this could indicate the business was started by a man named Schlop, there is no evidence to show this. The brewery must have opened late in 1859, as only five hundred barrels of beer were brewed that year. An 1860 industrial census listed Koch's brewery as having fifteen thousand dollars invested in it, with six employees. The fifteen hundred barrels of ale and twelve hundred barrels of beer produced that year ranked it in the middle of the forty or so breweries then operating in St. Louis. One of the employees was Antoine Koch, presumably a brother of Louis.

In 1874, Louis Koch took on Ferdinand Feldkamp as a partner in the business. Production at the brewery that year amounted to 13,594 barrels, ranking the firm thirteenth of the twenty-nine local breweries. Not much is known about Feldkamp, and the Koch & Feldkamp name lasted only until 1876. Feldkamp remained in the brewing industry a few more years, then opened a saloon at 412 Locust Street.

While Louis Koch is listed in the 1876 St. Louis city directory, he must have died sometime that year. The next year's directory lists his widow, Elizabeth, as the brewery head; in fact, the 1878 directory lists her as a brewer. In 1879, she is listed as the proprietor of the Louis Koch Brewery. Elizabeth Koch had to cope not only with the death of her husband, but also with stagnant business at his namesake plant. Production was down to 11,822 barrels in 1877, shrank to 11,319 the next year, then rebounded a bit to 12,500 in 1879. That year the national convention of the United States Brewers Association was held in St. Louis, and appearing in the front row of the group photo commemorating the event was a youthful looking Charles (Carl) Koch, son of Elizabeth and Louis.

NEW HANDS

George Schilling was a veteran of the St. Louis brewing industry, having spent many years as foreman at the Julius Winkelmeyer Brewing Association. He stepped down from that position in 1879 and proceeded to spend the summer months on a European vacation. Upon his return, he became a partner in Elizabeth Koch's brewery, with the business name changed to Koch & Schilling Brewing Company.

Philip Stock, presumably a member of the family that had long operated the Oregon Brewery in St. Louis, also became affiliated with Koch & Schilling at this time. Stock served as corporate secretary, while Schilling took on the title of president and superintendent. Stock and Schilling may have brought with them an infusion of cash, as a new mash tub was installed in the brewery in 1881. Other improvements were likely made as new technology was introduced into the brewing field during this era.

Elizabeth Koch must have been ready to exit the beer business, for in 1882 Charles F. Schneider, another brewing veteran, bought her out to become president of the new Schilling & Schneider Brewing Company. Schneider had spent many years working for his almost-namesake brewer Joseph Schnaider, managing the beer garden and saloon adjacent to Schnaider's brewery at Twentieth and Chouteau.

General Manager Anton Reck assisted Schilling and Schneider at their brewery. The partners operated their own malt house and in 1884 produced between sixteen and eighteen thousand barrels, all of which was sold in draft form. In addition to the brewery, the company operated a saloon in downtown St. Louis at 16 S. Broadway.

THE END (almost)

Merger mania first hit the U.S. brewing industry in the 1880s, fueled in part by British capitalists looking to invest their money away from home. It was the English pound that fueled the engine of the St. Louis Brewing Association (SLBA), which organized in 1889 to purchase eighteen local breweries. Among them was the Schilling & Schneider Brewing Company. Schilling & Schneider's corporate secretary Philip Stock must have been handy with a pen, as he likewise served in that role for both local and state brewers' associations. He also became secretary of the St. Louis–based board of the SLBA. Anton Reck responded to the SLBA takeover by fleeing north to purchase the Jehle brewery in nearby Alton, Illinois. It proved to be a good career move, as the Reck Brewing Company stayed in business until Prohibition.

In the meantime, the SLBA consolidated operations and closed a good number of the breweries it had acquired. The Schilling and Schneider branch stayed open only until 1891. By the next year, the buildings of the former Louis Koch brewery were either torn down or remodeled to make way for expansion of the SLBA's Green Tree branch, which operated until 1919.

AN UNLIKELY REVIVAL

That would be the end of the brewery's story but for some interesting twists of fate. Louis Koch's son Carl had stayed in the brewing industry, and Carl's son Charles Joseph likewise worked in the beer business. He survived the dry years by peddling supplies to home brewers, then returned to brewing after Repeal. His son Charles Joseph Koch Jr. followed in the family tradition, starting as an apprentice in the 1940s, graduating from the Siebel Institute in 1948, and serving as brewmaster at several breweries, including Burger and Hudepohl in Cincinnati and Wiedemann in Newport, Kentucky. His final brewmaster position was at the Wooden Shoe Brewing Company in Minster, Ohio.

One day Charles Jr. walked into a tavern in Minster and noted that the Wooden Shoe tap knob had been replaced by one from Burger. He asked the owner the reason and was told that Burger was becoming more popular because of its TV sponsorship of Reds baseball games. "That was the beginning of the end," Koch later recalled to the *Cincinnati Post*. "Small breweries couldn't support a baseball team!" He soon decided to exit the beer business, and he opened a successful chemical company.

That looked like the end of the Koch family's tenure in the brewing industry. Charles Jr.'s son Jim studied law and business at Harvard. But he dropped out of graduate school at age twenty-four and headed to the western U.S. to become an instructor with Outward Bound, a wilderness-education program. Later, his wild oats sown, Jim returned to graduate school and got a job with a

Boston think tank and consulting firm. Still, after several years there, Jim again began to grow restless. He enjoyed an occasional beer and noticed that American beer drinkers had few choices. Aside from the mass-produced U.S. lagers, the only other choices were imports that could easily grow stale. "Americans pay good money for inferior beer," Koch said in a *Reader's Digest* article. "Why not make a good beer right here in America?"

OLD FORMULA, NEW SUCCESS

Jim Koch recalled that several years before, when his father had been cleaning out his attic, he had run across some yellowed old beer recipes. After reviewing them, Jim's dad had commented, "Today's beer is basically water that can hold a head." Nonetheless, when Jim told his father he was quitting his job to open a brewery, he replied, "That is the dumbest thing I ever heard." But

Jim's dad relented, investing forty thousand dollars in his son's idea. Koch invested one hundred thousand dollars of his own savings, friends and relatives kicked in a like amount, and in 1984 the Boston Beer Company was born. For his new beer, Jim borrowed the formula from his great-great-grandfather's recipe, tweaked it a little, and brewed the first batch in his kitchen.

In 1985, Koch filled his briefcase with beer bottles and headed out for the bars of Boston, trying to sell them his product, which he decided to call Samuel Adams Boston Lager. He chose the name both for its local connections and for the fact that in addition to being the governor of Massachusetts and a revolutionary patriot, Adams had also done his own brewing (the book *100 Years of Brewing* commented on Adams's beer-making talents by reporting that he was "a brewer of, it must be confessed, very indifferent ale and beer.")

By the end of 1985, sales of Samuel Adams had reached five hundred barrels, ironically matching the 1859 production total met in St. Louis by Louis Koch during his first year in business. But from these small beginnings, Samuel Adams beer became a huge success. In 1988, sales grew to thirty-six thousand barrels as specialty beers began

Top: Pre-1874 ad for Louis Koch's brewery.

Bottom: Photo snapped in the spring of 2009 of the one-time residence of Elizabeth Koch, at 2300 S. 13th Street in St. Louis.

catching the consumers' fancy. While Boston Beer opened a small test brewery in its hometown, for many years most of its beer was brewed by the Pittsburgh Brewing Company, with help from Blitz-Weinhard, Miller, G. Heileman, and Stroh.

This led to a bit of a feud between Jim Koch and Anheuser-Busch scion August Busch IV when the latter grumbled about Samuel Adams being contract brewed. Koch responded to the *St. Louis Post-Dispatch*, "When competitors malign contract brewing, I say it's the same thing as if Julia Child came over to my house to cook dinner. It may be my kitchen, but it's her dinner." When Anheuser-Busch joined in a campaign with numerous micro-breweries to force brewers to list on their labels who was actually producing their beer, Koch fired back, "My advice to Anheuser-Busch is, 'Why don't you try a different way of competing and make a better beer?'"

Koch's Boston Beer Company has expanded both geographically and in terms of beer styles, offering various ales, lagers, stouts, seasonals, and over-the-top brews like the legendary Triple Bock and Utopia. The Hudepohl-Schoenling Brewery in Cincinnati was leased with an option to purchase in 1996. A $6.5 million expansion was undertaken, enabling Boston Beer to brew most of its product itself, with current sales above a million barrels per year and over 350 employees.

During the Ohio brewery expansion, two 195-barrel brew kettles were installed. Small by modern standards, Jim Koch nicknamed the kettles Charles and Louis after his brewing ancestors. "This is the kind of kettle my great-great-grandfather would have used making the original recipe," Koch told the *Cincinnati Post*. "There's no economic justification for them, they're just beautiful . . . there's a lot of art in brewing."

So the next time you sip a Samuel Adams Boston Lager, forget about the bewigged brewer/patriot and instead offer a toast to nineteenth-century St. Louis brewer Louis Koch, who first brewed a similar beer at a location that is now an Anheuser-Busch parking lot.

The office building, the only still-standing part of the Schilling & Schneider Brewery, is now a neighborhood tavern called "Big Daddy's."

Schorr-Kolkschneider Brewing Company

2537 Natural Bridge Avenue

Schorr Brewing Company	1902–1902
Schorr-Kolkschneider Brewing Company	1902–1924
	1933–1939

Top: Photo of the Schorr-Kolkschneider brewery about 1902. A note scribbled on the back of the photo says "Opening day," which may explain the bunting on the front of the brewery.

Bottom: 1930s label for "Healthful Refreshing S-K Lager Beer."

Facing page, top: Portrait of Jacob B. Schorr.

Facing page, bottom: Photo of John J. Schorr, the brewery's president in the mid-1930s.

While not as illustrious as such St. Louis brewing dynasties as the Busches, the Lemps, or the Griesediecks, the Schorr family nonetheless played a significant role in area beer history. Family members also branched out to breweries in other locations along the Mississippi River and elsewhere in the country.

A BACKGROUND IN BEER

The Schorr family's first brewery began production centuries ago in Bavaria. While one account gives the opening date as the 1660s, descendant Chuck Betz recalls seeing the year of 1522 inscribed on the still-existing building while visiting in the late 1990s. The brewery back in Germany had remained open until not long before Betz's visit.

It wasn't until the 1860s that the family turned its attention to the United States, when Johann Valentin Schorr and his sons migrated. They began operating one of the two breweries in the small town of Waterloo, Illinois, about twenty-five miles southwest of St. Louis. They were also involved in a brewery in Millstadt, Illinois, a village even smaller than Waterloo (and then known as Centreville).

Three of the Schorr brothers went on to local brewing prominence—Michael, who returned to Waterloo from St. Louis in the 1880s to run the surviving brewery there; John W., who was a partner in St. Louis's Excelsior Brewery and later headed the Tennessee Brewing Company in Memphis; and Jacob B., who in the 1870s went to work at Charles G. Stifel's City Brewery in St. Louis. The boys' career choices may have had something to do with the fact that they had brewing in their blood from both sides of their family. Their mother was the former Louisa Koechel, the daughter of Johann Koechel, who had started the first brewery in Waterloo.

A NEW BREWERY

Jacob Schorr spent twenty-eight years as the brewmaster at Stifel's. When he left, it was to strike out on his own, and he started construction of a new brewery on a wedge-shaped chunk of land in north St. Louis. The brewery had a brief life as the Schorr Brewing Company, but soon its name was changed to Schorr-Kolkschneider (or S-K). This likely indicates that partner Henry W. Kolkschneider had been convinced to ante up additional funds in order to help support the business. Their beer first hit the market on June 14, 1902. The new S-K brew was aged and naturally krausened in sixteen large wooden tanks layered at the bottom with beechwood chips, added to clarify the brew.

Henry Kolkschneider was born in Hanover, Germany, in 1853 and arrived in St. Louis in 1871. He worked for a year as a laborer in a lumberyard, then spent his first year in the beer business driving a delivery wagon for Joseph Schnaider's Chouteau Avenue brewery. He spent the next four years as a teamster for the Anthony & Kuhn brewery, where he first met Jacob Schorr, who as plant foreman was his boss. In 1876, Kolkschneider accepted a position as collector for the Hyde Park brewery in St. Louis, where he spent the next twenty-five years.

JACOB SCHORR

Schorr-Kolkschneider must have done pretty well after its rocky beginning, as in 1909 a new bottling department was built across the street from the brewery. The building was two stories, 66′ × 104′, and featured a covered driveway and wagon yard on one side. It was connected to the main brewery by an underground tunnel.

That same year Kolkschneider made the news when, after having his horse and buggy stolen, he did some detective work and after a few hours tracked down the thief. Although the wagon-jacker was in the vehicle when Kolkschneider found it, he escaped after a brief struggle.

Brewery President Jacob B. Schorr suffered a stroke in October 1915 and never recovered, passing away at home the next February at the age of sixty-five. Succeeding him as both president and brewmaster was his son John J. Schorr. Henry Kolkschneider continued as corporate vice president, treasurer, and general manager, while another of Jacob's sons, Clarence W. Schorr, was company secretary and plant superintendent. Brewery brass was rounded out by John Scheller, manager of the bottling department.

John J. Schorr had considerable experience in the brewing industry, having apprenticed under his father at Stifel's prior to attending the U.S. Brewers Academy in Chicago. He then worked at his uncle's Tennessee Brewing Company before returning to St. Louis, briefly plying his trade at the Green Tree Brewing Company before again working alongside his father at Stifel's and then at S-K.

Henry Kolkschneider received mention in a brewing trade magazine once more in April 1916 when it was mentioned he had taken out his final citizenship papers. Apparently his tardiness at doing so while the war raged in Europe was somehow

deemed newsworthy. Not long after he became a citizen, however, the Eighteenth Amendment became the law of his adopted land.

THE (NOT SO) DRY YEARS

The S-K brewery turned to production of near beer, malt extract, soda (including S&K Grape Beverage), and popsicles during the dark days of Prohibition. As with most such endeavors, sales were poor. Thus the Schorrs were compelled to switch tactics in order to keep their business afloat—by bootlegging real beer.

Actually, numerous breweries continued to pursue their now-illegal trade, and S-K must have succeeded at this for a while. Their first encounter with the law didn't come until July 24, 1924, when forty barrels of beer were seized by Prohibition agents from a truck leaving the brewery. Two days later, the feds returned and confiscated eighty-two barrels from inside the plant. Their suspicions were confirmed when chemists analyzed the beer and found the average alcohol content to be slightly over 5 percent.

Six men were each charged with six violations of the Volstead Act. They included company officers John, Albert, and Clarence Schorr and Fred Ficht, plus bookkeeper Walter Meyer and brewery employee Joseph Reichenberger. The three Schorrs and Ficht each had to post twenty-five hundred dollars bond in order to stay out of jail. Charges against the men included unlawful manufacture, removal, disposal, and transportation of "real beer" as well as not paying taxes on it. Since the company held a near-beer permit, it was only legal to have real beer in vats and not in bottles or kegs. The government also got court permission to padlock the brewery under the nuisance section of the Volstead Act. This served to restrain the officers from using the plant to manufacture any kind of beverage. The defendants were also requested to show cause as to why the plant shouldn't face closure for a year as punishment for its violations.

All of the men charged ended up pleading guilty. Albert Schorr was ill and unable to attend the trial, but the other three officers were each fined twenty-five hundred dollars and the two employees and the company fined five hundred each. Whether this misadventure prevented any more illegal beer from flowing out of the plant for the duration of Prohibition is unknown.

HAPPIER DAYS

Despite its earlier legal entanglements, the S-K brewery was ready to operate shortly after Prohibition ended. In April 1933, Schorr-Kolkschneider ordered a whopping one million bottles and twenty-five thousand wooden cases. A fifty thousand dollar rehabilitation fund was set up by the company, and thirteen thousand dollars would be spent for "automobile trucks." Contracts had also been signed to purchase malt and other raw materials. Soon, the plant's 360-barrel brew kettle was being fired up every day of the week except Sunday.

S&K lager beer came back on the market on July 15, 1933. "Fully Aged in Wood" was one of the reopened brewery's mottos. By the end of 1933, ten trucks were on the road delivering beer that was sold by the company's five salesmen. Two full-time bartenders were on staff serving visitors free samples at the brewery's sternwirthe (sampling room). Senator Harry S. Truman was one of those who took advantage of this hospitality, describing S-K as "tasty."

In June 1934, the *St. Louis Star-Times* published a lengthy article on the recently revived regional beer business. Included in an ad taken out by S-K was an illustration of its stockhouse with the following text:

> As you read this 767,250 gallons of fine, golden S-K lager are mellowing in 93 gigantic storage tanks of seasoned white oak. . . . In the same old painstaking way used many generations ago . . . we haven't yet turned to so-called modern speed and mass-production methods for the purpose of cutting corners and expenses.

John J. Schorr served as brewery president after Repeal. Joining him as corporate officers were his brother Clarence as secretary-treasurer and Fred Ficht as vice president. Ficht had an interesting connection to Schorr's former partner, Henry Kolkschneider—in addition to being his stepson, he was also his son-in-law, having married Henry's only child, Annie. John Schorr didn't get to enjoy the revived beer business for long, passing away in 1935 at age fifty-eight following an appendicitis op-

eration. Brother Clarence took over his role as master brewer. Other survivors included son William, who also worked at the brewery, and daughter Olivia, who was the wife of Alton, Illinois, brewer William Netzhammer.

A DOWNHILL SPIRAL

Unfortunately, the demise of the S-K brewery was not too far behind that of its former chief executive. By 1936, financial cracks were starting to show in the operation, when a suit was filed against the company by the Wellston Bottling Works, which served as the S-K distributor for St. Louis County. The suit involved a twenty-five thousand dollar bank note, which the brewery had apparently used to pay operating expenses, but which Wellston president David Massa insisted had been intended as collateral for a loan. We don't know the brewery's side of the story, because Schorr-Kolkschneider vice president Ficht declined to discuss the suit with reporters. Nor is it known how this suit was finally resolved.

Despite this turmoil, S-K did have enough cash to engage in a holiday print ad campaign later in 1936, encouraging patrons to "Spread good cheer—Be prepared for Christmas callers—have a good supply of stimulating, pep-provoking S-K Lager Beer on hand."

In June 1937, a new brewmaster was brought on board. Michael Schachtner, a 1910 graduate of the Siebel Institute with experience at breweries in Germany and Saginaw, Michigan, was hired to brew the S-K brands. These included the standard lager and a kulmbacher sometimes marketed as "Vat."

Financial difficulties finally caught up with the brewery in 1938, when it filed for bankruptcy protection in a last-ditch effort to stay afloat. In February 1939, the trustee reported to Federal Judge George Moore that S-K had lost $57,761 over the last eleven months. This prompted the court to issue an order that the brewery be closed. In August it was reported in *Modern Brewer* that the Natural Bridge Realty Company, a subsidiary of the brewery, was liquidated of fifteen pieces of property that brought $16,700. No date had been set for sale of the brewery, which the article mentioned had earlier been sold at auction, although the bid was not high enough to be accepted by the court. Meanwhile, former S-K employees scrambled to find new jobs in the industry. Brewmaster Schachtner landed a position as master brewer at the Kewaunee (Wisconsin) Brewing Company while Clarence Schorr became a salesman for the Wisconsin Malting Company.

A reason given by some for the demise of the Schorr-Kolkschneider Brewing Company was the fact that its beer was lousy. Henry Tobias, one of the last employees, and who later went to work for Anheuser-Busch, was quoted years later as blaming the oaken aging tanks for causing quality problems with the brew. He felt that filling the vats with water, which was done when the brewery was closed in the 1920s, had allowed resin to leach out of the wood, providing a medium for yeast infections that were then passed on to the beer. When sales dropped, beer stayed in the vats too long, which led to batches of bad beer being released to the public. Tobias also recalled carbonation problems with S-K bottled beer. Bottles from the same batch would range from flat and foamless to "spurters" from which most of the contents would eject upon opening. It seems not even brewers as savvy as the Schorrs were able to overcome these production problems.

The old brewery buildings served other businesses until 1969, when the brewhouse at 2537 Natural Bridge Avenue and several of the other structures were razed. The wrecking ball didn't get everything, though, as a couple of the buildings survive to this day. These include the original brewery stable and wagon shed, and the bottling works across the street built in 1909, recently occupied by a business but now vacant.

Right: 1906 newspaper ad, partially in German, from the *St. Louis Globe-Democrat*.

Below: Detailed photo of the brewery sometime after Repeal. Used with permission of Missouri Historical Society.

SCHORR-KOLKSCHNEIDER BREWING COMPANY

Natural Bridge Road und Parnell Strasse

Brauer von erstklassigem Bier

The Joseph Uhrig Brewing Company
(Camp Spring Brewery)

Eighteenth and Market streets

William Kraut and Joseph Uhrig	1846–1849
Joseph Uhrig & Co./Joseph Uhrig	1849–1876
Joseph Uhrig Brewing Company	1876–1880
Excelsior Brewing Company	1880–1889
Excelsior branch, SLBA	1889–1891

Top: Photo of Joseph Uhrig, from *The Makers of St. Louis: The Mirror*, 1906.

Bottom: Joseph Uhrig wooden bottle case.

Facing page: Early 1870s Joseph Uhrig embossed bottle.

The Joseph Uhrig Brewing Company, originally known as the Camp Spring Brewery, was established in 1846 by William Kraut and Joseph Uhrig. Both men had previously operated downtown St. Louis saloons—Kraut a place called the Henri-House and Uhrig (along with brothers Andreas and Ignatz) the Fulton Coffee House.

Joseph Uhrig was born in Lauterbach, Germany, in 1807. For generations his family had been in the river transportation business, which trade Joseph followed. He came to the United States at age twenty-nine, landing in Baltimore where he started running a ferry boat. Uhrig arrived in St. Louis in 1838, where he operated a flat boat and later a steamboat named *Pearl*. He was involved in various other enterprises as well. One of them, a brewery, began when Joseph's brother Ignatz bought a lot at Eighteenth and Market streets, which joined a lot owned by William Kraut on the banks of Chouteau's Mill Creek.

The Uhrig brothers must have already been contemplating opening a brewery, for on New Year's Day 1846 Kraut leased Ignatz Uhrig's lot, upon which was a small house, a beer saloon, and the foundation for a small brewery. Kraut agreed to finish building the brewery with his expenses applied as payment in lieu of rent. After running out of cash, Kraut had to borrow fifteen hundred dollars from Joseph Uhrig, who took out a one-year mortgage on the brewery and equipment. But by the end of the year, with brewing about ready to commence, Kraut and Uhrig decided to become partners in the business.

Once underway, their small plant was soon unable to keep up with demand. A bigger building was put up on adjacent land. The cost of this second brewery included:

$3,452.52 for a stone building
$1,000.00 for equipment
$541.50 for additional odd supplies

UHRIG TAKES OVER

William Kraut was one of many victims of St. Louis's 1849 cholera epidemic, leaving Joseph Uhrig to complete the new brewery on his own. Unlike some of the other area breweries, in an 1850 census Camp Spring reported doing all of its brewing by hand power rather than steam or horse. Nonetheless, it produced some six thousand barrels of beer that year, ranking second in town behind only the nearby Winkelmeyer plant.

Joseph Uhrig became sole owner of the Camp Spring Brewery in 1853 when he bought out the Kraut family heirs. The next year he began expanding a natural limestone cave beneath property he had earlier purchased at what would become the southwest corner of Jefferson and Washington. The original cave was just 40 feet long, but was expanded to 210 feet by 20 feet by 20 feet and lined in brick. The brewery was about half a mile from these cellars but was soon connected to them by a tunnel. Uhrig later spent $100,000 to have a narrow-gauge railroad installed inside the tunnel in order to more easily transport beer.

Above the cave, which would become famous as Uhrig's Cave, a large beer saloon, dance hall, gardens, malt house, and icehouse were built. Uhrig's Cave became one of the best-known beer gardens in the city. Among its attractions were live entertainment and railroad rides back and forth from the brewery to the cave.

Joseph Uhrig brought his brother Ignatz aboard at the brewery in the late 1850s, and for the next few years continued to see a slow but steady growth in beer sales. The Camp Spring Brewery produced nine thousand barrels of beer in 1857, ranking it seventh in production out of twenty-nine city breweries. The same year the brewery's beer was awarded top prize at the annual St. Louis Fair. Camp Spring was also the first brewery in St. Louis to produce bock beer. In connection with the release of this beer, an annual celebration was held every May Day on the cave grounds.

CONTINUED SUCCESS

By 1860, the Uhrigs' brewery was the fourth largest in the city. That year a future beer baron signed on to work at the brewery: eighteen-year-old August Uihlein, who was hired as bookkeeper, collector, and shipping clerk for twenty dollars a month plus free board. That was a big improvement over what Uihlein had been paid at the Schlitz brewery in Milwaukee—one dollar a month. By 1862, Uihlein had become Uhrig's general manager. Following the death of Joseph Schlitz, the Uihlein family took over the Milwaukee brewery and August returned there to help run it. Uihlein had likely become acquainted with Joseph Uhrig in Milwaukee, for in 1854 the latter had purchased nine acres of land in that city. There he built a mansion where he spent time every summer.

August Uihlein wasn't the only future brewing celebrity to pass through the brewery, as in the early 1860s Louis Schlossstein served as Camp Spring's foreman. He later became one of the owners of the Green Tree Brewery, but not before marrying Josephine Uhrig, widow of Ignatz, in 1863.

Annual beer production at Camp Spring was over twenty thousand barrels in the early 1870s, and Uhrig's Cave and the beer garden continued to thrive. The company also became one of the many shipping breweries in St. Louis, bottling its beer for export to places near and far.

Joseph Uhrig died in 1874 at his summer home in Milwaukee. His wife, Walburga, inherited the plant, with son-in-law Otto Lademann taking over daily management. Lademann was a native of Hereford, Germany, who had been a young Civil War hero. Upon returning to St. Louis he had served as the brewery's business manager.

NEW COMPANY, NEW OWNERS

In 1876, the brewery was incorporated as the Joseph Uhrig Brewing Company, but the next year production shrank to just over eighteen thousand barrels. This ranked tenth of the twenty-six breweries in St. Louis.

Mechanical refrigerating machines were being perfected in the late 1870s, and breweries were quick to utilize them. In September 1878, Uhrig had such a device installed by D. L. Holden and Brothers. Refrigerators of the era did not always work well once they were put in, but *The Western Brewer* reported that Uhrig's was "in successful operation." Unfortunately, brewery sales continued to shrink, to 15,604 barrels in 1878 and then 13,346 the next year (shoving Uhrig down to thirteenth in production out of twenty-five local breweries, no longer in the top half). The year 1879 was also notable in that a theatre company began holding productions at the cave/beer garden, which is regarded as a predecessor to today's Muny Opera in Forest Park.

The end came for the Joseph Uhrig Brewing Company in 1880. Early that year the brewery defaulted on a $20,000 note held by Mrs. Uhrig. She briefly ran the business, but in March creditors filed suit against the corporation for about $75,000. Mrs. Uhrig insisted that she had purchased the company in exchange for forgiveness of a $105,000 debt it owed to her. The brewery's creditors, however, were adamant that the property be sold. The legal wrangling came to an end six months later. While Uhrig's sales had been steadily declining, that of the Excelsior Brewing Company had been increasing. Excelsior had been leasing its Seventh Street brewery from Henry Koehler, brother of its president Casper Koehler. Excelsior management saw a golden opportunity to move across town to the Uhrig location.

In exchange for seventy-five thousand dollars, Excelsior obtained the real estate, buildings, cooperage, and stock on hand of the Joseph Uhrig Brewing Company. *The Western Brewer* opined that "the purchasers are believed to have obtained a great bargain." The sale did not include Uhrig's Cave, which the magazine stated was "now on the market."

LIFE WITHOUT UHRIG

The Excelsior Brewing Company successfully operated at the old Uhrig site through the next decade. It was a part of the St. Louis Brewing Association merger in 1889 and continued as a branch of the English-financed company.

On January 12, 1890, a tornado knocked down the ninety-foot-tall brewery chimney. Part of it fell upon a small house next door. While a woman and her baby were trapped in the rubble, they were rescued and discovered to be nearly unhurt. Soon,

though, the entire brewery became rubble, as the property was sold to a railroad company. In 1891, the former Uhrig/Excelsior plant was torn down to make way for Union Station.

The SLBA trotted the Excelsior name one block down the street to the former Winkelmeyer facility, where it would operate until 1916. Union Station, of course, still exists as a shopping mall and hotel, and incredibly the old site of the Uhrig brewery was once again home to a brewery when two brewpubs, the short-lived Bacchus Brewing Company and later the Route 66 Brewery and Restaurant, operated in the mall.

Just as the Uhrig Brewing Company wound up replaced by a more famous building, so did the old Uhrig's Cave and beer garden. In 1884, the property was sold to Thomas McNeary, who with his brothers installed electric lights and continued offering entertainment. But within a few years the site had been virtually abandoned. An indoor theatre was built there in 1900, and the early years of the twentieth century saw roller skating, bowling, and mushroom growing at the property. Then in 1908 the land was leased to the St. Louis Coliseum, and a ten-thousand-seat building known as the Coliseum was built. Enrico Caruso sang there, Johnny Weissmuller swam there, both major political parties held national conventions there, and teetotaling preacher Billy Sunday even gave lectures there. But like the Uhrig brewery, the Coliseum eventually saw its popularity fade.

In 1953, the Coliseum was demolished in order to make way for the Jefferson Bank. During demolition, the underground caverns were briefly exposed, giving spelunkers one final chance to see the old tunnel where, eighty years earlier, folks could ride a train from the Joseph Uhrig Brewing Company to the famous Uhrig's Cave and celebrate with a fresh Uhrig beer.

Above: Uhrig label from 1876, celebrating the country's centennial.

Left: Uhrig brewery scene, from *The Western Brewer*, 1879.

Wainwright Brewery Company

(Fulton Brewery and Busch / Wainright Brewery)

Fulton Brewery
21 Almond Street

Wainwright & Coutts	1831–c. 1841
Wainwright & Withnell	c. 1841–1846
Ellis & Samuel Wainwright	1846–1851
Samuel Wainwright	1851–1857

Busch/Wainwright Brewery
Gratiot, Cerre, Ninth, and Tenth

George Busch	1854–1855
Busch & Fritz	1855–1857
Fritz & Wainwright	1857–1870
Samuel Wainwright & Company	1870–1883
Wainwright Brewery Company	1883–1889
(new plant built near old with office at 1015 Papin)	
Wainwright branch, SLBA	1889–1922

Above: Portrait of Ellis Wainwright, from *The Western Brewer.*

Facing page: Photo of Samuel Wainwright from Scharf's *History of Saint Louis City and County.*

Today the name Wainwright is associated by informed St. Louisans with the Wainwright Building, which is one of the city's best-known pieces of architecture. A plaque on the building honors architect Louis Sullivan and his patron Ellis Wainwright, identified as a St. Louis capitalist. But over a century ago the Wainwright name would have been associated with beer. And unlike most prominent St. Louis brewing families, the Wainwrights hailed from England rather than Germany.

PIONEER BREWERS

Joseph Wainwright was the first member of the family to tread on American soil. He had worked at his father's successful ale brewery in Yorkshire, England, prior to migrating to Lawrenceville, near Pittsburgh, Pennsylvania, in 1818. He started a brewery there that was destined to last until Prohibition. It was actually his daughter Martha who first influenced St. Louis brewing, by marrying real estate mogul John Withnell in 1829. Two years later Withnell (who still has a street in south St. Louis bearing his name) moved to St. Louis to seek his fortune.

Martha Wainwright Withnell's brother Ellis may well have accompanied her husband to St. Louis. In November 1831 the *Missouri Republican* reported that a new brewery had opened at the corner of Main and Almond streets, four blocks from the local market. Partners in the business were Ellis Wainwright and Charles Coutts, the latter a stonecutter by trade. Their Fulton Brewery had only one local competitor (though others would soon follow) and ultimately became the first such business to have any lasting influence on the local industry, as the handful of previous St. Louis breweries had come and gone rather quickly.

The new concern initially brewed ale and porter, with common (unlagered) beer production added in 1841. Around this time Coutts sold his share in the business to Ellis Wainwright's brother-in-law John Withnell.

The Fulton Brewery (presumably named after steamboat pioneer Robert Fulton, which in turn may explain why decades later some Wainwright shell glasses were etched with the representation of a steamboat) grew slowly during the first half of the 1840s. But toward the middle of the decade the owners made a concerted effort to stimulate the sale of their ale by improving its quality. New machinery was installed, including a malt kiln of the latest design. An expert brewer named McKee was hired, who had experience in several East Coast plants and in the short-lived Missouri Brewery in St. Louis. The actions taken to improve the quality of the product at the Fulton Brewery were apparently successful. In 1846 the editor of the *Daily Missouri Republican* distributed samples of the brewery's malt liquor to "experts," who pronounced the beverages to be of "very superior quality," the equal to any produced in the East.

Ellis Wainwright's brother Samuel, who was born in

Pittsburgh in 1822 and had learned brewing at his father's plant, moved to St. Louis in 1846 to join Ellis at the brewery, buying out brother-in-law Withnell. Ellis Wainwright died during the cholera epidemic of 1849, and Samuel became sole owner of the Fulton Brewery in 1851 upon buying his late brother's share from his estate. By this time the brewery was one of the largest in town, producing three thousand barrels per year, most of it still ale and porter.

WAINWRIGHT MOVES

Samuel Wainwright made a bold business move in 1857, buying into George Busch's brewery at Ninth and Gratiot and abandoning the Fulton Brewery in the process. Busch, an older brother of Adolphus Busch, had built the plant in 1854. Charles A. Fritz became Busch's partner the next year. Fritz then found himself Samuel's partner when the latter bought out Busch. Rather than the English-style brews produced at the Fulton Brewery, the new partners began devoting their business to lager beer.

Under the leadership of Fritz (who was also president of the U.S. Savings Institution in St. Louis) and Samuel, George Busch's former brewery continued to flourish. It led the city in production in 1857, annual sales reached fifteen thousand barrels in 1859, and by 1866 Samuel Wainwright was wealthy enough to build a mansion at 1121 Morrison in St. Louis. Interestingly, the plant continued to be called "Busch's Brewery" for many years. The name wasn't abandoned until brother Adolphus and partner Anheuser had stopped calling their rival plant the Bavarian Brewery in favor of Anheuser-Busch.

In 1869 the Fritz and Wainwright brewery, which by then occupied the entire block bounded by Ninth, Tenth, Gratiot, and Cerre, was consumed by fire. A new, grander brewery was rebuilt on the ashes of the old. It featured a three-hundred-barrel brew kettle heated by steam instead of direct fire, the method still utilized by most of the local competitors. Below ground was a lagering cellar subdivided into fourteen tunnels. Each ran between 60 and 125 feet in length, and was generally 18 feet high and 18 feet wide. When filled to capacity, twenty-two thousand barrels of beer could be lagered in the brewery's caverns.

The partners also operated a large malt house at Stoddard (later Eleventh) Street and Chouteau.

In addition to barley malt, rice (which the brewery claimed improved the flavor and quality of its beer) was also processed.

Fritz and Wainwright continued in business together until 1870, when Charles Fritz retired after selling his share to Lorenz Lempel and Robert Jacob, with the new firm calling itself Samuel Wainwright and Company. By 1874 the rebuilt plant was selling thirty thousand barrels of beer a year, ranking it third in the city, narrowly trailing Lemp and Anheuser.

ENTER ANOTHER ELLIS WAINWRIGHT

Samuel Wainwright died in 1874, with his widow, Catherine, inheriting his share of the brewery. Their son Ellis, who was born in St. Louis in 1850 and named after his recently deceased brewing uncle, took over his father's role in managing the brewery and purchased Robert Jacob's share of the business in 1875.

Throughout this period the Wainwright brewery continued to prosper, with Ellis Wainwright emerging as a rather colorful character. After receiving a college education, he had learned the business at his father's brewery, and upon Samuel's death suddenly found himself an industry leader at the age of twenty-four. During the 1879 U.S. Brewers Convention, which was held in St. Louis, Ellis Wainwright became involved in an altercation with a temperance advocate named Bemis, who then sued for thirty-five thousand dollars in damages. Ellis admitted pushing Bemis to the ground, but claimed self-defense. The court awarded Bemis two cents in damages, which Ellis promptly paid as he walked out of the courtroom.

In 1883, the Wainwright Brewery Company was organized with capital stock of two hundred thousand dollars. The old premises, despite recent improvements, were sold to the St. Louis and San Francisco Railroad and a spectacular new plant was built nearby, with an office address of 1015 Papin. In 1884, Ellis Wainwright bought out remaining partner Lempel, making Ellis and his mother the only stockholders. They were assisted in the boardroom by corporate secretary William Haren. A St. Louis native, Haren started working for the brewery as a clerk in 1876, and would later become its general manager.

The new brewery was designed by the famous

local firm of E. Jungenfeld and Company and completed later in 1884. It featured three seven-story buildings and, to use the parlance of the time, was truly a "model brewery," a huge complex built using upwards of 3 million bricks. Strategically located, the site boasted two sets of railroad tracks connecting it to nearby railroad yards and to the Union Depot. Two giant De La Vergne refrigerating machines were installed, to keep all 650,000 cubic feet of the brewery cool. After opening, production quickly grew to ninety thousand barrels a year. As no bottling or shipping was done until later years (for a while export orders were actually declined)

the entire output, with the exception of some bottled in St. Louis by Jacob Furth, was consumed locally. The Wainwright brewery continued to maintain its position as the third largest in town, though it had been left way behind by A-B and Lemp, which grew so big thanks partly to their export trades.

Assisting Ellis in the management of the brewery was his mother, Mrs. Catherine D. Wainwright, a German woman described by Hyde and Conard as "a lady of exceptional force of character and excellent business ability." Her son Ellis turned out to be no slouch of a businessman himself. During one two-year stretch when he steered the managerial wheel, the net worth of the brewery doubled.

Owl Brew and Cabinet, Wainwright's two major lager labels after a bottling plant was built, were marketed so well that they were among the top-selling local bottled beers. Other Wainwright brands included Standard Lager, Bock, Erlanger, and Culmbacher. Brewery stock was increased to four hundred thousand dollars in 1886, indicating further improvements were being made, including a new cooling tower through which a million gallons of water cascaded daily.

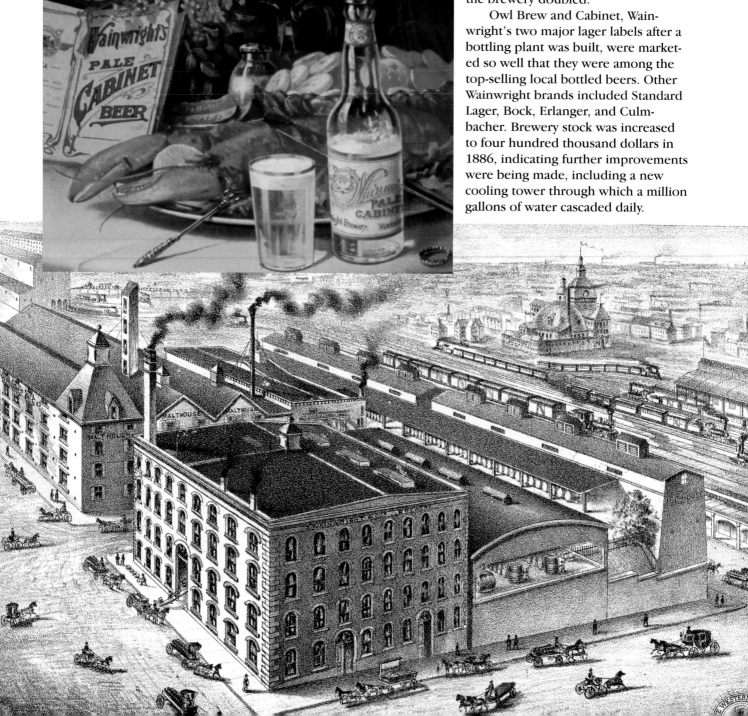

A MEGA-MERGER

The last decades of the twentieth century saw English capitalists investing heavily in overseas ventures, which included pieces of the United States brewing industry. In 1889, the Wainwright brewery was one of eighteen area breweries sold to the British syndicate known as the St. Louis Brewing Association (SLBA). The SLBA merger was a venture that Ellis Wainwright had helped put together, not surprising considering his English background. He was named president of the American branch of the operation, which continued day-to-day management of the breweries. Ellis also served as president of the United States Brewers Association during the years 1891 and 1892. He continued heading the SLBA until 1901, when he resigned, while retaining his seat on the corporate board of directors. By then his attention had drifted to New York City, where many of his other business interests were located.

Around this time, crusading St. Louis circuit attorney (and later Missouri governor) Joseph Folk began investigating a possible attempt by owners of the St. Louis and Suburban Railway Company to bribe government officials in order to receive additional franchises. Several prominent brewers were among those later indicted, including Ellis Wainwright, whose signature appeared on a $135,000 note that allegedly was part of the scheme, which came to be called the "boodle case."

While he always insisted that he had signed the note as a routine business matter, Ellis opted to leave the country rather than face the charges. He left New York and headed for Paris. With close to $4 million in the bank and an additional $60,000 per year streaming in from leases at the Wainwright Building, he began what would become a ten-year exile.

After traveling widely for a while, including tours of the Middle East and Siberian gold mines, with side trips hunting wolves, Ellis purchased a large home in Paris, where he conducted his U.S. business interests via telegram. While in France he lived an aristocratic life that included visits from nobility, rounds of golf, trips to health spas, winters on the Riviera, and joy rides in his forty-horsepower Mercedes.

ENTER ELLIS, AGAIN

Then, in April 1911, Ellis unexpectedly returned to St. Louis, declaring, "My God, I'm glad to be back in the best town in the world!" He surrendered to authorities, posted bond, and proceeded to leave for the St. Louis Club in the vehicle of his old friend August A. Busch. Within a short time, all criminal charges against him were dropped, the state's case weakened by time and the death of a star witness. Ellis soon returned to New York, buying a place on Park Avenue.

Ellis's namesake brewery had in the meantime continued on as one of the primary facilities of the SLBA, even after some of the breweries were closed and most of the conglomerate's other brands (including those of Wainwright) were dropped in order to concentrate on the Hyde Park label. In 1917, the company introduced the Colda brand of non-alcoholic beer, but it was not a success. The Wainwright brewery kept brewing until the advent of Prohibition, and continued producing non-alcoholic drinks until late in 1922. By then most of the SLBA's other facilities were either empty or being leased to other concerns.

In 1933, with the repeal of Prohibition a certainty, the SLBA became attractive again to investors. In June of that year, the firm of Stifel, Nicolaus and Company, which consisted partially of men who had been active in the pre-Prohibition SLBA, purchased the conglomerate's three remaining breweries—Lafayette, Hyde Park, and Wainwright. While brewing recommenced at the Hyde Park plant, the Wainwright brewery was used for other purposes. In 1943, the Hyde Park Brewing Association sold the property, consisting of twenty-two buildings on an eighty-thousand-square-foot tract, to a truck and terminal warehouse firm. Two years later part of the Wainwright brewery was dynamited to make way for a truck terminal. The old Wainwright brewery grounds were eventually swallowed up by the immense Ralston-Purina complex, the rest of the buildings torn down to make room for that growing St. Louis food products company. Visitors to the industrial site today are hard-pressed to imagine that it was once the home of a massive brewery.

Facing page, top: A reverse-on-glass sign showing an inviting restaurant table with a bottle of Wainwright's Pale Cabinet beer.

Facing page, bottom: Pencil drawing of the brewery in 1879, from *The Western Brewer.*

ELLIS WAINWRIGHT & THE WAINWRIGHT BUILDING

As befitting a third-generation St. Louis brewer, Ellis Wainwright lived a colorful and interesting life. Among the interests of the socially prominent Ellis were the St. Louis Jockey Club, of which he was a founding member; the St. Louis Public Library and the St. Louis Museum of Fine Arts, of which he was a trustee; and the art school of Washington University, of which he was president.

While his career as a brewer and his philanthropy are largely forgotten, the Wainwright name lives on in downtown St. Louis with the Wainwright Building at Seventh and Chestnut streets, which was placed on the National Register of Historic Places in 1968. This famous building had its origins in 1890, when Ellis's mother Catherine bought several lots with the intention of tearing down the small homes and store buildings then present and replacing them with a speculative office building. Ellis was reportedly a bit skeptical of the plan at first, perhaps preoccupied with his recent marriage to Charlotte Dickson. But he later grew interested in the project and commissioned renowned Chicago architect Louis Sullivan to design it. The use of steel frameworks and the development of the modern elevator had just recently liberated buildings from their old height limits, though most designers had continued to make their structures needlessly massive. Ellis simply asked Sullivan for a "skyscraper" of about ten stories and then gave the architect free rein. The end result was a building that would become one of the most influential in the history of architecture, one of the first skyscrapers ever designed.

In 1891, with the building nearing completion, Charlotte Wainwright suddenly grew ill from peritonitis and died at the young age of thirty-four. During their brief marriage, the Wainwrights had socialized with the elite of the city. In the months before her death, Charlotte had taken an ocean cruise to Europe with Lilly Busch, wife of Adolphus. Tall and elegant, and upon whom Ellis lavished furs and jewels, Charlotte was described in an article in *Leslie's Weekly* as the most beautiful woman in St. Louis. Ellis was crushed by her death.

To honor his wife, Ellis asked Sullivan to design a tomb. The result was the somewhat plain yet beautiful limestone "dome and cube" still found in Bellefontaine Cemetery and sometimes referred to as a miniature Taj Mahal. The oblique design is softened by delicately carved bands of floral and geometric motifs. Patterned after an Arab Muslim saint's tomb in Blida, Algeria, the Wainwright tomb is considered by many architectural historians to be one of Sullivan's masterpieces (the book *St. Louis: Landmarks & Historic Districts* called it "among the most perfect works of architecture in the country.") Ellis Wainwright's ashes, and his parents' remains, eventually joined Charlotte inside the memorial.

The Wainwright office building was completed in 1892. Villeroy & Boch, a familiar name to many stein collectors, provided the floral-patterned Mettlach encaustic tiles that covered the lobby floor. The building originally consisted of over two hundred offices and nine store spaces, with the Missouri State Brewers Association and the brewery architectural firm of E. Jungenfeld and Company among its tenants.

A 1956 poll of architects conducted by *Architectural Record* named the building one of the two most significant American commercial structures of the nineteenth century. Despite its architectural significance, at one time it appeared the building might be torn down to make way for a parking lot. Washington University had inherited most of Ellis's interest in the building, later selling it to a pair of local businessmen. The building was saved from the potential wrecking ball by the National Trust for Historic Preservation, which took an option on the building. Finally, the State of Missouri stepped forward, turning the building into a government office complex in 1981, which it still is. Coincidentally, the Wainwright Building is now home of the St. Louis office of the Missouri Division of Liquor Control, an agency with far-reaching regulatory control over the breweries under its jurisdiction.

The Wainwright Building in downtown St. Louis.

ELLIS WAINWRIGHT'S SAD DEMISE

Ellis Wainwright never remarried after his brief and tragic betrothal to Charlotte Dickson. But in 1922, at age eighty-two, he took up with a twenty-two-year-old divorcee named Rosalind Velva Kendall, shocking his friends by "adopting" the woman, who then took his last name and became his constant companion while set up in an adjacent New York apartment. She was an aspiring actress who called Ellis "Daddy" and accompanied him on strolls through Central Park. Ellis arranged a screen test for her, but her film career never got off the ground after the studio insisted that Ellis pay most of the cost of any movie in which she might appear. A year after her adoption, Rosalind supposedly accepted seventy-five thousand dollars from Ellis in exchange for her relinquishment of any rights to his estate (an agreement she would later claim she did not understand the terms of).

By 1924, Ellis Wainwright was quite sick, suffering from hardening of the arteries, and he returned to St. Louis, staying briefly at the Missouri Baptist Sanitarium. He then moved to a six-room suite at the Buckingham Hotel, overlooking Forest Park. There he became an almost total recluse. Ellis was cared for by a nurse and four attendants, and when maids arrived to clean his apartment, his handlers moved him from room to room so he wouldn't be seen, as he had developed an aversion to strangers. Visitors to the hotel looking for Ellis were told that he wasn't staying there. After his senility was made worse by a stroke, he began imagining he was bankrupt, suffered bouts of severe depression, and complained about a conspiracy to murder him. When he was no longer able to manage his own affairs, Ellis's heirs, lawyers, and friends began a long battle over his money. Rosalind had followed Ellis to St. Louis but, following instructions from lawyers, was kept away from him by a guard at the door and by household servants.

Ellis Wainwright finally passed away on November 6, 1924. Among those at his deathbed were some of his old brewing industry pals—Norman

Right: Bottle label used by Wainwright's sole bottler at the time, Jacob Furth & Co.

Below: Ellis Wainwright's tomb.

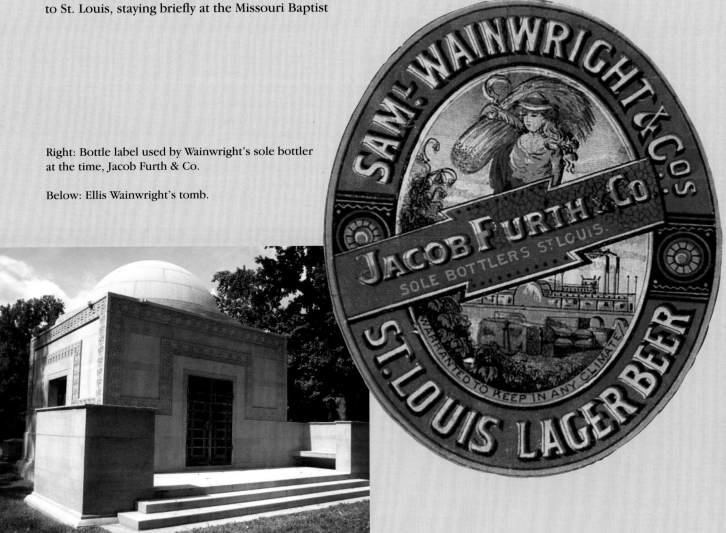

Jones, Herman Stifel, and William Haren. Shortly after his death a fight emerged between Rosalind, who was contesting a change in his will, and various Wainwright heirs, represented by Washington University lawyer Marion Early. Early leveled the charge that Rosalind's adoption had been fraudulent and that she had simply been Ellis's mistress; medical experts were called and testified to Ellis's growing lunacy in his final years. The matter was finally settled out of court, with Rosalind taking about one-quarter of Ellis's eight hundred thousand dollar estate. It was later revealed that lawyers had taken nearly half of her share.

Left: Scarce embossed Wainwright pilsner glass. Note the similarity of embossing to label on previous page.

Below: Brewery workers photo, taken near the Wainwright brewery loading docks. It is easy to guess the profession of the gentleman on the far right, with the broom.

While he gave his name to the brewery that for a time was the biggest in St. Louis, Julius Winkelmeyer was trained as a nail maker. Born in Wurttemburg, Germany, in 1816, Winkelmeyer learned his father's trade before coming to St. Louis in 1842. Two of his brothers had previously arrived, while another brother and sister were soon to follow. Winkelmeyer worked as a store clerk in his early St. Louis days. Shortly after his move to Missouri, he befriended Frederick Stifel, who hailed from the same part of Germany and was a trained brewer, being the son of a brewer from the town of Neuffen. In 1843, Winkelmeyer and Stifel launched a brewery at Second and Rutger streets. The pair made a good business duo, with Stifel attending to the brewing duties and the gregarious Winkelmeyer handling sales and planning.

Their business took the name Union Brewery and succeeded greatly in a St. Louis that was just beginning to grow. Construction of a bigger and better facility was started in 1846, on the north shore of Chouteau's Pond, on Market between Seventeenth and Eighteenth streets. A new building was completed the next year. The property was an ideal site for a brewery, primarily owing to the vast natural underground cavern system below it. This was extremely important for beer storage in the days before artificial refrigeration, and as a result numerous breweries sprang up in the neighborhood.

In the meantime, Frederick Stifel became Julius Winkelmeyer's brother-in-law when the latter wed his sister Christina Stifel on January 24, 1847. Christina had come to the United States at age sixteen in 1840, joining some of her siblings in Wheeling, West Virginia, before moving to St. Louis.

The duo's beer sales were growing so fast that another large brewery addition was started in 1848. The cellars fronting Market Street were completed and a new bar room and "summer house" finished the same year. More land near the brewery was purchased as well.

The year 1849 brought a horrible cholera epidemic to St. Louis. Among its victims were Frederick Stifel and his wife, Louise, who succumbed to the illness on the same day. Ironically, a cause of the epidemic was thought to be Chouteau's Pond, which had once been clean enough to be a popular recreation spot but had become badly polluted as the city started growing. The pond was drained in 1853, and the site was turned into a railroad yard after Union Station was completed in 1894.

THE FAMILY CARRIES ON

Julius Winkelmeyer continued running the brewery without Stifel. The new brewery building was completed shortly after his partner's death. An 1851 article in a local newspaper boasted that the Union Brewery was the largest brewery in the United States, a highly

Winkelmeyer / Union Brewery

352 S. Second Street

Stifel and Winkelmeyer	1843–1847

1714 Market Street (new site)

Stifel and Winkelmeyer	1847–1849
Julius Winkelmeyer	1849–c. 1857
Winkelmeyer & Schiffer	c. 1857–1860
Julius Winkelmeyer	1860–1867
Julius Winkelmeyer & Company	1867–1879
Julius Winkelmeyer Brewing Association	1879–1889
Winkelmeyer branch, SLBA	1889–1891
Excelsior branch, SLBA	1891–1916

Top: Portrait of Julius Winkelmeyer, reproduced from Scharf's *History of Saint Louis City and County.*

Bottom: This 1850s photo of the Winkelmeyer & Schiffer Union Brewery may be the oldest existing photo of a St. Louis brewery. Used with permission of Barb Cook.

returned to take over the old Louis Koch Brewery).

The Winkelmeyer Brewery became one of the first local "shipping" breweries. An early ad stated, "Lager Beer Shipped in Wood and Glass a Specialty. Manufacturer of Young's Extract of Malt." As with most other area breweries, the late 1870s and early 1880s were a time of expansion at Winkelmeyer. The brewery was not growing as fast as some of its local rivals, however, having dropped to eleventh (of twenty-three) in production by 1884.

SLBA SALE, NAME CHANGE

Still, the brewery was of interest to the British syndicate known as the St. Louis Brewing Association (SLBA), which absorbed Winkelmeyer and seventeen other area breweries in an 1889 merger. August Straub did not stick around long as an SLBA employee, retiring in 1890 to first take an eighteen-month European vacation, then devoting his attention to the International Bank of St. Louis before passing away in 1898. The Winkelmeyer brothers must have taken the money and run as well, since the SLBA quickly dropped their name from the plant. Their mother, Christina, had not only done well with the brewery, but her later investments also prospered. When she died at age eighty-nine in 1912, she was one of the wealthiest women in St. Louis.

Another of the SLBA breweries was the Excelsior Brewing Company, which beginning in 1880 operated in the former Uhrig brewery, just up the street from Winkelmeyer. When Excelsior closed in 1891, to be torn down in order to make way for Union Station, the SLBA moved the Excelsior name down the block to the Union/Winkelmeyer facility. The SLBA continued operating there until just before the dawn of Prohibition in 1916. The brewery was soon torn down. In the 1930s, the giant post office building that remains on the site today was constructed.

INTO THE TWENTY-FIRST CENTURY

While the Winkelmeyer brewery disappeared without a trace, the name still lives on in the form of rare brewery collectibles. The old brewery caves are still down there, of course, including a sealed entrance in the sub-basement of Union Station. Two other St. Louis buildings kept the family name alive as well.

One was the Winkelmeyer mansion at 4373 West Pine Boulevard in the Central West End. The huge house was built in 1890 by Christina Stifel Winkelmeyer and designed by her nephew, the German-trained St. Louis architect Otto Wilhelmi. More than a century later the house was serving

questionable claim. The seventy-five hundred barrels produced in 1850 did make it the largest beer plant in St. Louis, though. Another distinction of the Union Brewery noted in an 1850 industrial census was the fact that of the nine employees, one was a woman, unique in the St. Louis industry at the time. The record does not indicate if this was Christina Stifel Winkelmeyer, but it seems likely.

A man named George Schiffer was brought aboard as a brewery partner for a few years beginning in the late 1850s. The brewery weathered storm damage and a fire, and Winkelmeyer ended up owning the entire block surrounding it. Business was so good that an 1858 newspaper quoted Winkelmeyer as saying, "I cannot at this moment spare any lager, because I cannot very well supply my regular customers." Production had grown to sixteen thousand barrels in 1860, still tops in the city.

Julius Winkelmeyer died in 1867. Carrying on the business were his widow, Christina, and her brother Christopher A. Stifel. The latter had come to St. Louis in 1849 with brothers Charles and Jacob (Charles went into the local brewing business as proprietor of the City Brewery).

Joining the brewery as they grew up would be Winkelmeyer sons Christopher and Julius, and son-in-law August W. Straub, who had married daughter Julia Winkelmeyer. August Straub was no mere in-law, but rather the son of Pittsburgh brewer John Straub. He had worked in banking as a young man, then joined his family's brewery. Production figues for 1874 showed the Union Brewery producing 28,769 barrels, number four in the local industry behind E. Anheuser and Co., Lemp, and Wainwright.

In 1879, the brewery was incorporated as the Julius Winkelmeyer Brewing Association, with Christopher Winkelmeyer as president, August Straub as secretary-treasurer, and Julius Winkelmeyer as superintendent (replacing the recently departed George Schilling, who had stepped down earlier in the year to take a summer vacation and as a nursing home when it was purchased by the Ronald McDonald House for $372,500. Rather than remodel it for their purposes, the new owners announced plans to tear down the home and rebuild. Angry, preservation-minded neighbors tried to save the house and were encouraged by a unanimous preservation board vote that it should stay. However, this decision was overturned by the city planning commission, and in 2001 the Winkelmeyer mansion fell victim to the wrecking ball.

The Winkelmeyer Building downtown at Eleventh and Walnut streets had a better fate. This structure, also designed by Wilhelmi, was erected in 1902 for Christina Stifel Winkelmeyer as an investment property. It was purchased by the Atlanta-based company Ameritas in 1985 and remodeled. That same year it was placed on the National Register of Historic Places. Coincidentally, the regional office for the U.S. Postal Inspection Service occupies the building today, leaving the mail service in charge of two of St. Louis's old Winkelmeyer sites.

Facing page: Trade card can be dated to around 1879 by the red stamping of "Brewing Association" over the earlier "& Co."

Right: Embossed stemmed pilsner-style glass, utilizing the Winkelmeyer Brewery's "shaking hands" company logo.

Below: A true museum piece, this lithograph shows the brewery, bottles of Winkelmeyer beer, and several colorful characters, some fanciful. Used with permission of Missouri Historical Society.

Chapter 3

Brewers Deserving Honorable Mention

$\mathcal{O}$f all the breweries that have operated in St. Louis since the days of John Coons, only a few managed to reach great heights. This does not overshadow the fact that over the last two hundred years a huge number of breweries have called St. Louis home.

Why did so many breweries fail? For the same reasons that companies in other industries have failed and that companies in the future will continue to fail. Among the reasons may have been the following:

1. Poor management—Surely some operators were very good brewers but poor business managers or marketers. Many companies, especially in the early years, were set up as sole proprietorships, with no line of succession in case of the illness or death of the owner.

2. Money—Some breweries started out under-financed, may have managed their money poorly, or did not have owners with the business skills to ride out hard times. Others may have been victims of bad timing, opening or expanding during periods of economic downturn.

3. Bad product—During much of the 1800s, the process of brewing beer was not entirely understood. What at first was a good product may have changed, for reasons that were not always apparent. Bad beer likely would have been placed on the market only once. Even today brewers face the challenge of consistently producing a palatable product.

4. Reluctance to change—An inability to adapt to new and different economic, social, and industrial situations surely led to the demise of many breweries.

5. Bad luck—Some breweries were victims of fires, cellar collapses, or similar disasters. Owners without adequate insurance would have been hard-pressed to rebuild. The ultimate form of bad luck, national Prohibition, permanently wiped out many local breweries.

For whatever reasons they failed, the fact remains that all the closed breweries at least made an attempt to satisfy the tastes of thirsty beer drinkers. No matter how small they were, or how short of a period they were in business, these businesses were a vital part of the brewing history of St. Louis, and therefore deserve mention here.

John Coons

c. 1809–c. 1811 Location unknown

The city of St. Louis had its humble beginning in 1764 when Pierre Laclede, the junior partner in a fur trading company, chose the spot for his headquarters. It was just two years later when the first recorded brewery in the St. Louis region was noted by a British army captain named Pitman. He spoke of the Jesuit plantation in Kaskaskia, Illinois, "with a brewery." Also south of St. Louis, the Missouri town of Sainte Genevieve hosted a brewery as early as 1779. That year, the will of local citizen Michael Livernois, dated December 28, refers to François Colman as the village's "master brewer."

It would be safe to assume that somebody started producing some type of beer early in the history of St. Louis as well. Writing in 1883, historian Thomas Scharf mentioned that descendants of the early residents of the city spoke of "a fermented liquor" made in St. Louis prior to 1800 and that there was at least one primitive brewing site. However, existing documentation of a brewery does not appear until the October 19, 1809, appearance of John Coons's advertisement in the *Missouri Gazette* newspaper. While historian James Neal Primm speculated in *Lion of the Valley* that Coons had started his brewery "probably several years before," he gave no evidence. Nor is there any further information available on the brewing activities of John Coons. But we must assume that he was still plying the trade in 1811, for that year a census, as reported in the *Louisiana Gazette*, listed two breweries in the St. Louis district.

St. Charles Oct. 1st 1809   3t-63

Barley and Hops.
Purchased at John Coon's Brewery, and at the Printing Office.

St. Vrain & Habb

1810–1812 (?)
Bellefontaine Road north of city on Rocky Branch (at site of today's Bellefontaine Cemetery)

Pioneering brewer John Coons had competition early on in the St. Louis beer business with the establishment in 1810 of a brewery north of the city. It was owned by a former Spanish officer and large landholder named Jacques St. Vrain. Joining St. Vrain was his brewmaster Victor Habb, described in the *Louisiana Gazette* as "an experienced European brewer." Sometimes referred to as "Old Victor," Habb (also spelled Hab or Hobb) would have quite an interesting career in early St. Louis brewing.

St. Vrain's brewery was constructed of logs and destroyed by a fire in 1812. The *Louisiana Gazette* offered the following condolence on March 28 of that year: "Thus has a worthy and meritorious citizen been crushed, at a moment when he was on the eve of reaping some advantage from a valuable and useful establishment." This was just the first of countless brewery fires in St. Louis. Such establishments were highly susceptible to fire, with open flames needed for brewing, malting, and pitching of wooden vats and barrels.

The fire was an especially tough break for Habb. Apparently out of a job, just three months after the fire he gave public notice to his creditors that, in order to get out of debtor's prison, he was declaring bankruptcy. This strategy must have worked, for by August of 1812 Habb was advertising for one or two cooper's apprentices. This possibly indicates further brewing activity by Habb.

A letter written by local trader Christian Wilt to his uncle on December 26, 1813, helps paint a picture of the activities and problems at the St. Vrain brewery. He states that business was hindered by the scarcity of barley, which was not being grown locally (though it could be), that wild hops were available for use or they could be cultivated, and that a lack of coopers was further hindering area brewing. Wilt's letter also mentions the fiery destruction of the St. Vrain establishment, and that "Luttig is about erecting one [brewery] with St. Vrain's brewer—but for want of funds it will not do much—it is to be up town."

While there is no evidence that the prospective brewery mentioned in the letter ever opened, Victor Habb would continue to play a prominent role in the local brewing industry.

St. Louis Brewery (I)

Joseph Philipson c. 1815–1820
Matthew Murphy & James Nagle 1820–1820
Murphy, Nagle & Philipson 1820–1821
Joseph Philipson 1821–1821
John Mullanphy, owner; Simon Philipson, lessee 1821–1824
Thomas Biddle, Phoenix Brewery 1824–1825
John Mullanphy 1825–1829
West side of North Main Street at Carr Street, last house in north part of town

Joseph Philipson was a Jewish merchant who came to St. Louis from Europe via Philadelphia. He decided to start a brewery in St. Louis, the first evidence of which is a March

Portrait of John Mullanphy.

1815 ad in the *Missouri Gazette & Illinois Advertiser* soliciting barley for the St. Louis Brewery:

Barley Wanted
Cash will be given at the St. Louis Brewery for any quantity of Barley that may be delivered immediately or in the course of next summer. The Brewery is disposed to form contracts with such farmers as may be desirous of entering largely into the cultivation of this article and will furnish grain for seed to those who cannot in time procure it elsewhere.

The brewery may or may not have begun operations in that year. In May of 1816, the *Missouri Gazette* observed that "The St. Louis Brewery has got into operation." It is unclear if this refers to the business opening just for the year or for the first time. On the other hand, brewery historian Stanley Baron states that the brewery's first beer was not brewed until the fall of 1817. He states further that "Old Victor Habb" did the brewing for Philipson and that the brew was cooled in a dugout canoe that was placed outside the brewery.

There was soon some better equipment in the brewery, with the installation of steel rollers for grinding the malt. Joseph Philipson's brother Simon, back in Philadelphia, had heard about the superiority of this new system, which had recently been installed in some breweries in Europe and on the East Coast. He bought a set of the rollers and had them sent to St. Louis.

Victor Habb must have continued working at Philipson's brewery through 1819, as a newspaper ad that March mentions that he would be running a beer and vinegar cart through the city to supply the brewery's customers. But by 1820 he was out, for that year storekeeper James Nagle and a practical brewer named Matthew Murphy entered into an agreement with Philipson to operate the business. The new partners also did distilling on the premises.

Newspaper accounts indicate that obtaining sufficient barley for brewing was a continuing problem. Despite this, the 1821 St. Louis city directory (the earliest in existence) lauds the establishment, stating that the city had "one brewery, where is manufactured beer, ale and porter of a quality equal to any in the western country."

This Philipson/Nagle/Murphy partnership was brief, as later in the year Philipson resumed sole ownership. But a January malt house fire and other financial difficulties forced him to soon sell out to wealthy St. Louis businessman John Mullanphy, a native of Ireland. Philipson would go on to make his living as a musician.

While Mullanphy continued to use Matt Murphy as his brewer, he called on Victor Habb to bore out a new pump for the brewery. Habb completed the job, but when he presented Mullanphy with a bill for seven dollars, the latter declared the charge excessive and refused to pay. The dispute must have become a matter of principle, for it stayed in the court system long enough that Habb ended up spending fifty dollars on witness fees. Mullanphy had to pay his lawyer twenty dollars to handle the case, eighteen dollars more than the two dollar difference between Habb's asking price and what he was willing to pay.

John Mullanphy opted to lease the brewery shortly after acquiring it to Simon Philipson, who moved to St. Louis from Philadelphia to run his brother's old plant. The brewery may have suffered yet another fire in 1823. A somewhat cryptic ad placed that year by John Mullanphy in the *Gazetteer of Illinois and Missouri* states, "The subscriber will receive proposals to build the stone work of a Brew House, on the property lately belonging to Joseph Philipson."

Following the expiration of his lease in 1824, Simon Philipson relinquished the operation back to Mullanphy. But he tried to keep the malt rollers he had purchased years earlier, claiming they had not been a part of the 1821 sale. Mullanphy disagreed and again went to court, where he finally prevailed after the case wound all the way up to the Missouri Supreme Court.

In 1824–25, newspaper ads soliciting barley appeared for a concern called the Phoenix Brewery, operated by Thomas Biddle. While some historians have suggested this was a new brewery, it would seem likely this was just a continuation of the rebuilt St. Louis Brewery, as Biddle was a Mullanphy son-in-law. Biddle's brewing career was brief, and he would be killed in an 1831 duel with Missouri Secretary of State Spencer Pettis.

John Mullanphy continued to own and run the business, as indicated by 1827 ads for his "St. Louis Ale." But in November 1829, the St. Louis Brewery was destroyed by fire, never to be rebuilt. The owner blamed the blaze on arson and offered a reward of five hundred dollars for information on the perpetrator. The city offered an additional five hundred dollars bounty, but a suspect was never located.

James C. Lynch and Company

1826–1835 Location unknown

Jefferson Brewery (I), James C. Lynch & Son

1838–c. 1839 Location unknown

The St. Louis Brewery had no competition for a number of years, but a new brewery opened in 1826 when James C. Lynch and Company began selling its ale and porter. In the fall of 1827, Lynch advertised in the *Missouri Republican*:

New St. Louis Brewery
James C. Lynch begs to inform his friends and the public that he has commenced brewing for the season, and is now ready to supply orders for new beer, ale and porter. Having enlarged his concern they may depend on a regular supply.

In addition to making his own beer, Lynch also imported ale from Pittsburgh, with an ad in the spring of 1829 stating that he had on hand 120 barrels of his own product and 100 barrels of Pittsburgh ale, "which would enable him to supply his customers throughout the season." Without local competition after the 1829 burning of the St. Louis Brewery, Lynch was able to increase his company's output. An 1830 ad stated that he had four hundred barrels each of ale and porter available. The next year the *Missouri Republican* reported that he had opened a new bottling works "under the store of Mr. George Ogilvie opposite the brass foundry." Despite these successes, by 1835 Lynch was having financial problems, and the brewery was closed and the property sold.

James Lynch opened another brewery in partnership with his son in 1838. Known as the Jefferson Brewery, it was open only for a short time. Lynch then left the brewing industry and turned to real estate as a vocation.

Metcalfe / Jackson / Eagle (I) 1833–1838

William Metcalfe & Son 1833–1838
Samuel Jackson 1838–1839
John Latham, Eagle Brewery 1839–c. 1841
159-161 S. Second Street

The firm of William Metcalfe & Son was an early example of a "chain" brewery: a brewer with more than one location. When the Metcalfes established their brewery in St. Louis in 1833, they already had one in Cincinnati and another in Louisville. The brewery advertised that it was in St. Louis to stay and promised that the beer, ale, and porter it produced would be equal to any in the country.

The *Missouri Republican* urged its readers to patronize the business and reprinted an article from the *Cincinnati Republican* touting the "better beverage" produced by Metcalfe and Son with its "ambrosial sweetness." Free delivery was offered anywhere in the city, barrels were available for six dollars, and the brewery owners said they expected to purchase quantities of barley from area farmers. While the brewery succeeded for a while, with a 20 percent increase in barley purchases in 1834, by 1838 it was closed. The owners advised that they were leaving town and took out the following ad:

Brewery for Sale
For sale complete brewing establishment, stock, lease and utensils, occupant leaving St. Louis. Stock consists of thirty barrels of ale, together with, materials to wit: malt, barley, hops for an average brewing of 100 barrels; 20 barrels of vinegar: among the utensils and articles are the following: a boiler containing 28 barrels, malt mill with horse power, mash tub containing 40 barrels, oval water reservoir, heep tub containing 26 barrels; coolers containing 26 barrels, large copper beer pump with pipes, smaller cooler with several tubs, wire malt kiln 12 x 14; washing troughs, 260 half and quarter barrels and several brass faucets; one coal stove, one wood stove, and other articles too numerous to mention.

Evidence points to Samuel Jackson either buying or leasing the brewery after the departure of the Metcalfes. The 1836–37 city directory lists William Metcalfe & Son as brewers at 159–61 S. Second Street with Jackson a brewer at 159 S. Second. Thus it would appear that Jackson was at the time an employee at Metcalfe & Son. The 1838–39 city directory lists Jackson as a brewer with his residence on N. Second Street, but no brewery address is given so it's merely an assumption that he stayed on by himself at the Metcalfe site.

A paragraph concerning the brewery appeared in the *St. Louis Missouri Argus* on May 3, 1839. It stated the following:

> The brewery formerly owned by Mr. Metcalf has passed into the hands of Mr. Leetham. The present brewer Bob Wood, who was brought here from Philadelphia on two steamboats, is favorable known from the Torrid to the Frigid Zone and the countries round about. Send in your orders for "Wood's Best" and you'll find it in every respect "what it's cracked up to be," hard to beat.

In the 1840–41 city directory, the 161 S. Second address is listed as the Eagle Brewery of John Latham. These are the only historical references to Latham (Leetham). Although an Eagle Brewery is listed (with an unknown proprietor) in an 1848 newspaper listing of city breweries, it was likely a different entity.

St. Louis Brewery (II)

Isaac McHose & Ezra or Elkanah English c. 1835–1839
Isaac McHose and Ezra English 1839–1851
Ezra English 1851–c. 1857
English & Gilpin c. 1857–c. 1859
English & O'Neil c. 1859–c. 1860
Abraham McHose & Co. c. 1864–c. 1866
316 S. Second Street

A concern that would become the most famous early ale brewery in St. Louis had its beginning around 1835 (though some sources say earlier) when partners Isaac McHose and Ezra English bought a lot on S. Second Street. The next year they spent $509 on improvements and purchased additional nearby property. Their brewery, an ale and porter plant, adopted the name St. Louis Brewery and saw many years of steady growth. In 1837, McHose and English presented employees of the *St. Louis Argus* newspaper with a seven-gallon keg of their beer. The journalists opined that better beer "was never drank by a London alderman."

A *Missouri Argus* newspaper notice dated August 5, 1839, states that the brewing partnership of Isaac McHose and Elkanah English was being "dissolved by mutual consent." The same day a new partnership was formed by McHose and Ezra English. The kinship between the two Englishes is unknown, but plainly Ezra was, at least for a time, not directly involved in the brewery.

By 1841, annual production reached about three thousand barrels, likely the most of any local brewery, and the services of a reputable master brewer had been obtained. A cooperage shop was added the same year. In correspondence with a local newspaper, a subscriber signed "M" (presumably McHose) urged his fellow citizens to patronize the St. Louis Brewery. Advertisements from 1842 included claims that the brewery's ale was the equal to any produced in the country and was of greater purity than the competition. This was supposedly ensured by carefully choosing the brewing ingredients and using no "artificial or deleterious" materials, unlike those used by other brewers.

McHose and English tried to develop an export market as early as 1842. They advertised their product as made to keep during the hot summer months and thus well suited for the southern markets. It was also announced that they would do no bottling that year so as to not compete with their local retailers.

Instrumental to the brewery's success was the development of a natural underground cave as a retail establishment. It became known as English Cave and was located between Arsenal, Wyoming, Illinois, and Jefferson streets in today's Benton Park. The brewery had first used the cave for storing its ale and had made considerable improvements to it. Though renamed Mammoth Cave and Park in 1846, the English name stuck to it then as it has to the present. In June of 1846, the brewery was storing twelve hundred barrels of beer in one hundred hogsheads in the cavern. That same year marked the beginning of the brewery's annual "Christmas Raffle," which was a notable St. Louis tradition for several years.

In addition to serving ale in the cave, which offered relief from summer heat and winter cold, improvements were made to the nearby grounds. There was a beer garden, a forested area, and even a greenhouse. According to the *Daily Missouri Republican*, guests made their way to the cavern grounds to sample "the celebrated 'double x' ale, brown stout and porter" from what remained one of the city's largest breweries. By 1850, the cave and surrounding grounds had become one of the most popular resorts in the city. Entertainment offerings were increased with more bands, a "sail swing" and balloon ascensions. Passengers on the balloons included people, dogs, and horses. For a time the ascensions became such a fad that a newspaper editor commented that the craft were going up in "fleets."

In 1851, Ezra English became sole owner of the brewery and cave. Expansions to the brewery continued and the 1853–54 city directory indicated that a "coffee house" (a quaint term of the era for a saloon) was on the premises. English leased the cave to partners Karl & Praetsch in 1854, and he also took on partners in the beer business. The St. Louis Brewery did business as English & Gilpin in the late 1850s, then as English and O'Neil. The 1860 Census of Industry listed the St. Louis Brewery as having produced eight thousand barrels that year, ranking it in a tie for sixth out of twenty-eight area breweries.

By 1864, the brewery had become the property of Abraham McHose and Company. McHose was presumably the son of brewery cofounder Isaac McHose. The younger McHose had previously served as a local deputy constable. His partners in the business included Philip C. Schmidt and St. Louis Chief of Police Bernard Laibold. But after 1866 the brewery disappeared from city directories. This was the same year Benton Park was established as a public park, so perhaps that was in some way associated with the brewery's demise.

Other factors in the closing of the St. Louis Brewery may have been the continued public taste for lager beer over ale or the departure from the business of Ezra English. There are no clues as to why Ezra English left the brewery he cofounded. His son Ezra Jr. had taken over the Southern Cream Ale Brewery of Heitz, Schricker and Company in the early 1860s, and city directory information indicates that the elder English was assisting his son as a brewer there. That brewery was soon closed as well.

While it no longer served as an ale storage cave or a beer garden, English Cave did continue to serve industry. In the late 1880s, it was the site of a mushroom growing business and in the next decade was used as a storage area for the Paul-Wack Wine Company. Today the cave is of special interest to local spelunkers, who would like desperately to explore it. They are frustrated, however, by the inability to find an entrance.

Missouri Brewery (I) (Small & Rohr)

1837–1841 Location unknown

The brewing duo of Small & Rohr opened the Missouri Brewery in 1837. Late that year they were advertising their "Supreme Pale Ale, Porter and Beer" and soon "Champagne and Nut Brown Ale" were likewise available.

Other ads mentioned that the company had imported a brewer who had worked at some of the largest breweries in the "Atlantic Cities." These ads claimed that the brewery's beverages were considered by experts to be equal to if not better than any found in the city. Despite this, on January 6, 1841, another newspaper announcement ("Notice to Brewers") stated that the entire plant "in Central St. Louis, called the 'Missouri Brewery,' and formerly in the occupancy of Mr. George Roler is hereby offered for sale" by its creditors. Although readers of the *Daily Missouri Republican* were promised "a great bargain will be given to any one disposed to purchase," the brewery apparently never reopened.

As for the brewer whom Small & Rohr had "imported" from back east, he was Robert McKee, who continued in the St. Louis brewing industry. In 1842, McKee was serving as a brewer at the Fulton Brewery, and by the late 1840s he was working as a maltster.

Some possible 1840s–1850s breweries

In studying early St. Louis city directories, it is not always easy to discern whether a person listed as a brewer was conducting his own business or if he was employed at a brewery owned by others. In some cases a beer depot or distributor may have been misidentified as a brewery.

One such individual was Thomas Brumbaugh, who was listed in an 1838–39 directory as a brewer at 3 Poplar Street. He doesn't appear in the next directory, but in 1842 was again listed as a brewer, this time at Payne between Broadway and Second Street.

Several others fall into the same category. Whether or not these fellows owned or leased their own breweries, we recognize them here for their pioneering efforts. The following list gives their names, addresses, and years they appeared in a city directory:

1842—August Juxberg, Second between
      Plum and Poplar
      David Keller, Carondelet Avenue

between Marion and Barry
1845—Peter Gilliam, east side of Seventh,
north of Pine
Gordon Robertson, southwest
corner of Sixth and Biddle
H. Schroeder, Liberty Beer House,
Fourth & Franklin (an 1852 directory
likewise lists the Liberty Beer House
at 98 S. Second Street operated by a
man named Blowser)
1848—Henry Faatz, 43 Plum
1851—Leon Block, Ale & Porter, Sixth and
Market
1852—L. Block & Bros., Porter & Ale
Depot
1854—L. Block & Bros., Ale, Porter & Soda
Man., Fifth between Lombardi &
Hickory
1857—John H. Stark, Carondelet Avenue

Oregon Brewery

Stephen Stock/Stock Brothers 1842–c. 1864

Windeck & Heitcamp c. 1864–c. 1865

Mississippi Valley Brewery, John Neff c. 1865–c. 1866

Mississippi Valley Brewery, Reising & Chambers c. 1866–c. 1867

414 S. Seventh Street (between Barry and Marion)

The Oregon Brewery (it was not uncommon for a brewery to take its name from a distant state) stayed fairly small throughout its existence but had a remarkable twenty-five-year run on the west side of Seventh Street. It was opened by Stephen Stock in 1842.

Like many early breweries, Stock's facility was a brewpub, with an adjacent tavern operating probably for the duration of the business. The brewery was called Stock Brothers for a time, with Peter Stock joining in the beer making. When Stephen Stock retired in the mid-1860s, the brewery was taken over by Martin Windeck and Fritz Heitcamp, but they soon moved over to the Rocky Branch Brewery. John Neff took over at the Oregon/Stock facility, renaming it the Mississippi Valley Brewery. By 1867, the last year it appears in city directories, the Mississippi Valley Brewery was being operated by Phil J. Reising and William C. Chambers.

The Stock family later returned to the St. Louis brewing business in the person of Philip Stock, who was involved with the Koch/Schilling & Schneider Brewery in the 1880s and then served as corporate secretary for the St. Louis Brewing Association conglomerate.

John Gast 1844–c. 1850

63 Carondelet Avenue

Brewery historian James Lindhurst garnered the following information from city records: "In 1844, John Gast began brewing on a very small scale in a one-room plant 'on the west side of the paved street that leads across the lower bridge to Carondelet'. The brewhouse was a brick structure 16' × 13 1/2'."

The 1845 city directory shows Gast on the east side of Second Street south of Wood, while in 1847 the Gast Brewery address was shown as 63 Carondelet Avenue. The brewery is not included in the next year's guide, but there is a John Gass listed as a musical instrument maker.

The last documented evidence of John Gast's brewery is an 1850 industrial census, which lists his plant as a one-man operation, with a mere $400 invested in it and ranking last out of the seventeen local breweries, with annual production of just 150 barrels.

While that marks an end of existing information for the first Gast Brewery, fifty years later a wine-making division of Gasts started a new brewery in St. Louis.

Rocky Branch Brewery

W. F. Bartalls c. 1844–c. 1848

Blume, Zoller & Co. c. 1848–c. 1853

Charles Zoller c. 1853–c. 1858

Northeast corner Ninth and Tyler

Charles Zoller c. 1858–c. 1863

Peter Haxel c. 1863–c. 1865

Windeck & Co. c. 1865–c. 1868

Bellefontaine Road between Harrison and Dock

The Rocky Branch Brewery was established in north St. Louis around 1844 by W. F. Bartalls. At first both distilling and brewing were performed at the location on Ninth Street above the Rocky Branch creek. Within a few years new ownership in the form of Blume (also spelled Blum and Bloam), Zoller and Company had taken over.

Eventually Charles Zoller became the sole proprietor of the brewery/saloon. In the late 1850s a new brewery was built about a dozen blocks to the north as the address changed to the east side of Bellefontaine Road between Dock and Harrison. The 1860 industrial census lists Rocky Branch as producing forty-five hundred barrels, mid-pack in the St. Louis beer production race. By the mid-

1860s, Peter Haxel had replaced Zoller at the brewery's helm. He in turn gave way to Martin Windeck and Frederick Lueberring, who ran the facility for a couple of years prior to its closing.

A 1909 Sanborn Insurance Map shows a soda water factory and blow-pipe works at the original brewery location on the northeast corner of Ninth and Tyler, possibly a long-lasting brewery remnant.

Washington Brewery

Engleton and Schneider c. 1844–c. 1846

George Schneider c. 1846–c. 1853

John Ruedy and/or George Schneider c. 1853–c. 1857

54 S. Third Street (southwest corner of Third and Elm streets)

Charles Schneider & Co. c. 1857–c. 1860

Carondelet Avenue between Anna and Harper

For a small concern that opened prior to 1850, the early history of the Washington Brewery (it was a common practice to name breweries after founding fathers) and its proprietor George Schneider is fairly well documented. Credit for this comes from three sources: first, the reminiscences of longtime Iowa brewer Matthew Tschirgi that appeared in the 1903 book *100 Years of Brewing*; second, the brewery research done by James Lindhurst for his 1939 doctoral thesis at Washington University; and third, deed research done by dentist William Swekosky.

Reflecting on his days spent in St. Louis some sixty years earlier, Tschirgi, a native of Switzerland, recalled going to work at the already established brewery in 1845. He remembered that the daily capacity of the plant that year was only twelve barrels of ale, as at the time no lager beer was being brewed in any of the six breweries in the city (a timeline casting still more doubt on exactly when Adam Lemp started brewing lager beer). The largest brewery in town then had a twenty-five-barrel capacity.

Lindhurst's research revealed that Schneider erected a stone building on the southwest corner of Third and Elm in 1844. The 1845 city directory lists Schneider with a partner named Shtophel Engleton, but soon after only George Schneider was owner. Schneider must have been selling plenty of beer, as Swekosky discovered that he bought the brewery property from Edward J. Gay on August 1, 1846. He then built a three-story building next to the plant featuring a meeting place on the top floor called Washington Hall. Schneider also bought land and constructed a beer cave across Wyoming Street from English's Cave.

There was a beer saloon on the brewery site called the Washington Beer House, and Schneider also hosted one of the earliest beer gardens in St. Louis (later the site of a Liggett Tobacco Factory). Both the saloon and Washington Hall stayed open into the twentieth century, by which time the former had developed such an unsavory reputation that it was nicknamed the "Bucket of Blood."

The brewery was seriously damaged by a fire in December 1846 but was rebuilt, producing around nine hundred barrels in 1847. By 1850, production had increased to two thousand barrels. An 1850 industrial census lists the Washington Brewery proprietor as L. Schneider, and the brewery's history grows rather murky after that.

Swekosky states that George Schneider sold the property in 1853 but leased the plant until its closing in 1857. An 1853–54 city directory lists John Ruedy as the Washington Brewery's proprietor, perhaps indicating he was subletting the plant from Schneider.

While brewing was ended at Third and Elm not long after, the Washington Brewery name was apparently taken by the Schneider family to a new location on the east side of Carondelet between Anna and Harper. Charles Schneider was shown brewing there in an 1858–59 city directory, and the 1860 U.S. Census of Industry lists the Washington Brewery of Charles Schneider and Company operating a small brewery there (a different census that year lists the operator as Lorenz Schneider).

Laurel Brewery

Joseph Fischgens c. 1845–c. 1853

Jaeger & Neff c. 1853–c. 1857

Fred Groeninger c. 1857–c. 1859

Conrad Elliott c. 1859–1860

P.R. Alexander & Co. 1860–c. 1861

Northwest corner of Hickory and Eighth

The Laurel Brewery was another small yet persistent St. Louis brewery. It was possibly opened by 1845, as that year's city directory lists Joseph Fischgens (also spelled Fischgans) as a brewer at the location. However, two years later Fischgens's business was listed as a porter and ale depot, indicating that he was selling the brew of others. Lindhurst states that Fischgens did not build his two-story brick brewery until 1848.

In 1850, the three employees of the Laurel Brewery made one thousand barrels of beer, checking in at fourteen out of seventeen St. Louis breweries in production. An 1853 directory lists the brewery but no proprietor, indicating that Fischgens may have left around this time. A different directory the same year lists the operators as Jaeger and Neff. A few years later Anton Jaeger would go out on his own at the Gambrinus Brewery.

Fred Groeninger operated the Laurel Brewery in 1857, with a directory listing both him and Jaeger there. A couple years later the owner was Conrad Elliott, and in 1860 the brewery was briefly taken over by Peter R. Alexander and Company.

Charles S. Smith

c. 1845–c. 1845
146 Washington Avenue

The 1845 St. Louis city directory lists Charles S. Smith as a brewer at 146 Washington Avenue, with his dwelling on Green Street. No other information has been found on Smith or his brewery.

Samuel D. Smith & Co.

c. 1845–c. 1845
Washington Avenue and Seventh Street

An advertisement appeared in an 1845 city directory as follows:

The Genuine
Root Beer, Mead & Porter
manu. by
S.D. Smith & Co.
at the
Corner of Washington Ave. & Seventh St.
"A Purifier of the Blood"

The 1847 directory shows Samuel D. Smith at 108 North Fifth Street, but no further information on his brewing activities has been located.

National Brewery (I)

Wagner & Hay 1847–c. 1853
Frederick Wagner c. 1853–c. 1866
Hartman and Zepp c. 1866–c. 1869
Katz, Gansses & Co. c. 1869–c. 1870
Ottocar Steiger c. 1870–c. 1870
153–55 S. Second Street (east side of Second between Poplar and Plum)
608 S. Second Street (address change c. 1866)

The National Brewery opened around 1847, with Wagner and Hay as proprietors. In 1850, it had six employees and brewed twenty-two hundred barrels of beer to rank tenth of seventeen local breweries. It was within a couple blocks of the original Lemp brewery, near the current location of the Gateway Arch.

The 1853 city directory places the National Brewery on the east side of Second between Poplar and Plum, with the individual listings indicating F. Wagner was operating the brewery and coffee house at 155 S. Second.

Disaster struck in 1854 when the entire facility was destroyed by fire. National was quickly rebuilt, and grew from producing thirty-five hundred barrels in 1857 to five thousand in 1860, placing it in the top half of the St. Louis brewing pack.

Frederick Wagner continued running the saloon and brewery until at least 1865. National does not appear in the 1866 city directory. When it reappears in 1867 and 1868 guides, the new operators were John Hartman and Louis Zepp. These partners headed for a new location in 1869, taking the National name with them to a site again close to the new Lemp brewery.

On January 2, 1869, the *Missouri Democrat* reported that a brewery at Second and Elm, capable of making fourteen barrels of beer a day, "was put up for sale." Presumably this was the original National location. The brewery stayed open for a couple more years, and its final operators had two of the most unusual names in St. Louis brewing history. An 1869 city directory lists the owners as Katz, Gansses & Co., while the next year the proprietor was Ottocar Steiger. There is no further mention of National in available records, leaving its final years and demise something of a mystery. Two decades later, the old National site once again began serving the brewing industry. The Berliner Weiss Beer Brewing Company opened its doors at 608–10 S. Second Street in 1891. It lasted until 1905.

Mound Breweries (I & II)

1/ Schmidt & Primeau c. 1847–1848

Louis Primeau 1848–c. 1851

Labeaume and Tenth

2/ Franz Kerzinger c. 1850–c. 1858

Southwest corner of Broadway and Webster

It appears that two different breweries operated under the Mound Brewery tag, the name coming from the Native American mounds that were virtually wiped out during the early development of St. Louis (though it was still nicknamed the Mound City).

The first Mound Brewery appears in the 1847 city directory as the property of Schmidt and Primeau, located on the corner of Labeaume and Tenth. The Schmidt involved may have been John Schmidt, who two years prior was shown as a brewer on the east side of Carondelet south of Soulard. In 1842, a John Schmidt was operating the Baltimore Tavern on Second Street between Poplar and Plum. The fact that August Juxberg was listed as a brewer at the same location leads to the intriguing possibility that this brewpub was Schmidt's introduction to St. Louis brewing. Louis Primeau continued at the Mound Brewery without Schmidt for a few years. He may have dropped the Mound name, and he disappears from records after 1851.

The Mound Brewery name resurfaces in 1850 as the plant of Franz Kerzinger, at the southwest corner of Broadway and Webster. In 1852, Kerzinger built a five-story combination brewery, saloon, and home on the site. He also set up a large beer garden that quickly became a favored destination for many German societies. The garden featured various "perches" and "lookouts" scattered about, offering visitors commanding views of the city, along with a large grape arbor.

Beneath the brewery was a large cave that extended about three hundred feet. It featured two main passageways each eight feet tall and twenty-five feet wide, with stone arches and a smooth stone floor. In addition to serving as a beer storage cellar, the cave had a flowing spring, water from which was pumped upward into a reservoir for use by the entire facility. Appropriately enough called Kerzinger's Cave, when the cavern (at the southwest corner of Broadway and Tyler) and the beer garden were visited by a *Missouri Republican* reporter, he described the site as a "romantic resort." Historian Ernst Kargau said a bathhouse was added to the brewery's beer garden in the late 1850s and that the cave was a popular place of amusement until 1862.

As for the brewery, an 1857 list of St. Louis breweries lists it as "Kertzinger's Cave" with annual production of seven thousand barrels, ranking ninth of twenty-nine local breweries. After that, the brewery disappears from records. That such a large concern would meet such a quick demise could be indicative of a fire or other disaster, but no evidence of such an event could be found.

Buena Vista Brewery / George Busch

1848–c. 1860

134 S. Third Street (southwest corner Third and Plum streets)

George Busch was a much older brother of St. Louis brewing legend Adolphus Busch. While his activities are not as well documented as those of his brother, George nonetheless played a significant role in early St. Louis brewing history. George Busch first started a brewery in Belleville, Illinois, around 1834 (it later became known as the Belleville or Anderson Brewery).

In 1848, Busch established a malt house and brewery at the corner of Third and Plum streets in St. Louis. Known as both Busch's Brewery and the Buena Vista Brewery, 1850 production amounted to four thousand barrels, sixth in total production out of seventeen local breweries. With his business growing, Busch needed more lagering and storage space, so he constructed extensive cellars on property surrounded by Ninth, Tenth, Cerre, and Gratiot streets. Also needing more room for brewing, in 1854 Busch built what was then considered a large brewery on the property above the storage vaults. He took on a partner named Charles Fritz the next year, then in 1857 sold his remaining share to Samuel Wainwright.

The brewery he sold would grow to huge proportions and stay open until Prohibition. George Busch kept running his malting business and may well have continued to do some brewing at the old Third and Plum site. An 1860 city directory lists him as a brewer living at 166 S. Third, across the street from the malt house.

Busch sold his malting business to Tinker Brothers and Company in 1859, which then sold it to Wattenberg, Busch and Company in 1863, and two years later Adolphus Busch and Company became proprietors. The plant was operated by Charles Rueppele & Co. beginning in 1868, and taken over by Charles Ehlermann & Co. in 1877. It was finally closed in 1881 when the Ehlermann concern moved operations to Twenty-second and Scott streets. Though he didn't achieve the lasting fame of his little brother Adolphus, George Busch still had the distinction of operating a St. Louis brewery at a time when the former was a mere child.

Eagle Brewery (II)

Eagle Brewery 1848–c. 1851
Jacob Ellerman c. 1851–?
E. Longuemare c. 1857
Carondelet between Soulard and Lafayette

Assuming it was not the same Eagle Brewery listed in an 1840–41 city directory, the second Eagle Brewery first turns up on an 1848 brewery list. That guide shows no proprietor or location. An 1850 city directory places the brewery on Carondelet Avenue; an I. Herget and Co. is listed in an 1850 industrial census (with a tiny 400-barrel production and a whopping $450 invested in it), which may or may not have been Eagle.

An 1851 city directory lists the Eagle Brewery of Jacob Ellerman at 223 Carr Street (possibly a depot/office), while 1853 and 1854–55 city directories place it back on Carondelet, between Soulard and Lafayette.

The name of a proprietor at Eagle does not come to light until the 1857 *Handels-Zeitung* list that indicates it was E. Longuemare. This list also gives an annual production of two thousand barrels, twenty-fourth of twenty-nine local breweries.

While the Eagle name then disappears from record books, the Longuemare name resurfaces with Charles Longuemare, whom the 1860 Kennedy city directory lists as a brewer on the south side of Soulard between Carondelet Avenue and Seventh Street. An 1860 census lists Longuemare as proprietor of the Stern (*Star* in German) Brewery. Thus the historical trail leads to the conclusion that Longuemare had moved over to the Star Brewery rather than staying at Eagle, which was next door but by then likely closed.

Below: Busch's Brewery scene, circa 1859.

Franklin Brewery

Charles and Richard Brewer 1848–1852

Richard Brewer 1852–1855

Tinker Brothers and Co. 1855–c. 1866

John B. Fleming c. 1867–1876

Caddick & Co. 1876–1878

25 S. Seventeenth Street

The legend that Benjamin Franklin once said, "Beer is proof that God loves us and wants us to be happy," has been debunked (though he did make a similar statement in regards to rain, grape vines, and wine). However Franklin still had a brewery named after him that operated in St. Louis for some thirty years.

The Franklin Brewery was started in 1848 by the aptly named duo of Charles and Richard Brewer. Their small plant was located on the east side of Seventeenth Street between Market and Clark, thus counting several other breweries as its neighbors. The large Winkelmeyer and Uhrig breweries were located nearby at least partly because of the natural caverns in the area.

In 1851, the brewery did business under the name Brewer and Son, and under Richard Brewer alone thereafter. About 1855 the Franklin Brewery was sold to brothers George and Zachariah W. Tinker. The Tinkers were well-known area maltsters who must have gotten the itch to use their malt to brew some beer. George Tinker was a native of Pennsylvania, born in 1814 and a cousin of pioneering St. Louis brewer Samuel Wainwright. He worked in the malt house and as a foreman at his uncle's Winterton Brewery back in Pennsylvania prior to heading to St. Louis in 1850, where he worked briefly at his cousin's Fulton Brewery. The next year George Tinker and his brother Zachariah, who had lived in St. Louis since 1839, established the Z. W. and George Tinker malt house at 72 Plum Street. The company was the first malt manufacturer in town not connected with a brewery. The brothers sold their first sack of malt to George Schneider of the Washington Brewery.

Increased demand brought an expansion of the malt house, capacity being doubled in 1854. Three years later William Smith was brought into the firm, and the business further expanded. Over the years most of the breweries in St. Louis bought malt from the Tinkers and Smith, including powerhouse breweries like Lemp, Stifel, Uhrig, and Winkelmeyer.

George Tinker, brewer and maltster.

When the Tinker brothers bought the small Franklin Brewery in 1855, it is unclear whether the plant was brewing ale or the lager-style beer that was beginning to take over the local industry. The book *100 Years of Brewing* insists that Franklin was always an ale and porter producer. Then again, with their English heritage, the Tinkers may have simply decided for themselves to brew ale and porter. Further muddling the record, an 1860 census says they brewed sixty-four thousand gallons of lager beer, while another from the same year lists them as producing twenty-two hundred barrels, including four hundred of ale. The latter numbers ranked them thirty-second in production out of forty St. Louis breweries, and one of only two ale producers.

While their brewery stayed small, the Tinker brothers and William Smith became huge players in the malting business. In 1864, they built a new malting facility, named the Franklin Malt House, on land bounded by Ninth, Tenth, Franklin, and Wash streets. Another new plant called the Spring Water Malt House was built in 1866. With so much malting going on, the Tinkers opted to get out of the beer business. They sold the Franklin Brewery to John B. Fleming, who renamed it the Franklin Ale Brewery and brewed the top-fermenting variety of beer exclusively. During the brewing year 1873–74, Fleming produced 1,742 barrels. He continued in the business for just a couple years afterwards, and by 1876 the brewery had been taken over by Caddick & Company.

The new owners produced just 646 barrels for the year ending May 1, 1877, and only 428 the next year. This marked the end of production at the Franklin Brewery, although Caddick & Company continued selling imported ale out of its office at 210 N. Third Street for a couple more years. The brewery buildings were torn down in 1879 and a large malt house built on the site.

As for the Tinkers, after Zachariah died in 1872, brother George and partner William Smith continued malting under the firm name of Tinker and Smith. The business was incorporated in 1879 when George Tinker's son, named Zachariah after his uncle, joined the business. William Smith retired in 1887, and George Tinker exited the malting business in 1896. In the meantime, the Tinkers had helped start the Columbia Brewing Company in St. Louis, which opened a new brewery in 1892 and took over the family's Spring Water Malt House. Zachariah would later buy the Algiers brewery in New Orleans, rename it the Security Brewery, and operate both it and the Franklin Malt House in St. Louis. George Tinker had played a major role in the St. Louis brewing industry for many years when he died in 1904. In a strange twist of fate, just two days later William Smith, for fifty years his close friend and business associate, also passed away.

Missouri Brewery (II)

Fisher & Peters (?) 1850–c. 1852
Robert Peyinghaus & Co. 1852–1855
G. Bautenstrauch c. 1860
Eighteenth and Morgan streets

An 1850 city directory lists the Missouri Brewery of Fisher and Peters at 68 S. Main Street. It is conceivable that the Main Street address was just an office or depot and not the brewery site. If so, the Fisher & Peters firm may have been the original operators of the Missouri Brewery at Eighteenth and Morgan streets, which researcher James Lindhurst reported

. . . began operation in 1852 under the ownership of Robert Peyinghaus and Company. This new concern started the production of imitation Scotch ale, and was under the superintendence of an experienced European brewmaster.

The Missouri Brewery placed this ad in the May 17, 1854, issue of the *Daily Missouri Democrat*:

MISSOURI BREWERY
Corner of Eighteenth and Morgan Street. The undersigned announce to their friends and fellow citizens that they have engaged the services of an eminent London brewer, and are now prepared to furnish hotels, taverns and private families with a superior article of Missouri Ale and Porter, in wood or bottle, and hope to merit and secure a generous patronage.

James Conran
Rob't Pryinghaus

Sadly the partners' hopes were dashed, for in September of 1855 the master brewer sold his equipment and the brewery building was advertised as for lease. At least one brewer answered

the call for a lessor, as an 1860 census notes the Missouri Brewery of G. Bautenstrauch, located at Eighteenth and Morgan and a producer that year of eight hundred barrels, the third smallest of forty local breweries.

Jefferson Brewery (II)

Francis Hammer c. 1850–c. 1855
Adolph Meyerson (?) c. 1857
Wetekamp & Bruning 1857–c. 1860
North side of Franklin Avenue between Seventeenth & Eighteenth streets

The Jefferson Brewery, named after a U.S. president who was himself a brewer, first appears in an 1850 city directory with Francis Hammer as proprietor. Its location was the corner of Eighteenth Street and Franklin Avenue. Little is known about Hammer, including any connection he may have had to the various members of the Hammer family who, years later, would briefly become owners of the small brewery that was the foundation of Anheuser-Busch. Francis Hammer's last recorded appearance at his brewery and coffee house is in an 1853–54 city directory.

It is unclear if the brewery operated by Adolph Meyerson on Franklin Avenue (mentioned in an 1857 directory) is the Jefferson Brewery. But in the *Handels-Zeitung* brewery list that appeared the same year, the Jefferson Brewery is shown as the property of A. Wetekamp and Bruning, with the notation "Just Established." Whether that means the brewery itself was newly established, or if it was just a new partnership at an existing brewery, is open to speculation.

In addition to their brewery, August Wetekamp and Louis Bruning operated a saloon at what was then 381 Franklin Avenue. Brewer Ferdinand Bruning was also part of the team. The business was fairly successful in 1860, with a reported production of five thousand barrels, ranking it fifteenth out of forty St. Louis breweries.

For whatever reasons, the brewery did not last much longer, as it disappears from records, with the 1863 city directory listing Bruning & Wehrkamp (presumably the same two men) as a fancy goods and toy shop company.

Neither man was finished with the beer business though, as Wetekamp went on to run the Laclede Brewery for over a decade, while Bruning partnered briefly with William Linze at the Philadelphia Brewery.

Simon Ziegelmeyer c. 1850

Unknown location

An 1850 industrial census lists the brewery of Simon Zilmyer, in which twelve hundred dollars was invested, four men were employed, and three hundred barrels were produced. This ranked the brewery sixteenth in output of the seventeen listed.

Presumably this is the same brewer as Simon Ziegelmeyer, who in 1860 was operating the Carondelet Brewery and saloon in the village of Carondelet, just south of St. Louis. As the listings for Carondelet do not normally appear in St. Louis guides until the 1870s, his 1850 location may well have been a separate operation. The location of the 1850 brewery and any subsequent activity is lost in the dustbin of history.

Star Brewery

Constantine Schnerr 1851–c. 1857

Schnerr and Niemann c. 1857–c. 1858

Niemann and/or Longuemare and/or

Lungstras and Company c. 1858–c. 1863

George Rothweiler c. 1863–c. 1866

Rothweiler & Sutter c. 1866–c. 1868

1701 Carondelet (southwest corner of Soulard and Carondelet)

Constantine Schnerr had a lengthy career in St. Louis brewing, which one source says included founding the Star Brewery in 1851, prior to which he had worked as a foreman for Lemp's Western Brewery. Historian James Lindhurst further states that the duo of Gaul and Reinhardt "probably" operated the Star Brewery during 1853 and that the next year it was run by Reinhardt and Uager. He cites the latter pair as suffering the loss of thirteen hundred barrels of beer in the collapse of a storage cave.

While it is certainly possible Schnerr had relinquished control of his newly built brewery in favor of Reinhardt, Gaul, and Uager, no explanation is offered as to the reason. As no evidence connects Schnerr directly to the brewery until 1857, it's certainly plausible Gaul, Reinhardt, and/or Uager were the founders. It's equally plausible that Schnerr never left and the others were operating a different nearby brewery.

The Star Brewery was located on the southwest corner of Soulard and Carondelet. In 1857, it manufactured five thousand barrels of beer to rank thirteenth of twenty-nine area breweries. City directory listings indicate that Schnerr had been joined by a partner named Christoph Niemann, the operator of a nearby saloon and billiard hall. Despite his apparent success at the site, Schnerr chose to leave about 1858 to start another brewery on Park Avenue. Niemann stuck around on his own according to an 1860 city directory, though an industrial census the same year lists Charles Longuemare as Star's proprietor. Yet a different 1860 industrial census shows the firm of Lungstras and Company operating a fairly large brewery. Since Star is not listed elsewhere by this source, this may indicate yet another team in place there. Backing this theory are 1860 city directory listings showing Rudolph Lungstras as a brewer residing at the southwest corner of Soulard and Carondelet, with brewer Barnard Koenig living at the same location and Peter Lungstras across the street (the Lungstras family was also involved in a brewery in Nashville, Illinois).

This ownership confusion is cleared up in an 1863 city directory, where the Star Brewery is shown being run by George Rothweiler. As Rothweiler was an insurance agent and collector for the Second Ward of St. Louis, he likely acquired the brewery through liens or bankruptcy, helping explain the ownership turmoil of previous years.

The brewery was something of a family affair during the mid-1860s with Ludwig and Bernard Rothweiler joining George there. Christopher Sutter was taken on as a partner in 1866. The last year the brewery appeared in a city directory was 1868.

Philadelphia Brewery

Reid and Company c. 1853–c. 1857

Herschfield & Co. c. 1857–1859

Adolphus Deutelmoser 1859–c. 1864

Bruning & Linze c. 1864–c. 1866

Oberschelp & Anthony 1866–1868

Anthony & Kuhn 1868–1870

2616–20 Morgan Street

The Philadelphia Brewery had its origins around 1853, the year it appears in a city directory as the Calledonian (a reference to Scotland) Brewery of Reid and Company, located at Twenty-fourth and Morgan streets. Directories in 1857–58 list the operators as Herschfield and Company. Possibly part of that firm from the start was Adolph Deutelmoser, shown as proprietor in

1859-60 city directories and in an 1857 newspaper list that pegged production at sixty-five hundred barrels (eleventh in size out of twenty-nine breweries listed).

An 1860 industrial census tabs annual production at four thousand barrels, dropping the brewery's ranking to twenty-seventh of forty. This could indicate either falling popularity of Philadelphia's beer or some difficulty such as a fire. By 1864, the brewery was being operated by Louis Bruning and William Linze. The former had previously been a partner in the Jefferson Brewery. The latter was also a partner with Henry Anthony in a local malting company, and would later co-own a similar business with well-known area maltster Rudolph Schmidt.

Two years later Philadelphia was taken over by William Oberschelp and the aforementioned Henry Anthony, with Francis Kuhn purchasing Oberschelp's share a couple years later.

Anthony and Kuhn would end up becoming big players in the St. Louis brewing game, but it would not be at the Philadelphia Brewery, which they left in 1870 in order to pursue the trade at the cross-town Jaeger Brewery. This apparently marked the end of brewing at the Philadelphia plant, though for a number of years the grounds continued serving as a beer garden.

Salvator Brewery

F. Schaeffer & Co. c. 1853–c. 1858
Schaeffer, Boernstein & Co. c. 1858–c. 1860
(converted to a weiss beer plant c. 1864)
82 Carondelet Avenue

The Salvator Brewery was opened about 1853 by F. Schaeffer (also spelled Schaefer and Schaffer) and Company. It was located on the west side of Carondelet between Marion and Carroll, later known as 82 Carondelet Avenue. By 1857, production had reached thirty-six hundred barrels, ranking twenty-first of twenty-nine St. Louis breweries. Henry Boernstein, the owner of the *Anzeiger des Westens* newspaper, was Schaeffer's partner for a time. In the mid-1860s, the brewery was converted to a weiss beer plant by Milentz and Brother. Chapter 4 contains more information on its subsequent history.

J. Schneider

c. 1853
Corner of Wood and Miller

The brewery of J. Schneider is listed in an 1853–54 city directory. The historical trail from Schneider to this location does not lead to any other known local brewers or breweries.

Wash Street Brewery

Jacob Hamm c. 1853–1858
Hamm & Hoppe 1858–c. 1864
Jacob Hamm c. 1864–c. 1866
Robert Lungstras 1866–1867
Henry Seelinger 1867–1868
1502 Wash Street

The Wash Street Brewery was located, appropriately enough, at the southwest corner of Fifteenth and Wash (today's Cole Street). It was established by at least 1853 by Jacob (sometimes called John) Hamm, and as typical of the era also housed a saloon and the Hamm family residence. Like a number of the breweries started in St. Louis during the 1850s, it had a fairly

Left: Statement from the Philadelphia Brewery dated October 25, 1858.

substantial output from the start. In 1857, there were five thousand barrels of beer manufactured, ranking Hamm's thirteenth in size of twenty-nine breweries in the city.

City directories in 1859 and 1860 list the Wash Street Brewery's proprietors as Hamm and Hoppe. Charles Hoppe was also a partner in the St. Louis firm of Teichmann and Company, commercial merchants. In later years he and his sons would operate a local malt house. A total of sixty-eight hundred barrels was produced in 1860, enabling Wash Street to check in at number eleven on a list of forty breweries. However, such promising sales totals were not destined to continue. J. J. Hamm died around 1866, with his widow listed as running the brewery in that year's city directory. She would form a partnership with Robert Lungstras (possibly the same gentleman as former Star Brewery operator Rudolph Lungstras), who then ran the place himself in 1867. Henry Seelinger was the final proprietor of the Wash Street Brewery, which was listed for the last time in an 1868 city directory.

Rudolph Brisselbach

c. 1855–c. 1860
In the village of Carondelet?

American Breweries II lists Rudolph Brisselbach as brewing in St. Louis around 1855. Brewery historian James Lindhurst, citing an 1860 census of industry, states that Brisselbach was then operating one of the three breweries in Carondelet and producing some two thousand barrels per year.

Iron Mountain Brewery, from Compton & Dry *Pictorial St. Louis*, 1875.

Bellefontaine Brewery

Pearson, Smith & Co. 1856–c. 1860
49 N. Commercial Street

The Bellefontaine Brewery was established in 1856 by Pearson, Smith and Company at 49 N. Commercial Street, with an office at the corner of Third and Elm. It was in the middle of the pack in local production, churning out four thousand barrels in 1857 (eighteenth of twenty-nine breweries) and forty-five hundred barrels in 1860 (nineteenth of forty).

There is no mention of the brewery in the spotty records of the next few years. Such an abrupt and mysterious demise could indicate a fire or some other disaster. To further add to the confusion, an 1865 city directory lists John Williamson, formerly of the Lowell Brewery, as the proprietor of the Bellefontaine Brewery at 17 Locust (a site which one year later was a depot for the Southern Ale Brewery).

Iron Mountain Brewery

Gebhardt & Meyer 1856–1858
Adolph Gebhardt 1858–c. 1869
John Kueppert c. 1873–1875
2301 Jackson

One of the more colorful names in St. Louis brewing was the Iron Mountain Brewery, taking the title from a fledgling railroad company of the same name. The new railroad had a station on Lami Street near where the brewery was built in 1856 by John H. Meyer and Adolph Gebhardt. Located on the southwest corner of Jackson and Lami streets, like most breweries of the time, Iron Mountain also featured a saloon.

Meyer (also spelled Meier) was a native of Prussia who came to St. Louis in 1844 at the age of sixteen. He worked as a bricklayer, and beginning in 1851 ran a grocery store prior to his being bitten by the brewing bug. Meyer sold out to partner Gebhardt in 1858 in order to move to Red Bud, Illinois, where he would start a brewery with Emil Berger, who likely had been his foreman at Iron Mountain.

The Iron Mountain Brewery produced 4,500 barrels in 1857, increasing to 5,300 barrels in 1860 to rank fourteenth out of forty local plants. It was still operating in 1869 as it shows up in that year's city directory, but was not in such guides from 1870 through 1872. The next year it was listed again, with John Kueppert the operator. Production figures from 1873 show 2,027 half-barrels were made. Since most other breweries had their outputs listed in barrels, perhaps this indicates that half-barrels were the only way Iron Mountain beer came packaged.

Kueppert kept the brewery open for just a couple more years, with its final city directory appearance in 1875.

St. Louis Steam Brewery

A. A. Lebeau & Co. 1856–1858
J. F. Boyd & Co . 1858–c. 1860
263–65 N. Main Street

*N*ewspaper accounts indicate that the St. Louis Steam Brewery was erected in 1856 by A. A. Lebeau and Company. It was advertised as one of the most extensive plants in the southwest. In addition to producing ale, porter, and malt, the business also sold hops. The superintendent of the brewery was A. Wood, previously of the Phoenix Brewery in Pittsburgh, Pennsylvania. Wood would later open his own brewery in St. Louis.

The original owners didn't stick around for long, giving way to J. F. Boyd and Company, which consisted of James F. Boyd and David J. Beattie. Advertising their product as "unsurpassed" in the "Western country," in addition to selling their own brew the partners also imported Wood's "celebrated Pittsburgh ale and porter."

The Steam Brewery was the sixth-largest producer in St. Louis in 1860, churning out more than eight thousand barrels. The fact that it was soon out of business leaves one wondering why it met such a swift demise, as after 1860 it disappears from available records. Beer making may have ended, but in the mid-1860s the site served the brewing industry again as the Linze and Anthony malt house.

Broadway Brewery

John G. Zoller and partners 1857–1866
Southeast corner of Broadway and Palm

*T*he Broadway Brewery was established in 1857 by John G. Zoller and Company. Production that year of thirty-five hundred barrels placed it twenty-second of twenty-nine local breweries. It was located near the Rocky Branch Brewery of Charles Zoller; there may have been a connection between the two Zollers as Charles sold Rocky Branch after the new brewery opened, while staying in the saloon business.

Broadway was, like many other breweries of the era, a combination brewery and saloon (the term brewpub had not yet been coined). The Zoller family residence was also on site.

John Zoller had two partners in the operation in 1860—Julius W. J. Kurlbaum and Joseph Winterer. The latter moonlighted as a gardener, so perhaps it is safe to speculate that there was an especially attractive beer garden associated with the brewery. Production in 1860 was forty-eight hundred barrels, a respectable eighteenth out of forty local breweries. John Glason was Zoller's partner in 1865 and 1866, after which the Broadway Brewery disappears from records.

Fortuna Brewery

Joseph Ferie (and various partners) 1857–1879
1906 Franklin Avenue

*T*hough it remained in business for twenty-two years, the Fortuna Brewery is nonetheless quite obscure. Perhaps this should not be surprising as it stayed small throughout its existence. The first trace of Fortuna comes in the 1857 *Handels-Zeitung* list, which shows the proprietors as Matthaieus, Frei and Co., with no production figures and the notation "just established." The "Frei" listed was actually Joseph Ferie, who would end up brewing at the 1906 Franklin Avenue site for over twenty years. Ferie had a new partner named Zeil in 1859 and 1860. If this was the William Zeil who lived five blocks north of the brewery, he may have been the first and only "barber and cupper" (his occupation as shown in the 1860 Kennedy city directory) to also own a brewery.

Next Fortuna operated under a trio of owners. Ferie hooked up with lumber dealer Herman H. Bergesch (likely the same Bergesch who had earlier partnered with Theodore Brinckwirth at the Lafayette Brewery) and Michael Doettling under the firm name Bergesch, Ferie and Doettling. Doettling left the brewery in the early 1860s, and Joseph Ferie became sole proprietor by 1866. Then in the 1870s he had a partner named Seeger.

Fortuna produced 1,300 barrels (thirty-fifth in size of forty local breweries) in 1860, while 1,454 half-barrels were made during the 1873–74 brewing season. Production was just below 1,100 barrels in both 1877 and 1878, after which the brewery quietly passed from the St. Louis scene.

Jackson Brewery

J. G. Buttner 1857–1857
Jacob Steuber 1857–c. 1866
Jacob B. Decker c. 1866–1867
West side of Easton between Victor and Barton

According to the book *Lost Caves of St. Louis*, the Jackson Brewery was built in 1857, on the same block and in the same year as the Pittsburgh Brewery. J. G. Buttner is shown as proprietor in an 1857 city directory, but the 1857 *Handels-Zeitung* list gives the operator as Jacob Steuber. That year's production of two thousand barrels placed Jackson twenty-fourth out of twenty-nine local breweries.

Unlike some of the other breweries in the Soulard neighborhood, Steuber's remained small, producing fifteen hundred barrels in 1860. Jacob Steuber continued at the Jackson Brewery through at least 1865. Although not listed in an 1866 city directory, Jackson makes a final appearance in 1867 with Jacob B. Decker shown as proprietor.

Pittsburgh Brewery

Coste & Kraeling 1857–c. 1860
Coste & Sempler c. 1860
Coste & Leussler c. 1860–c. 1870
A. Leussler & Co. c. 1870–1876
2506 Carondelet Avenue (east side of Carondelet between Sidney and Victor)

The Pittsburgh Brewery, one of many built in the Soulard neighborhood, was established in 1857 by partners Coste and Kraeling. Felix Coste was the president of the St. Louis Building Savings Association and likely brought money to the table, so it can be assumed that partner Kraeling provided the practical brewing experience.

Pittsburgh hit the ground running, manufacturing five thousand barrels in its first year of operation, already placing it in the top half of the St. Louis brewing industry. An 1860 industrial census lists the operators as Coste and Sempler with annual production at an impressive eight thousand barrels, ranking Pittsburgh either sixth of twenty-eight or eighth of forty breweries listed, depending on the census. Later that year the firm was doing business as Coste and Leussler.

This company was a family affair, as Pauline Leussler had become the wife of Felix Coste. Around 1870 the brewery began operating under the name of August Leussler (presumably Pauline's brother) and Company and continued under that ownership until closing.

According to *Lost Caves of St. Louis*, the brewery opened a branch called "The Cave" at Rosati and Lynch. Both locations were still in operation in 1875, with the distinction of appearing that year on the Compton and Dry bird's-eye maps.

The Pittsburgh Brewery produced just over ten thousand barrels during the 1873–74 brewing season, but even so had fallen to sixteenth in production out of twenty-nine competitors. Its last listing in a city directory was in 1876. Pittsburgh is one of the few breweries closed at such an early date for which breweriana exists, in the form of unusually shaped amber pint bottles, which are very rare.

Uhrig/Apel

Ignatz Uhrig c. 1857–1860
Herman Apel c. 1860–c. 1864
Pratte Avenue between Locust and Washington

In addition to his involvement in the St. Louis saloon business and the large Camp Spring Brewery (with his brother Joseph), Ignatz Uhrig apparently ran a brewery of his own for at least a couple of years. He appears in the 1857 and 1858 city directories as brewing on Pratte Avenue between Locust Street and Washington Avenue. Uhrig died young in 1861, but the brewery must have continued on, as the 1864 directory lists Herman Apel brewing on Pratte Avenue near Locust. The brewery was likely closed shortly thereafter, as within a couple years Apel would spend a brief time as a partner with Charles Huber at the Jaeger/Gambrinus Brewery.

Above: Portrait of Ignatz Uhrig.

Left: The words "Lager Beer" are embossed on the reverse of this bottle.

A. Wood

c. 1857–c. 1858

122 Levee Street (?)

Beer made by A. & A. Wood was available in St. Louis as early as 1852, when the W. A. Yore Company at 81 Commercial Street made arrangements to import the products from the duo's brewery in Pittsburgh, Pennsylvania. Adam Wood had opened what became known as the Phoenix Brewery in Pittsburgh in 1843. The Yore building featured a large warehouse and underground cellar to store the Woods' beer.

In 1854, the Woods opened a malting plant at 79 Commercial Street, which was advertised as the most extensive in the West. However, it was destroyed by a fire in 1857. The previous year Wood had become superintendent of the newly opened Steam Brewery in St. Louis. The 1857 and 1858 city directories list Wood as a brewer at 122 Levee Street, after which he disappears from local records. It is somewhat unclear whether the Levee Street location was a new brewery or just Wood's home while he continued at Steam.

Atlantic Brewery

John Gaul c. 1859–1864

Fischer & Zeiner 1864–c. 1869

1304 Park Avenue

The Atlantic Brewery in St. Louis opened around the same time as the Pacific. It first appears in city directory records in 1860, when John (sometimes called Jacob) Gaul is cited as brewing and operating a saloon on the southwest corner of Park Avenue and Thirteenth Street.

According to John Rodabough's book *Frenchtown*, Atlantic began in 1859 with Johann Gaul building a two-story brick building at Park and Hamtramck (as Thirteenth Street was also known). The author also reported the following:

> By 1862 he devoted his time and building to the manufacture of beer kegs. Mrs. Gaul spent her time in a most interesting manner—she stole clothes.

It seems that for some time folks in the neighborhood were having items stolen from their clotheslines. Mrs. Gaul had supposedly publicly denounced such criminal behavior as the work of children. But one night she was caught in the act, and when authorities searched the Gaul household (presumably at the brewery) they found a collection of all sizes and types of clothing, described as "astonishing."

John Gaul stayed at the brewery through 1864, when it was taken over by partners John F. Fischer and Frederick Zeiner. Its last appearance in a city directory was in 1867, though Rodabough says it didn't close until 1869.

The Gaul name (or at least something close to it) is not just associated with Atlantic and the theft of laundry, but also with one of the more difficult riddles of St. Louis brewery history. An 1853–54 city directory lists a brewery operated by "Ranhardt and Gauld." Unfortunately it is one of two breweries on the list for which no address is given. Historian James Lindhurst states that Gaul and Reinhardt were "probably" operating the Star Brewery in 1853, with Gaul replaced the next year by a man named Uager. That March the *St. Louis Intelligencer* reported on the collapse of a brewery storage cave, causing the loss of thirteen hundred barrels of beer, which Lindhurst credited to Star. While this may have been the case, it seems just as likely that Gaul and partners either helped found Star and/or started brewing at the Atlantic site earlier than credited here.

Carondelet/South St. Louis Brewery

Jacob Fritz c. 1859

Simon Ziegelmeyer c. 1860

Ferdinand Gsell ?–1874

Alphonse Gsell 1874–1875

West side of Second Street between Grundy and Market

In his thesis on St. Louis brewing history, James Lindhurst cites an 1859 newspaper article indicating that Jacob Fritz was operating the Carondelet Brewery in the village of Carondelet, just south of St. Louis. It was one of three breweries then in Carondelet, the others being the Great Southern (Klausmann) Brewery and another operated by Rudolph Brisselbach. In 1860, the Carondelet Brewery was operated by Simon Ziegelmeyer.

Since Carondelet was a separate town prior to being absorbed by the city, its listings did not appear in early St. Louis city directories. By 1872–73, Carondelet had been annexed, and the plant appears in city directories from those years as the South St. Louis Brewery, Ferdinand Gsell proprietor. In its final year or so of operation the brewery was operated by Alphonse Gsell.

David H. Evans

c. 1859–c. 1860

191–93 N. Main Street (?)

According to historian James Lindhurst, by 1857 the firm of David H. Evans was shipping into St. Louis some thirteen thousand barrels of malt liquor per year. While this would seem to indicate that the Evans operation was merely a beer depot, 1859 and 1860 city directories list Evans as a brewer located at 191–93 N. Main Street. A different city directory from 1860 lists the Main Street concern as a wholesale wine and liquor business, with the firm of Evans and Carey (David H. Evans and David Carey) running a saloon at 126–28 N. Third Street. This casts some doubt on whether or not Evans was actually brewing.

Schnerr's Brewery

c. 1859–c. 1868

1206 Park Avenue

After leaving the Star Brewery in the late 1850s, Constantine Schnerr headed to the southwest corner of Rosati Street and Park Avenue for his next brewing venture. As typical of the time, Schnerr ran a brewery, operated a saloon, and lived on the premises. Evidence indicates the site was likely chosen due to the presence of storage cellars dug there previously for the Star and possibly other breweries.

The new establishment was similar in size to Schnerr's old Star Brewery, with production in 1860 tabbed at six thousand barrels. This ranked in size either eleventh of twenty-eight or thirteenth of forty St. Louis breweries, depending on which census report you favor. Despite this early success, by 1870 the brewery was no longer operating. It would continue to serve the brewing industry, however, by becoming the Forster Malt House and later the A. Griesedieck Malt House.

Schnerr's Brewery is mentioned in a couple of different historical accounts. According to historian Ernst Kargau, Schnerr's Garden was located near the brewery before its 1860s closing. It included a dance hall, "in which the

conduct was at times improper"—the police sometimes became involved. Historian John Rodabough stated that the Schnerr Brewery was sold to Anton and Henry Griesedieck and that Christian Zainer, "a brewer of rare skill and formerly with the Atlantic Brewery and later with Schnerr, was also part of the package purchase."

The Schnerr Brewery was located just down the street from Atlantic and made a final appearance in an 1868 city directory, one year later than Atlantic's last listing. Brewing in the neighborhood had given way to malting.

Southern Ale Brewery

Heitz, Schricker and Company c. 1859–c. 1864

Ezra English Jr. c. 1864–c. 1866

English & Quinlaven c. 1866–c. 1867

English and Remmer c. 1867–c. 1867

241 S. Fourth Street (rear)

The Southern Ale Brewery had its origins in the late 1850s as Heitz, Schricker and Company. Primary members of the firm were Charles Heitz and Adam Schricker, who with his brother (we assume) Michael Schricker also owned a brickyard described as "near English's cave." Heitz was likely the brewery's foreman since he lived at the 241 S. Fourth Street location. Both 1859 and 1860 city directories list the site as the alley near Hazel between Third and Fourth streets.

Judging by the German names of the early owners, the site was possibly not an ale brewery at the outset, but by 1864 it had been taken over by Ezra English Jr., son of the pioneering St. Louis ale brewer. That year's city directory identifies the plant as a cream ale brewery.

In 1866, the directory showed both Englishes living at the brewery. The elder Ezra was still listed as a brewer so must have been pitching in, while Ezra Jr. was listed as a partner with Edward Quinlaven in the Southern Ale Brewery, with an office at 17 Locust Street and a depot at 251 Biddle.

Ezra English Sr. does not appear in the 1867 city directory so may have died around this time. Ezra Jr. must have gained a new partner in Henry Remmer, as the directory shows both of them brewing at the location, described as the alley between Chouteau, Convent, Third, and Fourth.

Right: The "E.Q." on this Southern Ale Brewery bottle is thought to stand for either "English & Quinlaven" or "Edward Quinlaven."

Thomas/Angelbeck

Julius Thomas c. 1859–c. 1860

Frederick Angelbeck c. 1860–c. 1866

Southwest corner of Mallinckrodt and Bellefontaine

In the 1859 and 1860 city directories, Julius Thomas is listed as a brewer located on Mallinckrodt below Broadway. A different 1860 guide does not mention Thomas, but does list a grocer named Frederick Angelbeck operating at Mallinckrodt and the corner of Bellefontaine (aka Broadway).

Angelbeck is shown as a both a brewer and grocer in the 1864 and 1866 directories. Famous St. Louis brewer Adam Lemp was another who combined running a grocery store and brewing. He had a longer beer career than Angelbeck, whose small brewing sideline soon ended.

Berscher/Baacke

Berscher and Co. c. 1860

John Hornby (?) c. 1864

Ferdinand Baacke c. 1865

South side of Franklin between

Twentieth and Twenty-first streets

An 1860 city directory lists the brewery of Berscher and Company on Franklin Avenue near Twentieth Street. This was just up the street from the Fortuna Brewery, with the Jefferson Brewery a couple more blocks away. The only other evidence of this brewing location comes from an 1865 city directory, listing Ferdinand Baacke as a brewer on the south side of Franklin between Twentieth and Twenty-first.

An 1864 city directory shows a brewery operated by John Hornby on Franklin Avenue between Twenty-third and Twenty-fourth streets. Given the tendency of some addresses to fluctuate during the era, it could have been the same brewery or a neighbor.

John Gankman

c. 1860

Unknown location

An 1860 census of industry lists John Gankman as a brewer that year of 500 barrels (250 each of ale and beer), placing him in a three-way tie for last place in production out of twenty-eight St. Louis breweries. There

are no clues as to if this was a continuation of an earlier business, the predecessor of a later business, or simply a short-lived operation.

Jeffery Jefferson

c. 1860

98 S. Fourteenth Street

A pair of 1860 city directories lists Jeffery Jefferson as brewing and residing at 98 S. Fourteenth Street. A census of industry that same year lists his production as five hundred barrels of ale. Nothing else is known about Jefferson or his operation.

Laclede Brewery

Charles Stolzh c. 1860

Wetekamp & Co./A. Wetekamp c. 1864–1877

101–7 Twenty-second Street

The Laclede Brewery took its name from Pierre Laclede, the youthful fur trapper who chose the site for a trading post that would eventually become the city of St. Louis. The brewery made its first recorded appearance in an 1860 industrial census as the property of Charles Stolzh. That year thirteen hundred barrels of beer were produced, ranking Laclede thirty-fifth in production out of forty local breweries.

By 1864, the brewery had been taken over by Wetekamp and Company, which consisted of August Wetekamp and Bernard Schmucker. Shortly thereafter Wetekamp became sole proprietor. He had moved to the Laclede Brewery from the Jefferson Brewery, where Schmucker was a grocer just down the street.

Laclede was located at the southwest corner of Estelle and Naomi streets and not far from the Grone Brewery. It produced 4,166 half-barrels of beer during the 1873–74 brewing season. By then the brewing firm's name was again Wetekamp & Company.

The fairly low production figures didn't stop *1875 Pictorial St. Louis* from praising Wetekamp & Co. as "another of those vast manufacturing establishments which supplies St. Louis and the west with lager" and mentioning a "large outside trade." Within a couple of years the brewery was closed, making a final city directory appearance in 1877.

Laclede also receives mention in the book *Lost Caves of St. Louis*. On July 15, 1965, authors Hubert and Charlotte Rother learned that a large tunnel had been exposed by workmen in the Mill Valley area. Upon arriving at Twenty-second Street, half a block south of Market, they found a north-south tunnel on the west side of the street. Inside the cave they saw walls and an arched ceiling composed of large, rough-hewn stones. The day before, when the tunnel was first unearthed, a brown jug and an 1861 dime had been found. The cellars were filled in a few hours after the Rothers left.

The foreman at the construction site told them two other caves had been uncovered farther south on Twenty-second Street. The available evidence led the authors to conclude that "the Grone Brewery and the Laclede Brewery originally used a portion of the same cave."

Lion Brewery

George Schneider c. 1860

John Weyand 1866–1869

2840 Carondelet Avenue

The first trace of the Lion Brewery is in the 1860 Kennedy city directory, which lists George Schneider as a brewer living and working at Dorcas Street and the northeast corner of Carondelet Avenue. It is historically unclear whether this was the same George Schneider associated with the Washington Brewery in the 1840s, the George Schneider who started what would eventually become Anheuser-Busch in the 1850s (right across the street from Lion), or a completely different gentleman.

Written record of the Lion Brewery does not reappear in city directories until the 1866–69 editions, all of which list John M. Weyand as a brewery proprietor and saloon operator at the former Schneider address. Weyand (referred to as Martin Weygand in the 1869 directory) also lived at the 2840 Carondelet (now South Broadway) location.

Today, the former brewery site is literally on the doorstep of the Anheuser-Busch brewing complex.

Pacific Brewery

Kunz and Hoffmeister c. 1860–c. 1872

Henry Kunz c. 1872–c. 1872

Northwest corner of Sixteenth and Singleton

Henry Kunz was born in Baden, Germany, on June 30, 1830, and came to St. Louis in 1854. While Kunz would become well known in St. Louis brewing circles through his activities as a maltster, he began his local beer career as a brewer. By 1860, he was a partner in and living at the Pacific Brewery. Kunz's co-owner at Pacific was Philip Hoffmeister. Depending on which census one believes, in 1860 the duo produced either one thousand barrels (twenty-third of twenty-eight local breweries) or four thousand barrels (twenty-seventh of forty) at the brewery located on the northwest corner of Sixteenth and Singleton.

Hoffmeister remained at Pacific until around 1872, when the city directory lists Kunz only. The brewery closed soon thereafter as Kunz decided to concentrate on his already established malting business. By 1875, William Goerger started operating the closed brewery's Pacific Malt House. A new malt house was later built a block up the street, and it kept the Pacific name.

Henry Kunz had started operating his own malt house at 1313 Ann Avenue after his service in the Civil War. He continued there long after exiting the brewing end of the business. His malt house burned to the ground in 1891 but was quickly rebuilt as a three-story stone and brick structure. Both the Pacific and Kunz malt houses operated into the first decade of the twentieth century. Henry Kunz incorporated his malt company in 1905 with partner Leo Rassieur, and he passed away two years later at age seventy-seven.

Henry Kunz,
Pacific Brewery.

Laclede Brewery, from Compton & Dry *Pictorial St. Louis,* 1875.

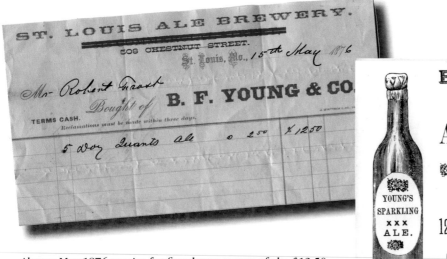

Above: May 1876 receipt for five dozen quarts of ale, $12.50.

Right: Early 1870s city directory ad.

Charles Schumann

c. 1860
Unknown location

An 1860 industrial census lists Charles Schumann's brewery as a producer of five hundred barrels, tied for last place in output among forty area breweries. However, an 1860 city directory shows Schumann as a clerk at the National Brewery and saloon of Frederick Wagner, where he also lived. Assuming this was the same person, perhaps he had gone from National into business for himself. Just to add a little more confusion, there was also a Charles Schuchmann who operated a brewery in Belleville, Illinois, around the same time.

St. Louis Ale Brewery (B. F. Young and Company)

Cooper & Conger c. 1862–1864
B. F. Young and Co. 1864–1884
514–16 N. Second Street

The St. Louis Ale Brewery, known for most of its existence as B. F. Young and Company, was the last of the early area ale breweries to close its doors, managing to stay in business for over twenty years. In its early days the brewery was the property of Richard F. Cooper and William J. Conger. It was located on the southeast corner of Palm and Second streets with an office at 313 N. Commercial Street (later moved to 508 Chestnut).

Cooper had previously operated an ale brewery in Alton, Illinois, with his brother Goldsbor-

ough. This brewery met a disastrous ending on February 6, 1862. As reported by the local paper (which got its details from none other than Richard Cooper), the brewery was burnt to the ground after an exploding boiler sparked a fire. Cooper said he had been near the boiler but was saved from serious injury after being knocked down and covered by debris, preventing materials from crashing down on him. He told the reporter that losses amounted to sixteen thousand dollars with no insurance coverage. Just three days before the explosion, Cooper had taken out an "indenture" where he mortgaged basically all of the brewery's assets (including a writing desk and horses) to cover overdue notes worth $5,860. Holder of the indenture was Richard Cooper, Esquire, of Cooperstown, New York. Unless somebody got the horses out of the brewery stable, he was left holding the entire bag.

Richard F. Cooper bounced right back into the business at the St. Louis plant, but he and partner Conger weren't around for long, as in 1864 the St. Louis Ale Brewery was taken over by B. F. Young and Company, which at least in its early years consisted of Bernard F. and John M. Young. For a fellow who was destined to be in the local beer business for so long, next to nothing is known about B. F. Young.

Available production figures show that the brewery was producing between eight hundred and eleven hundred barrels per year from the mid- to late 1870s. But by 1884 production had slipped below five hundred barrels. Still, the company was doing its own malting as well as bottling its ale and porter. The St. Louis Ale Brewery made its final city directory appearance in 1884.

LOWELL BREWERY

ALE AND PORTER.

JOS. SCHMITT & CO.,

ST. LOUIS, MO.

SOLD IN BARRELS, HALF AND QUARTER BARRELS,
And In Quart and Pint Bottles by the Dozen.

DEPOT—NO. 31 COMMERCIAL STREET,
Between Chestnut and Pine,
Where Saloons, Steamboats and Families can ALWAYS BE SUPPLIED.

Henry Brinkmyer

c. 1863

1084 Broadway

Henry Brinkmyer is listed as a brewer in an 1863 city directory. The next year he was listed as a baker. This indicates either an error in one of the directories or a man capable of making a variety of yeasty products.

Lowell Brewery

John Williamson & Co. c. 1864–c. 1866

Joseph Schmitt & Co. c. 1866–c. 1867

Joseph Schmitt c. 1867–c. 1869

Northeast corner of Bryan Avenue and Broadway

An 1864 city directory contains an ad for the Lowell Brewery of John Williamson and Company. It lists an address of 77 Commercial (likely a depot) and the company members as Williamson, local merchant Charles Giraldin, and a man named Ferdinand whose last name is illegible on the microfilm of the directory. The next year's directory lists Williamson at the Bellefontaine Brewery at 17 Locust Street. This could well be an error, or else Williamson had jumped ship.

By 1866, the brewery's proprietors were Joseph Schmitt and Company, which consisted of Joseph and Anthony Schmitt. They likewise took out a directory ad, which touted the Lowell Brewery's ale and porter available in full, half, and quarter barrels as well as pint and quart bottles (by the dozen). The Schmitt's ad promised their retail location was "where saloons, steamboats and families can always be supplied." The brewery depot and office were located at 31 N. Commercial Street (between Chestnut and Pine).

The Lowell Brewery is listed identically in 1867 and 1868 directories, with Joseph Schmitt as sole operator and the brewery site finally being listed at the northeast corner of Bryan Avenue and Broadway. The 1869 directory reveals that the brewery's office had moved to 707 N. Second Street, its last appearance in available records.

St. George Brewery

Cornelius Oehler c. 1864

Southwest corner of Carondelet and Lancaster

An 1864 city directory lists Cornelius Oehler as proprietor of the St. George Brewery and saloon on the southwest corner of Carondelet Avenue and Lancaster. No other information has surfaced on this nineteenth-century St. Louis brewpub.

Fritschle/Minnehaha/National (II)

Charles Fritschle and Co. 1865–c. 1867

Zepp & Hartman, National Brewery c. 1868–c. 1870

C. Wagner, National Brewery c. 1870

John Hartman c. 1875

Southwest corner of Cave and Seventh streets

(southwest corner of Carondelet Avenue and Cherokee)

The Minnehaha Brewery presents an intriguing enigma to hardcore St. Louis brewery historians. The unusual name crops up in several odd places, but it never manages to appear in any city directories. The first trace of this brewery appears in an 1865 directory that lists Charles C. Fritschle as a brewer on Seventh Street at the junction of Carondelet Avenue. Additional information comes from a pair of manuscripts written by William G. Swekosky, a St. Louis dentist and researcher of historical buildings. He states that

National Brewery (II), from Compton & Dry, *Pictorial St. Louis*, 1875.

Fritschle and partner Louis Zepp built a two-story frame brewery in 1865. Prior to that, Fritschle was a baker on Plum Street, while Zepp ran a nearby saloon on Carondelet Avenue and Lux Street. Swekosky claims that the saloon was the only retail outlet for beer from the new brewery, which was first called the Minthalia and later the Minnehaha Brewery. While Dr. Swekosky gives no explanation for the choice of these names (no information could be found for Minthalia, and Minnehaha was Hiawatha's lover in an epic 1855 Longfellow poem), he notes that the brewery sat above a cave on the southwest corner of Seventh and Cave streets on land leased from Dr. N. N. DeMenil.

In August of 1866, Fritschle and Company borrowed twelve hundred dollars from DeMenil, with a deed listing numerous brewery items, including an iron safe, used as collateral for the loan. This infusion of cash was not enough to save the struggling business, and the lease was foreclosed upon by DeMenil in June of 1867.

This did not mark the end of brewing or Zepp's activities at the location, however. By the next year, Zepp and a new partner, John Hartman, took over the National Brewery on Second Street. By 1869, they had moved the National name and their brewing operation down to the former Fritschle & Zepp site. A brewer identified in a city directory as C. Wagner ran the business in 1870, the last time it shows up in such a guide. Some beer making may have continued at the site, however. The Compton and Dry maps of 1875 show the frame brewery and a circular brick wall that had been built at the cave's entrance. The building is identified as National Brewery, John Hartmann (the name appears in records with both one and two "n's") proprietor.

When Lee Hess bought the DeMenil mansion in 1945, it contained a safe with the name "Minnehaha" on it. He later dumped it into a hole in the yard. According to one source, Hess tore down the brewery in 1946, while a neighbor claimed it had been torn down around 1920. In their book *Lost Caves of St. Louis*, Hubert and Charlotte Rother state that DeMenil stored perishable food in the cave beneath his house, "and when the nearby Minnehaha Brewery needed storage cellars, DeMenil leased the brewery's owners a portion of his cave." According to the Rothers, both the Lemp and Minnehaha breweries used portions of the cave, and "in order to prevent the yeast germ from flying from one's

kegs to the other, a wall was built between the two respective properties underground."

Minnehaha supposedly used a portion of the cave called the Entrance Chamber, so named when the cave was opened to tourists. While exploring the cave, the Rothers found an air shaft they claimed was used by the brewery as an ice chute and hoist. The Rothers also cite Falstaff historian Pat Doyle: "We have also heard that the Cherokee Brewery at one time produced a brand of beer called Minnie-Ha-Ha" and that "there, too, could be some connection between the Cherokee Brewery and the original Minnie-Ha-Ha Brewery which we know used a portion of the Lemp Cave."

Historian Stephen Walker in *Lemp: The Haunting History* takes a similar view, referring to Minnehaha as a brand of the Cherokee Brewing Company aged in the Minnehaha Cave, part of which lies beneath the Lemp Mansion. A new bottling house built by the Lemp Brewing Company in 1901 took over part of the former "Minnehaha" brewery property. The authors could locate no connection between the Cherokee Brewery and the Minnehaha name. The brewery safe is the moniker's only solid link to the St. Louis brewing industry.

Halm/Mick

Joseph Halm 1865–c. 1869
Henry Mick, Lion Brewery c. 1869–1872
N. Schaeffer & Co. c. 1874
1627 Second Carondelet Avenue

Joseph Halm was a partner in the Phoenix Brewery with Christian Staehlin (who was St. Louis city treasurer in addition to being a brewery owner) from 1860 through 1864. When he left, it was to start his own brewery just up the

Right: Ad for J. H. Mick's Loewen ("Lion") Brewery.

street, described in city directories as the west side of Second Carondelet Avenue between Lafayette and Geyer.

Halm continued brewing at this location for a few years and was succeeded by Henry Mick. In an ad for Mick's brewery, it is referred to as the Loewen Brauerei, indicating a possible connection between him and the original Lion Brewery, which closed around the same time. Mick left the second site in 1872 to take over a brewery in Edwardsville, Illinois. This marked the end of city directory appearances for the St. Louis brewery, though beer making may have continued at the location for a time. *American Breweries II* lists the brewery of N. Schaeffer, operating in 1874–75 at Second and Carondelet streets, likely a corruption of the brewery's address and the last evidence of any brewing there.

Cairns, Brandon and Company

c. 1866

Eleventh Street between Market and Clark

In 1860, John Cairns was a St. Louis soda manufacturer, operating a plant on S. Eleventh Street near Market Street. He must have decided to branch out into brewing, for an 1866 city directory lists Cairns, Brandon and Company (John Cairns, George Brandon, and George Shebley) as ale brewers operating out of the soda plant of Cairns & Company (Cairns and just Shebley).

It is possible that the partners were only bottling ale produced by someone else, but whatever the case it was a short-lived sideline, as no other references to the company's brewing activities have been located.

Friederich Mueller

c. 1866

99 Buel Street

In an 1866 city directory, Friederich Mueller is shown brewing and residing at 99 Buel Street. Nothing else is known about this operation.

Charles C. Fuller

c. 1870

217 Washington Avenue

Evidence for this brewery consists of an 1870 city directory listing.

Benton Brewery

c. 1873–1874

East side of Fourteenth Street between Penrose and Ferry

An 1873 city directory shows the Benton Brewery and proprietor Bernard Sternberg at the above address. The next year's directory refers to the business as the Benton Brewing Company.

Production figures for 1873–74 (preserved on a sheet salvaged from the Falstaff Brewing Corporation) show that the Benton Brewery sold 676 half-barrels of beer in a six-month period. Another company, with a somewhat illegible name (G?opel, St. Louis Co.) is shown as selling a mere twenty-seven half-barrels in a six-month period. It is unclear if the latter company was a successor to the Benton Brewery or a completely different operation, but both quickly passed from the local brewing scene.

Joseph Guggemos

c. 1890–c. 1893

3027 N. Eleventh Street

Joseph Guggemos is listed in an 1890 city directory as a brewer at 3027 N. Eleventh Street, which was a block south of the Great Western Weiss Beer Brewery. The 1891 directory lists the Guggemos brewery address as the southwest corner of Branch and Eleventh streets. The plant's product may also have been weiss beer; the record is unclear.

In 1892, Guggemos was running a saloon at 923 North Broadway and residing at 1127 N. Thirteenth Street. While he had a tiny role in St. Louis brewing, Guggemos would soon move to Omaha, Nebraska. According to *American Breweries II*, he and his family would be associated with two different breweries there. One of these would keep brewing until statewide Prohibition in 1917, while the other did the same and was later resurrected by the Metz Brewing Company, which stuck around until 1961.

Ideal Brewery

1897–1899

1629 S. Thirteenth Street

The Ideal Brewery was hailed as a new brewery in the May 15, 1897, issue of *The Western Brewer*. Three months later that publication announced that the business had been incorporated with a capital stock of thirty thousand dollars, one-half paid. The stockholders were company President Peter M. Kling, Rudolph Menkel, and corporate Secretary Gustav A. Senn.

Two years later *The Western Brewer* announced that Ideal had "gone out of existence," with the stockholders taking formal action to surrender the company charter. It further stated that the plant was to be sold. It's possible that brewing continued briefly after this, because Ideal does not appear on the "Breweries Closed" list of *American Brewer* until February 1900.

A 1908 Sanborn insurance map shows the 1629 S. Thirteenth Street brewery address as a small building located behind a bakery at 1636 S. Fourteenth Street. Further details about this brewery, such as just exactly what the product was, are lacking.

Scotch Hop Ale Company

1913–c. 1916

729 Clark Avenue

Hop Ale Company, Incorporated
c. 1934?–c. 1935?
3838 Laclede Avenue

A 1908 Sanborn insurance map indicates that 729 Clark Avenue was home to a Wesco Supply Company warehouse. It would soon be the site of a brewery, as announced by *American Brewer* in September 1913: "The Scotch Hop Ale Company, of St. Louis, Missouri, has been incorporated with a capital of $10,000." The incorporators were E. M., O. M., and L. S. Roberts. The company also appears in 1915 and 1916 city directories. The new brewery was in the midst of the old Chinatown section of St. Louis. When Busch Stadium was built downtown in the 1960s, Cardinals fans could see the former brewery location from their seats—it wasn't far from third base.

With the Prohibition movement growing in strength in the 1910s, many breweries began

Top: 1930s cardboard from the Hop Ale Company, Inc.

Middle: Circa 1916 bottle cap.

Bottom: Tip tray issued during World War I, emphasizing that Scotch Hop Ale was non-intoxicating.

making low- or no-alcohol products. This may well have been the case with Scotch Hop Ale, though the historical record is unclear. Toward the end of national Prohibition, the brewery was resurrected as Hop Ale Company, Incorporated. City directory listings from 1934 indicate this company had been capitalized at five thousand dollars in 1930 and consisted of E. Mason Roberts, president; Earl W. Kersten, vice president; and Hilda Kersten, secretary-treasurer. It isn't known if this version of the company ever got into ale production; if so, the venture was short-lived. The main building on Laclede Avenue still stands but offers no clues.

The Heimsheimer Brewing Co.

c. 1913
Location unknown

On April of 2009, a collector from the state of Washington placed a paper-labeled pre-Prohibition bottle of pilsner beer from the Heimsheimer Brewing Company of St. Louis for sale on eBay. The label had been perforated to show the date December 19, 1913 (12-19-13).

Research of St. Louis city directories, *American Breweries II*, and the *1913 Brewers Hand Book* showed no evidence of a brewery having ever operated in St. Louis by that name. It is the suspicion of the authors that the Heimsheimer Brewing Company was some version of a contract brewer that had its beer brewed and bottled by a local brewer and never operated as an actual brewery. This illustrates that new information on the old St. Louis brewing industry still surfaces from time to time.

Label evidence suggests that the brewer of Heimsheimer Pilsener was the Independent Breweries Company, as the perforations on the label and the use of a clear bottle are similar to that company's contract-brewed Davenport Pale brand.

Missouri Brewing Company (III)

c. 1934–1937
120 Iron Street

Even though the company operated in the 1930s, information on the post-Prohibition version of the Missouri Brewing Company is hard to find. It was located just off Broadway Avenue in south St. Louis, and label evidence indicates the brewery produced beer for the local Roebock liquor store.

Michelob Brewing Company

Research Pilot Brewery 1981–2008
Michelob Brewing Company 2008–present
#1 Busch Place

Anheuser-Busch opened this brewery, then known as the Research Pilot Brewery, in 1981. It is the least known of all St. Louis breweries and is actually a brewery within a brewery. Located in the nine-story building immediately to the south of the A-B brewhouse, today it is formally part

Left: Bottle case from the short-lived Missouri Brewing Co. (III).

Above: Front entrance to the Michelob Brewing Co.

of the Michelob Brewing Company.

Capable of producing a brew as small as ten barrels, the Michelob Brewing Company name was established on April 1, 2008. It plays an important part in the overall success of the parent company. The Michelob Brewing Company not only serves as a training ground for interns, trainees, and up-and-coming brewmasters, but also allows for the testing of new equipment and the evaluation of new raw materials. With the basic ingredients of beer being agricultural products, the quality of the annual crops is subject to the whims of Mother Nature. For test and evaluation purposes, the Michelob Brewing Company's small capacity allows for the brewing of test batches when a new crop of hops or barley is received.

The small brewery also serves the brewing department of Anheuser-Busch InBev's New Products Group by providing small batches of never-before-produced beers. Among the many products developed there have been Jack's Pumpkin Spice Ale, Wild Blue Lager, and Bare Knuckle Stout, along with the complete Michelob family of beers: Porter, Marzen, Honey Lager, Pale Ale, Dunkel Weisse, and Irish Red.

The Michelob Brewing Company is a complete brewery from brew kettle to packaging, including a bottling line and pasteurizer. It is not open to the public.

THREE NON-BREWERS
(listed here to dispel myths that have appeared elsewhere)

1. Jacob Brandenburger, c. 1867. He is listed as a brewer in *American Breweries II* and in an 1867 city directory as brewing and residing at 214 Cherry Street. While it's certainly possible Brandenburger was operating his own brewery, the fact that the directory lists City Brewery as the name of his business leads to the conclusion that he was instead running a depot for the brewery of that name. The City Brewery of Charles Stifel was a well-established St. Louis brewery at the time and operated a depot and office on Cherry Street in the 1860s.

2. Engle & Faber Brewing Company, c. 1890. This is named as a brewery in *American Breweries II*. While much of the information in that book is based on published material, none on Engle & Faber was located in the process of researching this book. In a book written by beer label expert Bob Kay, a label is pictured for a beer produced by this company, although it does not explicitly state who the brewer actually was. This is just not enough proof to list it as a brewery.

3. Theo. Schwer and Company, c. 1891. In their book *Lost Caves of St. Louis*, the Rothers state that "The Theo. Schwer and Company Brewery was located at 709–15 Lynch Street, which is one block south of Sidney Street and near Carondelet, now South Broadway. The brewery was in operation for a single year in 1891 and bottled a brand of beer known as 'Our Favorite.'" However, the 1891 book *Commercial and Architectural St. Louis* states that Schwer and Company was a mere bottling firm, not a brewery.

Pen and Sunlight Sketches of St. Louis (1898) sets the record completely straight, revealing that Theo. Schwer founded his company in 1887. He was joined as a partner in August 1890 by Ben Heyl, forming Theo. Schwer and Company. The fact that they were still in business eight years later points to them as having had some success. The same source also states that Our Favorite beer was brewed especially for Schwer & Co. by the Anheuser-Busch Company, quite convenient since the bottling company was right next door to that brewery.

Above: Display of brews developed by the Michelob Brewing Co.

Right: Footed etched glass advertising the Our Favorite contract brand from Theo. Schwer and Company. One of the rarest of pre-Prohibition St. Louis beer glasses.

Chapter 4

Weiss Beer Breweries

The word *weiss* means white in German, and the brewing of weiss-style beer has a long tradition in Germany. It is so named because of its pale appearance, which is a result of the use of wheat in addition to barley malt. While fairly popular in the mid-nineteenth century, weiss beers later became marginal styles. However, they have recently grown in popularity in both Europe and America. Varieties include hefeweizen (literally "yeast wheat") and the darker dunkelweizen.

One of the best-known weiss beers is the type known as Berliner weiss, so named because it was popular in Berlin. It uses two-thirds wheat malt and one-third barley malt (some pre-Prohibition beers called Berliner in the United States may have also used some corn). The resulting beer is highly effervescent, with a rather low alcoholic content, similar to today's "light" beers. Because it is brewed with top fermenting yeast (and is therefore an ale), weiss beer undergoes a secondary fermentation in the container when bottled, leaving a residue of yeast at the bottom.

Weiss beer is well known among local breweriana collectors owing to the distinctive, often brown, bottles in which it was placed. These bottles used ceramic stoppers with the brewery name usually embossed on them. The fact that many St. Louis weiss beer breweries were associated with saloons also indicates that it was available in draft form.

The weiss style was never a mainstream product in America, and weiss beer breweries were tiny compared to their lager-brewery brethren, typically located in a single building or two and with a small brewing capacity. They did very little advertising, and the owners could hardly be considered "beer barons." Nonetheless, St. Louis was home to many of them, and the fact that some operated for long periods of time attests to a loyal following. Thus they deserve at least a chapter in St. Louis brewing history.

Many German immigrants brought their white beer brewing tradition with them to St. Louis. The 1860s and 1880s were particularly popular times for the opening of weiss beer breweries. Two of the earliest establishments turned out to be the longest lasting and were also notable for being operated for a number of years by women.

The following listings include all known St. Louis weiss beer breweries. The four operations for which considerable information is known are discussed first, followed by the remaining breweries listed in the order in which they opened.

Hannemann/Columbia
(2543–45A Dodier Street)
Carl Hannemann 1857–c. 1865
Lena Hannemann c. 1865–c. 1874
Hannemann & Deuber c. 1874–1884
Lena Hannemann 1884–?
Columbia Weiss Beer Brewery,
Samuel King ?–1900
Columbia Weiss Beer Brewery,
J. T. Muench, receiver 1900–1901
Columbia Weiss Beer Brewery,
Leonard Gross 1901–1909
Columbia branch, Missouri Weiss Beer
Brewing Co. 1909–1919

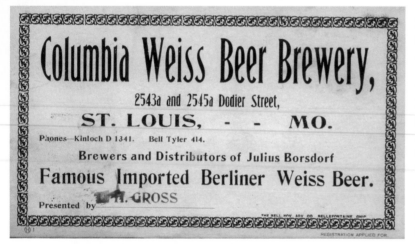

Beer Brewery and was operated by Samuel King. Soda was bottled in addition to white beer.

King went bankrupt in 1900, after which the brewery was taken over by Leonard H. Gross. In the decade prior to Prohibition it was operated as the Columbia branch of the Missouri Weiss Beer Brewing Company with Gross as corporate president. Although brewing ended with the enactment of national Prohibition, the Columbia branch remained open under the guidance of Otto Thoma and his sons. They bottled soda and, under the banner Columbia Products, served scofflaw home brewers by canning Columbia and Bavarian brand malt extracts. Domestic and imported hops, porcelain stoppers, and bottle cappers were also sold. Otto Thoma died in 1930, and the business closed around five years later.

In 1857, Carl Hannemann opened a weiss beer brewery in north St. Louis at what was then the Plank Road (Twentieth Street) and Hebert Street. Changes in street designations later altered the brewery address to Twenty-fifth and Dodier streets, and still later to 2543–45A Dodier. The Hannemann family operated the brewery and an adjacent tavern for decades. Following the death of Carl Hannemann his widow, Lena, took over the business. George Deuber was her partner/brewer in the 1870s–80s. He would later be a partner in the American Weiss Beer Brewery in St. Louis.

Before the turn of the century the former Hannemann site became known as the Columbia Weiss

Top left: View of "peak-a-boo" Columbia Weiss trade card, when opened up.

Center: Back of same trade card.

Top right: Columbia Weiss bottle with the tapered sides typical of most pre-Prohibition weiss beer bottles from St. Louis.

Salvator/Milentz/Stettner & Thoma
(1535 South Broadway)
Salvator Brewery, F. Schaeffer & Co.
c. 1853–c. 1858
Salvator Brewery, Schaeffer & Boernstein
c. 1858–c. 1860
Louis Milentz & Bro. c. 1860–c. 1873
Laura Milentz c. 1873–c. 1882
Henry Rooke c. 1882–1884
Henry Rooke Soda Water Company
1884–1886
Stettner & Thoma 1886–1906
(130 Sidney Street)
Stettner & Thoma 1906–1909
Stettner & Thoma branch, Missouri Weiss
Beer Brewing Co. 1909–1919

South of downtown, at South Broadway and the corner of Marion Street, Louis F. Milentz and his brother Carl began brewing weiss beer in the 1860s. They were unique in having taken over a non-weiss plant established as the Salvator Brewery around 1853. In 1857, Salvator was being run by F. Schaeffer & Co., and produced thirty-six hundred barrels of beer.

Soon after that Schaeffer was joined by a new partner named Henry Boernstein, the owner of the daily *Anzeiger des Westens* newspaper. It is unclear when the Milentzes took over the plant and changed production to white beer, but they first appear in a city directory in 1864. Bottle evidence suggests they operated under the name Praemium Weiss Bier Brauerei.

After the death of Louis Milentz his widow, Laura, took over his share of the business. She ran the brewery herself and with family members until the 1880s, when it was sold to Henry Rooke. He continued manufacturing beer as well as soda, kept the word "Praemium" on his bottles, and in 1884 incorporated as the Henry Rooke Soda Water Company.

In 1886, ownership changed to partners Christopher Stettner and Otto Thoma. While Stettner was trained as a brewer, Otto Thoma and his brother Leo came from a family that had run an inn in Altenschwald, Baden, Germany. The boys arrived in the United States as teenagers in 1881. Otto worked as a waiter and bartender before entering the beer business. Leo Thoma left for Kansas City in 1898 to open his own weiss beer plant.

Stettner & Thoma was successful enough that a new facility was opened at 130 Sidney Street in 1906. This brewery merged with the Columbia Weiss plant in 1909 upon the incorporation of a $60,000 stock company called the Missouri Weiss Beer Brewing Company. Stockholders included Christopher Stettner, Otto Thoma (named corporate vice president), Robert Dougherty, Joseph Tenge, Leonard Gross (corporate president), and Frank W. Feuerbacher, a well-known St. Louis maltster and a partner in the Green Tree brewery. Both breweries remained open under their old names, as branches of the new company.

Business was good for the new Missouri Weiss Beer Brewing Company. In 1914, both the Columbia and the Stettner & Thoma branches installed new bottling equipment. But like the rest of the industry, they were forced to cease brewing a few years later following the enactment of Prohibition. The Thoma family closed its namesake branch but kept the Columbia branch open, selling supplies to home brewers into the mid-1930s.

Top: Seldom seen bottle label from Stettner & Thoma.

Center: Porcelain bottle stopper of the style used by all St. Louis weiss beer breweries after 1880 until Prohibition.

Wittemann-Rost
(211–13 St. George Street)
Wittemann, Rost & Company 1888–1896
(1825 Arsenal Street)
Wittemann-Rost Brewing Co. 1896–1909
(315 Chestnut Street?) 1909–1911

Also involved in the 1909 Missouri Weiss Beer Brewing Company merger was another major St. Louis weiss beer producer, the Wittemann-Rost Brewing Company. Cofounder Otto Rost was born in Berlin in 1844. He came to the United States in 1860 and served in the Union army from 1865 to 1868. After living in Austin, Texas, he came to St. Louis in 1877 to work in the shoe and leather business. Partner John Wittemann, a native of Bad Ems, Germany, worked in the St. Louis shoe manufacturing business, where he became acquainted with Otto Rost. He became Rost's father-in-law when Rost married Elizabeth Wittemann.

With his job in the shoe business becoming obsolete, Otto Rost felt a career change was in order, so in 1887 he went to Europe to study the art of weiss beer brewing. The next year the Wittemann,

Rost & Company brewery was launched at 211–13 St. George Street. The company succeeded, and a new brewery was opened at 1825 Arsenal Street in 1896 (today the site of a gas station directly across Interstate-55 from Anheuser-Busch). At this time the Wittemann-Rost Brewing Company name was also adopted.

Wittemann-Rost was possibly unique among local weiss beer brewers in that it also produced at least one other style of beer. An existing label for the company's Pale Ale brand is evidence of this.

John Wittemann died in 1906, and two years later Otto Rost was ready to retire, so he entered negotiations with the men organizing the Missouri Weiss Beer Brewing Company. Rost was felled by a severe stroke on New Year's Day, 1909, rendering him helpless and mute. He passed away six months later. In the meantime, Missouri Weiss purchased the assets of Wittemann-Rost. The plant at Arsenal and Lemp was then closed, although city directories in 1910 and 1911 mysteriously list the Wittemann-Rost Brewing Company at 315 Chestnut.

Above: Wittemann-Rost workers photo. Probably all the employees of the brewery are in this image.

Royal Breweries, Incorporated
(1030–40 Victor Street) 1934–1935

One St. Louis company actually attempted to revive the weiss beer industry following the repeal of Prohibition. The plant of Royal Breweries, Incorporated was established in 1934 at 1030–40 Victor Street. This was literally in the backyard of the old Anthony & Kuhn brewery, which had later been converted into the Green Tree Brewing Company bottling shop and the Frank Feuerbacher Malting Company malt house.

Royal's corporate brass included William E. Willis as president, Arthur O. Straub as assistant president, John T. Davy as vice president, and Jack Hirrlinger as secretary-treasurer. Royal even made an overture to reopen the former Waterloo Brewing Company brewery in Waterloo, Illinois. But by January 1935, after only a few months in operation, the company declared bankruptcy. Court papers listed Royal's liabilities at $10,775 and assets of just $4,000. William Willis testified that "internal dissension in management and poor judgment in the selection of a beer to produce" were responsible for the

brewery's failure.

Thus did the history of weiss beer brewing in St. Louis come to an end, at least until the microbrewing revolution.

Top: The one-time Wittemann-Rost brewery, as it looked in the early 1960s.

Above and left: Matchbook and bottle label from the Royal Breweries. This label is the only example known to the authors.

Other St. Louis Weiss Beer Breweries

Numerous other weiss beer breweries, some of which were open for many years, also operated in St. Louis. Embossed bottles exist from many of these breweries, and even for a few that slipped under the radar screen of city directories. Information on these breweries follows:

August Offer c. 1864–c. 1868
(southeast corner of Twentieth and Davis streets)
City directories list Offer as a white beer brewer also living and operating a saloon on the premises.

Christian Koch c. 1864–c. 1867
(1149 Broadway)
City directories show Koch brewing white beer and living on location.

Louis Loos/Stamm & Co.
Louis Loos c. 1864–c. 1866
(65 S. Seventh Street)
Stamm & Co. (Charles Stamm and Fred Keisel) c. 1866–c. 1867
Loos appears in an 1864 city directory, Stamm and Co. in an 1866 guide. The Stamm and Kiesel (an alternate spelling) families were also involved in a brewery in Trenton, Illinois, in the mid-1860s. The St. Louis brewery doubled as a residence for all three proprietors.

William Ochsner c. 1864–c. 1866
(123 S. Seventh Street)
This white beer brewer appears in 1864 and 1866 city directories.

Edward Thode c. 1864
(191 S. Seventh Street)
Thode is shown as a brewer of white beer in an 1864 city directory.

Charles Pesseux c. 1864
(136 N. Fifth Street)
Pesseux is listed as a brewer in an 1864 city directory. He may have left St. Louis that year as he was also running a white beer brewery in Springfield, Illinois, in 1864 and for several years after.

Schultz/Schultz & Co.
Frederick Schultz c. 1885–1889

(1108 S. Eleventh Street)
Frederick Schultz & Co. 1889–?
(513 S. Fourth Street)
Schultz's brewery was listed in brewing industry publications such as *The Western Brewer*. It is also listed in *American Breweries II* as operating under the name Berlin Weiss Beer Brewing Company.

American Weiss Beer Brewery
American Weiss Beer Co. 1885–1886
(4117 N. Broadway)
American White Beer Co. 1886–1888
(1940–42 N. Broadway?)
American Weiss Beer Brewery 1888–1891
(1904–6 N. Broadway)
American Weiss Beer Brewery, August Hauschild 1891–1894
American Weiss Beer Brewery, Lohmueller and Deuber 1894–c. 1898
American Weiss Beer Brewery, Chas. Lohmueller c. 1898–1901
Despite operating for at least fifteen years, little information exists on this company.

St. Louis Weiss Beer Brewing Company
Great Western Weiss Beer Brewery Company 1887–1888
(3107–13 N. Eleventh Street)
St. Louis Weiss Beer Brewery Company 1888–1901
St. Louis Weiss Beer Brewery Company, Henry Bresser 1901–1905
St. Louis Weiss Beer Brewery Company 1905–1907
First listed in an 1887 city directory under the Great Western name, this brewery was operated the rest of its life under the St. Louis tag. Proprietor Henry Bresser also operated a grocery store and lived a couple of blocks from the brewery.

Schroeder's Berliner Weiss Beer Company
c. 1888–c. 1890
(834 Chouteau Avenue)
c. 1890–1916
(1013 Paul Avenue)
Despite it having been in business for around thirty years, little is known about this operation.

August Spitzbarth 1889–c. 1893
(3905 Kossuth Avenue)
Assumed to be a weiss beer brewer, further information is lacking.

The Berliner Imported Weiss Beer Company 1891–1905
(608–10 S. Second Street)
This company operated from the same address as the National Brewery decades earlier. It must have had some financial difficulties early on as an 1891 issue of *The Western Brewer* indicates it was sold that November 7 by court order for a mere $251.

Pilsner Weiss Beer Brewery Company ?–c. 1896
(1877 S. Thirteenth Street)

1899 (1701–3 Singleton Street)
Information on this business is likewise lacking. The Singleton location was near the malt house of William Goerger.

Carl Meyerhofer c. 1886
(address unknown)
Is listed in an 1886 edition of *The Western Brewer* as a new brewery in St. Louis.

C. W. Fries 1888–1891
(806 S. Second Street)
Is listed as a new brewery in an 1888 issue of *The Western Brewer* and also appears in *American Breweries II*.

Ernest Koenig Brewing Co. c. 1892
(Dekalb Street)
This operation was listed as a new brewery in the May 1892 edition of *The Western Brewer*. It must have been around for a while, as three different styles of bottles filled by the company exist, but no further evidence has surfaced.

Abraham/Adam Koplazinsky c. 1911
(address unknown)
Is listed in *American Brewer* as both opening (Abram.) and closing (Adam) in April 1911.

Bottles exist for two St. Louis weiss beer breweries for which no further documentation was located. They are:

1. National/Natural Bridge White Beer Brewery (both the Hannemann/Columbia and the August Offer breweries were located near the Natural Bridge Plank Road. One of them may have been bottling under this name, or it could have been a separate operation).

2. F. Raake

Top: Tin sign framed in wood.

Right: Twenty-four-bottle case from Schroeder's Berliner.

Chapter 5

Craft and Contract Brewers

While Gambrinus, the legendary king of Flanders, is the unofficial patron saint of the brewing industry, the craft brewing segment of the industry should honor former president Jimmy Carter. On October 14, 1978, Carter signed Public Law #95-458, which allowed for tax exemption on the yearly home brewing of one hundred gallons of beer for one person and two hundred gallons per household. It also gave birth to an entire generation of home brewers.

As defined by the Brewers Association of Boulder, Colorado, there are three distinct types of brewery operations within the craft brewing industry. The first is a microbrewery, which produces fewer than fifteen thousand barrels per year and may either self-distribute its beer or distribute it through the traditional three-tiered system. The three-tiered system of distribution, called for by state laws enacted at the Repeal of Prohibition, requires that breweries sell their beer to a wholesale distributor who in turn sells it to the retail outlet. No one is allowed to own more than one element. This was put into place to avoid the abuses to the system that occurred prior to Prohibition, when the breweries owned and operated both the brewery and the retail outlet. O'Fallon Brewing Company is a local example of a microbrewery that sells through the three-tier system.

The second type of brewery is a brewpub, defined as a combination restaurant-brewery that sells 25 percent or more of it beer on site. Morgan Street Brewery is a St. Louis brewpub. The third type is a regional craft brewer, one that sells between fifteen thousand and two million barrels per year and is independently owned and operated. The Saint Louis Brewery, Inc., fits into this category. In addition to marketing in seven states through the three-tiered system, its owners also operate the Schlafly Tap Room and Schlafly Bottleworks in the traditional brewpub style.

Fritz Maytag of the Anchor Brewing Company in San Francisco can be credited with saving an entire style of beer (steam beer) by purchasing a failing brewery in 1966. But he cannot really be considered the first microbrewer. That laurel goes to Jack McAuliffe, who opened the New Albion Brewing Company in Sonoma, California, and placed his beer on the market in March of 1977. The legendary Bert Grant receives the honor of being the owner of the first brewpub, the Yakima Brewing and Malting Company, which opened July 1, 1982, in Yakima, Washington. Development of the growing craft-brewing industry in the state of Missouri had to wait until after Dave Miller and others worked to change state law, paving the way for the Saint Louis Brewery to become the first craft brewer in the state of Missouri.

The following lists all the modern day brewpubs that operated in the city of St. Louis through 2009 and also some representative contract brewers.

The Saint Louis Brewery, Incorporated/ The Schlafly Tap Room
(2100 Locust Street) 1991–

The Saint Louis Brewery, Inc., maker of Schlafly brand beers, was incorporated on August 22, 1989, by partners Tom Schlafly, Dan Kopman, Charles Kopman, and Joe Tennant. Their plans called for opening a brewpub, but brewpubs were then illegal in the state of Missouri. At the same time, Dave Miller and several other home-brewing enthusiasts were working to change state beer laws. Advocates of the change succeeded by vote of the Missouri legislature in the spring of 1990. Section 311.195 of the Missouri Statutes provided for special licenses allowing smaller breweries to produce a maximum of twenty-three hundred barrels per year and also to hold a retail liquor license. The following year, the Saint Louis Brewery's Schlafly Tap Room became the first brewpub in the state to receive such a license. Since that time Tom Schlafly has successfully worked to have laws further modified to allow for higher production limits and off-premise sales.

The Schlafly Tap Room is housed in the former Swift Printing Company building, which is on the National Register of Historic Places. It was built for and occupied by the Lambert-Deacon-Hull Printing Company from 1902 until 1939, when Swift moved in. Heavily damaged in a 1976 firestorm, which swept the Midtown neighborhood, the building was so disfigured that it was used as background for the 1981 movie *Escape from New York*. It rose from ruins into a spacious brewpub, and today the brewery's corporate offices are located on the third floor of the south wing of the building.

Following the installation of a fifteen-barrel brewing system, manufactured by Diversified Metal Engineering Ltd. (DME), the Tap Room opened for business on December 26, 1991. It was the first new commercial brewery to open in St. Louis since 1934. The first out-of-house draft beer accounts for Schlafly brands included Joe Edwards's Blueberry Hill restaurant and music club in University City, Cardwell's in Clayton, and the Trainwreck Saloon in Brentwood.

Both the Tap Room restaurant and its brewing operation were a success from the start. Production reached 2,222 barrels in 1995. The owners decided they wanted to package Schlafly beer in bottles but lacked a facility for doing so. Between the spring of 1996 and the summer of 2003, the brands were brewed and bottled under contract by the August Schell Brewing Company in New Ulm, Minnesota. This enabled production to increase to more than

Left: Tom Schlafly (on right) seated with Dan Kopman; both are holding glasses of Tom's namesake brew.

Below: The Saint Louis Brewery's second brewery, located in Maplewood, Missouri.

ten thousand barrels in 2002. Upon the opening of the Schlafly Bottleworks in Maplewood in 2003, all bottling was transferred there. Combined production at both St. Louis and Maplewood for 2008 was more than twenty-four thousand barrels. At the Bottleworks, tours are provided on a daily basis and an exhibit highlighting the history of the St. Louis brewing industry is displayed.

Dave Miller, the original head brewer, honed his skills as a home brewer and has written many books on the subject. He left Schlafly in 1994 to be the head brewer at Blackstone's in Nashville, Tennessee, from which he recently retired. Dave was quoted in the 1994 May/June issue of *Brewing Techniques* as saying, "I had the greatest hobby in the world and I had to go and turn it into a job." Longtime Saint Louis Brewery employees include Stephen Hale, a college classmate of Dan Kopman's, who served as the assistant brewer when the brewery opened. Hale left for a brief period of time in 1994, but returned to serve as the head brewer. Hale also had the great fortune of meeting his wife, the former Sara Choler, on the job while she was serving as the brewery's first quality control employee. Tom Flood, the Tap Room's first restaurant manager (and currently the facilities manager for both locations) holds the distinction of having left the employment of the company five times and having been hired six times. James "Otto" Ottolini, whose ingenuity, inventiveness, and brewing skills are legendary, is credited with overseeing the majority of the equipment installation and subsequent improvements to both the Tap Room and the Bottleworks. He has gone on to head up brewing at the Bottleworks. The longest tenured employee, bartender Paul Jensen, was hired in 1991 prior to the Tap Room's opening, and holds court on a full-time basis behind the main bar.

Business at both Schlafly facilities has thrived under the guidance of Tom Schlafly and Dan Kopman. Their brewpubs are noted for interesting menus and the large number of beer styles always on tap. Annual events include Burns' Night, the Cod and Cask Festival, an Oyster and Stout Festival, Hop in the City, and the yearly anniversary party.

Above: Recent photo of the Morgan Street Brewery.

Morgan Street Brewery (721 N. Second Street) 1995– Owners/operators Steve and Vicki Owings and partners Dennis and Randy Harper opened the second brewpub in post-Prohibition St. Louis history on September 1, 1995. For the location of their Morgan Street Brewery they chose the city's historic Laclede's Landing district. The building is one of the oldest on the Landing, dating from the late 1880s. It was built for the Schoelhorn-Albrecht Machine Company, a manufacturer of capstans (machines for lifting heavy weights using cable) for Mississippi River barges.

Morgan Street's brewing equipment, located (and easily viewed) on the first floor, includes a 21-hectoliter (17.4-barrel) system constructed by AAA Metal Fabrication. The bar and dining facility are also on the first floor, with another bar on the second floor and banquet facilities in an adjacent building. The brewmaster at the Morgan Street Brewery is Marc Gottfried, who was hired as a brewing assistant at age nineteen in 1996 and has served as the head brewmaster since 1998. Gottfried began brewing in his basement at age thirteen and today serves as the vice president of the Master Brewers Association of the Americas—District St. Louis.

Morgan Street brews lager beer exclusively, and production for 2008 was 688 barrels, all sold in house. As the Morgan Street Brewery's silver anniversary nears, it continues offering a varied menu with at least four styles of beer on tap.

Bacchus Brewing Company

(1820 Market Street) 1999–2000

Located within the revitalized St. Louis Union Station (once site of the pre-Prohibition Joseph Uhrig and Excelsior breweries), Bacchus took over a location formerly occupied by Dierdorf & Hart's Steak House. Owner Davide Weaver, along with a silent partner, opened the brewpub in January 1999. Davide's mother, Rita Weaver, was the head chef and his wife, Gina Weaver, managed the staff and helped with marketing. Davide Weaver chose the name (despite its close association with wine) in an effort to emphasize the historic relevance of brewing beer and the fact that Bacchus is often associated with drinking and having a good time.

Off-premise sales at Blueberry Hill, Vito's, Riddle's, and Velvet were very successful. But high rental cost per square foot, along with a lack of nearby free parking and the fact that mall traffic was less than promised, led to an early demise for Bacchus. The brewpub closed in January 2000. Four months later the location reopened as the Route 66 Brewery.

Route 66 Brewery and Restaurant

(1820 Market Street), 2000–2005

The father-son team of Rao and Shashi Palamand opened the Old 66 Brewery in suburban Crestwood in 1998. They relocated to 1820 Market Street in the Union Station mall under the slightly altered Route 66 Brewery name, in the former site of the Bacchus Brewing Company. Rao Palamand, a food chemist with over twenty years' experience at Anheuser-Busch, had previous brewpub experience and helped supervise brewing.

Route 66 Brewery and Restaurant opened on May 1, 2000, with a fifteen-barrel brewing system supplied by Liquid Assets. Mike Wilson served as

manger, and in the spring of 2004 Mike Kilian was serving as the brewmaster. Plagued with the same high rent as the previous occupant, Route 66 closed on January 23, 2005. The brewing equipment is now in use at the Highland Restaurant and Brewery in Kirkwood.

City Grille and Brewhaus

(3914 Lindell Boulevard) 2005–2006

Little is known about this brewpub, as it enjoyed only a very brief existence. Located in the building that formerly housed the Playboy Club, the City Grille and Brewhaus opened quietly on December 2, 2005, and by January 18, 2006, had new owners. The brewpub, which used a seven-barrel capacity brewing system manufactured by the Pub Brewing System, was closed in March 2006.

Top: Tap handle from Bacchus Brewing Company.

Above: Logo for a short-lived brewpub.

Below: Route 66 Brewery scene.

Square One Brewery and Distillery

(1727 Park Avenue) 2006–

Located in the historic Lafayette Square neighborhood of south St. Louis, Steve and Molly Neukomm opened Square One Brewery at the corner of Park Avenue and Eighteenth Street on February 20, 2006. Their historic building was constructed in 1883, and in the early 1900s was acquired by Anheuser-Busch, which operated it as a "tied house," a saloon serving A-B products exclusively. Steve Neukomm purchased the building in 1985, and following a major fire in June of 2004 decided that it was time to come "back to square one" and rebuild the location as a brewpub.

Steve Neukomm's entry into the brewing industry occurred in September of 1999 when he took over the operation of the former Heartland Brewing Company, located between the Missouri towns of Washington and Labadie. The Neukomms

includes a sixteen-liter still from the Iberian Copper Works of Portugal and a fifty-five-gallon still manufactured by Vendome of Louisville, Kentucky. Square One is producing rum and vodka under the name Spirits of St. Louis. The brewpub features a varied menu, numerous beers on tap, and an outdoor seating area.

Buffalo Brewing Company
(3128 Olive Street) 2008–

Owner Dushan Manjencich opened the Buffalo Brewing Company brewpub on March 17, 2008. He had previously owned and operated the Yippie-ie-O Grille in St. Charles, Missouri, as well as other area nightspots. He purchased the 3.5-barrel DME brewing system from the closed Gentlemen Jim's of Poughkeepsie, New York.

Dave Johnson handles the brewing chores. Buffalo's brands include Buffalo Gold, Chili Beer, Buffalo Drool, Vanilla Brown, ESB, Maibock, Rye IPA, and Extra American Stout. The cozy brewpub features an array of food selections.

also own and operate the Augusta Brewing Company, which features a beer garden located along the Katy Trail in Augusta, Missouri.

In 2009, Dr. John Witte, formerly of the Trailhead Brewing Company in St. Charles, handled the brewing operations, using a ten-barrel brewing system manufactured by JV Northwest Incorporated. In late 2008, Square One became the first modern microdistillery to operate in St. Louis. Equipment

Above: Some friends of the authors entering the Square One Brewery.

Below: Pouring a draft beer inside the Buffalo Brewing Company. A stuffed buffalo head is partially visible above the bar.

Mattingly Brewing Company
(3000 S. Jefferson Avenue) 2008–

Owned and operated by brothers Douglas and Michael Mattingly, this brewpub had its grand opening the week of June 16, 2008, in the city's Benton Park neighborhood. Brewing equipment arrived in September 2008, and the first beers were tapped that November. Drew Huerter does the brewing for Mattingly using home-styled equipment, which includes four four-barrel fermenters. The number of beers available has gradually grown and the brewpub offers a widely varied menu.

Amalgamated Brewing Company
(1821 Cherokee Street) 2009–

Doing business as The Stable, this brewpub is located in a portion of the former William J. Lemp Brewing Company complex. The building was used by Lemp as a horse stable, garage, and loading area. Business partners Aaron Whalen, Jesse Jones, Paul Pointer, and Marc Naski held their grand opening on June 21, 2008. Plans call for brewing lager beer exclusively; the first of the house-brewed and sold beers, Helles, was released on May 29, 2009. Marc Naski does the brewing with equipment originally used at the Custom Brew Haus in Clayton. The fermenting and lagering tanks came from Bavarian Brewery Technologies. A microdistillery is also operated on the premises.

Cathedral Square Brewery
(3914 Lindell Boulevard) 2009–

Scheduled to open to the public in the spring of 2010, the Cathedral Square Brewery represents the reincarnation of brewing in the former Playboy Club building, which operated for a short time as the City Grille and Brewhaus before closing in 2006. Using the previously installed seven-barrel Pub system, brewer Brian Neville will be producing Belgian-style ales for owner Dr. Gupreet Padda. While the facility is under construction, Neville has been able to brew using the existing equipment, so the beers have been offered around town at several locations and events.

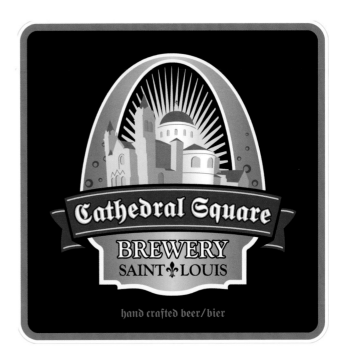

St. Louis Contract Brewers

A contract brewer is defined as one who handles the label design, formulation, distribution, sales, and marketing of a beer, while the product is brewed and packaged by another operating brewery. The practice has a rich history in St. Louis, going back to at least 1876 when Anheuser-Busch contract brewed Budweiser for Carl Conrad.

Another noted local contract brew was the 905 beer brand. It first appeared in 1886 and was sold by the W. Schneider Wholesale Wine and Liquor Company of St. Louis. In the post-Prohibition years it could be found at the local 905 liquor store chain and was produced at various breweries.

Recently, three contract brewing companies have operated in St. Louis. Two of them are attempts at reviving former great St. Louis brewing industry names, while the other was the effort of a local entrepreneur and former home brewer who decided to enter the industry.

Griesedieck Brothers Brewing Company

Attempting a revival of the original company, eighth-generation brewer Raymond A. Griesedieck reincorporated Griesedieck Brothers Brewing Company in 1992. By 2000, two of his relatives had also joined the company, and in 2002, Griesedieck Brothers beer was once more available in St. Louis on draft as Golden Pilsener. By 2006, the brand had made its way into bottles. Griesedieck Brothers Golden Pilsener is currently brewed and packaged by the Sand Creek Brewing Company of Black River Falls, Wisconsin, while the Griesedieck Brothers Brewing Company self-distributes the brand.

Established 1840

Lemp Brewing Company

Lemp was re-created once again in 2004 by Steve DeBellis, when Lemp Lager was contract brewed by The Lion Brewery of Wilkes-Barre, Pennsylvania. The O'Fallon Brewery of O'Fallon, Missouri, began brewing Lemp Jurassic Dark the next year. In late 2008, production of Lemp Lager was moved to the Stevens Point Brewery of Stevens Point, Wisconsin. The long-awaited return of Lemp brand beer brewed in St. Louis occurred on Friday, February 13, 2009. On that day it became available on tap at the Lemp Mansion. This Lemp beer had been brewed down the street at The Stable brewpub.

Hill Brewing Company, Incorporated (a.k.a. Hill Craft Beer Company)

Ray Hill, who started out as a home brewer in 1998, operates his namesake company along with business partner Mario Wayne, who serves as executive vice president of sales and marketing. Under a joint venture announced in April 2007, Ray Hill's American Pilsner brand beer was contract brewed for him by Anheuser-Busch. A-B also purchased a 49 percent share of the company, which was then renamed Hill Craft Beer Company. The beer was distributed in St. Louis, Kansas City, and Washington, D.C. During the InBev takeover of A-B in the fall of 2008, the contractual agreement was terminated, and construction began on a brewpub in Ferguson, Missouri. Tentatively named Ray Hill's Brewhouse, it is located in a building that once served as a St. John's Liquor Store, with a scheduled opening in October 2009. Ray Hill's Brewhouse purchased a fifteen-barrel brewing system formerly used at Linden's Brewing Company in Fort Collins, Colorado, with a two-unit kegger.

Chapter 6

Affiliated Industries and Organizations

o record of the brewing history of St. Louis would be complete without the mention of a number of people and organizations that have played a major role in support of the local brewing industry. From those who collect brewing industry artifacts and history, industry professionals, architects, and suppliers, to labor unions, festivals, and museums, they have all played a part in the long and colorful story.

Barry-Wehmiller Companies, Incorporated

(Formerly known as the Barry-Wehmiller Machinery Company)

s a leading city in the U.S. brewing industry, St. Louis also attracted a large number of affiliated industries. Products of these businesses included malt, cooperage, machinery, boxes, chemicals, ice, cans, bottles, asphalt flooring, wagons, advertising signs, hoses, belts, bottling equipment, brewer's pitch, bungs, and more.

Barry-Wehmiller is one St. Louis–based brewery supply company that rose to prominence in the pre-Prohibition era and continues to be a big player in the beer business to this day. Its origins date to March 30, 1885, when Thomas J. Barry purchased half-interest in a small machine shop on South Broadway. Known as Essmueller & Barry, Millwrights and Machinists, the shop served local malt houses and breweries by doing repair work and by providing elevation, conveyor, and transportation equipment.

The company moved to Twenty-first and Walnut streets in 1890, where Barry was soon joined by his brother-in-law Alfred H. Wehmiller, who entered the business as a draftsman in 1894. The two men took over the business and incorporated in 1897 as the Barry-Wehmiller Machinery Company with Thomas Barry as president. In 1901, Barry-Wehmiller sold its first continuous-motion pasteurizer to the Anheuser-Busch Brewing Association. Development of a bottle soaking and washing machine for refillable bottles led the new

company from selling its equipment mostly in St. Louis and the American southwest to becoming a worldwide supplier to the brewing industry and a dominant company within it. Thomas Barry died in 1903 and was replaced as corporate president by Alfred Wehmiller.

In 1913, the company's St. Louis office and manufacturing plant were moved to a new and larger facility located at 6501 W. Florissant Avenue. This site provided the company with excellent access to the local railroads, allowing it an easy means of transportation of larger machinery. That same year the company began work on equipping a giant new bottling shop at the Joseph Schlitz Brewing Company in Milwaukee, and its national sales continued expanding until passage of the Eighteenth Amendment. Branches had been opened in New York, Los Angeles, Fort Worth, and Birmingham, England.

A later article in *American Brewer* stated the following about Barry-Wehmiller's situation beginning in 1919: "With a bleak outlook for the future and a new plant that had been occupied for only six years, the company intensified its attention to other industries and considerable success was attained in the dairy and soft drink industries." Barry-Wehmiller also tripled its international business during the Volstead days.

Alfred Wehmiller passed away in 1927, with his widow, Lillie, succeeding him as company president. Upon Repeal, Barry-Wehmiller aggressively re-entered the U.S. brewing industry. A 1938 expansion included the installation of a five-ton crane for loading and unloading materials. Local companies such as Falstaff, Hyde Park, and Griesedieck-Western used the company's equipment. During World War II, Barry-Wehmiller served the war effort by producing materials that included twenty-millimeter shells and gun turret components.

Frederick Wehmiller obtained a degree in mechanical engineering from MIT and succeeded his mother as company chief in 1951. He died suddenly in 1957 at age forty-five. At that time his brother Paul Wehmiller was elevated to chairman of the board, with William A. Chapman becoming corporate president, a position he held until his death in 1975. Chapman was succeeded by his son Robert. In 2009, Robert H. Chapman was still president and CEO of the company, which had more than four thousand employees. Chapman and his family own around 70 percent of Barry-Wehmiller, which has corporate headquarters at 8020 Forsyth Boulevard in Clayton, Missouri. Barry-Wehmiller today operates a variety of companies around the world that produce packaging and conveying equipment. In addition, engineering services are provided not only for the brewing industry, but also for the agricultural, soft drink, and chemical industries. Recent acquisitions have increased the company's annual revenue to more than $1 billion. The company has also developed a small pasteurizer designed for use in brewpubs and microbreweries.

In a 2007 interview with the *St. Louis Business Journal*, President Chapman said of his company, "We are trying to build a great American company serving global markets." Barry-Wehmiller has indeed come a long way from the machine shop on Broadway.

Brewers and Maltsters Local #6

Known today as Teamsters Local #6, the former Brewers and Maltsters union local in St. Louis is the oldest chartered local in the state of Missouri. Local #6 received its charter as an affiliate of the United Brewery Workers Union at a meeting in Baltimore, Maryland, on August 29, 1886. In attendance were delegates from New York City, Newark, Detroit, Philadelphia, and Baltimore. St. Louis did not send a delegate but gave its vote to the delegates from New York.

Five years earlier, around 250 journeyman St. Louis brewers had struck for shorter hours and higher pay in accordance with union resolutions. According to *The Wetsern Brewer*, the strike was quickly and amicably settled. Following a boycott, the union signed its first contract with the Anheuser-Busch Brewing Association in 1891. As a symbol of its success, the local acquired a permanent headquarters in 1911, upon purchasing the former Shepard School building in south St. Louis. The building was adjacent to the recently closed Home Brewing Company. Following remodeling, the school was renamed Gambrinus Hall and served as the union headquarters until the new Gambrinus Hall (constructed adjacent to the original building) opened in 1965.

Joseph J. Hauser served as secretary-treasurer from 1910 through 1924 and again from 1934 until 1946. Robert F. Lewis (1914–1997) served as the local's secretary-treasurer from 1946 until 1977. Lewis led his members out of the CIO in 1952 after

Left: December 1936, Barry-Wehmiller ad from *Modern Brewery Age*.

Above: Teamsters Local #6's hard-charging Robert F. Lewis.

the president of the international union failed to fire three officers who had taken the Fifth Amendment when testifying before the Dies Committee in Congress. The Dies Committee had been set up to investigate "un-American activities." Local #6 then became affiliated with the Teamsters. Twenty-one years later the national union (the Union of United Brewery, Flour, Cereal, Soft Drink and Distillery Workers of America) likewise joined the Teamsters.

In his 1960 book *The Enemy Within*, dealing with the McClellan Committee's crusade against Jimmy Hoffa and corrupt labor unions, Robert Kennedy described Lewis as "a tough, honest and outspoken union leader." He was a golfer, hunter, fiery speaker, and uncanny negotiator who dressed like a fashion model. Lewis was willing to take on brewery management as well as national and international union leaders whom he felt were not doing their work in the best interests of the membership. He would only negotiate for his own union and staunchly refused to be part of any national negotiations. A number of other locals would wait for Lewis to sign a contract and then accept the same offer, knowing that they could not negotiate a better one. He had a standing offer that "anytime any members feel they can do a better job, all they have to do is get 15 per cent of the membership's support and I'll resign."

In 1973, Lewis negotiated a precedent-setting agreement with Anheuser-Busch allowing older employees to take early retirement at age sixty with full pay guaranteed until age sixty-five. This allowed

for speeding the modernization of the St. Louis plant while keeping the younger members employed. Upon Lewis's retirement in June of 1977, August A. "Gussie" Busch Jr. was quoted in the June 25/26, 1977 edition of the *St. Louis Globe-Democrat* as saying that "Lewis was costly but never dull. He was tough but always fair and honest in his dealings. I've respected him more than any other labor leader I've ever known. He's going to be missed."

The Teamsters Local #6 still has offices in the Gambrinus Hall located at 3650 Wisconsin Avenue; Bob Gartner serves as the business agent.

Above and right: Two pre-Prohibition St. Louis Brewers and Maltsters union badges.

Brewery Collectibles Club of America (BCCA)

Founded in St. Louis in April of 1970 under the name Beer Can Collectors of America (BCCA), today this premier breweriana collector's club goes by the name Brewery Collectibles Club of America (still BCCA) and maintains its office at 747 Merus Court in Fenton, Missouri. An article in the *St. Louis Globe-Democrat* on October 20, 1969, featuring the collection of Denver Wright Jr., led to other local collectors contacting Wright, and they soon organized the club.

Today, members of the organization collect a large variety of breweriana including cans, bottles, labels, coasters, lithographs, and virtually anything else with a brewery name on it. The BCCA has a steady membership of around four thousand, representing all fifty states and many other countries. The club has published two books on beer cans, known as *United States Beer Cans, Volumes I and II,* which include not only the history of the beer can but also color photos of thousands of different cans.

There are more than one hundred local chapters worldwide. The BCCA hosts a late-summer national convention (or CANvention) at sites around the country, and the St. Louis–area chapter—the Gateway Chapter—hosts a number of annual shows. St. Louis was the host city for the 1971 and 1995 CANventions.

Falstaff International Museum of Brewing

As part of the St. Louis Bicentennial observation, the Falstaff Brewing Corporation opened what was believed to be the first brewing museum in the nation. Located at 1923 South Shenandoah Avenue, across the street from the main entrance to Falstaff's Plant #10, the new visitor center and museum opened on April 27, 1964. In the November 1964 issue of *Modern Brewery Age*, it was hailed by Harvey A. Beffa, then chairman of the board at Falstaff, as "a permanent tribute to the community's brewing heritage."

Originally called Stein Hall when constructed by the Griesedieck Brothers Brewery Company, the building was first opened on September 2, 1954, and cost $140,000. While housing the stein collection of Edward J. Griesedieck, then president of that brewery, it was also intended to serve as a meeting place for employees, wholesalers, visitors, and civic organizations. In its first year of operation it was recorded that the Stein Hall had hosted 21,776 guests.

The new Falstaff museum featured more than three hundred display items, some dating back to the 1820s. Exhibits included the original twelve-barrel brew kettle of Adam Lemp; a hand-operated bottle-corking machine and a horizontal steam engine (both formerly used in the Lemp Brewing Company); and a tabletop model of a Barry-Wehmiller pasteurizer. Today, all of these items are exhibited at the Missouri History Museum in Forest Park. The Falstaff museum also featured beer glasses, bottles, steins, tavern furniture, advertising pieces, and early brewing tools.

The museum also unveiled six pen-and-ink drawings by local artist Donald Langeneckert. The drawings depict various stages of local brewing history including: 1820–1840, Aging Beer in Caves; 1840–1860, Firing the Brew Kettle; 1860–1880, Cutting Ice on the Mississippi; 1880–1900, Brewery Wagon on Broadway; 1900–1920, A Toast to the Fair; 1920–1940, Beer Is Back.

The building housing the museum was known as the Falstaff Inn and served as the brewery's visitor center in addition to hosting meetings and events. The museum was closed in 1975 following the takeover of the Falstaff Brewing Corporation by Paul Kalmanovitz. Kalmanovitz not only shut down the museum, but he also ordered employees to box up the steins on display and send them to him

Left: Membership application for the Brewery Collectibles Club of America (BCCA), showing the many breweriana items that members collect.

out in California. His instructions included throwing away all of the other items, even though many were on loan from the public. While some donors did get their items back and others were salvaged, this marked an undignified ending for the Falstaff Museum.

Master Brewers Association of the Americas—District St. Louis

*D*edicated to promoting, advancing, and improving the professional interests of brewery and malt house production and technical personnel, the Master Brewers Association of the Americas (MBAA) was founded in Chicago on March 21, 1887. District St. Louis, the largest of the twenty-four worldwide districts, was formed on October 27, 1887, and was headed in 2009 by President Bradley Seabaugh. Marc Gottfried of the Morgan Street Brewery serves on the district board of governors and as vice president of District St. Louis. The national convention was held here in 1891, 1904, 1940, 1944, 1953, 1975, and 1984. Local brewmasters who have served as national president include Edward Wagner, 1904–1908; William Carthaus, 1912–1917; Andrew Steinhubl, 1983–1984; Warren Peter, 1991–1992; and George Reisch, 2008–2009.

St. Louis Brewers Heritage Festival

Sharing a common passion for beer, seven local brewers took part in the original St. Louis Brewers Heritage Festival held May 10–12, 2007, in Forest Park. Participating breweries—Alandale Brewing Company, Anheuser-Busch, Augusta Brewery, Morgan Street Brewery, O'Fallon Brewery, Saint Louis Brewery, and Square One Brewery—poured fifty different beers. As a tribute to the local industry, the Missouri History Museum opened a display featuring the pre-Prohibition history of brewing in St. Louis called *From Kettle to Keg*, which remained open until January 2009. Bob Lachky, Tom Shipley, and Jay Cunningham of Anheuser-Busch and Dan Kopman of the Saint Louis Brewery organized the festival.

"Here's to Beer," a campaign to raise the awareness of beer and promote the entire brewing industry, was created in 2006 and funded entirely by Anheuser-Busch. The campaign provided the financial support for the St. Louis Brewers Heritage Festival.

The 2008 Festival provided sixty beers for tasting and was organized similarly to the first, being held May 8–10 in Forest Park. The Griesedieck Brothers Brewing Company joined the original seven brewers from the 2007 event, along with the local home brewers club, the St. Louis Brews. Despite severe rainstorms, attendance exceeded eighteen thousand, making it the third-largest brewers' festival in the United States.

In an effort to avoid the early May rainstorms of the two previous festivals, the third annual event in 2009 was held on June 5–6, and the location was changed to the upper fields east of the Muny Opera. With the weather cooperating, it made for a delightful event. Over sixty beer styles were presented by eleven local brewers. The "Festival Beer" (of which the various brewers make their own versions) was the home brew champion "Ted O'Neill's Dry Stout." New brewers that year included the recently opened Amalgamated Brewing Company, Buffalo Brewing Company, and Mattingly Brewing Company in addition to Trailhead Brewing Company of St. Charles, Missouri.

St. Louis Brewery Architects

With St. Louis firmly established as a brewing center by the 1870s, it was natural for some local architects to turn their attention to brewery design. The most famous of these was Edmund Jungenfeld, who came to St. Louis in 1864. Like Adolphus Busch, Jungenfeld was a native of Mainz, Germany. As a young man, Jungenfeld attended technical schools, worked, and traveled throughout Europe. Early in his career he worked for a railroad. In the United States he quickly gained a reputation for his skills in designing public buildings as a partner with local architect Thomas Walsh. These included buildings in Missouri—the "Four Courts" and county jail buildings in St. Louis and the normal school in Warrensburg—as well as in Illinois: the Blind Asylum in Jacksonville, the Insane Asylum in Anna, and the normal school in Carbondale.

Jungenfeld's career as a brewery architect took off in 1869, when he was commissioned by Adolphus Busch of the Anheuser brewery to begin work on what historian Bill Vollmar described as "the most modern and coordinated brewery in the United States." A new brewhouse erected in 1869 was the first step toward this goal. By the time of his premature death at age forty-four in 1885, Jungenfeld was responsible for drawing plans for the complex of buildings that allowed annual production at Anheuser-Busch to rise from twenty-five thousand to three hundred thousand barrels. In a one-year period beginning in the fall of 1877, seven new buildings or additions were completed. Many other breweries in St. Louis and throughout the country would likewise turn to Jungenfeld for design work.

With the peak of his career corresponding to the early development of artificial refrigeration, Jungenfeld not only designed buildings to house such machines, but also with partners C. G. Mayer and J. Koenigsberg formed the Empire Refrigerating Company in 1882. This company and his architectural firm were both located in the Empire Building at 919 Olive Street.

An illustration of the esteem in which Jungenfeld was held is the fact that after his death his successors retained the name E. Jungenfeld and Company. The business continued as brewery design and engineering experts, with the three main figures Robert W. Walsh, Frederick Widmann, and C. D. Boisselier.

A wonderful book was published by the company in 1895, titled *A Portfolio of Breweries and Kindred Plants Designed by E. Jungenfeld & Co.,*

Above: An 1895 view of the offices of E. Jungenfeld & Co., from that architectural firm's *Portfolio* publication.

St. Louis. Photos included one of a busy "draught-ing" office featuring eleven men dutifully design-ing away; five pages of Anheuser-Busch brewery buildings, plus the residence and private stable of Adolphus Busch; and numerous views of sixteen other local breweries the firm had helped develop.

In the 1890s, E. Jungenfeld and Company moved its offices to the Wainwright Building. In 1898, the company decided to change its name to Widmann, Walsh and Boisselier. The partners emphasized that there would be no changes in the business. They explained that the modification was made "owing to the confusion occasionally occur-ring and consequent wordy explanations required from time to time regarding the personnel of our firm." Boisselier later left the firm, but Widmann

and Walsh continued designing brewery buildings up to the dark years of Prohibition.

Another local architectural firm that played a large role in the brewing industry was operated by the Janssen family. E. C. Janssen was advertis-ing his services in *The Western Brewer* as early as 1883. From his office at 506 Olive Street, Janssen described himself as an "architect and builder of breweries and malt houses." He designed the large American Brewing Company, opened in St. Louis in 1890, and later was a partner in the Wagner Brew-ing Company in Granite City, Illinois.

When Oscar Janssen joined the business it be-came known as Janssen and Janssen. The company once again designed breweries following Repeal. In the early 1940s, the firm name became Oscar

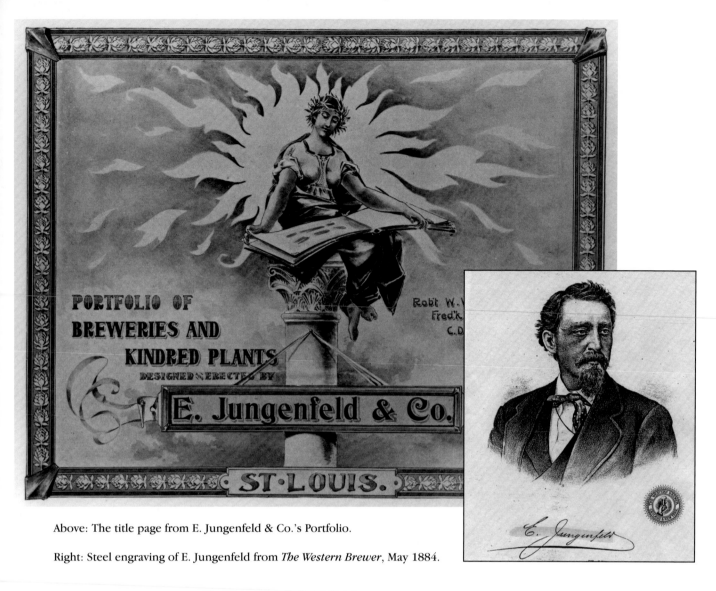

Above: The title page from E. Jungenfeld & Co.'s Portfolio.

Right: Steel engraving of E. Jungenfeld from *The Western Brewer*, May 1884.

Janssen Architects and Engineers, with an office in the Chemical Building. Local brewers employing the company for their fast-growing plants included Anheuser-Busch, Columbia, Griesedieck-Western, and Griesedieck Brothers, as well as Storz in Omaha.

At least one other well-known design firm specializing in breweries maintained a local office. Architect and engineer Wilhelm Griesser also had offices in New York, Pittsburgh, and Denver. A 1912 ad bragged that Griesser had "built the two largest breweries ever built in this country."

St. Louis Brews—The Home Brewers

The St. Louis Brews is a club dedicated to the brewing, evaluation, and responsible consumption of home-brewed beers. The group was formed after John Sterling posted a sign-up sheet in 1985 on the bulletin board of the home brew supply store Bacchus and Barleycorn—

St. Louis, which was located at 7713 Clayton Road. Little could he have guessed that, two decades later, the home brew club he started would have 145 members.

After reading a book published by local home brewer Dave Miller, Sterling contacted Miller, who became the club's original technical programs director. Miller went on to publish numerous books on home brewing and became the head brewer for the Saint Louis Brewery in 1991. Later, Miller took a position with the Blackstone Restaurant and Brewery in Nashville, Tennessee, retiring in 2009. The St. Louis Brews meets at 7:00 p.m. on the first Thursday of every month at the Anheuser-Busch Conference Center on Soccer Park Road in Fenton.

The original officers in 1985 were Clay Biberdorf, president; Dave Miller, vice president; John Sterling, secretary; and Jason Held, treasurer. Today, the officers are Dan Stauder, president; Josh Eberhardt, vice president; Paul Murphy, treasurer; Tim Fahner, secretary; and William Nordmann, brewmeister.

Chapter 7

The Choicest Product of the Brewers' Art

While the brewing history of St. Louis continues to unfold on a daily basis, most of the breweries and their workers are long gone, and most of the buildings have been destroyed. With them went the chance to ever taste their beer.

What does remain is the "breweriana," the advertising and packaging items used by the breweries. These items run the gamut from large wooden barrels to bottle caps and everything in between. They range from gorgeous artwork and intricate signs to the utilitarian. Much of this breweriana is being lovingly preserved by collectors.

As we close the book on St. Louis brewing history, we will leave you with some of these items.

Lemp cloth banner from the early 1900s.

Falstaff cone top beer can
marketed in the late 1940s
and a Crowntainer beer can
distributed by Griesedieck
Brothers after World War II.

Early 1900s Anheuser-Busch self-framed tin sign.

Celluloid-over-cardboard from the late 1890s, advertising the National
Brewery's flagship brand, White Seal beer.

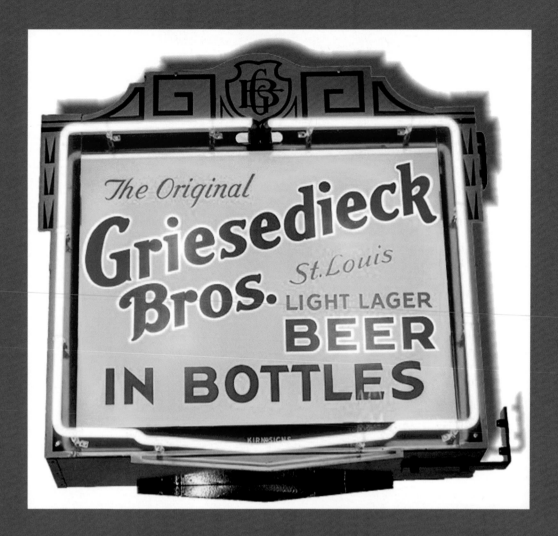

1930s GB double-sided outdoor light-up pole sign, framed with neon, and a Falstaff box neon from 1934 that could be used as either a back-bar or window display.

This ABC electric clock from the 1930s still keeps good time.

Wonderfully detailed lithograph issued by the Union Brewing Company
shortly after it opened in 1898.

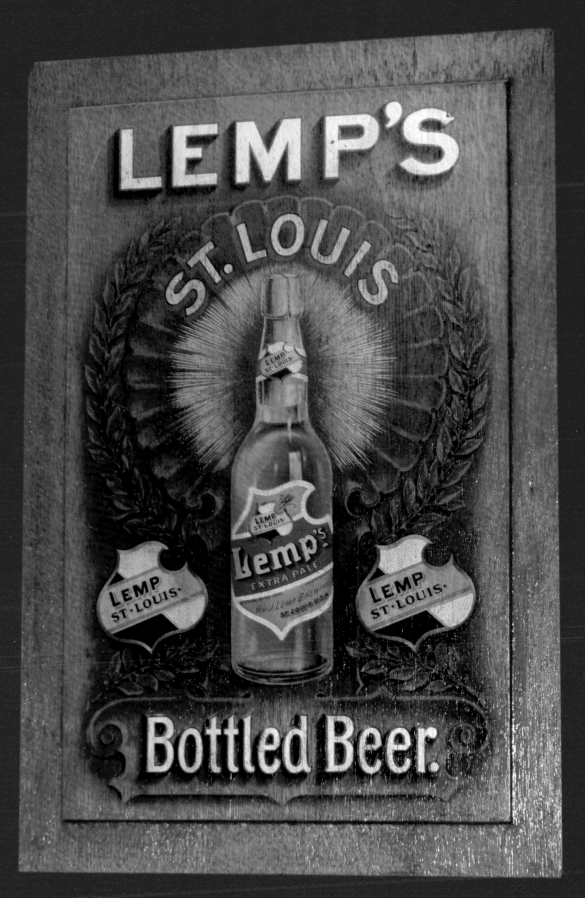

The label design on the bottle found on this Meyercord (decal on wood) dates the sign to the early 1900s.

Two great steins. On the left, one of the pre-Prohibition ABC Masters' back-bar series. On the right, a late 1890s 1.0-litre stein produced by the Columbia Brewery.

Chalk back-bar statue issued for a number of years after
World War II by Falstaff.

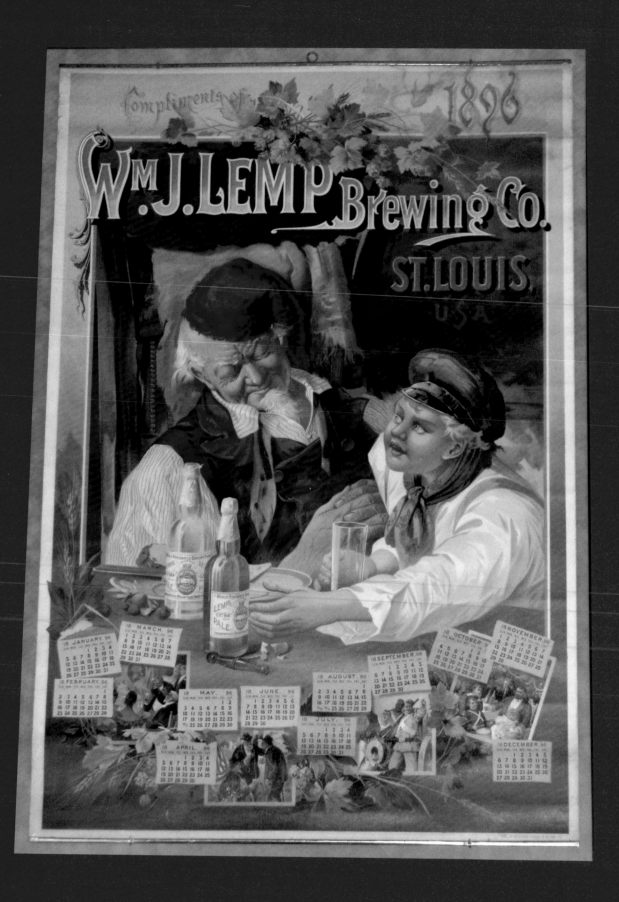

This 1896 Lemp calendar is unusually detailed.

Pre-World War I felt and cloth pennant from Anheuser-Busch.

Two colorful 1930s tin-over-cardboard signs. The Falstaff Super-X brand was short-lived and not a sales success.

Teddy Roosevelt provides a toast to Lemp beer in this early 1900s die-cut
tin sign.

The gentleman on this early 1900s tray was trademarked by Lemp as
"The Connoisseur."

Bibliography

Books

Ambrose, Stephen E. *Undaunted Courage*. New York: Simon & Schuster, 1996.

Anderson, Will. *The Beer Book*. Princeton, N.J.: The Pyne Press, 1973.

Baron, Stanley. *Brewed in America*. Boston: Little, Brown and Company, 1962.

Bartley, Mary. *St. Louis Lost: Uncovering the City's Architectural Treasures*. St. Louis: Virginia Publishing, 1998.

Billon, F. L. *Annals of St. Louis in Its Territorial Days*. Self-published, 1888.

Brink's Illustrated Historical Atlas of Randolph County, Illinois. Philadelphia: Brink & Co., 1875.

Bull, Donald, and Manfred Freidrich. *Register of United States Breweries, 1876–1976*. Trumbull, Conn.: Bullworks, 1976.

Bull, Donald, Manfred Freidrich, and Robert Gottschalk. *American Breweries*. Trumbull, Conn.: Bullworks, 1984.

Cochran, Thomas C. *The Pabst Brewing Company*. New York: New York University Press, 1948.

Coleman, Alix, and Steven Price. *All the King's Horses*. St. Louis: Anheuser-Busch, Inc., 1983.

Compton, Richard J., and Camille Dry, *Pictorial St. Louis*. St. Louis: Compton & Co., 1875, 1979, 1997.

Courtaway, Robbi. *Wetter Than the Mississippi: Prohibition in St. Louis and Beyond*. St. Louis: Reedy Press, 2008.

Cox, James. *Notable St. Louisans*. St. Louis: Benesch Art Publishing Co., 1900, 1908.

Cox, James. *Old and New St. Louis*. St. Louis: Continental Printing Co., 1894.

Dacus and Buel. *A Tour of St. Louis*. St. Louis: Western Publishing Co., 1878.

Darby, John F. *The Personal Recollections of John F. Darby Mayor of St. Louis*. St. Louis: Hawthorn Publishing Co., 1835, 1880.

Devoy, John. *A History of St. Louis and Vicinity*. St. Louis: J. Devoy, 1898.

Faherty, William B. *The St. Louis Portrait*. Tulsa: Continental Heritage, Inc., 1978.

Ford, James E. *A History of Jefferson City*. Salem, Mass.: Higginson Book Co., 1994.

Gill, McCune. *The St. Louis Story*. St. Louis: Historical Records Association, 1952.

Gregory, Ralph. *A History of Washington Missouri*. Washington: The Washington Missourian, 1991.

Griesedieck, Alvin. *The Falstaff Story*. St. Louis: Simmons-Sissler Company, Inc., 1951.

Hagen, Harry M. *Saint Louis Portraits of the Past*. St. Louis: Riverside Press, 1976.

Hannon, Robert E. *St. Louis: Its Neighborhoods and Neighbors, Landmarks and Milestones*, St. Louis Regional Commerce and Growth Association, 1986.

Harris, NiNi. *A History of Carondelet*. St. Louis: Patrice Press, 1991.

Hyde and Conard. *Encyclopedia of the History of St. Louis*. St. Louis: Southern History Co., 1899.

Kargau, Ernst D. *Mercantile Industrial and Professional St. Louis*. St. Louis: Nixon-Jones, 1902.

Keithahn, Charles F. *The Brewing Industry*. Federal Trade Commission, December 1978.

Kirschten, Ernest. *Catfish and Crystal*. Garden City, N.Y.: Doubleday and Company Inc., 1960.

Krebs, Roland, and Percy Orthwein. *Making Friends Is Our Business*. The Cuneo Press, Inc., 1953.

Morrison, Andrew. *The Industries of St. Louis*. J. M. Elstner & Co., 1885.

O'Rear, G. W. *Commercial and Architectural St. Louis*. St. Louis: Jones and O'Rear, 1888.

Plavchan, Ronald J. *A History of Anheuser-Busch, 1852–1933*. New York: Arno Press, 1976.

Primm, James Neal. *Lion of the Valley, St. Louis Missouri from 1764–1980*. Boulder: Pruett Publishing Co., 1980.

Reavis, L. U. *The Railway and River Systems of St. Louis*. St. Louis: Woodward, Tiernan & Hale, 1879.

Reedy, William Marion, ed. *The Makers of St. Louis*. St. Louis: The Mirror, 1906.

Rich, H. S. & Company, ed. *One Hundred Years of Brewing*. Chicago: H.S. Rich & Co., 1903.

Rodabough, John. *Frenchtown*. St. Louis: Sunrise Publishing Company, 1980.

Ronnenberg, Herman. *Beer and Brewing in the Inland Northwest, 1850–1950*. Moscow: University of Idaho Press, 1993.

Rother, Hubert and Charlotte. *Lost Caves of St. Louis*. St. Louis: Virginia Publishing, 1996.

Scharf, Thomas. *History of St. Louis City and County, Vol. II*. Philadelphia: Louis H. Everts & Co., 1883.

Schlafly, Tom. *A New Religion in Mecca*. St. Louis: Virginia Publishing, 2006.

Smith, Gregg. *A History of Suds and Civilization from Mesopotamia to Microbreweries*. New York: HarperCollins Publishers, 1995.

Stevens, Walter B. *History of St. Louis the Fourth City, 1763–1909*. St. Louis: S. J. Clarke Publishing, 1909.

Story, C. C. *Men of Affairs of St. Louis: A Newspaper Reference Book*. St. Louis: Press Club of St. Louis, 1915.

Tarver and Risk. *The Western Journal of Agriculture, Manufacturers*. Charles & Hammond Printers, 1892.

Tolzmann, Don, ed. *The German Element in St. Louis*. St. Louis: Genealogical Publishing Co., 2000 translation.

Toft, Carolyn. *St. Louis Landmarks and Historic Districts*. St. Louis: Virginia Press, 2002.

Van Wieren, Dale P. *American Breweries II*. West Point, Pa.: East Coast Breweriana Association, 1995.

Van Ravensway, Charles. *St. Louis, An Informal History of the City and Its People, 1764–1865*. St. Louis: MHS Press, 1991.

Yenne, Bill. *Beers of North America*. New York: Gallery Books, 1986.

Walker, Stephen P. *Lemp: The Haunting History*. St. Louis: The Lemp Preservation Society Inc., 1988.

Wilderman, A. S. and A. A., ed. *History of St. Clair County*. Chicago: Munsell Publishing, 1907.

Newspapers

Belleville News-Democrat, February 18, 1979.

Cape Girardeau Republican, October 1914.

Carondelet News, January 20, 1906; November 30, 1907; November 3, 1933.

Cincinnati Post, November 19, 1905.

Columbia Missouri Statesman, November 24, 1854.

Daily Missouri Democrat, May 17, 1854.

Dogtown Dispatch, October 5, 1983.

Jackson Journal, July 16, 1975.

Los Angeles Times, January 23, 1987.

Louisiana Gazette, November 30, 1809; April 26, 1810; May 3, 1810; May 24, 1810; June 21, 1810; March 28, 1812.

Missouri Argus, November 27, 1835; September 23, 1836; October 18, 1837; May 5, 1839; September 21, 1839; December 5, 1840.

Missouri Gazette, October 19, 1809; May 24, 1810; October 21, 1815; May 25, 1816; December 7,

1816; May 31, 1820.

Missouri Republican, July 16, 1823; October 11, 1827.

New York Times, June 12, 1966.

Riverfront Times, August 23, 2000; May 30, 2001; September 11, 2008; March 12, 2009.

Sacramento Bee, January 9, 1995.

Sauce Magazine, June 2008.

South Side Journal, February 5, 2008; April 1, 2008.

St. Louis Argus, November 27, 1835; September 23, 1836.

St. Louis Business Journal, February 21, 1983, June 18, 2002; May 18, 2007, September 21, 2007.

St. Louis Globe-Democrat, October 24, 1899; June 25, 1907; June 26, 1907; September 8, 1921; September 9, 1921; September 29, 1921; August 5, 1924; November 7, 1924; October 31, 1925; September 17, 1927; January 10, 1930; April 2, 1933; June 23, 1933; July 21, 1933; October 2, 1933; March 9, 1934; June 6, 1934; November 8, 1934; December 7, 1934; January 20, 1935; March 22, 1935; March 23, 1935; April 26, 1935; November 12, 1935; November 30, 1935; December 13, 1935; February 2, 1936; February 25, 1936; September 16, 1936; December 23, 1936; April 18, 1937; April 20, 1937; July 2, 1937; October 26, 1937; June 29, 1938; October 2, 1939; October 17, 1942, February 4, 1944; August 14, 1945; September 7, 1948; July 5, 1954; July 21, 1957; December 15, 1957; April 28, 1964; April 10, 1968; June 9, 1974; April 29, 1975; June 13, 1975; June 28, 1975; April 14, 1984; August 9, 1984.

St. Louis Inquirer, February 1989; August 1990; October 1997; January 2003

St. Louis Post-Dispatch, September 12, 1924; September 22, 1924; April 7, 1933; April 8, 1933; June 1, 1933; June 23, 1933; June 25, 1936; July 8, 1937; March 16, 1939; March 17, 1939; April 4, 1939; July 28, 1939; December 16, 1940; February 4, 1941; September 14, 1943; July 4, 1954; February 29, 1964; October 12, 1969; December 2, 1973; June 9, 1974; April 27, 1975; September 28, 1975; February 3, 1976; March 11, 1979; January 18, 1981; May 19, 1981; June 28, 1987; July 16, 1987; July 30, 1989; November

3, 1991; October 30, 1994; August 18, 1995; April 21, 1996; July 21, 1996, July 28, 1996; June 8, 1998; June 27, 1998; December 30, 1999; October 22, 2000; April 11, 2003; May 24, 2008; May 25, 2008; May 28, 2008; May 29, 2008; May 30, 2008; June 1 2008; June 3, 2008; June 11, 2008; June 12, 2008; June 13, 2008; June 14, 2008; June 15, 2008; June 16, 2008; June 17, 2008; June 19, 2008; June 20, 2008; June 24, 2008; June 26, 2008; June 27, 2008; June 29, 2008; July 4, 2008; July 6, 2008; July 8, 2008; July 9, 2008; July 10, 2008; July 12, 2008; July 13, 2008; July 14, 2008; July 15, 2008; July 16, 2008; July 17, 2008; July 20, 2008; August 15, 2008; August 16, 2008; August 17, 2008; August 19, 2008; September 11, 2008; September 17, 2008; September 30, 2008; October 7, 2008; November 7, 2008; November 12, 2008; November 13, 2008; November 19, 2008; December 9, 2008; January 8, 2009; January 22, 2009; January 24, 2009; February 24, 2009.

St. Louis Republic, July 12, 1908; July 8, 1910.

St. Louis Republican, December 1879.

St. Louis Star, October 10, 1929; March 13, 1933.

St. Louis Star, The City of St. Louis and Its Resources, 1893.

St. Louis Star Times, June 6, 1934; November 17, 1948.

St. Louis Sun, September 30, 1989.

Wall Street Journal, January 5, 1982, April 7, 1983

Washington Missourian, August 1, 1990.

Periodicals

All About Beer, February/March 1993.

American Brewer, February 1900, July 1900, September 1900, June 1901, September 1901, November 1901, January 1902, April 1902, August 1902, November 1904, January 1905, February 1905, September 1905, January 1906, June 1906, October 1906, January 1907, March 1908, June 1908, August 1908, September 1908, February 1909, March 1909, April 1909, September 1909, November 1909, December 1909, August 1910, March 1911, April 1911,

October 1912, January 1913, March 1913, May 1913, June 1913, October 1913, November 1913, December 1913, July 1914, January 1915, February 1915, March 1915, May 1915, December 1915, January 1916, April 1916, June 1916, September 1916, December 1916, March 1934, May 1934, June 1934, October 1934, November 1934, February 1935, April 1935, June 1935, July 1935, October 1935, December 1935, February 1936, March 1936, April 1936, May 1936, October 1936, November 1936, February 1937, October 1937, February 1938, June 1938, August 1938, September 1938, December 1938, January 1939, February 1939, March 1939, May 1939, June 1939, August 1939, October 1939, January 1940, February 1940, October 1940, November 1940, December 1940, January 1941, March 1941, December 1941, January 1942, April 1942, February 1942, September 1942, January 1943, March 1943, May 1943, July 1943, August 1943, September 1943, November 1943, January 1947, February 1947, March 1947, June 1947, November 1947, February 1957, March 1957, April 1957, July 1957, November 1957, December 1957, January 1958.

American Brewers Review, June 15, 1938.

Beer Distributor, July 1959.

Brewer and Maltster, December 1913, March 1915, May 1915, March 1916, May 1916, June 1916, August 1916, September 1916, December 1916, November 1917, September 1918, November 1918.

Brewers Hand Book, The Supplement to The Western Brewer, 1907, 1913.

Brewers Digest, July 1942, January 1944, August 1944, September 1944, September 1952.

Brewers Journal, September 1895, March 1935, May 1935, June 1935, July 1935, December 1935, February 1936, June 1936, October 1936, November 1936, June 1938, July 1940, January 1944, August 1946, September 1954, August 1955.

Bulletin of the Missouri Historical Society, January 1960, January 1966, July 1966.

Business Week, April 13. 1963; July 30, 1966, "How Falstaff Brews New Markets"; March 24, 1973.

Dun's Review and Modern Industry, August 1966.

Financial Week, January 5, 1993.

Forbes Magazine, January 1, 1956 "Brewers"; May 1, 1957 "Hop Scotch Brewers"; December 15, 1976; July 31, 1995.

Gateway Heritage, Missouri Historical Society, fall 1987.

Kirkwood Historical Review, March 1975.

Modern Brewer, September 1934, January 1936, February 1937, November 1937, April 1938 (article by F. P. Hankerson, "The History of Brewing in St. Louis"), July 1938, February 1939, October 1939.

Modern Brewery Age, April 1933, January 1936, June 1936, June 1937, August 1938, February 1939, August 1939, October 1940, January 1946, February 1946, April 1946, May 1946, June 1946, March 1948, April 1948, June 1948.

On Tap, Griesedieck Brothers Brewery Co., November 1954, September 1955.

Newsweek, January 7, 1980.

P.O.V., September 1999.

Reedy's Mirror, December 18, 1914.

St. Louis Commerce, July 1956, April 1980, January 1981.

St. Louis Scene, April 1964.

St. Louisan, November 1974, "The Death of a Beer Dynasty," by Don Crinklaw; January 1976.

Smithsonian, June 1988.

Society for Industrial Archeology (newsletter), Volume 35, Summer 2006.

The Brewers Bulletin, July 8, 1954.

The Soulard Restorationist, Fall House Tour 1986.

The Western Brewer, October 1877, October 1878, January 1879, March 1879, May 1879, October 1879, December 1879, January 1880, April 1880, May 1880, July 1880, August 1880, October 1880, November 1880, December 1880, July 1881, November 1881, December 1881, January 1882, February 1882, March 1882, June 1882, July 1882, August 1882, October 1882, December 1882, February 1883, May 1883, June 1883, September 1883, November 1883, May 1884, June 1884, July 1884, September 1884, December 1884, July 1885, December 1885,

April 1886, May 1886, August 1886, September 1886, March 1888, May 1888, June 1888, August 1888, February 1889, July 1889, August 1889, December 1889, February 1890, March 1890, April 1890, October 1890, November 1890, June 1891, August 1891, October 1891, November 1891, December 1891, January 1892, April 1892, June 1892, October 1892, November 1892. June 1893, July 1893, August 1893, August 1894, August 1895, September 1895, January 1896, May 1896, June 1896, September 1896, November 1896, December 1896, January 1897, February 1897, March 1897, May 1897, June 1897, August 1897, September 1897, January 1898, February 1898, May 1898, June 1898, October 1898, January 1899, February 1899, March 1899, April 1899, May 1899, June 1899, July 1899, August 1899, September 1899, October 1899, January 1900, February 1900, April 1900, July 1900, November 1900, April 1901, February 1902, April 1902, March 1903, November 1903, January 1904, February 1904, March 1904, May 1904, September 1904, January 1906, January 1907, May 1907, June 1907, July 1907, August 1907, October 1907, November, 1907, December 1907, January 1908, February 1908, March 1908, April 1908, May 1908, June 1908, July 1908, August 1908, September 1908, January 1911, February 1911, March 1911, April 1911, July 1911, October 1911, December 1911, January 1912, February 1912, March 1912, April 1912, May 1912, July 1912, August 1912, October, 1912, November 1912, December 1912, February 1914, May 1914, June 1914, October 1914, November 1914, December 1914, January 1915, February 1916, June 1916, July 1916, January 1917, February 1917, March 1917, April 1917, May 1917, June 1917, September 1917, December 1917.

Time, July 11, 1955.

West End Word, July 3, 1985.

World Trade, March 1993.

_____, *The Greater Belleville*, James Allen Reed, 1910, 1913

Related Material

Anheuser-Busch Brewing Association, Trade Journal, 1884, 1895.

Anheuser Busch Fact Book, Anheuser-Busch, 1977, 1980, 1984, 1991–92, 1993, 1994–95.

A Simple Story of the Origin and Unprecedented Growth of the Anheuser Busch Brewing Association, 1889.

Baden Through the Years, Baden Women's Club, 1956.

Beer Barons of St. Louis, Gateway Chapter Cemetery Tour, by Gregg Kreyling.

Book of St. Louisans, The St. Louis Republic, 1906, 1912.

City of St. Louis, Atlas of, 1883.

Cole County Illustrated Sketch Book and Directory of Jefferson City and Cole County.

Der Sechszehnten Convention, St. Louis September 1904.

Encyclopedia Britannica.

Falstaff Family Album, The Falstaff Brewing Corporation.

Falstaff Shield, The Falstaff Brewing Corporation.

Gates Family History, by Christine Hawes-Bond.

Greentree Breweries Incorporated corporate records.

History of St. Louis, Commercial Statistics, Improvements of 1853.

Kramer Manuscript.

Letter from Louis Haenni to Henry Nicolaus.

Missouri Embossed Beer Bottles (website) by Bruce Mobley.

Missouri Manufacturers, 1874.

Missouri State Gazetter and Business Directory, 1889–1890.

Pen and Sunlight Sketches of St. Louis. Chicago: Phoenix Publishing Co., 1892.

Portfolio of Breweries and Kindred Plants, E. Jungenfeld and Co., St. Louis, 1895.

Research Company of America, New York, 1939, 1942, 1949, 1952, 1955, 1959, 1962, 1965, 1967, 1970, 1972, and 1974.

St. Louis Brewing Association mortgage and legal records.

St. Louis City Directories and Sanborn Insurance Maps, various years.

St. Louis, Her Trade, Commerce and Industries, 1882–1883.

St. Vincent Deutschen Waisen-Vereins, Golden Jubilaum, June 13, 1900, courtesy Hal and Jerry Leeker.

Souvenir Program from "Swiss Day" at the Fair, August 19, 1904, Charles J. Peat.

Swekosky, Dr. Wm G., manuscript, Missouri Historical Society Archives, Historic Preservation Papers.

The Story of Falstaff, Its Heritage and Transition, Falstaff Brewing Corporation.

Thoma family website at aol.hometown.

United States Brewers Guide, 1630–1864.

United States Securities and Exchange Commission, Section 14A, filed August 15, 2008.

Wing's Brewers Handbook, 1884.

What's Brewing in Soulard, Soulard Restoration Group, Russell and Nancy Farber.

Unpublished Master's Theses

Lindhurst, James. "History of Brewing in St. Louis, 1804–1860." Master's thesis, Washington University, 1939.

Quinn, Mary Jane. "Local Union No. 6, Brewing, Malting and General Labor Departments, St. Louis, MO." Master's thesis, University of Missouri, 1947.

Some of the material in this book previously appeared in the following publications: *Beer Cans and Brewery Collectibles* (the magazine of the Brewery Collectibles Club of America); *American Breweriana Journal* (the magazine of the American Breweriana Association); *The Breweriana Collector* (the magazine of the National Association of Brewerina Advertising); and *Can-A-Gram* (the newsletter of the Gateway Chapter of the Brewery Collectibles Club of America).

Index

1866 U.S. Brewers Convention, 7, 67
1879 U.S. Brewers Convention, 11–12, 65, 183, 195
1904 St. Louis World's Fair, 4, 16–17, 37–39, 68, 70, 73, 90, 125, 136
905 beer, 277

A

ABC Brewing Company, 14–17, 20–21, 45, 81–89, 102, 135–136, 253
ABC Brewing Corporation, see ABC Brewing Company.
A-B, see Anheuser-Busch.
ABC Old English Ale, 87
Adams, Cassilly, 38
Alexander, P.R. & Co., 211–212
Alpen Brau beer, 20–21, 71–74, 79, 90, 118, 135–136
Altgeld, John, 177
Amalgamated Brewing Company, 29, 245, 252
American Brewers' Association, 163
American Brewing Company, see ABC Brewing Company.
American Can Company, 87
American Weiss Beer Brewery, 234, 238
Anderson Brewery, 213
Angelbeck, Frederick, 224
Anheuser, E. and Company, 7–8, 10–12, 30–31, 34–36, 50
Anheuser, Eberhard, 7–8, 10, 12, 32–34, 56
Anheuser-Busch Brewing Association, see Anheuser-Busch.
Anheuser-Busch Companies Inc., see Anheuser-Busch.
Anheuser-Busch Companies, see Anheuser-Busch.
Anheuser-Busch InBev, 50–51, 112, 232
Anheuser-Busch Inc., see Anheuser-Busch.
Anheuser-Busch, 10, 12–14, 18–51, 55
Anthony & Kuhn Brewing Company, 8, 11–13, 52–55, 112, 122, 237
Anthony, Henry, 11, 52–55
Anti-Saloon League, 17, 116, 171
Antler, Henry, 80
Apel, Herman, 53
Arsenal Brewery, 7–9, 14, 82–84, 166–169, 179, 182
Atlantic Brewery, 222–223
Augusta Brewing Company, 28, 244, 252
Autenreith, Charles, 162

B

Baacke, Ferdinand, 224
Bacchus Brewing Company, 28
Bach, Louis, 145
Bachmann, Herman, 75
Baltimore Tavern, 213
Banner beer, 74
Barnes, Lynn, 140
Barry, Thomas J., 247
Barry-Wehmiller, 110, 247–250
Bartalls, W.F., 210
Bauer, A.H., 135
Bauer, I.J., 162
Baur, Oscar, 87–88
Baur, Robert, 87–88, 115
Bautenstrauch, G., 9, 216
Bavarian Brewery, 7–9, 11, 27, 32–34, 125, 147, 195
BCCA, 250
Beattie, David J., 220
Beck, Christian, 68
Becker, Charles F., 10, 160
Becker, F. Otto, 37
Beer Can Collectors of America, see BCCA.
Beffa, Harvey, 94, 96–98
Beffa, Jr., Harvey, 97–98
Bellefontaine Brewery, 9, 219, 227
Bellefontaine Cemetery, 39, 55, 198
Benton Brewery, 229
Benton Park, 6
Bergen, L., 127–128
Berger, Emil, 219
Bergesch, Herman, 9, 220
Berliner Weiss Beer Brewing Company, 212, 239
Berliner weiss beer, 233
Berscher & Co., 224
Berscht, 66
Bevo Mill, 39–40, 51, 123
Bevo beverage, 18, 39–40, 91, 123
Biddle, Thomas, 5, 176, 206
Bierman, Fred A., 110
Birsner, Harry, 118
Blatz, Valentine, 36
Block, Leon & Bros., 210
Blowser, 210
Blume, 210

Boernstein, Henry, 218
Boisselier, C.D., 252–253
Bongner, Julius, 68
Bosewetter, Richard, 67
Boston Beer Company, 28, 182, 184–185
Boyd, James F., 9, 220
Brailey, James S., Jr., 135
Brandenburger, Jacob, 232
Brandon, George, 229
Brauneck, Charles, 146
Breidenbach, Henry, 64, 176
Breitner, Edward, 56
Bremen Brewery Company, 9, 56–57
Bresser, Henry, 238
Brewer, Charles, 215
Brewer, Richard, 215
Brewers and Maltsters Local #6, 11, 13–14, 124, 126,
    248–249
Brewery Collectibles Club of America, see BCCA.
Brinckwirth, Fredericka Lanvers, 142
Brinckwirth, Griesedieck & Nolker,
Brinckwirth, Louis, 142–143
Brinckwirth, Louisa, 142–143
Brinckwirth, Theodore, 6, 9, 141,220
Brinckwirth, Griesedeick & Nolker, see Brinckwirth-
    Nolker Brewing Company.
Brinckwirth-Nolker Brewing Company, 12–13, 141–143,
    179–180
Brinkmyer, Henry, 227
Brisselbach, Rudolph, 137, 219, 222
Brito, Carlos, 50
Broadway Brewery, 9, 220
Brookings, W.T., 173
Brumbaugh, Thomas, 209
Bruning, Ferdinand, 216
Bruning, Louis, 9, 216
Buchholz, William, 138
Buckingham Hotel, 199
Budweiser Beer and Wine Company, 77
Budweiser (or Bud) Light beer, 47
Budweiser beer, 12–13, 20, 33–35, 37, 39, 43–44, 48, 90,
    119, 166, 246
Buehner, Christian, 59
Buena Vista Brewery, 213–214
Buffalo Brewing Company, 28–29, 244, 252
Burton Ale and Porter Brewing Company, 160–161
Busch, Adolphus, III, 21–22, 41–42, 51
Busch, Anna, 10, 33
Busch August A., III, 26, 45–51, 165, 197
Busch August, IV, 48–51
Busch August A. "Gussie," Jr., 21–22, 24–26, 41–43, 45,
    48, 51, 249
Busch August A., Sr., 21, 39–41,51
Busch Bavarian beer, 23–24, 43
Busch Lager beer, 23, 43–44

Busch, Adolphus, 10–12, 14, 33–34, 37, 39, 51, 124, 128,
    130, 140, 166, 175, 182, 195, 213–214, 252–253
Busch, George, 7, 213–214, 194–195
Busch, Lily, 10, 33, 39, 198
Busch, Ulrich, 10, 33
Busch's Brewery, 7, 9, 213–214
Buttner, J.G., 221

C

Cabinet beer, 196–197
Caddick & Co., 215
Cairns, John, 229
Caldwell & Watson, 12
Calledonian Brewery, 217
Camp Spring Brewery, 7–9, 190–191, 221
CANvention, 250
Capone, Al, 88–89
Caray, Harry, 118–119
Carey, David, 223
Carling Brewing Company, 23, 127, 134, 181
Carondelet Brewery, 20–21, 58–61, 111, 137, 217
Cathedral Square Brewery, 29, 245
Cavanaugh, James, 160
Centennial Malt House, 65
Central Brewing Company, 17, 61
Cerveceria Cuahtemoc, 65
Chambers, William C., 210
Chapman, William A., 248
Cherokee Brewery, 13, 62–63, 77, 112, 125, 228
Choler, Sara, 242
Chouteau Avenue Brewery, 10, 12–13, 64–65
Chouteau Avenue Crystal Ice and Cold Storage, 65
Chouteau's Pond, 7, 201
City Brewery, 5–7, 9, 66–68, 100, 102, 232
City Grille and Brewhaus, 28–29, 243–245
Clark Avenue Brewery, 10, 122–123
Class, George, 177
Clowder House Foundation, 69
Clydesdales, 41, 44, 48–49
Colman, Francois, 205
Colton, H.J., 97
Columbia branch, Missouri Weiss Beer Brewing Co.,
    234–235
Columbia Brewing Company, 15, 17, 20–23, 25, 61,
    69–74, 83, 85, 95, 97, 215
Columbia Pale beer, 70
Columbia Products, 234
Compton, William, 58–60
Conrad, Carl, 12, 33–34, 246
Conrades, Edwin, 68
Conrades, Louise, 69
Conran, James, 216
Consumers Brewing Company, 7, 17, 63, 75–78, 115,
    118, 121, 125, 135–136

Continental Building, 96
Coons, John, 4, 204–205
Cooper & Conger, 226
Cooper, Richard F., 226
Corkery, J.F., 106
Coste & Sempler, 221
Coste, Felix, 9, 221
Courtaway, Robbi, 116
Courtney's Ale, 73
Coutts, Charles, 194
Crown Cork and Seal, 15
Crowntainer can, 118–119
Cullen-Harrison Act, 20
Cunningham, Jay, 252
Custer's Last Fight, 38
Custom Brew Haus, 245

D

D'Oench, William, 7–8, 10, 32–33
Dacey, James A., 86
Damhorst, Herman, 122
Davy, John T., 237
De Menil, N.N., 228
DeBellis, Steve, 121, 246
Decker, Jacob, 221
Dennig, Louis S., 133
Denny, Charles, 130
Dependahl, Charles, Jr., 98
Deuber, George, 234, 238
Deutelmoser, Adolphus, 9, 217
Diageo-Guinness, 51
Dierberg, James, 154
Dill, Arthur, 59–61
Doettling, Michael, 220
Dory, John, 66
Dougherty, Robert, 235
Drosten, W.J., 80
DuBois Brewing Co., 34
Duffy, A.J., 160

E

E. Jungenfeld & Co., see Jungenfeld, E. & Co.
Eagle Brewery
   (I), 207–208
   (II), 8, 214
Ebel, Louis, 169
Eberhardt, H.G., 162
Eberhardt, Josh, 254
Eckerle, Nicholas, 138
Eckerle, Theobald (Theodore), 9–10, 124, 167
Eder, Henry, 133–134
Edmond, Luiz Fendando, 50
Ehlermann, Charles & Co., 12, 213

Eighteenth Amendment, 40–41, 68, 71, 123, 129, 140, 187
Ellerman, Jacob, 214
Elliott, Conrad, 9, 211–212
Elschepp, Rudolph, 139
Emmet Brewery, 127
Empire Brewing Company, 16–17, 79–80
Ems, Nick, 58–61
Engle & Faber Brewing Company, 232
Engleton, Shtophel, 211
English, Elkanah, 208
English, Ezra, Jr., 209, 223
English, Ezra, Sr., 5–6, 9, 208–209, 223
Ernst, George, 59
Essmueller & Barry, 247
Evans, David H., 223
Excelsior Brewery, 8–9, 12–13, 70, 81–84, 87, 167, 180, 186, 190–193, 201–202

F

Faatz, Henry, 210
Fahner, Tim, 254
Fairbanks & Co., 12
Falstaff alumni, 93
Falstaff Brewing Corporation, 7, 15–17, 19–26, 41, 58, 66, 69–70, 74–75, 78, 90–103, 114, 116, 152, 154, 229, 250
Falstaff Inn, The, 250–251
Falstaff International Museum of Brewing, 25, 154, 250
Falstaff beer, 15, 19, 96, 148, 152, 158–159
Falstaff, Sir John, 90, 94, 96
Farley, M.F., 162
Feasting Fox, 39
Federal Trade Commission, 25
Feickert, Jacob, 155
Feldkamp, Ferdinand, 182
Felker, Bernard, 105
Fellhauer, Martin, 162
Ferie, Joseph, 9, 220
Feuerbacher mansion, 112
Feuerbacher, Frank, 55, 109–110
Feuerbacher, Max, 8, 64, 108–109, 111, 237
Ficht, Fred W., 187–188
Finney, James, 5–7, 66
Finney, William, 5–7, 66
Fischer, John F., 222
Fischer, Oscar, 94, 96
Fischgens, Joseph, 211
Fisher, Charles, 164
Fisher, George K., 135
Fisher & Peters, 216
Fleischbein, Jacob, 176

Fleming, John B., 215
Flood, Tom, 242
Folk, Joseph, 197
Forest Park Brewing Company, 17–18, 84, 91–92, 102–103, 115
Forster, August, 128, 133
Forster, C. Marquard, 10, 127–133, 179–180
Forster, Frank, 71, 123, 129, 180
Fortuna Brewery, 9, 220, 224
Fox, Walter W., 106
Franklin Brewery, 9, 215–216
Franklin Malt House, 215–216
Friedrich, John Michael, 63, 160–161
Fries, C.W., 239
Fries, L.P. & Son, 12
Fritschle, Charles, 227
Fritz, Charles A., 7, 9, 195, 213
Fritz, Jacob, 167, 222
Fruend, L.A., 73
Fuller, Charles C., 229
Fulton Brewery, 5–7, 209, 215
Furth, Jacob, 196, 199

G

Gambrinus Brewery, 8–9, 52–53, 182, 212, 221
Gambrinus Hall, 126, 248–249
Gambrinus, 35, 52–53, 240
Gankman, John, 224
Garrison Development, 151
Gartner, Bob, 249
Gast Bank Note and Lithographing Company, August, 104
Gast Bottling Company, 106
Gast Brewery, Inc., 20, 104–107
Gast Brewing Company, 16–17
Gast Wine Company, 104
Gast, Alex, 104–105, 136
Gast, Felix, 105
Gast, Ferdinand, 105, 135–136
Gast, John, 104, 210
Gast, Leopold, 104
Gast, Paulus, 16, 104–105
Gast, Ulysses, 105
Gateway Chapter BCCA, 250
Gaul, John, 222
Gay, Edward J., 211
GB Stein Hall, 120–121
Gebhardt, Adolph, 9, 219
German Brewery, 9–10, 36, 124–125
Gilliam, Peter, 210
Gilpin, 208–209
Giraldin, Charles, 227
Glason, John, 220
Goerger, William, 225, 239

Gottfried, Marc, 242, 251
Gottschalk, Charles W., 9, 32
Grace Company, W. R., 25
Grant, Bert, 240
Grant's Farm, 39, 43, 48
Great Southern Brewery, see Klausmann Brewing Company.
Great Western Weiss Beer Brewery Company, 238
Green Tree Brewery, 8–10, 12–13, 55, 59, 64, 108–112, 125, 130, 179–180, 182–193, 187, 191, 235, 237
Greenberg, Lou, 89
Gretchen Inn, 39
Griesedieck, Brewing Company, A., 13, 76, 177–180, 223
Griesedieck Beverage Company, 18–19, 91–92
Griesedieck Brewing Company (see Griesedieck Brothers Brewery)
Griesedieck Brothers Brewery, 7, 20, 23, 25, 42, 78, 90–101, 246, 250, 252, 254
Griesedieck-Western Brewery Company, 23, 92, 110, 134, 181, 247, 254
Griesedieck, Alvin "Buddy," 19, 92–96, 135
Griesedieck, Anton, 7, 76, 90, 95, 114–116, 118, 177, 179
Griesedieck, Bernard, 114–115
Griesedieck, Edward J., Jr., 96, 98, 120
Griesedieck, Franz (Frank), 6, 77, 115, 142
Griesedieck, Henry A., "Hank," 120
Griesedieck, Henry C., 77–78, 85, 135–136, 177
Griesedieck, Henry, Jr., 17, 114–115, 135–136
Griesedieck, J. Edward, 116
Griesedieck, Johann, 114
Griesedieck, Joseph, Jr., 96
Griesedieck, Louisa, 77
Griesedieck, Mathilda, 130
Griesedieck, Papa "Joe," 18–19, 90–96, 103, 115, 116, 150, 156, 158
Griesedieck, Raymond A., 91, 116
Griesedieck, Robert Anton "Bubby," 120
Griesedieck, Robert, 118
Griesedieck, William H., 120
Griesser, Wilhelm, 162, 164–165, 254
Grimm, John, 58
Groeninger, Fred, 211–212
Grone Brewery, 12–13, 115, 122–123, 161, 224–225
Grone Cafeteria, 123
Grone Construction, 123
Grone, Henry, 10, 53, 65, 122, 179
Grone, Herman, 123
Grone, John G., 122
Grone, Josephine, 143
Grone, Rosa, 115
Gronenbold, 176
Gross, Leonard H., 233–235
Grupo Modelo, 50
Gsell, Alphonse, 222
Gsell, Ferdinand, 222

Guggemos, Joseph, 229
Gull, Rudolph, 118–119
Gundlach Brewery, 138
Gutting, Ferd, 97–98

H

H. Grone Brewery, see Grone Brewery.
Haase, Louis H., 79, 135–136
Habb, Victor, 4–5, 205–206
Hafferkamp, Robert, 125
Hale, Stephen, 242
Halm, Joseph, 228–229
Hamilton, Paul, 65
Hamilton, Wendy, 65
Hamm, Jacob, 9, 219
Hammer, Carl, 32
Hammer, Dr. Adam, 7, 32
Hammer, Francis, 216
Hammer, Philip, 7, 32
Hannemann, Carl, 7, 233–234
Hannemann, Lena, 233
Haren, William A., 180, 195, 200
Harney, M.C., 135
Harper, Dennis, 27, 242
Harper, Randy, 27, 242
Hartman, John, 212, 227
Hartung, Frank, 143
Hauptmann, Peter, 63
Hauschild, August, 238
Hauser, Joseph J., 248
Hawes, Richard S., Jr., 86
Haxel, Peter, 210–211
Hay, 212
Healy, William, 105
Heartland Brewing Company, 243
Hecker Brewery, 127
Hehner, Philip, 81, 167
Heidbreder, John F., 10, 65, 160
Heil, Henry, 79
Heim's Brewery Company, 13, 77, 179
Heimsheimer Brewing Company, 231
Heitcamp, Fritz, 210
Heitz, Charles, 9, 223
Hek beverage, 91, 115
Held, Jason, 254
Herbst, George, 44
Herget, I. & Co. 214
Herold, Ferdinand, 63–63, 77, 112
Herold, Robert F., 63, 77, 125
Herold, Theodore, 125, 179
Hermann, Charles F. & Co., 12
Herschfield & Co., 217
Hertel, Fred, 177
Heyl, Ben, 232

Hickory Brewery, 9
Hiemenz, Jacob, 81–82
Hill Craft Beer Company, 246
Hill, Ray, 246
Hirrlinger, Jack, 237
Hoelzer, Fred, 58–59
Hoelzle, Charles, 81
Hoffmeister, Philip, 9, 225
Home Brewing Company, 11, 17, 124–126
Holden, D.L. 191
Hoover, E.J., 170–171
Hop Ale Company, 231
Hoppe, Charles, 9, 12, 219
Hornby, John, 224
Howard, Martin J., 110
Huber, Charles, 53, 221
Huber, Ignatz, 81
Huber, J., 81
Huelsing, J.P., 118
Huerter, Drew, 29, 245
Hunicke, Julius, 128
Huppert, William, 140
Hyde Park beer, 23, 143, 181, 197
Hyde Park Breweries Association, see Hyde Park Brewery.
Hyde Park Brewery, 10, 13, 20, 23, 71, 73, 90, 116, 123, 127–134, 187, 197, 247

I

Ideal Brewery, 230
Independent Breweries Company (IBC), 7, 10, 15–17, 70–71, 75, 77–81, 85, 90–91, 102, 104–105, 114–115, 124–125, 133, 135–136, 148, 169, 231, 240
Independent Realty Company, 71, 136
Independent Realty Investment Company, 86
International Shoe Company, 19, 116–117
Iron Mountain Brewery, 8–9, 219–220
Ittel, Simon, 82

J

Jackson Brewery, 9, 137, 221
Jackson, Samuel, 207
Jacob, Robert, 10, 12, 127–128
Jaeger, Ambrose, 53
Jaeger, Anton, 8–11, 52–53, 212
Jaeger, Nicholas, 53
Jannus, Tony, 152
Janssen & Janssen, 36, 253
Janssen, E.C., 83–84, 253
Jefferson Brewery
    (I), 9, 207
    (II), 216–218
Jefferson, Jeffery, 224
Jehle brewery, 183

Jensen, Paul, 242
Jessel, George, 73
John O'Brien Company, 83, 111
Johnson, Dave, 244
Jones, C. Norman, 131, 140, 180–181, 199
Jones, Edward D., 134
Jones, Jesse, 245
Jungenfeld, E. & Co., 12, 36–37, 57, 62, 115, 124–125, 160, 176, 196, 198, 252–254
Jungenfeld, Edmund, see Jungenfeld, E. & Co.
Juxberg, August, 209, 213

K

Kalmanovitz, Paul, 26, 98–100, 154, 250
Kanne, Louis, 88–89
Katz, Gansses & Co., 212
Keisel, Fred, 238
Keller, David, 209
Kendall, Rosalind Velva, 199
Kersten, Earl W., 231
Kersten, Hilda, 231
Kerzinger, Franz, 213
Kerzinger's Cave, 213
Ketterer, Lorenz, 176
Kiel, Henry, 163
Kilian, Mike, 243
Kimpel, John, 12
King, Samuel, 233–234
Klausmann Brewery Company, 13, 58, 137–140, 179–180
Klausmann, Carl, 8, 137–138
Klausmann, Maria, 137–139
Kling, Peter M., 230
Knapp, A.S., 86
Koch, Antoine, 182
Koch, Charles (Carl), 183
Koch, Christian, 238
Koch, Elizabeth, 182–184
Koch, Jim, 28, 185
Koch, Charles Joseph, Jr., 183
Koch, Louis, 9, 28, 167, 182
Koechel, John, 145, 186
Koechel, Louisa, 186
Koehler, August W., 76
Koehler, Casper, 9, 15, 65, 70, 81–85, 135–136, 157, 192
Koehler, Henry, 14, 81–84, 191
Koehler, Hugo, 14, 17, 71, 135–136
Koehler, Henry, Jr., 85
Koehler, Julius, 70
Koehler, Oscar, 82–83
Koenig, Barnard, 217
Koenig, Ernest, 239
Koenigsberg, J., 252
Kolb, Elizabeth, 167
Kolkschneider, Henry W., 186–188

Koplazinsky, Abraham, 239
Koplazinsky, Adam, 239
Kopman, Charles, 27, 240
Kopman, Dan, 27, 240–241, 252
Kovarik, Joseph, 58
Krauss, Caroline, 109
Krauss, Chris, 138
Krauss, John, 109, 138, 140, 179
Kraut, William, 190
Krey Packing, 134
Krug, 75, 93
Kueppert, John, 219–220
Kuester, John H., 160
Kuhn, Francis, 11, 52–55, 218
Kuntz, Michael, 6, 141
Kunz, Henry, 9, 65, 122, 225
Kupferle Brothers, 12
Kurlbaum, Julius, 220

L

LB Redevelopment, 150
Labatt USA, 50–51
Lachky, Bob, 252
Laclede Brewery, 216, 224–225
Lademann, Otto, 10, 191
Lafayette Brewery, 6, 9, 90, 141–143, 177, 180
Laibold, Bernard, 209
Lami Brewery, 120, 219
Langeneckert, Donald, 250
Latham, John, 207–208
Laubketter, Fred, 79
Laurel Brewery, 52, 211–212, 240
Lazarus, Meyer, 88
Lebeau, A.A. & Co., 220
Leisse, Hubert, 167
Lemp Brewing Company (Brewery), 9, 11–16, 18–19, 29, 36–37, 51
Lemp Mansion, 16, 19, 150–151, 155–157, 228, 246
Lemp, Adam, 6, 9–10, 75, 86, 128, 144–146, 154, 224, 250
Lemp, Charles, 148, 155–156
Lemp, Edwin, 25, 148, 154
Lemp, Elsa, 15, 18, 156
Lemp, Frederick, 16
Lemp, Hilda, 15, 156
Lemp, William J., III, 22, 157
Lemp, William J., Jr., 17–18, 147–148, 150–152, 155–158
Lemp, William J., Sr., 10–12, 15–16, 19, 65, 76, 90, 146–148, 150, 154–156
Lemp, Lillian (Handlan), 157
Lemp, Louis F., 147–148
Lemp's brew kettle, 6, 154
Lempel, Lorenz, 167, 195
Leussler, August, 9, 221

Lewis, Robert F., 248–248
Liberty Brewing Company (Brewery), 10, 13, 63, 160–161
Lierheimer, Lance, 27
Limberg, Ellie, 157
Limberg, Rudolph, 15, 70, 157
Lincoln Brewery, 124
Lind, Leroy, 110
Link, Ernst, 122
Linze, William, 216–218, 220
Lion Brewery, 225, 228–229, 246
Lipsius, F., 82
Liquor Dealers' Benevolent Association, 165
Lite beer, 26, 46–47
Livernois, Michael, 205
Loebs, George, 62–63
Loebs, Henry, 63
Loebs, Jacob, 63
Lohmueller, Charles, 238
Long, Dennis "Denny," 45–48
Longuemare, Charles, 9, 214, 217
Longuemere, E., 214
Loos, Louis, 238
Love, J.A., 105
Lowell Brewery, 219, 227
Lueberring, Frederick, 211
Lungstras, Peter, 217
Lungstras, Robert, 219
Lungstras, Rudolph, 217, 219
Lutz, Albert, 162–163
Lynch, James C., 5, 207

M

Manhattan Brewing Company, 87–89
Manjencich, Dushan, 28, 244
Manufacturers Railway Co., 37
Maritzen, August, 115
Marth Brewing Corporation, 59, 178
Master Brewers Association of the Americas, 17, 95, 134, 242, 251
Matthaieus, Ferie & Co., 220
Mattingly Brewing Company, 29, 245
Mattingly, Douglas, 245
Mattingly, Michael, 245
Mayer, C.G., 252
Maytag, Fritz, 240
McAuliffe, Jack, 240
McCourtney, J. Spencer, 136
McHose, Abraham, 108, 208–209
McHose, Isaac, 5–6, 208–209
McKee, Robert, 209
McNeary, Thomas, 193
Medart, J. Reynolds, 80
Meier Brothers, 62

Menkel, Rudolph, 230
Meramec Brewing Company, 121
Mertens, J. Adolph, 73
Metcalfe, William & Son, 207–208
Meyer, Dick, 43, 45
Meyer, John H., 219
Meyer, Walter, 187
Meyerhofer, Carl, 239
Meyerson, Adolph, 216
Michelob Brewing Company, 231–232
Michelob Light beer, 46
Michelob beer, 15, 38, 46, 231–232
Mick, Elmer, 112
Mick, Henry, 228–229
Milentz, Laura, 235
Milentz, Louis F., 235
Miller Brewing Company, 14, 25–28, 34, 45–49, 51, 185
Miller Brothers Brewery, 7, 13, 77, 114
Miller Lite beer, (see Lite beer)
Miller, Dave, 240, 254
Miller, Herman, 76
Miller, John, 98
Miller, Robert, 76, 144, 177
Minnehaha Brewery, 227–228
Mississippi Glass Company, 12
Mississippi Valley Brewery, 210
Missouri Anti-Saloon League, 171
Missouri Brewery, 194
   (I), see Small & Rohr.
   (II), 9, 216
   (III), 231
Missouri Historical Society, see Missouri History Museum.
Missouri History Museum, 28, 120, 154
Missouri Weiss Beer Brewing Company, 233, 235–236
Model Bottling Machinery Company, 102
Moeller, Otto, 79
Moerschel, Jacob, 79
Moran, William, 10, 127
Morgan Street Brewery, 27, 242, 251–252
Morton, Earl P.,
Mound Brewery (I) (II), 213
Mueller, Friederich, 229
Muench, J.T., 233
Mullanphy, John, 5, 205–206
Murphy, James T., 88
Murphy, Matthew, 5, 205–206
Murphy, Paul, 254
Mutual Brewing Company, 17, 162–165

N

Nagle, Frank, 77
Nagle, James, 5, 206
Narragansett Brewing Company, 96–97, 101

Naski, Marc, 245
Nation, Carrie, 16–17
National Brewery
    (I), 212
    (II), 9, 227–228
National Brewery Company, 17, 108, 114–115, 130
National Liquor Dealers' League, 165
National/Natural Bridge White Beer Brewery, 239
Natural Light beer, 26, 46
Neff, John, 210–212
Netzhammer, William, 188
Neukomm, Steve and Molly, 28, 243
Neville, Brian, 245
New Albion Brewing Company, 240
New Bremen Brewery, see Bremen Brewery Company.
Newton, Jere, 94, 97
Nicolaus, Henry, 69, 109–110, 123, 127, 130–132,
    180–181
Nicolaus, Katie, 130
Nicolaus, Louis J., 131–132, 181
Niemann, Christoph, 217
Nolan, Patrick Henry, 162–165
Nolker, Fred, 143
Nolker, William F., 6, 141–142
Nordmann, William, 254

O

O'Fallon Brewing Company, 240, 246, 252
O'Neil, Mary, 60
Obenier, Frank, 135
Oberschelp, William, 52, 218
Obert Brewing Company, 20–21, 116, 135, 148, 168–178
Obert Louis, III, 174
Obert, Charles L., 173
Obert, Elizabeth M., 171, 175
Obert, Harry, 169–170, 174
Obert, Louis, Jr., 169, 171, 173
Obert, Louis, Sr., 7, 14, 148, 166–168, 175
Obert, William A., 171, 173
Obert, William F., 175
Ochsner, William, 238
Oehler, Cornelius, 227
Offer, August, 238–239
Oheim Brothers saloon, 16
Old 66 Brewery, 151, 243
Oregon Brewery, 8–9, 210
Otto, Edward F., 135
Ottolini, James "Otto," 242
Owings, Steve and Vicki, 27, 242

P

Pabst Brewing Company, 14–16, 22–26, 36–38, 43, 46,
    51, 100

Pabst, Colonel Gustav, 15, 156
Pabst, Frederick, 16, 156
Pacific Brewery, 9, 225
Padberg, Lorenz F., 162–163, 165
Padda, Dr. Gupreet, 245
Painter, William, 15
Palamand, Rao, 151, 243
Palamand, Shashi, 151, 243
Pale Minstrel beer, 140
Peacock, Dave, 50
Pearl beer, 114, 177–178
Pearson, Smith & Co., 9, 219
Peerless Brewing Company, 59, 111
Pesseux, Charles, 238
Peswich Brewery, 167
Peter, Warren, 251
Peters, Edgar, 116, 118
Peters, Raymond, 116, 118
Peyinghaus, Robert, 216
Pfund, Frederick, 124
Phelan, J. Leo, 105
Philadelphia Brewery, 8–9, 52, 54, 64, 108, 217–218
Philipson, Joseph, 5, 205–206
Philipson, Simon, 5, 205–206
Phoenix Brewery, 9, 59–60, 76, 176–178, 180, 205–206,
    220, 222, 228
Pilsner Weiss Beer Brewery Company, 239
Pittsburgh Brewery, 8–9, 221
Plamandon, A.D., 85–86
Playboy Club, 243, 245
Pointer, Paul, 151, 155, 245
Posdorf, August, 110
Praemium Weiss Bier Brauerei, 235
Prather, Charles, 116
Primeau, Louis, 213
Prohibition, 17–20, 40–41, 65, 68–71, , 81, 85–86,
    89–93, 97, 102–103, 105, 110, 115–116, 123, 128–130,
    135–136, 140, 143, 148–152, 154–156, 165, 170–171,
    173–174, 176, 178, 181, 183, 187–188, 194, 197, 204,
    213, 229–235, 237, 240, 242–243, 246–247, 252–253
Prudential Bar Fixture Company, 65
Pulitzer, Joseph, 167

Q

Quinlaven, Edward, 223

R

Raake, F., 239
Ragan, Elsie, 60
Rassieur, Leo, 62, 225
Rassieur, Theodore, 69
Rathgeber, Fred, 138
Reck, Anton, 183

Red Feather beer, 82
Reichenberger, Joseph, 187
Reid & Company, 217
Reinhardt, 217, 222
Reisch, George, 251
Reising, Phil J., 210
Remmer, Henry, 223
Remmers, Oliver, 106
Research Pilot Brewery, 231
Ritter, August, 131, 133
Ritter, Otto, 128, 131
Roarty, Mike, 46
Roberts, E.M., 230
Roberts, L.S., 230
Roberts, O.M., 230
Robertson, Gordon, 210
Robinson, R.D., 86
Rocky Branch Brewery, 8–9, 205, 210
Roebock Liquors, 60, 231
Roler, George, 209
Rolling Rock beer, 49
Rollins, F.P., Jr., 73
Rombauer, E.R., 115
Rooke, Henry, 235
Rost, Otto, 236
Rother, Charlotte, 63, 126, 178, 225, 228
Rother, Hubert, 63, 126, 178, 225, 228
Rother, Max, 105
Rothweiler, Bernard, 217
Rothweiler, Ludwig, 217
Route 66 Brewery & Restaurant, 28, 243
Royal Breweries, Inc., 25, 237
Ruedy, John, 211
Ruepple, Charles, 213
Ruff, Casper, 141

S

SABMiller, 49–51
Saint Louis Brewery Inc. (Tap Room), 27–28, 240–242, 252, 254
Salvator Brewery, 218, 235
Samuel Adams Boston Lager, 182, 184
Sand Creek Brewing Company, 246
Sand, John S., 170
Saussenthaler, Peter, 82
Schachtner, Michael, 188
Schaefer, I.W., 177
Schaeffer, F. 218, 235
Schaeffer, N. 228–229
Scheller, John, 187
Schiffer, George, 9, 202
Schilling & Schneider Brewing Company, 9, 13, 179, 182, 185, 210
Schilling, George, 183

Schlafly Bottleworks, 28–29, 240–242
Schlafly, Tom, 27, 240–242
Schlitz, Joseph Brewing Company 14, 22–26, 34, 36, 43, 46–47, 51, 96, 119, 191, 247
Schlop Brewery, 9, 182
Schlossstein, Louis, 108–111, 130, 179, 191
Schmaltz, George, 58
Schmid, Francis, 9, 56
Schmidt, John, 213
Schmidt, Philip C., 209
Schmitt, Joseph, 227
Schmoll, John, 105–106
Schmucker, Bernard, 224
Schnaider, Joseph, Jr., 64–65
Schnaider, Joseph, Sr., 8–13, 64–65, 108, 109, 178, 181, 183, 187
Schnaider's Brewery, see Chouteau Avenue Brewery.
Schnaider's Garden, 12, 64–65
Schneider, Charles, 9, 183, 211
Schneider, George, 7, 32, 211, 215, 225
Schneider, L., 211
Schneider, Lorenz, 211
Schneider Wholesale Wine and Liquor Company of St. Louis, W., 246
Schnerr, Constantine, 9, 217, 223
Schnerr's Brewery, 9, 223
Schorr Brewing Company, 186
Schorr, Albert, 187
Schorr, Clarence W., 187–188
Schorr, Jacob, 16, 67, 186–187
Schorr, Johann Valentin, 186
Schorr, John J., 186–188
Schorr, John W., 68, 82
Schorr-Kolkschneider Brewing Company, 16, 20–21, 135, 148, 169, 186–189
Schreiber, William, 56–57
Schricker, Adam, 223
Schroeder, H., 210
Schroeder, Liberty Beer House, H., 210
Schroeder's Berliner Weiss Beer Company, 238–239
Schuerman, Henry, 140
Schultz, Frederick, 238
Schumacher, F.W., 68
Schumann, Charles, 9, 226
Scotch Hop Ale Company, 230–231
Schwer, Theo., 232
Seabaugh, Bradley, 251

Sect Wine Company, 83–84
Seeger, 220
Seelinger, Henry, 219
Seibel, Conrad, 12, 147
Senn, Gustav A., 230
Shaw's Garden, 12
Shea, John G., 152
Shebley, George, 229
Shield, The (Falstaff), 93
Shipley, Tom, 252
Shupp, Bessie M., 116
Shupp, Reverend W.C., 171
Siemon, Frederick, 124
Small & Rohr, 5–6, 209
Smith, Charles S., 212
Smith, Samuel D., 212
Smith, William, 215–215
South St. Louis Brewery, 222
Southern Ale Brewery, 223
Southern Brewery, 9, 140
Sparling, Lowell, 140
Spengler, Tobias, Jr., 9, 56
Spengler, Tobias, Sr., 9, 56–57
Spitzbarth, August, 239
Spori, Louis, 56
Sportsman's Park, 42–43, 161
Spot, the Hyde Park dog, 129
Spring Water Malt House, 70
Sproul, Frank, 77
Sproul, Louisa, 77
Square One Brewery, 28, 243–244, 252
St. George Brewery, 227
St. Louis Ale Brewery, 11, 226
St. Louis and Suburban Railway, 197
St. Louis Breweries Limited (SLBL), 179–180
St. Louis Brewers Heritage Festival, 28, 252
St. Louis Brewery Company, 176–178
St. Louis Brewery
    (I) 5–6, 9, 205–207, 214, 222
    (II), 12, 208
St. Louis Brewing Association (SLBA), 7–10, 14–16,
    18, 57, 62–68, 70, 75, 77, 81–82, 86, 90, 108, 110,
    114–115, 122–123, 125, 127–131, 135, 137–143, 148,
    160–161, 168–169, 176–183, 190, 193–194, 197,
    201–202
St. Louis Brews, The, 254
St. Louis Coliseum, 7, 193
St. Louis Lager, 31, 37, 42, 50
St. Louis Refrigerator and Wooden Gutter Company, 12
St. Louis Refrigerator Car Company, 37
St. Louis Retail Liquor Dealers' Association, 163
St. Louis University, 28
St. Louis Weiss Beer Brewing Company, 238
St. Vrain, Jacques, 4–5, 205
Stable, The, 151, 245–246

Staehlin, Christian, Jr., 8–9, 176–178
Staehlin, Christian, Sr., 9, 176, 228
Staehlin, George, 176
Stag beer, 23, 134
Stamm, Charles, 238
Stark, John H., 210
Star Brewery, 214, 217, 219, 222
Star-Peerless Brewery, 174
Stauder, Dan, 254
Steam Brewery, 9, 220
Steiger, Ottocar, 212
Steinberg, Mark C., 71, 136
Steinhubl, Andrew, 251
Steinkauler, Adelbert, 7, 166
Steinkauler, Guido, 7, 9, 166–167
Sterling, John, 254
Stern Brewery, 9, 214
Sternberg, Bernard, 229
Stettner & Thoma, 235
Stettner, Christopher, 235
Steuber, Jacob, 9, 221
Steuver, Anton C. (Tony), 135–136
Steuver's Cottage Restaurant, 125–126
Stevens Point Brewery, 246
Stifel, Carl, 20, 69
Stifel, Charles G., 7, 9–10, 12, 16, 53, 65–68, 179, 232
Stifel, Christina, 66, 201–202
Stifel, Christopher A., 66, 201–202
Stifel, Frederick, 6, 66, 201
Stifel, Herman, 69, 135, 181
Stifel, Jacob, 66
Stifel, Nicolaus and Company, 130, 197
Stifel, Otto, 16, 66–69, 90, 92, 179–181
Stifel, Otto F. Union Brewing Company, 16, 20, 22–23,
    58, 66–69, 90
Stifel's City Brewery, 12–13, 66–69, 179, 128, 186, 202
Stock, Peter, 210
Stock, Philip, 179, 183, 210
Stock, Stephen, 124, 180, 210
Stock Brothers, 9, 210
Stokes, Patrick, 45, 48–49
Stolzh, Charles, 9, 224
Stork Inn, 39
Straub, Arthur O., 237
Straub, August W., 202
Straub, John, 202
Strelinger, Gilbert, 105
Stroer, Joseph, 181
Strutmann, R.G., 59
Stumpf, Frederick, 75
Stumpf, Otto, 75
Stumpf, William (Wilhelm), 7, 9, 75–76, 78, 147
Stumpf's Brewery, 9, 75–76, 90, 114–115, 177
Stumpf's Cave, 75
Stutz, William, 125

Sullivan, John, 148
Sullivan, Louis, 194, 198
Sutter, Christopher, 217
Sutter, Daniel, 162
Swekosky, William, 211, 227–228
Swift Printing Company, 27, 240

T

Tannhauser beer, 166, 168, 170, 173
Tap Room, 240–242
Tapper, The, 97, 101
Tenge, Joseph, 235
Tennant, Joe, 27, 240
Tennessee Brewing Company, 82–83, 168, 186–187
Terre Haute Brewing Company, 87–89
Thamer Brewing Company, 7, 76, 114, 177
Thamer, Julius, 76
Thannberger, Maria, 55
Thannberger, Mathilde, 55
Thode, Edward, 238
Thoma, Leo, 235
Thoma, Otto, 234–235
Thomas, Julius, 224
Thomas, Dwight D., 86
Thompson, Jeff, 166
Tinker and Smith Malting Company, 215
Tinker Brothers & Co., 9, 213
Tinker, George, 215, 216
Tinker, Zachariah W., 15, 135, 215
Tobias Spengler & Son, 56–57
Tobias, Henry, 189
Tower Grove Park, 12
Tracy, Nellson N., 80
Tschirgi, Matthew, 211

U

U.S. Brewers Academy, 16, 91, 95, 115, 147, 160, 187
Uhrig Brewing Company, 12, 34
Uhrig, Ignatz, 137, 190–191, 221
Uhrig, Joseph, 6–10, 81, 137, 190–193, 221
Uhrig, Josephine, 191
Uhrig, Maria, 137
Uhrig, Mary, 109, 130
Uihlein, August, 12, 191
Union Brewing Company, 6, 9, 16, 55, 58, 66–69, 90, 92, 180, 201
Union Station, 7, 28, 193, 201–202, 243
United States Brewers Association, 7, 17, 67, 147, 183, 197
United States Brewmasters' Association, 102
Urban, Dominic, 7, 32

V

Vahlkamp, Henry, 91
Van Nort Brothers Electric Company, 160
Van Blascum, J.C., 179
Veeck, Bill, 42
Villeroy & Boch, 160, 198
Vogel, Edward, Jr., 118–120
Vollmar, Bill, 252
Vollmer, Karl K., 71, 73, 97
Volstead Act, 18, 20, 41, 85, 187, 247
Vordtriede, E.H., 109

W

Wagenhaeuser, Anton, 75–76
Wagenhauser, Henry, 114
Wagner Brewing Company, 17
Wagner, C., 227–228
Wagner, Ernest, 77
Wagner, Frederick, 9, 212, 225
Wagner, John, 144
Wagner, Edward, Jr., 102–103, 116
Wagner, Edward, Sr., 17, 84, 102–103, 135, 251
Wahl & Henius, 102, 133
Wahl, Fred, 65
Wahl, Peter, 167
Wainwright Brewery, see Wainwright Brewing Company.
Wainwright Brewing Company, 12–13, 86, 127, 179, 194–200
Wainwright Building, 198, 253
Wainwright Withnell, Martha, 194
Wainwright, Catherine D., 196, 198
Wainwright, Charlotte, 198
Wainwright, Ellis, 5–7, 14, 127, 179–180, 194–200
Wainwright, Samuel, 7, 9, 194–195, 213, 215
Walsh, Mrs. Stella S., 171
Walsh, Robert W., 252
Walsh, Thomas, 252
Walther, Adolph, 95, 110
Walther, Louis, 19, 94
Wash Street Brewery, 8–9, 219
Washington Beer House, 211
Washington Brewery, 9, 32, 211, 215, 225
Washington Hall, 211
Washington University, 16, 67, 128, 148, 198, 200, 211
Wattenberg, Busch and Company, 213
Wattenberg, Ernst, 33
Wayne, Mario, 246
Weaver, Gina, 243

Weaver, Davide, 28, 243
Weaver, Rita, 243
Wehmiller, Alfred H., 247
Wehmiller, Frederick, 247
Wehmiller, Paul, 247
Weiss beer, 233–239
Weiss, Mathias, 9, 124, 166–168
Wellenkoetter, Henry B., 86
Wellman, Frank, 79
Wellston Bottling Works, 188
Wesley, Marie, 60
Western Brewery, Lemp's, see Lemp Brewing Company.
Western Cable Railway Company, 147
Wetekamp, August, 9, 216, 224
Weyand, John, 225
Whalen, Aaron, 245
Whelan, John, 122
White Seal beer, 115
Widmann, Frederick, 252
Widmann, Walsh & Boisselier, 36, 253
Wilhelmi, O.J., 202–203
Will, Louis, 138
Williamson, John, 219, 227
Willis, William E., 237
Wilson, Mike, 243
Windeck, Martin, 210–211
Wineburg, Robert, 100
Winkelmeyer Brewery (Brewing Ass'n.), 12–13, 201–203
Winkelmeyer Building, 203
Winkelmeyer, Christina Stifel, 201–203
Winkelmeyer, Christopher, 179, 181, 202
Winkelmeyer, Julia, 202

Winkelmeyer, Julius, 6, 9, 13, 66, 183, 201–202
Winterer, Joseph, 220
Winterman, H.L., 80
Withnell, John, 194
Witte, Dr. John, 244
Wittemann, Elizabeth, 236
Wittemann, John, 236
Wittemann-Rost Brewing Co., 236–237
Women's Christian Temperance Union, 17
Wood, A., 220, 222
World's Columbian Exposition, 37
Wright, Denver, Jr., 250

Y

Yippie-ie-O Grille, 244
Young, Bernard F., 11, 226
Young, John M., 226
Young, Paul F., 57

Z

Zainer, Christian, 223
Zeil, William, 220
Zeiner, Frederick, 222
Zepp, Louis, 130, 212, 227–228
Ziegelmeyer, Simon, 137, 217, 222
Ziegenhain, Henry, 135
Zoller, Charles, 9, 210–211
Zoller, John, 220

COLUMBIA BANNER
BEER
"THE COCK
O' THE BAR"
COLUMBIA'S
BANNER
COLUMBIA BREWING CO.
ST. LOUIS U.S.A.